Social Policy for Children & Families

Social Policy for Children & Families

A Risk and Resilience Perspective

Jeffrey M. Jenson
University of Denver

Mark W. Fraser
University of North Carolina, Chapel Hill

SAGE Publications
Thousand Oaks ■ London ■ New Delhi

For information:

Sage Publications, Inc.
2455 Teller Road
Thousand Oaks, California 91320
E-mail: order@sagepub.com

Sage Publications Ltd.
1 Oliver's Yard
55 City Road
London EC1Y 1SP
United Kingdom

Sage Publications India Pvt. Ltd.
B-42, Panchsheel Enclave
Post Box 4109
New Delhi 110 017 India

Printed in the United States of America

Library of Congress Cataloging-in-Publication Data

Social policy for children and families: A risk and resilience
perspective/Jeffrey M. Jenson, editor, Mark W. Fraser, editor.
  p. cm.
Includes bibliographical references and index.
ISBN 1–4129–0413–7 (pbk.)
  1. Children—Government policy—United States. 2. Child welfare—United
States. 3. Youth—Government policy—United States. 4. Family policy—United
States. 5. Developmental psychology. 6. Child development.
I. Jenson, Jeffrey M., 1953- II. Fraser, Mark W., 1946-
HV741.S623 2006
362.82′0973—dc22   2005008153

This book is printed on acid-free paper.

06   07   08   09   10   9   8   7   6   5   4   3   2

Acquiring Editor:	Arthur T. Pomponio
Editorial Assistant:	Veronica Novak
Project Editor:	Beth A. Bernstein
Copy Editor:	Ron Harris (Print Matters, Inc.)
Typesetter:	C&M Digitals (P) Ltd.
Indexer:	Molly Hall
Cover Designer:	Michelle Lee Kenny

Contents

Foreword

M any young people in the United States grow up in circumstances that place them at risk for school failure, delinquency, substance abuse, and other social problems. Some children are born with disabilities that condition their capacity to learn. Others are raised in dangerous environments characterized by unsanitary conditions or are exposed to toxic substances that lead to developmental delays and learning problems in school. A significant number of American children and youth live in unsafe neighborhoods or neglectful families. Sadly, many of these children develop antisocial behaviors that alienate them from peers and teachers as they begin their formal education.

In most cases, parents find ways to offset biologic and environmental risk by providing the social, emotional, and financial supports that are necessary to raise a healthy child or adolescent. However, despite their best efforts, some parents find it impossible to create the opportunities and environmental conditions that help their children succeed at school and in the community. The result is seen in a young person's decision to drop out of school, use illicit drugs, or participate in any number of antisocial behaviors as an adolescent or young adult. Lack of opportunities and environmental supports also contributes to childhood depression and eating disorders, and may increase the likelihood that some youth will leave home to test their independence or escape abusive circumstances by living on the street or with friends. Such children and youth are often referred to public programs and become the concern of elected officials, policymakers, and practitioners.

How should we help? Finding effective solutions to the complex problems facing American children, youth, and families is one of our nation's foremost public policy challenges. Child and family policies have vacillated widely over time, depending upon prevailing philosophical beliefs about the most effective way to help vulnerable children, youth, and families. Resultant programs and interventions for children and families have been plagued by inconsistency and by a fragmented service delivery system that often fails to consider the multiple needs of young people and their parents. In some cases, bureaucratic obstacles have worked to reduce innovations in policy or program responses.

Child, youth, and family policies are implemented in the nation's health, mental health, child welfare, juvenile justice, and education systems. Each of these systems is large and complex, and each operates in partial isolation from the other. My experience in the U.S. House of Representatives reveals a need for fresh thinking about the individual and social problems facing American children and families. New frameworks are necessary to help elected officials and policymakers design and deliver integrated policies and programs across all systems of care for children, youth, and families.

In this book, Jeffrey M. Jenson and Mark W. Fraser outline a risk and resilience framework that offers promise for innovations in policies targeting vulnerable families. The model is based on knowledge gained from studying the risk and protective factors associated with the onset and persistence of such problems as delinquency and substance abuse. It suggests that policies and programs targeting known causes and correlates of child and adolescent problems are most likely to be successful in preventing problem behaviors and supporting children and families.

Jenson and Fraser have asked an impressive group of scholars to apply this framework to policy design in child welfare, education, mental health, health, developmental disabilities, substance abuse, and juvenile justice. Each chapter author has addressed the issue of policy and service integration across different systems of care. Case examples are used to illustrate innovative approaches and to illustrate ways that service integration might be achieved. Borrowing from ecological theorists, Jenson, Fraser, and colleagues emphasize the importance of policy design at the individual, family, social, and community level. The result is a book filled with promising ideas about the best ways to deliver a more comprehensive attack on the multiple problems facing young people.

The ideas expressed in this book represent an important shift in thinking about conventional policy development processes. A risk and resilience perspective—combined with principles emphasizing the integration of policy across different systems of care—is a logical progression in the process of creating policies for children, youth, and families. Elected officials and policymakers would do well to read and apply the principles expressed in this book to the problems faced by American families.

—Mark Udall
U.S. House of Representatives,
Colorado 2nd Congressional District

Acknowledgments

The ideas expressed in this volume address many of the most pressing problems confronting children, youth, and families in American society. We thank each of the chapter authors for the careful and rigorous thought they devoted to advancing new and innovative approaches to public policy. A book such as this owes a great debt to many people behind the scenes. Thanks to Diane Wyant of the University of North Carolina at Chapel Hill and Jenifer Rinner of the University of Denver for administrative and technical support in manuscript preparation. Finally, special thanks to Mary, Alex, and Katy Fraser and to Mary, Nils, and Anna Jenson for the daily reminders of what it means to be a family.

—Jeffrey M. Jenson

—Mark W. Fraser

Introduction

M uch has been written about risk and protective factors associated with social and health problems. Begun some 30 years ago, research to trace the causes of problem behavior in young people has led to a new understanding of the individual, interpersonal, social, and environmental factors that affect developmental outcomes. In recent years, attention has also been directed to increasing our understanding of resilience, commonly thought of as a child's capacity to overcome adverse life conditions (Fraser, Kirby, & Smokowski, 2004; Werner & Smith, 1992). Knowledge of these characteristics has been widely used to improve the efficacy of prevention and treatment programs for vulnerable children and families (Biglan, Brennan, Foster, & Holder, 2004; Hawkins, Catalano, Kosterman, Abbott, & Hill, 1999).

The intention of this book is to show that principles of risk, protection, and resilience also hold great promise for the design and delivery of social policies and programs for children and families. Knowledge gained from longitudinal investigations of risk, protection, and resilience in children and youth has rarely been applied to social policy. We hope that this book will help students, practitioners, policymakers, and researchers apply what might be called the principles of risk and resilience to the design of social and health policies.

Organization of the Book

The core section of the book is formed by seven chapters devoted to child welfare, education, mental health, health, developmental disabilities, substance abuse, and juvenile justice policies. Chapter authors identify key policies in their respective areas and evaluate the degree to which principles of risk, protection, and resilience can be used to improve existing programs and services. Recommended readings, questions for discussion, and web-based resources are provided for each of the seven core chapters. In this regard, authors follow a similar outline in which they

- trace the purpose of social policy in a substantive area;
- describe the incidence and prevalence of problems experienced by children and youth receiving services;
- articulate common risk and protective factors associated with the onset or persistence of the relevant problem behavior;
- identify historical and current policies that have been developed to address these problems;
- evaluate the degree to which such policies have been based on principles of risk, protection, and resilience;
- identify strategies to incorporate elements of risk, protection, and resilience in new policy directives; and
- discuss ways to integrate social policy for children, youth, and families across policy and service domains.

In Chapter 2 Peter Pecora examines child welfare policies and programs aimed at children, youth, and families. In describing a key service domain for children, youth, and families, Pecora traces the history and evolution of American child welfare policy and offers suggestions about ways to incorporate principles of risk, protection, and resilience in a key service domain.

Public schools touch the lives of a majority of American children and families. Changes in educational policy since 2000 are having a profound effect on teachers, parents, and children and youth in elementary, middle, and high schools. In Chapter 3 Andy Frey and Hill Walker discuss the landmark No Child Left Behind Act and its sweeping implications for the character of public education across the country. They note that educational reform is closely linked to political ideology and societal values pertaining to educational access and opportunity. Frey and Walker conclude by offering an agenda for reform.

In Chapter 4 Mary Fraser reviews the effectiveness of mental health policies for children, youth, and families. Current *system of care* (SOC) approaches are among the promising policy and program directives she identifies. Fraser notes the frequency of co-occurring problems found among youth and suggests that the integration of mental health, juvenile justice, and substance abuse policies be a public policy priority.

Kathleen Rounds and Thomas Ormsby trace the development of key public health policies in the United States in Chapter 5. They outline recent changes in the health care delivery system and assess their impact on children and families. Recommendations for integrated health policy based on risk, protection, and resilience are offered.

Recognizing and understanding developmental disabilities commonly found among children and youth has become a focus of policy debate in recent years. In Chapter 6, Susan Parish and Alison Whisnant discuss changes in policy for children with developmental disabilities in the past several decades. Using a risk and protective factor perspective, they offer recommendations for improving service delivery to children and youth with developmental disabilities.

In Chapter 7 Jeffrey Jenson, Elizabeth Anthony, and Matthew Howard review recent trends in the prevalence, etiology, prevention, and treatment of adolescent substance abuse. They trace the origins of policies aimed at young substance abusers and comment on the relative effectiveness of alternate policy approaches. Jenson and colleagues conclude that principles of risk, protection, and resilience have been influential in improving the efficacy of prevention and treatment programs for young people and reflect on the implications of these findings for substance abuse policy.

In Chapter 8 William Barton traces changes in juvenile justice policy since the creation of the juvenile court. He identifies the tension found in public policy between competing program goals of rehabilitation and punishment. Barton concludes with cautious optimism about the application of public health principles to juvenile justice policies and programs.

In the final chapter of the book, we expand on our framework for using principles of risk, protection, and resilience to develop more fully integrated policies for children, youth, and families. We argue that integration of policy and programs across service domains should be a goal of future policy directives targeting children, youth, and families. Considerations are given to developmental processes of children and youth in the design of this framework. Recommendations for ways to advance a public health framework based on risk, protection, and resilience in policy design, implementation, and evaluation are offered.

Summary

We hope the framework described in this book stimulates innovative ideas about the design of policies for vulnerable children and families. Principles of risk, protection, and resilience, too often ignored in policy discussions, hold great promise for improving the efficacy of social policies for children and families. In more precisely addressing risk and promoting protection, policies in fields ranging from child welfare to substance abuse may produce services and programs that more effectively help children and families prevail over adversities.

References

Biglan, A., Brennan, P. A., Foster, S. L., & Holder, H. D. (2004). *Helping adolescents at risk: Prevention of multiple problem behaviors.* New York: Guilford.

Fraser, M. W., Kirby, L. D., & Smokowski, P. R. (2004). Risk and resilience in childhood. In M. W. Fraser (Ed.), *Risk and resilience in childhood: An ecological perspective* (2nd ed., pp. 13–66). Washington, DC: NASW.

Hawkins, J. D., Catalano, R. F., Kosterman, R., Abbott, R., & Hill, K. G. (1999). Preventing adolescent health-risk behaviors by strengthening protection during childhood. *Archives of Pediatrics and Adolescent Medicine, 153,* 226–234.

Werner, E. E., & Smith, R. S. (1992). *Overcoming the odds: High risk children from birth to adulthood.* Ithaca, NY: Cornell University Press.

1

A Risk and Resilience Framework for Child, Youth, and Family Policy

Jeffrey M. Jenson

Mark W. Fraser

S ocial policies and programs for American children, youth, and families have undergone frequent shifts in philosophy and direction in the past century. Many policy frameworks—selective eligibility, universal prevention, rehabilitation, punishment—have contributed to the conceptual bases for services, programs, and interventions targeting young people. The most consistent characteristic of American social policy for children, youth, and families may be the sheer inconsistency of efforts aimed at helping the nation's most vulnerable populations.

Recent advances in understanding the developmental processes associated with the onset or persistence of childhood and adolescent problems warrant new thinking about policies and programs. We now know more than we ever have about why some children and adolescents develop social and health problems, and—in the case of such problems as sexually transmitted diseases, drug use, and delinquency—why some youths appear to make choices that lead to poor outcomes at home and in the school and community. Unfortunately, this knowledge is not yet systematically applied to policy or program design. The result is poorly specified, inadequately integrated, and often duplicative services for children and families. The motivation for this volume comes from the growing recognition that knowledge gained from understanding the developmental trajectories of children who experience social and health problems must be used to craft more effective policies and programs.

Coming of Age in America

Children, youth, and families face enormous developmental challenges in American society. At no time in the country's history have young people and their parents been confronted simultaneously by such a wide array of positive and negative influences and opportunities. Most children and youth become healthy adults who participate in positive—or "pro-social"— activities and are guided by interests that lead to meaningful and fulfilling lives. For some American children and youth, however, the path to adulthood is filled with risk and uncertainty. Because of the adversities they face, the prospect of a successful future for such young people is sometimes bleak.

The health of America's children and youth at the turn of the 21st century can be graphically conceptualized as a portrait of contrasts. Some rates of problem behavior—most notably violent offending and teen pregnancy— have decreased significantly in the past 8 to 10 years. Following a period of rapid increase between the late 1980s and 1995, the violent juvenile crime rate returned to its pre-1988 level and has remained stable since 1996 (Snyder, 2003). Encouragingly, teen birth rates among females between 15 and 17 years old declined 24 percent between 1996 and 2001. Only 25 births per 100,000 young women were recorded in 2001 (Centers for Disease Control and Prevention, 2001).

The promising news illustrated by a reduction in the prevalence of some types of childhood and adolescent problems is juxtaposed against disturbing accounts of school violence, persistent rates of substance use by young adolescents, the introduction of new and dangerous drugs, and unacceptably high rates of childhood poverty. Thirty-seven accounts of school violence were recorded in the nation's schools between 1974 and 2000 (Vossekuil, Fein, Reddy, Borum, & Modzeleski, 2002). The nation's deadliest school incident occurred in Littleton, Colorado, where, in April 1999, 14 students and one teacher died at Columbine High School following a shooting spree by two alienated and angry classmates. Sporadic acts of school violence have occurred in virtually every region of the United States in the years following Columbine.

Drug use among American youth continues to impose significant individual and societal costs upon the nation. Since 1991, reports have shown an increasing trend among young adolescents in the prevalence of smoking, alcohol consumption, and other drug use (Johnston, O'Malley, & Bachman, 2004). Despite recent leveling of these trends, the number of eighth-grade students reporting lifetime use of any illicit drug increased from 19 percent in 1991 to 23 percent in 2003. Illicit drug use among 10th-grade students increased from 31 percent to 41 percent between 1991 and 2003. Particularly concerning is evidence indicating that 12 percent of the nation's high school seniors tried ecstasy in 2002, an increase from 6 percent in 1996 (Johnston et al., 2004).

Many social and health problems are related to poverty. Nearly 17 percent of children under the age of 18 live in poverty in the United States, a condition that significantly affects individuals, families, and communities (U.S. Census Bureau, 2003). Children are more likely than all other age groups in the country to be poor (Cauce, Stewart, Rodriguez, Cochran, & Ginzler, 2003). Youth of color are disproportionately represented in poverty. At the turn of the millennium, childhood poverty rates varied markedly by race and ethnicity—26 percent for American Indians, 24 percent for African Americans, and 23 percent for Hispanics. This compares to 11 percent for Asian and Pacific Islanders and 8 percent for non-Latino whites (Dalaker & Proctor, 2000). Poverty has negative effects on several key outcomes during childhood and adolescence, including school achievement and delinquency (Brooks-Gunn & Duncan, 1997). Poverty is also associated with adverse consequences during adulthood and later stages of life (McCord, 1997). The persistent nature of behaviors typified by involvement in antisocial conduct, or arising from environmental conditions such as poverty, requires well-reasoned and innovative policy and program responses.

Policy and Program Responses to Childhood and Adolescent Problems

Experts from criminology, education, medicine, psychology, public health, sociology, and social work agree that there is no single pathway leading to school failure, drug use, delinquency, and other problems. Rather, it is the accumulation of risk—the sheer number of adversities and traumas confronted by children and families—that seems to disrupt normal developmental trajectories (Rutter, 2001). Jessor and Jessor's (1977) assertion in the mid-1970s that a small group of youth engages simultaneously in a variety of dangerous and costly problem behaviors has been well supported in the past 25 years. Indeed, the same academically marginalized youths who are involved in drug use may also be at risk of sexually transmitted diseases and violent victimization from family members or partners. Despite the fact that we know far more about these youths, their friends, and their families (e.g., Elliott, Huizinga, & Menard, 1989; Huizinga, Loeber, & Thornberry, 1994; Loeber, Farrington, Stouthamer-Loeber, & Van Kammen, 1998; Robins & McEvoy, 1990; White, Loeber, Stouthamer-Loeber, & Farrington, 1999), few innovative policy strategies for reducing the number of children and adolescents who experience problems have been introduced. One of the looming challenges for advocates and experts is to find ways to incorporate into public policies and programs the new knowledge emerging from research.

Currently, social policies and programs for children, youth, and families in the United States are highly fragmented. Many policies aimed at improving conditions for vulnerable and high-risk populations fail to consider the number, nature, or severity of problems experienced by American families. Other policies and resultant programs are duplicative, leading to a host of eligibility and implementation conflicts in the areas of child welfare, mental health, substance abuse, juvenile justice, education, and others.

The application of theoretical and empirical evidence to the design of social policies and programs aimed at improving the lives of children, youth, and families is limited. Social policy is often hurriedly created in the context of significant community events or trends that have attracted public attention and compel legislation. In some cases, policies developed in reaction to specific events lead to decisions that fail to account adequately for unforeseen or unintended long-term consequences. A case in point is that of the extensive juvenile justice reforms implemented across the country in the early to mid-1990s. Faced with increased rates of gang activity and violent youth crime, nearly all states enacted reforms emphasizing strict sanctions and punishments for young offenders. Many of these reforms—most notably boot camp programs and the extensive use of judicial waivers for serious offenders (i.e., where some juvenile offenders were prosecuted in criminal courts and exposed to adult rather than juvenile sanctions)—subsequently produced mixed or ineffective results (Jenson, Potter, & Howard, 2001).

We have learned quite a lot about the causes and progression of childhood and adolescent problems in the past several decades. Advances in understanding the life course development of problem behavior among children and youth, however, have been used primarily to enhance prevention and treatment strategies (Biglan, Brennan, Foster, & Holder, 2004). Aside from the ecological perspective (Bronfenbrenner, 1979, 1986), conceptual models that inform the design and direction of social policies for children, youth, and families are sorely lacking. In this book, we argue that a public health framework rooted in ecological theory and based on principles of risk and resilience is beginning to define a new and useful conceptual model for the design of social policy across the substantive areas of child welfare, education, mental health, health, developmental disabilities, substance use, and juvenile justice.

Public Health Frameworks for Social Policy

Public health frameworks for understanding and preventing childhood and adolescent problems have become widely used to promote positive youth outcomes in the emergent field of prevention science (Biglan et al., 2004; Hawkins, Catalano, & Miller, 1992). At its core, a public health approach to ameliorating youth problems considers the presence or absence of risk and protective factors in the design and selection of interventions. Closely related to principles of risk and protection is the concept of resilience, the ability to overcome adverse conditions and to function normatively in the face of risk. A public health perspective for policy development aimed at children, youth, and families must incorporate the key concepts of risk, protection, and resilience.

Risk and Protection

In the context of childhood and adolescence, risk factors are individual, school, peer, family, and community influences that increase the likelihood of such problem behavior as dropping out of school or becoming a juvenile delinquent. The identification of risk factors for a variety of childhood and adolescent problems has gained widespread acceptance in the prevention field in the past decade (Biglan et al., 2004; Gottfredson & Wilson, 2003; Romer, 2003). Its origins, however, date to the late 1970s and early 1980s, when researchers and policymakers began placing greater importance on understanding the individual, family, social, and community factors that commonly occurred in the lives of troubled children and youth (Rutter, 1979, 1987). The emphasis on understanding the underlying causes of childhood and youth problems led investigators to identify specific factors that were consistently associated with the occurrence of adolescent problem behaviors. This approach, adapted from public health efforts to identify risk factors associated with such problems as smoking and heart disease, led to the use of "risk-based" strategies to prevent childhood and adolescent problems (Hawkins et al., 1992).

Risk Factors

The earliest risk factor models were primarily lists of the correlates of adolescent problems (e.g., Garmezy, 1971). These models were drawn from previous research that identified risk factors for adolescent problem behaviors such as substance abuse and delinquency (e.g., Hawkins, Jenson, Catalano, & Lishner, 1988). Early models often failed to consider the temporal relationship of risk factors to the occurrence of specific behaviors or to examine the additive and interactive effects of risk factors. Recent reviews of risk factors for adolescent problem behaviors (e.g., Fraser, Kirby, & Smokowski, 2004; Fraser & Terzian, in press; Hawkins, Herrenkohl, Farrington, Brewer, Catalano, & Harachi, 1998; Jenson & Howard, 2001; Thornberry, 1998) have improved on earlier efforts by limiting their selection of studies to those in which the risk factor clearly preceded a problem behavior. Longitudinal studies have also been conducted to better understand the processes by which risk factors influence behavior over the course of childhood and adolescence (e.g., Hawkins, Catalano, Kosterman, Abbott, & Hill, 1999; Loeber et al., 1998; Spoth, Redmond, & Shin, 1998). We adopt Fraser and Terzian's (in press) definition of a risk factor in this book:

> Broadly defined, the term *risk factor* relates to any event, condition, or experience that increases the probability that a problem will be formed, maintained, or exacerbated (p. 5).

This definition recognizes that the presence of one or more risk factors in a person's life may increase the likelihood that a problem behavior will occur at a later point in time. The presence of a risk factor does not ensure or guarantee that a specific outcome—school failure, for example—will eventuate. Rather, its presence suggests an increased chance or probability that such a problem may develop. Common risk factors for childhood and adolescent problems by level of influence are shown in Table 1.1. These and other factors are discussed in relation to specific topics presented in Chapters 2–8.

Closely linked to risk factors are protective factors, which are characteristics and conditions that buffer exposure to risk.

Protective Factors

Experts favoring less of a deficit-based model to understanding childhood and adolescent problems have advocated a framework based on characteristics that *protect* youth from engaging in problem behaviors. There is some debate about the exact definition of *protection* and about how to put protective factors into practice (Fraser et al., 2004; Rossa, 2002). Most

Table 1.1   Common Risk Factors for Childhood and Adolescent Problems by Level of Influence[a]

Environmental Factors

    Laws and norms favorable to antisocial behavior

    Poverty and economic deprivation

    Low economic opportunity

    Neighborhood disorganization

    Low neighborhood attachment

Interpersonal and Social Factors

    Family communication and conflict

    Poor parent–child bonding

    Poor family management practices

    Family alcohol and drug use

    School failure

    Low commitment to school

    Rejection by conforming peer groups

    Association with antisocial peers

Individual Factors

    Family history of alcoholism

    Sensation-seeking orientation

    Poor impulse control

    Attention deficits

    Hyperactivity

a. Adapted from Fraser et al., 2004; Jenson & Howard, 1999; and Hawkins et al., 1998.

investigators agree that protective factors are attributes or characteristics that lower the probability of an undesirable outcome (Benard, 2004; Rutter, 1987; Werner & Smith, 1992). There is disagreement, however, about the independence of protective factors in relationship to risk.

The knowledge base associated with the concept of protection began emerging in the 1980s, when investigators such as Rutter (1979) and Werner and Smith (1982) observed that certain positive attributes appeared to operate in the presence of risk or adversity. The exact definition of a protective factor, however, quickly became a topic of debate. Most of this debate has centered on the confusion created when both risk and protective factors are conceptualized as representing the opposite ends of a single continuum (Pollard,

Hawkins, & Arthur, 1999). For example, consistent family management practices are often identified as important in producing positive outcomes in children. Inconsistent family management is construed as a factor leading to poor outcomes. In simple terms, consistent family management is identified as a protective factor whereas inconsistent family management is seen as a risk factor. Using risk and protection in this manner establishes the two concepts as polar opposites, with one pole representing positive outcomes and the other pole representing negative outcomes.

Therein lies the current debate among social scientists. Put succinctly, the questions are the following: (1) Do risk and protective factors represent measurable levels of an attribute or characteristic that has two poles along a single continuum? or (2) Are risk and protective factors separate and independent constructs?

We view protection as a concept that operates as a buffering agent to risk exposure and offer the following definition from Fraser and Terzian (in press):

> protective factors (are) resources—individual or environmental—that minimize the impact of risk (p. 12).

This definition views protective traits as individual characteristics or environmental conditions that *interact* with specific risk factors present in a child or in his/her environment. We believe that protective factors operate in three ways. They serve to (1) reduce or buffer the impact of risk in a child's life, (2) interrupt a *chain* of risk factors that may be present in a young person's life (e.g., disrupt a potential chain of risk that begins with peer rejection and leads to involvement with antisocial peers and then to delinquency), and (3) prevent or block the onset of a risk factor (Fraser & Terzian, in press).

Table 1.2 shows common protective factors discussed by authors in subsequent chapters.

Resilience: When a Child Prevails Over Adversity

Resilience is one's capacity to adapt successfully in the presence of risk and adversity (Garmezy, 1986; Luthar, 2003; Olsson, Bond, Burns, Vella-Brodrick, & Sawyer, 2003). Numerous examples of young people and adults who have "overcome the odds" associated with the negative effects of risk come from child welfare (Festinger, 1984), juvenile justice (Vigil, 1990), substance abuse (Werner & Smith, 2001), and other service delivery settings. We conceptualize resilience as the outcome of a process that takes into account level of risk exposure and the presence or absence of

Table 1.2   Common Protective Factors for Childhood and Adolescent Problems by Level of Influence[a]

Environmental Factors
- Opportunities for education, employment, and other pro-social activities
- Caring relationships with adults or extended family members
- Social support from non-family members

Interpersonal and Social Factors
- Attachment to parents
- Caring relationships with siblings
- Low parental conflict
- High levels of commitment to school
- Involvement in conventional activities
- Belief in pro-social norms and values

Individual Factors
- Social and problem-solving skills
- Positive attitude
- Temperament
- High intelligence
- Low childhood stress

a. Adapted from Fraser et al., 2004; Jenson & Howard, 1999; and Hawkins et al., 1998.

protective factors. When exposure to risk is high, evidence suggests that most children and adolescents experience some type of problem or developmental difficulty (Cicchetti & Rogosch, 1997). Protective factors exert influences on developmental outcomes where risk is high, but they may be relatively benign in circumstances where risk is low (Fraser, Richman, & Galinsky, 1999).

Sameroff and colleagues (Sameroff, 1999; Sameroff & Fiese, 2000; Sameroff & Gutman, 2004) have used the phrase *promotive factor* to refer to attributes or characteristics that have positive effects on people's lives, irrespective of the level of risk exposure. They argue that promotive factors (e.g., high intelligence) have direct effects on child and adolescent outcomes. Tests of the direct impact of promotive effects have been relatively limited to date (Sameroff, Bartko, Baldwin, Baldwin, & Siefer, 1999).

Increasingly, experts are viewing resilience as the outcome of an interactive process involving risk, protection, and promotion. Thus, adaptation—expressed through individual behavior—is interpreted as an interactive product involving the presence or absence, level of exposure, and the strength of the specific risk, protective, and promotive factors present in a person's life.

Applying Principles of Risk and Resilience to Social Policy

Applications of public health principles have primarily been used to develop specific clinical or programmatic interventions in school and community prevention settings (Cicchetti, Rappaport, Sandler, & Weissberg, 2000; Luthar & Cicchetti, 2000; Marsten, 2001). The result has been impressive. Recent research identifies a number of efficacious risk-based interventions aimed at preventing child and adolescent problems such as substance abuse (Foxcroft, Ireland, Lister-Sharp, Lowe, & Breen, 2003; Gottfredson & Wilson, 2003) and delinquency (Catalano, Arthur, Hawkins, Berglund, & Olson, 1998; Catalano, Loeber, & McKinney, 1999). Research and governmental entities, concerned with improving the dissemination of effective programs, have made lists of effective interventions available to practitioners, educators, and the general public (Campbell Collaboration Library, 2004; Center for the Study and Prevention of Violence, 2004; Schinke, Brounstein, & Gardner, 2002). This, in turn, has led to greater use of empirically based interventions by members of the practice community.

A logical next step in the application of the risk and resilience model requires extending the framework to the development of a broader cross section of programs and public policies (Fraser & Galinsky, 2004). To date, only limited examples of this process exist. Investigators in the public health field have applied principles of risk, protection, and resilience to design prevention strategies that target risk factors for AIDS. Evidence suggests that the implementation of this approach has led to reductions in the spread of AIDS in many parts of the world (Sorenson, Masson, & Perlman, 2002).

A second example of using a public health framework to affect program and policy change comes from innovations in substance abuse prevention. Hawkins, Catalano, and Associates (1992) have created a theoretically based prevention process designed to help community leaders develop and implement effective substance abuse prevention programs. The Communities That Care (CTC) program is based on the social development model (SDM), a general theory of human behavior that integrates perspectives from social control theory (Hirschi, 1969), social learning theory (Bandura, 1989), and differential association theory (Sutherland, 1973; Matsueda, 1982). The SDM specifies the mechanisms and causal pathways by which risk and protective factors interact in the etiology of various behaviors, including adolescent drug use (Catalano & Hawkins, 1996). The model proposes that four protective factors inhibit the development of antisocial behaviors in children: (1) *bonding,* defined as attachment and commitment to family, school, and positive peers

(Garmezy, 1986); (2) *belief in the shared values or norms* of these social units; (3) *external constraints* such as clear, consistent standards against drug use (Hansen, Malotte, & Fileding, 1988; Scheier & Botvin, 1998), and (4) *social, cognitive, and emotional skills* that provide protective tools for children to solve problems (Rutter, 1987) that assertively and confidently perform in social situations (Werner & Smith, 1982), and that resist influences and impulses to violate their norms for behavior (Hansen, Graham, Sobel, Shelton, Flay, & Johnson, 1987).

In the CTC model, coalitions are formed to engage in systematic prevention planning that requires communities to identify prevalent risk and protective factors for adolescent problems in their localities. Following the assessment of such factors, communities are encouraged to select prevention strategies on the basis of available empirical evidence (Hawkins et al., 1992). Although the CTC model falls short of satisfying the criteria for a formal policy, it does initiate a process whereby knowledge of risk and protective factors becomes an integral part of program design. The model is currently undergoing a 5-year test in seven states.

As implied in the preceding examples, applying principles of risk and resilience to policy design requires an understanding of the developmental trajectories associated with the onset or persistence of child and adolescent problems. Figure 1.1 illustrates the process involved in applying a public health perspective to policy and program design for children, youth, and families.

Two additional elements in this model—ecological theory and life course development—are outlined briefly next.

Ecological Theory and Life Course Development

Mentioned earlier, we use an ecological perspective to provide a context for thinking about principles of risk, protection, and resilience over the course of child development. The ecological perspective is well known and widely applied in education, practice, and research across social work and many disciplines (Bronfenbrenner, 1979, 1986; Germain, 1991; Fraser, 2004). Ecological theory posits that development is deeply affected by interactions between the biological and psychological characteristics of the individual child and conditions in his/her environment. Environmental conditions are usually described as family, peer, school, and community influences (Bronfenbrenner, 1979, 1986). An ecological perspective views child development as a product of transactions between an organism and the context or, in the vernacular of social work, the influence of events that

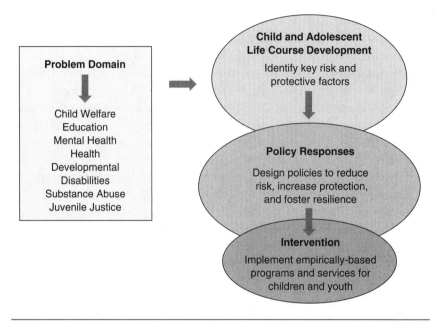

Figure 1.1   A Risk and Resilience Framework for Child, Youth, and Family
Policy

occur in the lives of young people within their family, peer, school, and
community settings.

We believe social policies for children, youth, and families must be framed
in an ecological perspective that considers the influence of the context. For
example, a child referred to the juvenile justice system lives within some type
of family unit, attends a local school, and has a network of peers. Evidence
indicates that both unique and interrelated risk and protective factors
increase or decrease the likelihood of problem behavior within each of these
domains (Fraser, 2004; Jenson & Howard, 1999). Social policies are, therefore, most likely to be effective when they address the myriad of influences
that lead to the onset of problem behavior for young people. In earlier work,
we have discussed risk and protective factors in the context of the ecological
perspective as a way to explain the onset and prevention of childhood and
adolescent problems (Fraser, 2004; Jenson, 2004). However, knowledge
of such factors has seldom been used as a lens through which to examine
social policy for children, youth, and families. Our intention is to show how
principles contained in the ecological perspective can be used to create integrated policies that may cut across traditional policy boundaries found within
systems of care for American children, youth, and families.

Summary

Knowledge gained from studies of risk, protection, and resilience has significantly affected our understanding of the onset and persistence of childhood and adolescent problems. Principles of risk, protection, and resilience have also been helpful in improving the conceptual and methodological rigor of prevention and treatment programs for children and youth (Kaftarian, Robinson, Compton, Davis, & Volkow, 2004). To date, these principles have not been systematically applied to social policies for children and families. This chapter has outlined a public health framework for child and family policy based on risk, protection, and resilience. Tenets of ecological theory and life course development were introduced as essential parts of the framework. In subsequent chapters, we more fully examine the utility of a public health framework for child and family policy.

References

Bandura, A. (1989). Human agency in social cognitive theory. *American Psychologist, 14,* 1175–1184.

Benard, B. (2004). *Resiliency: What we have learned.* San Francisco: WestEd.

Biglan, A., Brennan, P. A., Foster, S. L., & Holder, H. D. (2004). *Helping adolescents at risk. Prevention of multiple problem behaviors.* New York: Guilford.

Bronfenbrenner, U. (1979). *The ecology of human development: Experiments by nature and design.* Cambridge, MA: Harvard University Press.

Bronfenbrenner, U. (1986). Ecology of the family as a context to human development: Research perspectives. *Development Psychology, 22,* 723–742.

Brooks-Gunn, J., & Duncan, G. J. (1997). The effects of poverty on children. *The Future of Children, 7,* 55–71.

Campbell Collaboration Library. (2004). [Database]. Retrieved on July 17, 2004, from http:/www.campbellcollaboration.org/Fralibrary.html

Catalano, R. F., Arthur, M. W., Hawkins, J. D., Berglund, L., & Olson, J. J. (1998). Comprehensive community and school based interventions to prevent antisocial behavior. In R. Loeber & D. P. Farrington (Eds.), *Serious and violent juvenile offenders: Risk factors and successful interventions* (pp. 248–283). Thousand Oaks, CA: Sage.

Catalano, R. F., & Hawkins, J. D. (1996). The social development model: A theory of antisocial behavior. In J. D. Hawkins (Ed.), *Delinquency and crime: Current theories* (pp. 149–197). New York: Cambridge University Press.

Catalano, R. F., Loeber, R., & McKinney, K. (1999). School and community interventions to prevent serious and violent offending. *Juvenile Justice Bulletin,* October. Office of Juvenile Justice and Delinquency Prevention. Washington, DC.

Cauce, A. M., Stewart, A., Rodriguez, M. D., Cochran, B., & Ginzler, J. (2003). Overcoming the odds? Adolescent development in the context of urban poverty. In S. S. Luthar (Ed.), *Resilience and vulnerability: Adaptation in the context of childhood adversities* (pp. 343–363). Cambridge, UK: Cambridge University Press.

Center for the Study and Prevention of Violence. (2004). *Blueprints for violence prevention.* Retrieved on July 16, 2004 from: http:/www.colorado.edu/cvsp/ publications/blueprints.html

Centers for Disease Control and Prevention. (2001). *Births: Final data for 2001, National vital statistics report.* Washington, DC: Author.

Cicchetti, D., Rappaport, J., Sandler, L., & Weissberg, R. P. (Eds.). (2000). *The promotion of wellness in children and adolescents.* Washington, DC: Child Welfare League of America.

Cicchetti, D., & Rogosch, F. A. (1997). The role of self-organization in the promotion of resilience in maltreated children. *Development and Psychopathology, 9,* 787–815.

Dalaker, J., & Proctor, B. D. (2000). *Poverty in the United States: 1999* (U.S. Census Bureau Report Series P60–210). Washington, DC: U.S. Government Printing Office.

Elliott, D. S., Huizinga, D., & Menard, S. (1989). *Multiple problem youth: Delinquency, substance use, and mental health problems.* New York: Springer-Verlag.

Festinger, T. (1984). *No one ever asked us: A postscript to the foster care system.* New York: Columbia University Press.

Foxcroft, D. R., Ireland, D., Lister-Sharp, D. J., Lowe, G., & Breen, R. (2003). Longer term primary prevention for alcohol misuse in young people: A systematic review. *Addiction, 98,* 397–411.

Fraser, M. W. (2004). The ecology of childhood: A multisystems perspective. In M. W. Fraser (Ed.), *Risk and resilience in childhood: An ecological perspective* (2nd ed., pp. 1–12). Washington, DC: NASW.

Fraser, M. W., & Galinsky, M. J. (2004). Risk and resilience in childhood: Toward an evidence-based model of practice. In M. W. Fraser (Ed.), *Risk and resilience in childhood: An ecological perspective* (2nd ed., pp. 385–402). Washington, DC: NASW.

Fraser, M. W., Kirby, L. D., & Smokowski, P. R. (2004). Risk and resilience in childhood. In M. W. Fraser (Ed.), *Risk and resilience in childhood: An ecological perspective* (2nd ed., pp. 13–66). Washington, DC: NASW.

Fraser, M. W., Richman, J. M., & Galinsky, M. J. (1999). Risk, protection, and resilience: Towards a conceptual framework for social work practice. *Social Work Research, 23,* 131–144.

Fraser, M. W., & Terzian, M. A. (in press). Risk and resilience in child development: Practice principles and strategies. In G. P. Mallon & P. McCartt Hess (Eds.), *Handbook of children, youth, and family services: Practice, policies, and programs.* New York: Columbia University Press.

Garmezy, N. (1971). Vulnerability research and the issue of primary prevention. *American Journal of Orthopsychiatry, 41,* 101–116.

Garmezy, N. (1986). On measures, methods, and models. *Journal of the American Academy of Child and Adolescent Psychiatry, 25,* 727–729.

Germain, C. B. (1991). *Human behavior in the social environment: An ecological view.* New York: Columbia University Press.

Gottfredson, D. C., & Wilson, D. B. (2003). Characteristics of effective school-based substance abuse prevention. *Prevention Science, 4,* 27–38.

Hansen, W. B., Graham, J. W., Sobel, J. L., Shelton, D. R., Flay, B. R., & Johnson, C. A. (1987). The consistency of peer and parent influences on tobacco, alcohol, and marijuana use among young adolescents. *Journal of Behavioral Medicine, 10,* 559–579.

Hansen, W. B., Malotte, C. K., & Fileding, J. E. (1988). Evaluation of a tobacco and alcohol abuse prevention curriculum for adolescents. Special Issue: The role of the schools in implementing the nation's health objectives for the 1990's. *Health Education Quarterly, 15,* 93–114.

Hawkins, J. D., Catalano, R. F., & Associates (1992). *Communities that care: Actions for drug abuse prevention.* San Francisco, CA: Jossey-Boss.

Hawkins, J. D., Catalano, R. F., Kosterman, R., Abbott, R., & Hill, K. G. (1999). Preventing adolescent health-risk behaviors by strengthening protection during childhood. *Archives of Pediatrics and Adolescent Medicine, 153,* 226–234.

Hawkins, J. D., Catalano, R. F., & Miller, J. Y. (1992). Risk and protective factors for alcohol and other drug problems in adolescence and early adulthood: Implications for substance abuse prevention. *Psychological Bulletin, 112,* 64–105.

Hawkins, J. D., Herrenkohl, T., Farrington, D. P., Brewer, D. D., Catalano, R. F., & Harachi, T. W. (1998). A review of predictors of youth violence. In R. Loeber & D. P. Farrington (Eds.), *Serious and violent juvenile offenders: Risk factors and successful interventions* (pp. 106–146). Thousand Oaks, CA: Sage.

Hawkins, J. D., Jenson, J. M., Catalano, R. F., & Lishner, D. L. (1988). Delinquency and drug abuse: Implications for social services. *Social Service Review, 62,* 258–284.

Hirschi, T. (1969). *Causes of delinquency.* Berkeley, CA: University of California Press.

Huizinga, D., Loeber, R., & Thornberry, T. P. (1994). Urban delinquency and substance abuse: Initial findings (Research Summary Series). Washington, DC: U.S. Department of Justice, Office of Juvenile Justice and Delinquency Prevention.

Jenson, J. M. (2004). Risk and protective factors for alcohol and other drug use in adolescence. In M. W. Fraser (Ed.), *Risk and resiliency in childhood: An ecological perspective.* (2nd ed., pp. 183–208). Washington, DC: NASW.

Jenson, J. M., & Howard, M. O. (1999). *Youth violence. Current research and recent practice innovations.* Washington, DC: NASW.

Jenson, J. M., & Howard, M. O. (2001). Causes and prevention of youth violence. *Denver University Law Review, 77,* 629–660.

Jenson, J. M., Potter, C. C., & Howard, M. O. (2001). American juvenile justice: Recent trends and issues in youth offending. *Social Policy and Administration, 35,* 48–68.

Jessor, R., & Jessor, S. L. (1977). *Problem behavior and psychosocial development: A longitudinal study of youth.* New York: Academic.

Johnston, L. D., O'Malley, P. M., & Bachman, J. G. (2004*). Drug use, drinking, and smoking: National survey results from high school, college, and young adult populations.* Washington, DC: U.S. Government Printing Office.

Kaftarian, S., Robinson, E., Compton, W., Davis, B. W., & Volkow, N. (2004). Blending prevention research and practice in schools: Critical issues and suggestions. *Prevention Science, 5,* 1–3.

Loeber, R., Farrington, D. P., Stouthamer-Loeber, M., & Van Kammen, W. B. (1998). *Antisocial behavior and mental health problems.* Mahwah, NJ: Lawrence Erlbaum.

Luthar, S. S. (2003). *Resilience and vulnerability: Adaptation in the context of childhood adversities.* Cambridge, UK: Cambridge University Press.

Luthar, S. S., & Cicchetti, D. (2000). The construct of resilience: Implications for interventions and social policies. *Development and Psychopathology, 12,* 857–885.

Marsten, A. S. (2001). Ordinary magic: Resilience processes in development. *American Psychologist, 56,* 227–238.

Matsueda, R. L. (1982). Testing control theory and differential association: A causal modeling approach. *American Sociological Review, 47,* 489–504.

McCord, J. (1997). *Violence and childhood in the innercity.* Cambridge, UK: Cambridge University Press.

Olsson, C. A., Bond, L., Burns, J. M., Vella-Brodrick, D. A., & Sawyer, S. M. (2003). Adolescent resilience: A concept analysis. *Journal of Adolescence, 26,* 1–11.

Pollard, J. A., Hawkins, J. D., & Arthur, M. W. (1999). Risk and protection: Are both necessary to understand diverse behavioral outcomes in adolescence? *Social Work Research, 23,* 145–158.

Robins, L. N., & McEvoy, L. (1990). Conduct problems as predictors of substance abuse. In L. N. Robins & M. Rutter (Eds.), *Straight and devious pathways from childhood to adulthood* (pp. 182–204). Cambridge, UK: Cambridge University Press.

Romer, D. (2003). Prospects for an integrated approach to adolescent risk reduction. In D. Romer (Ed.), *Reducing adolescent risk: Toward an integrated approach* (pp. 1–9). Thousand Oaks, CA: Sage.

Rossa, M. W. (2002). Some thoughts about resilience versus positive development, main effects, versus interaction effects and the value of resilience. *Child Development, 71,* 567–569.

Rutter, M. (1979). Protective factors in children's responses to stress and disadvantage. In M. W. Kent & J. E. Rolf (Eds.), *Primary prevention of psychopathology: Vol. 3. Social competence in children* (pp. 49–74). Lebanon, NH: University Press of New England.

Rutter, M. (1987). Psychosocial resilience and protective mechanisms. *American Journal of Orthopsychiatry, 57,* 316–331.

Rutter, M. (2001). Psychosocial adversity: Risk, resilience, and recovery. In J. M. Richman & M. W. Fraser (Eds.), *The context of youth violence: Resilience, risk, and protection* (pp. 13–41). Westport, CT: Praeger.

Sameroff, A. J. (1999). Ecological perspectives on developmental risk. In J. D. Osofsky & H. E. Fitzgerald (Eds.), *WAIMH handbook of infant mental health: Vol. 4. Infant mental health groups at risk* (pp. 223–248). New York: Wiley.

Sameroff, A. J., Bartko, W. T., Baldwin, A., Baldwin, C., & Siefer, R. (1999). Family and social influences on the development of child competence. In M. Lewis & C. Feiring (Eds.), *Families, risk, and competence* (pp. 161–186). Mahwah, NJ: Lawrence Erlbaum.

Sameroff, A. J., & Fiese, B. H. (2000). Transactional regulation: The developmental ecology of early intervention. In J. P. Shonkoff & S. J. Meisels (Eds.), *Handbook of early childhood intervention* (2nd ed., pp. 135–159). New York: Cambridge University Press.

Sameroff, A. J., & Gutman, L. M. (2004). Contributions of risk research to the design of successful interventions. In P. Allen-Meares & M. W. Fraser (Eds.), *Intervention with children and adolescents: An interdisciplinary approach* (pp. 9–26). Boston: Allyn & Bacon.

Scheier, L. M., & Botvin, G. J. (1998). Relations of social skills, personal competence, and adolescent drug use: A developmental exploratory study. *Journal of Early Adolescence, 18,* 77–114.

Schinke, S., Brounstein, P., & Gardner, S. (2002). *Science-based prevention programs and principles, 2002.* DHHS Pub No. (SMA) 03–3764. Substance Abuse and Mental Health Services Administration, Rockville, MD.

Snyder, H. N. (2003). Juvenile arrests 2001. *Juvenile Justice Bulletin,* December. Office of Juvenile Justice and Delinquency Prevention. Washington, DC.

Sorenson, J. L., Masson, C. L., & Perlman, D. C. (2002). HIV/Hepatitis prevention in drug abuse treatment programs: Guidance from research. *NIDA Science and Practice Perspectives, 1,* 4–12. National Institute on Drug Abuse. Washington, DC.

Spoth, R., Redmond, C., & Shin, C. (1998). Direct and indirect latent variable parenting outcomes of two universal family-focused preventive interventions: Extending a public-health oriented research base. *Journal of Consulting and Clinical Psychology, 66,* 385–399.

Sutherland, E. H. (1973) Development of the theory [Private paper published posthumously]. In K. Schuessler (Ed.), *Edwin Sutherland on analyzing crime.* Chicago: University of Chicago Press.

Thornberry, T. P. (1998). Membership in youth gangs and involvement in serious and violent offending. In R. Loeber & D. P. Farrington (Eds.), *Serious & violent juvenile offenders. Risk factors and successful interventions* (pp. 147–166). Thousand Oaks, CA: Sage.

U.S. Census Bureau. (2003). *Statistical abstract of the United States.* Washington, DC: Author.

Vigil, J. D. (1990). Cholos and gangs: Culture change and street youth in Los Angeles. In R. Huff (Ed.), *Gangs in America: Diffusion, diversity, and public policy* (pp. 142–162). Thousand Oaks, CA: Sage.

Vossekuil, B., Fein, R. A., Reddy, M., Borum, R., & Modzeleski, W. (2002). *The final report and findings of the Safe School Initiative: Implications for the prevention of school attacks in the United States.* United States Secret Service and United States Department of Education. Washington, DC.

Werner, E. E., & Smith, R. S. (1982). *Vulnerable but invincible: A longitudinal study of resilient children and youth.* New York: Adams, Bannister, & Cox.

Werner, E. E., & Smith, R. S. (1992). *Overcoming the odds: High risk children from birth to adulthood.* New York: Cornell University Press.

Werner, E. E., & Smith, R. S. (2001). *Journeys from childhood to the midlife: Risk, resilience, and recovery.* New York: Cornell University Press.

White, H. R., Loeber, R., Stouthamer-Loeber, M., & Farrington, D. P. (1999). Developmental associations between substance use and violence. *Development and Psychopathology, 11,* 785–803.

2

Child Welfare Policies and Programs

Peter J. Pecora

Purpose and Overview of Child Welfare Policy

The child and family social services delivery system in many areas of the country remains overburdened. In 2002, nearly 2 million U.S. children were reported as abused and neglected. Compared with 1990 reports, this represents an increase of some 46 percent in officially reported victims.[1] The United States federal government recently estimated that 532,000 children were placed in foster care in family and non-family settings and 813,000 children were served throughout that fiscal year (U.S. Department of Health and Human Services, 2004).[2] As shown in Table 2.1, the numbers of

This chapter draws from material in the third edition of *The Child Welfare Challenge*. I appreciate the advice from that textbook's co-authors James Whittaker, Anthony Maluccio, Richard Barth, and Robert Plotnick. Special thanks to Fran Gutterman, Adrienne Hahn, Martha Jenkins, and Betsey Rosenbaum of Casey Family Programs, and the legislative advocacy staff of the Child Welfare League of America for the policy briefs and position statements that informed the legislative policy section. Finally, foster care alumni, practitioners, and foster parents have taught us much about the real impacts of policy; we appreciate the time they have devoted to improving the child welfare system.

Table 2.1   Children in America: Selected Facts and Figures

National Child Demographics

Child population under age 18 in 2003[1]	73,043,506
White children under 18 in 2003[2]	58.6%
Nonwhite children under 18 in 2003[3]	41.4%
Children and youth under 14 in 2003[4]	77.4%
Children and youth age 14–17 and older in 2003[5]	22.6%

Who Cared for America's Children in 2002?

Both parents[6]	68.7%
Mother[6]	22.8%
Father[6]	4.6%
Grandparent[6]	1.8%
Other relative[6]	1.1%
Foster parent[6]	0.3%
Nonrelative[6]	0.8%
Number of women with no husband present who were raising their own children under 18 years[7]	8,145,233

The Most Vulnerable Children

Children living in families with incomes below the poverty line in 2002[8]	12 million
National poverty rate for children under 18 in 2003[9]	17.7%
Referrals for possible child abuse or neglect in 2002[10]	1.8 million
Children substantiated or indicated as abused or neglected in 2002[11]	896,000
Children who died as a result of abuse or neglect in 2002[12]	1,400
(1.98 deaths per 1,000)	
Children in foster care on September 30, 2003[13]	523,000

| Children adopted from the public foster care system during the fiscal year ending September 30, 2002[14] | 53,000 |
| Children waiting to be adopted from the public foster care system as of September 30, 2002[15] | 126,000 |

Sources: Adapted with permission from "A National Fact Sheet 2004." Copyright © Child Welfare League of America.

1. U.S. Census Bureau, Population Reference Bureau (2004). Special tabulations of the supplemental survey. Washington, DC: Author.

2. U.S. Census Bureau (2003). National population estimates: Sex, age, race, and Hispanic origin. Washington, DC: Author.

3. Ibid.

4. U.S. Census Bureau (2003). National population estimates: sex and age. Washington, DC: Author.

5. Ibid.

6. U.S. Census Bureau. (2003, June). Household relationship and living arrangements of children under 18 years, by age, sex, race, Hispanic origin, and metropolitan residence: March 2002 (Table C2). Available online. Washington, DC: Author.

7. Estimate from the 2002 Community Population Survey of the U.S. Census Bureau. U.S. Census Bureau, American Community Profile. (2003). Table 1. General Demographic Characteristics. Last retrieved August 19, 2004, from: http://www.census.gov/acs/www/Products/Profiles/Single/2002/ACS/Tabular/010/01000US1.htm

8. National Center for Children in Poverty (NCCP), Columbia University. (2003). *Low-income children in the United States (2003)*. Available online. New York: Author. In 2001, 16.3% of children under age 18 lived in poverty—more than any other age group in America. U.S. Bureau of the Census. (2003, September). People in families with related children under 18 by family structure, age, and sex, iterated by income-to-poverty ratio and race: 2002 below 100% of poverty. All races (Table POV03). Available online. Washington, DC: Author.

9. U.S. Census Bureau (2004, August). American Community Survey, Data Profiles 2003. Washington, DC: Author.

10. U.S. Department of Health and Human Services, Children's Bureau, Administration on Children, Youth and Families, National Clearinghouse on Child Abuse and Neglect Information. (2003). *Child Maltreatment 2002*. Washington, DC: Author, p. xiii.

11. Ibid, p. xiii.

12. Ibid, p. 51.

13. U.S. Department of Health and Human Services, Administration for Children and Families Administration on Children, Youth and Families, Children's Bureau. (2004). Adoption and Foster Care Analysis and Reporting System (AFCARS). 2002 data, as updated during May 2004. Washington, DC: U.S. Government Printing Office.

14. U.S. Department of Health and Human Services, Administration for Children and Families, Children's Bureau. *The AFCARS report–Preliminary FY2001 estimates as of March 2003.* (8): 1–7. Washington, DC: U.S. Government Printing Office. (See http://www.acf.dhhs.gov/programs/cb/publications/afcars/, p. 4.)

15. Ibid, p. 4.

children in placement have risen substantially since 1980, but they have shown a slow and steady decrease since 2000, with the decrease in out-of-home care attenuated by lower reunification rates. People of color are underrepresented among child welfare staff, and there are insufficient services to ensure that children achieve permanency by returning home or being placed with guardianship or adoptive families.

However, new resources and ideas are reshaping child welfare practices in many locales. Notably, agencies in Illinois, New York City, and other areas are making successful efforts to reduce the length of stay of children in out-of-home care, to reduce the level of restrictiveness of child placements, and to increase the proportion of children placed with relatives or clan members. In addition, the number of children being adopted or securing a form of permanency through guardianship has increased over the last two decades as some states have significantly decreased the time to adoption (Avery, 1998; U.S. Department of Health and Human Services, 2003a). These innovations may expand further with new initiatives under way. These include child welfare demonstration waivers, expedited adoptive parent assessments, expedited approvals of subsidy applications, increases in judicial personnel, and heightened attention by the agencies and courts to the need for more timely permanency planning. Consider the example of New York City, where the number of children in foster care has been reduced, and 2,793 children placed in out-of-home care were adopted in 2003 (New York City Administration for Children's Services, 2004). Though the child welfare system is burdened, professionals, families, and advocates across the country are experimenting with new policies and procedures designed to find for children safe and permanent living arrangements.

In this chapter, we review risk and protective factors related to why children and their families become involved in the child welfare system and the major social policies that are directed toward these families. In addition, the ways in which concepts of risk and protection are implemented in these policies are examined. Drawing from innovative projects and programs across the country, we conclude with a discussion of current policy issues and recommendations for improving child welfare services.

Mission and Goals of Child Welfare Services

The mission of child welfare has historically been to respond to the needs of children reported to public child protection agencies as abused, neglected, or at risk of child maltreatment. Recently, there has been more emphasis on looking beyond public and private child welfare agencies to involve communities as a whole in the protection and nurturing of children. In addition, efforts to formulate collaborative community strategies aimed at preventing and responding to child abuse and neglect have increased. Our knowledge of the interplay of risk and protective factors at the levels of child, parent, family, neighborhood, and community has grown to include the need to look beyond the typical parent–child dyad. Although all children have highly individual needs and characteristics, they live in the context of a family structure. Families, in turn, reside in the context of a culture and a neighborhood. Finally, communities are centered in the context of social, economic, cultural, and political environments (Child Welfare League of America, 2003).

A child welfare system that fails to incorporate and draw upon the richness and strength embodied in this context of family life is a system that cannot effectively respond to the needs of vulnerable children and troubled families. Although agency mission statements provide the overall context for service, it is essential that key goals or outcomes are specified to help guide such functions as establishing strategic plans, program structures, funding, and practice guidelines within a context of philosophical values (American Humane Association, 1998).

Key Goals and Outcomes for Child Welfare Services

The field of child welfare services is gaining more clarity and consensus about its primary mission. A primary goal and two secondary goals exist for child welfare services: first and foremost, the primary goal is to protect children from harm. The second goal is to preserve existing family units, which we understand to include both birth family and relative families as appropriate. The third goal is to promote children's development into adults who can live independently and contribute to their communities—a goal that may require a variety of permanency planning alternatives such as family reunification, placement with relatives, different forms of guardianship (depending upon local law), adoption, and *planned* long-term foster care or kinship care with legal safeguards such as guardianship (Pecora, Whittaker, Maluccio, & Barth, forthcoming; U.S. Department of Health and Human Services, 2003a). There is some debate in the field about placing child safety as a goal superior to family support. Indeed, many family advocates and some researchers argue that without a simultaneous emphasis on child safety and family support, neither will happen in an equitable manner. In a similar vein, the capacity of the system to support families and promote positive developmental outcomes for children in custody has been the subject of much criticism and debate (Berrick, Needell, Barth, & Johnson-Reid, 1998; Maluccio & Pecora, forthcoming). The key components of each of these major goals (also called "outcome domains") are summarized next.

Safety

A core goal for child welfare services is keeping children safe from child abuse and neglect. This includes children living with their birth families, children returned home to their families, and children placed in out-of-home care. In terms of concrete outcomes, citizens should be looking to child welfare services to *prevent children from being maltreated* and to *keep families safely together* including families that may be functioning at a minimum standard of parenting. Child welfare workers operate on the philosophical basis that all children have a right to live in a safe environment and receive protection from abuse and neglect. For example, the focus of child protective services (CPS) should be to deliver services that are preventive, nonpunitive, and geared toward parent rehabilitation through identification and treatment of the factors that underlie maltreatment.

At the most general level, there is a firm consensus regarding the mission of child protective services: It is designed to protect children from child maltreatment committed by their parents or other caretakers. But, in translating this broad mandate into policy guidelines and practice, the consensus breaks down in a variety of areas, such as defining what constitutes child abuse or neglect, establishing standards for agency intervention, and specifying what comprises a minimum standard of parenting (popularized by the question, "What is a good enough parent?"). It also is a policy and practice area that would benefit from increased attention to research findings emerging on risk, resilience, and protective factors as staff members assess family safety and child development.

Permanency

When the state steps in to protect an abused or neglected child, it is not enough for the state to make the child safe; the state must also consider the child's needs for permanent and stable family ties. In addition to protecting a child, the state should ensure that the child will be brought up by stable and legally secure permanent families, rather than in temporary foster care under the supervision of the state. This principle has been well established in federal law: first by the Adoption Assistance and Child Welfare Act of 1980, and then by the Adoption and Safe Families Act of 1997. Adapted from Hardin (1992), the text in the accompanying box summarizes the arguments for permanency and the outcomes that we expect when children are afforded permanent homes.

Why Should We Care About Permanency Planning for Children?

Although permanency alone does not guarantee a normal healthy childhood, it is a key factor in the successful upbringing of children for a number of reasons. First, many mental health experts have concluded that stable and continuous caregivers are important to normal child development. (See, for example, Goldstein, Freud, & Solnit, 1973; Rosenberg, 1987; and Rutter, 1981). Children need secure and uninterrupted emotional relationships with adults who are responsible for their care in order to learn how to form healthy relationships later in life.

Second, children need parents who are fully committed to caring for them, and it is easier for parents (whether biological, foster, or adoptive) to maintain a strong commitment to the child when their role is secure. Not having parents who provide unconditional love and care can represent a profound insult to a child's self-image (Fanshel & Shinn, 1978; Wald, 1976; Weinstein, 1960). Children are likely to feel more secure under the control of parents than under that of child welfare agencies. In addition, fully committed parents are more likely to provide conscientiously for the child's needs.

Third, having a permanent family adds a critical element of predictability to a child's life, thereby promoting a sense of belonging. Being in foster care and never knowing when or where one might be moved can impose great stress on a child. With a permanent family, a child can form a more secure sense of the future and can better weather other difficulties and changes in childhood and adolescence. (Casey Family Programs, 2003a; Maluccio, Fein, & Olmstead, 1986).

Fourth, autonomous families generally are more capable of raising children than the state (Goldstein, Freud, & Solnit, 1973; Rutter, 1981, 1989). Decision making for children in state-supervised foster care tends to be fragmented and diffuse because it is shared by social workers, professional therapists and evaluators, foster parents, court personnel, and biological parents. Full-time permanent parents, who concentrate far more personal commitment and time on the child than any professional, are best able to make fully informed and timely decisions for a child.

In terms of concrete outcomes, citizens should be looking to child welfare services for a number of permanency-related outcomes, including *purposeful case plans* that explicitly address the child's legal status and need for permanency planning. If permanent placement is an important goal for abused and neglected children, it follows that service plans for such children should be designed, in part, for that purpose. Whether a service plan has been logically designed to achieve a safe and permanent home for the child is a key indicator to measure the appropriateness of the plan and, ultimately, to measure the plan's success, and that of the child welfare agency.

Other outcomes (framed in italics to help distinguish them from one another) include children being *placed in the least restrictive placement* possible, *with siblings* whenever possible, with *minimal placement moves or disruptions*, and with a *timely resolution of their legal status,* so that they can be adopted by a caring adult if a birth parent is unable to care for them.

Adapted from Hardin, M. (1992). *Establishing a core of services for families subject to state intervention* (pp.11–12). Washington, DC: American Bar Association. Reprinted by permission.

Child Well-Being

Achieving child well-being means that a child *is safe from child abuse or neglect*. This requires that a *child's basic needs are met* and that the child be able to *grow and develop* in an environment that provides consistent nurture, support, and stimulation. In this outcome domain, we include the need for children to develop a healthy sense of identity, an understanding of their ethnic heritage, and skills for coping with racism, sexism, homophobia, and other forms of discrimination that remain prevalent in our society. Although there are limits to what child welfare services can provide, the system should promote standards of parenting that will, at a minimum, provide a child with the developmental opportunities and emotional nurturance needed to grow into an adult who can live as independently as possible.

Family Well-Being

Family well-being means that a family has the capacity to care for children, to fulfill their basic developmental, health, educational, social, cultural, spiritual, and housing needs. It implies that child welfare staff members have some responsibility for locating these essential services and supports and for helping to sustain or promote the parents in their child-rearing roles.

Each of these outcome domains is exemplified, albeit imperfectly, by six federal outcome standards as shown in Table 2.2 (Milner, Mitchell, & Hornsby, 2001). A U.S. Government Accounting Office report (2004) summarized the issue this way:

> It is against these benchmarks for statewide data indicators that a state is measured. Any state whose performance is found to fall short of substantial conformity (based upon data analysis and an on-site review of individual cases) is given an opportunity to develop and implement a plan to improve performance and avoid the withholding of federal funds. AFSA also required HHS to prepare and submit to Congress an annual report on the performance of each state on each outcome measure. Source: McDonald, Salyers, & Shaver (2004, p. 5)

Theoretical Frameworks Underlying Child Welfare Policies and Programs

A number of theoretical orientations, including ecological models, child development theories, social learning and social support theories, and risk and protective factor frameworks, underpin the design of policies and programs in child welfare.

Table 2.2   Six National Standards for Child Welfare

Standard	Description	Benchmark
Recurrence of Maltreatment	Of all children who were victims of substantiated or indicated child abuse and/or neglect during the first 6 months of the period under review, the percentage that had another substantiated or indicated report within 6 months.	A state passes if 6.1 percent or fewer of children who were victims of abuse or neglect experience another incident of abuse or neglect within 6 months.
Neglect in Foster Care	Of all children in foster care in the state during the period under review, the percent that were the subject of substantiated or indicated maltreatment by a foster parent or facility staff.	A state passes if 0.57 percent or fewer children in foster care experience maltreatment by a foster parent or facility staff.
Foster Care Re-entries	Of all the children entering care during the year under review, the percent of those children entering foster care within 12 months of a prior foster care episode.	A state passes if 8.6 percent or fewer children entering care during a year under review enter foster care within 12 months of a previous foster care episode.
Stability of Foster Care Placements	Of all those children who have been in foster care less than 12 months from the time of the latest removal, the percent of children experiencing no more than two placement settings.	A state passes if 86.7 percent or more of children in foster care less than 12 months experience no more than two placement settings.
Length of Time to Achieve Reunification	Of all children who were reunified with their parents or caretakers at the time of discharge from foster care, the percent reunified within less than 12 months of the time of the latest removal from the home.	A state passes if 76.2 percent or more children reunified with parents are reunified within 12 months of their latest removal from the home.
Length of Time to Achieve Adoptions	Of all the children exiting foster care to adoption during the year under review, the percent of children exiting care in less than 24 months from the time of the latest removal from the home.	A state passes if 32 percent or more of the children adopted from foster care are adopted within 24 months of their latest removal.

Source: From McDonald, J., Salyers, N. Shaver, M. (2004). *The foster care strait jacket: innovation, federal financing & accountability in state foster care reform—A report by Fostering Results.* Urbana-Champaign, IL: Children and Family Research Center at the School of Social Work, University of Illinois at Urbana-Champaign. Reprinted with permission.

Ecological Developmental Models

Child characteristics interact with the experience of child maltreatment and child welfare services such as foster care to produce outcomes. These characteristics include genetic factors, risk factors such as poverty, racism and dangerous living environments, and family of origin characteristics and functioning (Cicchetti & Lynch, 1993; Fraser, 2004). In addition, other factors, such as family characteristics and functioning, child and family supports, and the quality and nature of services provided by various community agencies, interact with the experiences of child maltreatment to produce certain outcomes.

The ecological perspective delineated by Cicchetti and Lynch (1993) suggests that the family is a powerful microsystem that has protective and ameliorative functions for youth. In terms of outcome areas, it is important to assess a range of domains, including mental and physical health, adaptive functioning, cognitive functioning, and social functioning. The ecological model espoused by Bronfenbrenner (1979, 1986) posits that individual development occurs and can only be understood within the context of the family and its larger social–environmental context. In this model, the interplay of factors at the individual, family, and environmental levels is necessary to understand individual behaviors. The ecological perspective requires identifying and analyzing risk and protective factors at the level of the child, the level of his or her family, and the broader societal level: Children's development arises from the complex interplay of these interwoven elements.

Developmental Theory

Five approaches related to child development theories are especially relevant to child welfare practice. First, *attachment theory* addresses relationships and traumas occurring prior to age 2 (e.g., Ainsworth, 1989; Weinfield, Ogawa, & Sroufe, 1997). Second, *trauma theory* (Briere 1992), as it relates to the effects of abuse and neglect, offers explanations for variations in the types and impact of abuse and for the impact of immediate or delayed intervention. Third, the *ecological perspective* offers useful concepts addressing the relative importance of individual, familial, and societal contexts (e.g., Bronfenbrenner & Morris, 1998; Garbarino, 1992, Pecora, Whittaker, Maluccio, & Barth, 2000). Fourth, *risk and protective factor frameworks* have descriptive utility for explaining resilience in children and youth and for identifying predictors of adult outcomes. Protective factors can be personal assets (e.g., social competence) and environmental assets (e.g., supportive parents or other relatives) that buffer or suppress risk (Catalano & Hawkins, 1996; Fraser, 2004; Rutter, 1989). Fifth, Erikson's *stages or steps in child development* are useful in understanding and predicting child adjustment sequelae, including how children may adjust to foster care (Downs & Pecora, 2004; Erikson, 1985).

Social Learning and Social Support Theories

Chamberlain (2003) and colleagues have implemented one of the most promising evidence-based models of treatment foster care in child welfare. Based on social learning theory, Social learning theory, widely applied in child welfare practice, emphasizes the complex nature of social situations and holds that human behavior occurs within an interactive social context.

Social support theory is beginning to be recognized as important as we continue to document with more compelling data that placement disruptions and school dislocation result in poor adult outcomes (e.g., Pecora, Kessler, Williams, O'Brien, Downs, English, White, Hiripi, White, Wiggins, & Holmes, 2005; Pecora, Williams, Kessler, Downs, O'Brien, Hiripi, & Morello, 2003; Ryan & Testa, 2004). This is consistent with what we know about the buffering effects of a positive social support system (Casey Family Programs, 2003a; Maluccio, Pine, & Tracy, 2002). Such a perspective stresses the value of providing consistent supports to children, birth parents, and foster families.

Risk and Protective Factors for Problems Leading to Involvement with the Child Welfare System

Conceptually, risk and protective factors are those elements that influence, respectively, the chances of adverse outcomes and optimal development for children who are exposed to maltreatment. This analysis is built upon the elaboration of the framework outlined in Chapter 1 of this volume. (See also Fraser, Kirby, & Smokowski, 2004.) A number of risk factors are associated with child maltreatment or behavioral problems that require child welfare agency involvement. As shown in Table 2.3, these include family poverty, parental substance abuse, parental mental illness, parental history of child maltreatment, social isolation, lack of employment resources in the community, and neighborhood gangs and crime.

Research on protective factors associated with child maltreatment is more limited but is informed by the larger protective factor literature. Several studies have outlined general factors that differentiate resilient children from those who have serious adjustment problems. Protective factors appear to fall into three general categories that include individual characteristics, family characteristics, and the presence of supportive others (Garmezy, 1985; Rutter, 1990; Werner, 1989). Individual characteristics include attributes such as self-sufficiency, high self-esteem, and altruism. Family characteristics include supportive relationships with adult family members, harmonious family relationships, expressions of warmth between family members, and mobilization of supports in times of stress. Finally, community supports refer to supportive relationships with people or organizations external to the family. These external supports provide positive and supportive feedback to the child and act to reinforce and reward the child's positive coping abilities (Hodges, 1994).

We see the more important protective factors as those emerging from the family and community context. These include parental competence, positive disciplinary approaches, caregivers and advocates, social support, positive peer networks, and presence of extended family members. Inclusion in community activities and availability of medical, educational, and financial resources to allow parents to provide appropriate care for their children are also critical protective characteristics.

It is important also to note the compelling connections between poverty and child maltreatment. Low-income families are less likely to have access to adequate food, safe housing, and prenatal or other medical care. They tend to have fewer social supports and experience more stress in child-rearing—all of which can increase the risk of child maltreatment. Generally, poverty has a direct negative influence on maternal behavior and subsequently on the quality of parenting children receive (Brooks-Gunn, Klebanov, & Liaw, 1995). For children generally, living in poverty is associated with a host of negative consequences, including poor physical health, diminished cognitive abilities, emotional and behavioral problems, and reduced educational attainment (Brooks-Gunn & Duncan, 1997).

Cultural Issues Related to Risk and Protection in Child Welfare

Although the literature is sparse, differences in risk and protective factors by race and ethnicity should also be considered in program and policy design. Hodges (1994) notes the importance of considering the needs of families and communities of color:

Table 2.3   Common Risk Factors for Child Abuse and Neglect

Risk Factors	*Protective Factors*
Child Risk Factors	**Child Protective Factors**[a]
• Premature birth, birth abnormalities, low birth weight, exposure to toxins in utero • Temperament: difficult or slow to warm up to others • Physical/cognitive/emotional disability, chronic or serious illness • Childhood trauma • Antisocial peer group • Age • Child aggression, behavior problems, attention deficits	• Birth Order—first born • Health Status—healthy during infancy and childhood • Activity Level—multiple interests and hobbies, participation and competence • Disposition—good-natured, precocious, mature, inquisitive, willing to take risks, optimistic, hopeful, altruistic, personable, independent • Developmental Milestones—meets or exceeds age-appropriate expectations • Self-concept—high self-esteem, internal locus of control, ability to give and receive love and affection • Perceptive—quickly assesses dangerous situations and avoids harm • Interpersonal Skills—able to create, develop, nurture, and maintain supportive relationships with others, assertive, good social skills, ability to relate to both children and adults, articulate • Cognitive Skills—able to focus on positive attributes and ignore negative • Intellectual Abilities—high academic achievement
Parental/Family Risk Factors	**Parental/Family Protective Factors**[b]
• Personality factors • External locus of control • Poor impulse control • Depression/anxiety • Low tolerance for frustration • Feelings of insecurity • Lack of trust • Insecure attachment with own parents • Childhood history of abuse • High parental conflict, including domestic violence • Family Structure—single parent with lack of support, high number of children in household • Social isolation, lack of support	• Structure—rules and household responsibilities for all members • Family Relational Factors—coherence and attachment, open exchange and expression of feelings and emotions • Parental Factors—supervision and monitoring of children, a strong bond to at least one parent figure, a warm and supportive relationship, abundant attention during the first year of life, parental agreement on family values and morals, emotional availability (parental accessibility and capacity for reading the emotional cues and meeting the emotional needs of the infant)

(Continued)

Table 2.3 (Continued)

Risk Factors	Protective Factors
• Parental psychopathology • Substance abuse • Separation/divorce, especially high conflict divorce • Age • High general stress level • Poor parent–child interaction, negative attitudes and attributions about child's behavior • Inaccurate knowledge and expectations about child development • Mental health problems, including maternal depression • Cultural "mis-match" (when a parent has a perception of normative development that is incongruent with that of the broader society and its service providers)	• Reciprocity–mutually satisfying relationships are built between an infant/young child and a parent • Family Size—four or fewer children spaced at least two years apart • Socioeconomic Status—middle to upper SES • Extended Family—nurturing relationships with substitute caregivers such as aunts, uncles, and grandparents • Other positive social network support
Community/Social/ Environmental Risk Factors	**Community/Social/ Environmental Protective Factors**[c]
• Low socioeconomic status of the neighborhood • Stressful life events • Lack of access to medical care, health insurance, adequate child care, and social services • Parental unemployment; homelessness • Social isolation/lack of social support • Exposure to racism/discrimination	• Positive peer relationships • Extended family in close proximity • Schools—academic and extracurricular participation and achievements, close relationship with a teacher(s) • Reliance on informal network of family, friends, and community leaders for advice

Source: This table is adapted from Coll & Magnuson (2000); Garbarino & Ganzel (2000); Hodges (1994); Osofsky & Thompson (2000); and U.S. Department of Health and Human Services Administration for Children and Families Children's Bureau, Administration for Children and Families, Office on Child Abuse and Neglect (2003b).

a. Much of the research on protective factors has focused on individual traits. This category of protective factors refers to factors that are learned (self-care and interpersonal attributes) as well as factors for which the individual has no control (birth order, gender). (Garmezy, 1983, 1985; Rae-Grant, Thomas, Offord, & Boyle, 1989; Rutter, 1979, 1981, 1985, 1987, 1990; Werner, 1989).

b. Family characteristics also act as protective factors (Garmezy, 1983, 1985; Rae-Grant, Thomas, Offord, & Boyle, 1989; Rutter, 1979, 1981, 1985, 1987, 1990; Werner, 1989).

c. Community characteristics include individuals and institutions, external to the family, that provide educational, emotional, and general supportive ties with the family unit as a whole or with individual family members. (Garmezy, 1983, 1985; Rae-Grant, Thomas, Offord, & Boyle, 1989; Rutter, 1979, 1981, 1985, 1987, 1990; Werner, 1989).

Assessing for risk of child abuse and neglect offers special challenges to practitioners who are unfamiliar with the diversity in culture of families of color. Families of color often have different family structures (Lynch, & Hanson, 1992; Mindel, Habenstein, & Wright, 1988), child rearing practices (Lynch, & Hanson, 1992; Mindel, Habenstein, & Wright, 1988), gender and family roles (Lynch & Hanson, 1992; Mindel, Habenstein, & Wright, 1988), and relationships to community (Lynch & Hanson, 1992; Mindel, Habenstein & Wright, 1988). Failing to accurately assess for these cultural differences might yield an incomplete assessment of the family, especially as it relates to family strengths. Lack of resources related to poverty might also obscure a practitioner's ability to identify strengths (p. 1).

The preceding discussion offers a brief overview of the individual, family, and community protective factors that serve as a buffer to some children during stressful and or abusive situations. However, given differences in family structure, child-rearing practices, and relationship to community, the degree to which the preceding factors apply to families of color is unclear. Certainly some of the protective factors associated with, for example, middle or upper socioeconomic status and academic success are universal across ethnic and class background. However, other factors may have a greater or lesser impact on families of color. From Hodges (1994), these include:

- *Active Extended Family*—fictive or blood relatives who are active in the child's life; provides material resources, child care, supervision, parenting, and emotional support to the child (Wilson, 1984).
- *Church or Religious Affiliation*—belongs to and actively participates in a group religious experience (Werner, 1989).
- *Strong Racial Identity*—exhibits racial pride, strongly identifies with ethnic group through clubs, organizations, political, and social-change movements.
- *Close Attachment to the Ethnic Community*—resides in the ethnic community, easy access to ethnic resources, including social services, merchants, media (newspaper), and demonstrates a commitment to the ethnic community.
- *Dispositional Attributes*—activity level, sociability, average intelligence, competence in communication (oral and written), internal locus of control (Werner, 1989).
- *Personal Attributes*—high self-esteem, academic achievement, assertiveness, quality of adjustment to single-parent household.
- *Supportive Family Milieu*—cohesiveness, extensive kinship network, nonconflictual relations.
- *External Support System*—involvement of absent fathers, male role models, supportive social environments of various ethnic communities.

Risk, Resilience, and Protection in Child Welfare Policy

Child welfare policy is slowly but steadily being shaped by advances in research and practice in risk, resilience, and protective factors. Landmark books such as *Neurons to Neighborhoods* reinforce infant and young child stimulation principles outlined by earlier pioneers and make them accessible to a broader audience (Shonkoff & Phillips, 2000). Berrick, Needell, Barth, and Johnson-Reid (1998) and Maier (1978) emphasize the importance of paying attention to child development fundamentals such as attachment theory and social learning in designing child welfare policy and programs. Advances in the treatment of child abuse and neglect have emphasized in a modest way how children with varied psychological makeups and differing amounts of social support respond differently to various healing approaches (Briere, 1992). Ecological and diversity perspectives underscore the vital roles that broader community networks and environments play in services and healing.

Over the past five decades major research studies (e.g., Fanshel & Shinn, 1978), "program scandals" (Wooden, 1976), class action lawsuits, and effective advocacy by adoptive parents precipitated a wide range of policy reforms. These include:

- Strategically focused family-centered services to strengthen parenting;
- Child-centered early intervention and remedial services based on increased understanding of early brain development;
- Attempts to embed substance abuse treatment services within child welfare, or at least to strengthen linkages across service delivery systems such as mental health, education, and juvenile justice;
- Use of least restrictive placement environments that facilitated the closure of hundreds of residential institutions; and
- Permanency planning for children to secure a stable family if their birth parents are unable to care for them within a reasonable period of time.

Two other significant transformations bear mentioning. First, service system leaders in child protective services, family support, and foster care have identified community collaborations as essential for effective services (Larner, Stevenson, & Behrman, 1998; Morgan, Spears, & Kaplan, 2003). Second, the field recognized the need to move children of all races and ages to more permanent family situations while also being cognizant of the need to nurture child development if children remained involved in the child welfare service system beyond a 3-month protective services intervention (Berrick, Needell, Barth, & Johnson-Reid, 1998; Maluccio, Fein, & Olmstead, 1986). In contrast, what has also emerged is the realization that major forms of racial disproportionality exist in the provision of services and achievement of permanency outcomes (Chibnall, Dutch, Jones-Harden, Brown, Gourgine, Smith, Boone, & Snyder, 2003; Hill, 2001; Hines, Lemon, Wyatt, & Merdinger, 2004). A discussion of this and other policy issues follows.

Key Child Welfare Policy and Legislation

A number of public policies influence program provisions and impact the families served by child welfare services. Key federal policies that are most related to child welfare are summarized in Table 2.4. These include adoption, child protection, income support, education, early intervention, family support, and foster care. Medical care, which is also important for child welfare, is discussed more thoroughly in Chapter 5 of this volume.

Current Policy Challenges[3]

A number of policy challenges face child welfare services, some of which are underscored by the mixed success the United States is having in meeting the basic needs of children; ensuring their safety, health, relationships, and opportunities; and supporting families as the foundation for positive child development. A cross section of policy challenges follows.

Early intervention services are underfunded and lack federal leadership. Early intervention services have long been recognized in helping families avoid involvement with the child welfare system. Best practices for early intervention programs involve a range of family-centered services that focus on meeting the needs of the child within the context of his or her family and larger environment. For example, in the course of early intervention, parents may be referred to job assistance or adult education and may receive assistance in obtaining housing and health care. Child-centered early intervention programs have been linked with improved child development across multiple domains (Graham & Bryant, 1993; Karoly, Kilburn, Caulkins, & Cannon, 2000). Clearly, with better prevention strategies in place, we could strengthen families and avoid much child maltreatment.

(Text continues on page 47)

Table 2.4   A Select List of Child Welfare–Related Federal Legislation[a] Listed by Year of Passage

Legislation	Purpose	References
Supplemental Social Insurance (SSI)	SSI is a means-tested, monthly income program for the elderly and people with disabilities. The program is federally financed and generally federally administered, although some states supplement federal payments and a few states administer their own programs directly. Children with disabilities have been able to receive SSI since the program's inception in 1972, and children's eligibility is based on functional limitations (Social Security Administration, 2000). Parental income and assets relative to family size are used to determine whether or not a child can receive SSI.	Light (1973), Stein (1984)
Child Abuse Prevention and Treatment Act of 1974 (P.L. 93–247)	Provides some financial assistance for demonstration programs for the prevention, identification, and treatment of child abuse and neglect; mandates that states must provide for the reporting of known or suspected instances of child abuse and neglect.	
Juvenile Justice and Delinquency Prevention Act of 1974 (P.L. 93–415)	Provides funds to reduce the unnecessary or inappropriate detention of juveniles and to encourage state program initiatives in the prevention and treatment of juvenile delinquency and other status offenses.	Costin, Bell, & Downs (1991)
Title XIX of the Social Security Act	Mainly provides health care to income-eligible persons and families. One of the sections of this Act established the Early and Periodic Screening, Diagnosis, and Treatment program, which provides cost-effective health care to pregnant women and young children.	

Legislation	Purpose	References
The Education for All Handicapped Children Act of 1975 (P.L. 94–142)	Act requiring and supporting education and social services to handicapped children. The Act requires states to (1) offer programs for the full education of handicapped children between the ages of 3 and 18, (2) develop strategies for locating such children, (3) use intelligence testing that does not discriminate against the child racially or culturally, (4) develop an individualized education plan (IEP) for each child, and (5) offer learning opportunities in the *least restrictive educational environment* possible, with an emphasis on mainstreaming—integrating handicapped children into regular classrooms.	Costin, Bell, & Downs (1991), Singer & Butler (1987)
The Individuals with Disabilities Education Act (IDEA) (Began as the Education for All Handicapped Children Act of 1975– P.L. 94–142)	The Individuals with Disabilities Education Act (IDEA) began as the Education for All Handicapped Children Act of 1975 (P.L. 94–142) and gave all children with disabilities the right to a free and appropriate public education. This watershed civil rights law resulted from sustained advocacy by parents of children with disabilities. Special education has been shaped by the six core principles that formed the nucleus of the Education for All Handicapped Children Act: (1) zero reject, meaning schools could not opt to exclude any children with disabilities from instruction; (2) nondiscriminatory evaluation, by which every child receives an individualized, culturally and linguistically appropriate evaluation before being placed in special education; (3) IEP, a plan delineating current performance, progress on past objectives, goals, and services for the school year, and evaluation of outcomes; (4) least restrictive environment, which is the goal that children with disabilities are educated to the extent possible	Parish & Whisnant (2005)

(Continued)

Table 2.4 (Continued)

Legislation	Purpose	References
	in settings with nondisabled children; (5) due process, which codifies the legal steps to ensure school's fairness and accountability in meeting the child's needs and how parents can obtain relief via a hearing or by second opinions; and (6) parental participation, whereby parents have the right to access their child's education records and participate in IEP planning (Kirk, Gallagher, & Anastasiow, 1993, pp. 51–52).	
	The second part of IDEA that is important for children served by child welfare agencies is early intervention, which has as its purpose the provision of prevention and treatment services to improve cognitive, social, and emotional development of the youngest children (under the age of 3). Children receiving early intervention services either are considered at risk for delayed development or have been identified as having a developmental disability (Ramey & Ramey, 1998).	
P.L. 101–476	Act modifying services for special education students.	
Title XX of the Social Security Act (as amended by the Omnibus Reconciliation Act of 1981)	Through a block grant arrangement, provides states with federal funds for a variety of social service programs.	Mott (1976)
The Indian Child Welfare Act of 1978 (P.L. 95–608)	Strengthens the standards governing the removal of Native American children from their families. Provides for a variety of requirements and mechanisms for tribal government overseeing and services for children.	Miller, Hoffman, & Turner (1980), Plantz, Hubbell, Barrett, & Dobrec (1989)

Legislation	Purpose	References
The Adoption Assistance and Child Welfare Act of 1980 (P.L. 96–272)	A child welfare reform legislation that uses funding incentives and procedural requirements to promote placement prevention and permanency planning.	Pine (1986)
Independent Living Initiative (P.L. 99–272)	Provides funding for services to prepare adolescents in foster care for living in the community on an independent basis.	Mech (1988)
P.L. 99–457	Mandates health, rehabilitation, education, and social services to children who have special needs from birth.	
Family Support Act of 1990	Establishes new initiatives for financial assistance for low-income families.	
1990 Farm Bill (P.L. 101–624)	The Food Stamp Program was re-authorized until 1995 as part of this bill.	http://thomas.loc.gov; http://www.connectforkids.org
Personal Responsibility and Work Opportunity Reconciliation Act (PRWORA). This funds the Temporary Assistance to Needy Families (TANF)	The largest income transfer program for poor families is Temporary Assistance to Needy Families (TANF). This is part of the nation's welfare system—administered by the states and funded jointly by state and federal governments. Low-income families of children with disabilities can also receive income transfers through TANF, which is the limited welfare program enacted in 1996 by the Personal Responsibility and Work Opportunity Reconciliation Act (PRWORA). TANF replaced Aid to Families with Dependent Children (AFDC), requires parents to work, and limits receipt of cash benefits to a lifetime maximum	

(Continued)

Table 2.4 (Continued)

Legislation	Purpose	References
	of 60 months. TANF allows states to exempt up to 20 percent of their welfare caseload from work requirements, but states have the discretion to establish more strict work participation rules.	
More Recent Child Welfare Legislation:		
Foster Care Independence Act of 1999 (P.L. 106–169) and the Educational Training Voucher Provisions	The Foster Care Independence Act of 1999 (P.L. 106–169) authorized the Education Training Voucher (ETV) program. Congress provided federal funding of $42 million for the first time in FY 2003 and increased funding to $45 million for FY 2004. In both years, the president requested $60 million in his budget.	
	The voucher program is a component of the Chafee Independent Living Program, which helps older youth leaving foster care get the higher education, vocational training, and other education supports they need to move to self-sufficiency. Up to $5,000 per year is available to a young person for the cost of attending college or vocational school.	
	ETV funds are distributed to the states using the same formula as the Chafee Independent Living Program under the Foster Care Independence Act. If a state does not apply for funds for the ETV program, the funds are reallocated to other states based on their relative need. Although states are generally doing a good job of distributing these funds, more foster youth could take advantage of the vouchers if their availability were more widely known. An additional $60 million is needed for ETVs for youth leaving foster care at age 18 and those adopted from foster care at age 16 or older (Child Welfare League of America (CWLA), 2004).	

Legislation	Purpose	References
Keeping Children and Families Safe Act	Reauthorizes the Child Abuse Prevention and Treatment Act (CAPTA). Authorizes funds for grants to state child welfare agencies, competitive grants for research and demonstration programs, and grants to states for the establishment of community-based programs and activities designed to strengthen and support families, all of which support services to prevent and treat child abuse and neglect. The Act amends the Adoption Reform Act of 1978 (Adoption Opportunities), focusing on the placement of older foster children in adoptive homes with an emphasis on child-specific recruitment strategies and efforts to improve interjurisdictional adoptions.	
	This Act also includes amendments to the Abandoned Infants Assistance Act, making aid a priority to infants who are infected with the HIV virus, have a life-threatening disease, or have been exposed perinatally to a dangerous drug. The Act also includes an amendment to the Family Violence Prevention and Services Act, extending from FY 2004 through FY 2008 authorization of appropriations for specified family violence prevention programs.	
The Adoption Incentive Program (P.L. 108–145)	The Adoption Incentive Program was first enacted as part of the Adoption and Safe Families Act in 1997 to promote permanence for children. In 2003, Congress passed the Adoption Promotion Act of 2003 (P.L. 108–145) to reauthorize the program with modifications.	

(Continued)

Table 2.4 (Continued)

Legislation	Purpose	References
	The Adoption Incentive Program is designed to encourage states to finalize adoptions of children from foster care, with additional incentives for the adoption of foster children with special needs. States receive incentive payments for adoptions that exceed an established baseline.	
	The Adoption Promotion Act revises the incentive formula in current law, creating four categories of payment. A state may receive	

- $4,000 for each foster child adopted above the established baseline of foster child adoptions;
- $6,000 for each foster child adopted whom the state classifies as having special needs, as long as the state also increases its overall adoptions;
- $8,000 for each older foster child adopted above the baseline of older foster child adoptions, as long as the state also increases its overall adoptions (an older child is defined as a child age 9 or older); and
- $4,000 for each older foster child adopted above the baseline of older foster child adoptions when the number of older foster child adoptions increases, but the overall number of foster child adoptions does not increase.

Legislation	Purpose	References
	The law also resets the target number of adoptions a state must reach to receive a bonus payment. Because not all states qualified for the bonus in 2003, a new target was established for adoptions, based on the number of adoptions in 2002 rather than the old formula, which created a number based on fiscal years 1995–1997. Under the new law, to receive a payment in any of the categories (overall adoptions, special-needs adoptions, or older-child adoptions), a state must exceed the number of adoptions in these categories set in FY 2002. For any subsequent year, the baseline is the highest number of adoptions in 2002 or later. (CWLA, 2004).[b]	
Adoption Opportunities Program (Title II of the Child Abuse Prevention and Treatment Act, P.L. 108–36).	The Adoption Opportunities Program provides discretionary grants for demonstration projects that eliminate barriers to adoption and provide permanent, loving homes for children who would benefit from adoption—particularly children with special needs.	
	Several resources and supports exist under the Adoption Opportunities Program to assist in the adoption of children. For example, the Collaboration to Adopt US Kids recruits homes for children waiting to be adopted through its National Recruitment Campaign and has developed a network of adoptive parent groups. Adopt US Kids also maintains a national Internet photo listing of waiting children.	

(Continued)

Table 2.4 (Continued)

Legislation	Purpose	References
	The Adoption Opportunities Program has also funded the National Resource Center on Special Needs Adoption, which provides technical assistance and training on current issues in special-needs adoption—such as compliance with federal laws and regulations, permanency planning, and cultural competence—to state, tribal, and other child welfare organizations.	
	In addition, it funds the National Adoption Assistance Training Resource and Information Network which provides free information on adoption subsidies to parents interested in adopting children with special needs, and a booklet on adoption assistance programs available in each state. Adoption Opportunities funding has also helped establish the National Adoption Information Clearinghouse (NAIC), a comprehensive information center on adoption.	
Runaway, Homeless, and Missing Children Protection Act	Runaway, Homeless, and Missing Children Protection Act (which reauthorized the Runaway and Homeless Youth Act) authorizes funds for the establishment and operation of centers to provide shelter, protection from sexual and other abuse, counseling, and related services to runaway and homeless youth under 18 years of age. The Act authorized local groups to open "maternity group homes" for homeless pregnant teens or for those that have been abused.	

Legislation	Purpose	References
	These homes are required to educate runaway youth about parenting skills, child development, family budgeting, health and nutrition, and related skills to promote long-term independence and the health and well-being of youth in their care.	
Legacy Provisions in the American Dream Downpayment Act	The LEGACY (Living Equitably: Grandparents Aiding Children and Youth) Act directs the Secretary of Housing and Urban Development to carry out: (1) a 5-year pilot program in connection with the supportive housing program, known as Section 202, to provide assistance to private nonprofit organizations for expanding the supply of intergenerational dwelling units for intergenerational families (families headed by an elderly person); and (2) a 5-year demonstration program for Section 8 rental assistance to families headed by a grandparent or relative who is raising a child.	
	The bill makes grandparent-headed and relative-headed families eligible for (1) the Family Unification Program, (2) HOME program ECHO units, and (3) fair housing initiatives training, education, counseling, and outreach. It also directs the secretary and the director of the Bureau of the Census to conduct a joint study of such families' housing needs.	

(Continued)

Table 2.4 (Continued)

Legislation	Purpose	References
Extending Food Stamps to Eligible Immigrant Children	Once barred from participating in the Food Stamp program by the Welfare Reform Act of 1996, immigrant children became eligible for Food Stamps as of October 1, 2003, as a result of a provision in the 2002 Farm Bill.	
Protect Act (Amber Alert System)	The Amber alert system, a national system to quickly alert the public about child abductions, was signed into law in April, 2004.	

Source: From Pecora, P., Whittaker, J., Maluccio, A., & Barth, R. *The Child Welfare Challenge: Policy, Practice, and Research,* copyright © 2003, reprinted with permission from Transaction Publishers.

A number of other pieces of legislation are important to child welfare services but are not summarized in this table, including the Social Security Act of 1935, amendments to the Act passed in 1939, 1950, 1962, 1965, 1967, 1974, and 1983, some of which are also known as the title amendments of Title IV, IV-A, IV-B, IV-E, IV-F, and V. These title amendments established, terminated, or altered a wide range of income assistance, medical, social service, and other programs. For more information, see Costin et al. (1991), DiNitto and Dye (1989), Stein (1991).

a. Compiled from Pecora, Barth, Whittaker, & Maluccio (forthcoming), and summaries prepared by the Public Policy Team of Casey Family Programs with the consultation of Children's Defense Fund, Child Welfare League of America, American Public Human Services Association, and the Alliance for Children.

b. Child Welfare League of America. (2004). Adoption. A fact sheet in the CWLA 2004 Legislative agenda. In *Making children a national priority.* Washington, DC: Author.

However, to implement these strategies, a more unified leadership with a cohesive plan for family support is needed at the federal and state levels. For example, communities interested in early intervention will need to invest public resources in evidence-based programs that support parents and strengthen families. We must also raise the public affordable child care and increase awareness among policymakers about the importance of *family economic security*. This need is emphasized by the large proportion of children entering child welfare as a result of parental neglect. As previously mentioned, more effective mental health and substance abuse interventions for parents would also reduce youth entry into foster care.

A risk, resilience, and protective factor perspective undergirds the philosophy supporting early intervention. Early intervention should disrupt risk processes, promote protective mechanisms, and stimulate resilience. Ideally, early intervention services promote well-being and optimal development by providing comprehensive community-based support services to help improve child developmental outcomes. Yet these services are underfunded and states lack the flexibility to use federal funds designated for placement services for family support programs.

Family support services are not backed by coherent funding strategies. These services, which include parent hotlines, crisis nursery services, environmental adaptations, personal assistance, and mental health and crisis intervention, provide support and training for children and families, and are often "lifeline" services. These allow families to care for their children at home rather than seeking expensive, and generally publicly financed, out-of-home care (Bruns & Burchard, 2000).

The goals of family support services include enabling families to raise children at home by reducing stress and by strengthening and enhancing caregiving capacities (Walton, Sandau-Becker, & Mannes, 2001). Utilization of formal support services by family caregivers plays a significant role in reducing the burdens and stress associated with caring for a child and helping families obtain services for unmet needs. Family support services across the United States are usually jointly financed by the federal and state governments, often with Medicaid resources, and typically administered by state or county governments. Not surprisingly, given the differences among the states in the provision of social services, there is variability in the level of funding allocated for family support and in the types of available services (Parish, Pomeranz, & Braddock, 2003). Consequently, these services are often not only underfunded, but also among the first to be cut during periods of economic downturn.

Block-granting of key child welfare funding mechanisms requires additional discussion. A number of federal leaders have submitted proposals to Congress under which states would be allowed to use federal foster care funds not only to support children in out-of-home care but also to support child abuse prevention and postadoption services. For example, several proposals have been made to change the system for funding key child welfare programs, including foster care entitlement under Title IV-E of the Social Security Act. One such proposal is described in the accompanying text box.

These and other proposals can be seen as efforts to address the family support issue. But the downside to these proposals is that the overall budget support for children's services would decrease if all the areas under that legislative area are considered. Based on what occurs with block-granting of Medicaid and food stamps, families would no longer have an entitlement. Educational efforts are needed to inform the public and policymakers of the importance of policies that preserve the open-ended entitlement for key child welfare programs. In addition, we need to raise awareness among policymakers and the public that funds should be tied to performance-based results (Casey Family Programs, 2004).

Policies and funding to treat mental health and substance abuse problems must be redesigned. Fragmented funding streams and policies fail to encourage effective treatment of co-morbid conditions that are much more common in child welfare than previously thought (Kessler & Magee, 1993). For example, substance abuse problems are present in a significant percentage of the families where children are placed in out-of-home care (Besharov, 1994). Many agency administrators are diverted from other activities in order to "braid" or cobble together multiple sources of funding to cover the costs of programs; their efforts highlight the critical need for more coordination at the federal and state levels to maximize the effectiveness of existing resources (Johnson, Knitzer, & Kaufmann, 2003).

Differential approaches to child protective services intake need additional testing. New intake approaches are attempting to divert low-risk families to supportive programs other than child protective services. These approaches need further testing and evaluation in order to inform policymakers' decisions concerning the roles of law enforcement; medical, legal, and social services personnel; and voluntary agencies.

Kinship care funding, licensing, and practice policies need to be aligned. More than 6 million children—approximately 1 in 12—are living in households headed by grandparents or other relatives. U.S. Census data tell us that 2.4 million grandparents are taking on primary responsibility for the basic needs of their grandchildren. Kinship caregivers often lack the information and range of supports they need to fulfill their parenting role. In an effort to remedy this situation, a group of child and aging advocacy and research organizations has prepared *Kinship Care Fact Sheets*. These sheets provide

Overhaul of Foster Care Eyed
Cheryl Wetzstein

The nation's foster care system would undergo sweeping changes, akin to welfare reform, under a bill recently introduced by House Republicans. "The way the federal government pays for foster care is perverse," said House Majority Leader Tom DeLay, Texas Republican and co-sponsor of the Child Safety, Adoption, and Family Enhancement Act. "We are spending billions of dollars to pay for the room and board of children in temporary foster care, but doing little else to actually improve these children's lives," he said.

The bill, introduced by Rep. Wally Herger, California Republican and chairman of the House Ways and Means subcommittee on human resources, is "like welfare reform for child welfare," said one congressional aide. As in the 1996 welfare reform, the bill would combine major child-welfare funding streams into a capped grant to states. The grant would grow $200 million a year, and when per-child adoption-bonus payments are added in, child-welfare funding is estimated to increase from $7.7 billion in 2005 to nearly $11 billion in 2014.

Congress also would remove outdated child-welfare rules, giving states more flexibility in how to spend their funds. However, states would have to ensure "better outcomes" for children, such as stronger efforts to prevent children from entering state care and improved management of children's cases when they are in care.

"This bill is designed to fundamentally change the child-welfare system to focus on outcomes rather than process," said Mr. Herger, who has been holding hearings for months on child-welfare issues.

House Democrats have not endorsed the bill, saying their Child Protective Services Improvement Act, introduced in 2003, is better. The Herger bill correctly provides more resources, but caps the grant—which "threatens the safe haven needed when children must be removed from their homes," said Rep. Benjamin L. Cardin, Maryland Democrat. Foster care is the "safety net of last resort for our most vulnerable children, and I cannot see the wisdom in cutting a hole in that net," said Mr. Cardin, who said the Herger bill erred in not requiring states to pay relatives who become legal guardians of foster children or resolving work force problems in child welfare.

Separately this week, leaders in child welfare and law enforcement said they are working together to respond more effectively when foster children run away, are abducted from care, or otherwise become "lost in the system."

The number of "missing" foster children is unknown, said Shay Bilchik, president and chief executive of the Child Welfare League of America, which, in collaboration with the National Center for Missing and Exploited Children, has released its first in-depth report on "Children Missing from Care."

The problem is likely to grow, however, because the number of teens and preteens in foster care steadily has risen. About 40 percent of children in foster care are 13 or older, compared with 25 percent in 1997, and older foster children are more likely to run away, said Bryan Samuels, director of the Illinois Department of Children and Family Services.

state-specific data and information directing kinship caregivers to support services that can help make their jobs easier (Children's Defense Fund, 2004). Twofold legislation was recently introduced by Senator Hillary Clinton to provide special tax breaks for these once-again parents and, perhaps more important, to establish "kinship navigators" to advise these parents. However, more work needs to be done to help resolve the policy inconsistencies in licensing and support of these families.

Tribal access to federal child welfare services funding should be increased and existing infrastructure should be improved. Consistent with their cultures, Native American tribes have exercised jurisdiction over their children, but they have seriously underdeveloped services. Tribal entities need to build a variety of service infrastructures such as management information systems and quality improvement programs. However, Native American tribes are not allowed to access Federal Title IV-E funds directly. This lack of direct access to key federal funds diminishes the effectiveness of tribal foster care programs.

Agency policies should promote better assessment and support of gay, lesbian, bisexual, and transgendered youth in out-of-home care. Mallon (1999) and others have described how child welfare service delivery systems have not encouraged staff members and foster parents to protect and nurture gay, lesbian, bisexual, and transgendered youth. Such youth are vulnerable to victimization, depression, suicide, and placement disruption because of their sexual orientation. Special efforts are needed both to assess the needs of these youths and to devise supportive services for them.

Cross-systems collaboration should be strengthened. When the risk factors and other root causes of parent need for child welfare services are identified, it is clear that a more integrated approach to family support and children's services is essential. Economic supports, education, mental health, domestic violence, law enforcement, juvenile justice, and child welfare need to work more toward a common purpose and minimize operating in isolation from each other. For example, co-morbid conditions such as depression and drug abuse require interdisciplinary approaches.

Transition policies and support for emancipating youth must be overhauled. Too many graduates of the foster care system are under-trained and underemployed. Many of these people are part of a large group of "marginalized youth." Alumni of foster care vary widely in their level of preparation for emancipation from foster care in terms of education and income (Cook, Fleishman, & Grimes; 1991; Goerge, Bilaver, Lee, Needell, Brookhart, & Jackman, 2002; Pecora, Kessler, Williams, Downs, English, &

White, in press). Society needs to promote investment in culturally relevant services, support, and opportunities to ensure that every youth in foster care makes a safe, successful transition to adulthood. Independent living preparation must be redesigned to start at age 10, not at the current age of 17. A comprehensive transition plan should be developed for every child. It should include planning for supportive relationships, community connections, education, life skills assessment and development, identity formation, housing, employment, physical health, and mental health (Casey Family Programs, 2001; Massinga & Pecora, 2003). Employment training and experience should be expanded for many youth while they are in care. Policies and incentives should ensure that no young person leaves foster care without housing, access to health care, employment skills, and permanent connections to at least one adult.

All youth in high school should receive the tutoring and employment experiences that build work-related skills. Youth preparing to emancipate must have greater access to experiential life skills and classroom-based training. Systems change is essential. The MacArthur Foundation transition scholars have documented how major American institutions have not kept pace with societal changes that require new ways of working to remove barriers to youth as they transition to adulthood (Carnegie Council on Adolescent Development, 1989).

Policies should provide fiscal incentives to improve high school graduation rates and to support postsecondary education and training for children and youth in foster care. The federal Higher Education Act (HEA) gives virtually no consideration to the special needs of children and youth in foster care. Congress is currently considering changes to the HEA that might provide an opportunity to improve this policy and the programs it supports (Casey Family Programs, 2003b). Policy innovations are needed to strengthen elementary and secondary education programs, including special education initiatives. In addition, federal and state policies must maintain the financial viability and array of services within the Medicaid and SCHIP programs for youth in foster care, and ensure that no young person leaves foster care without access to appropriate health care (Cook, Fleishman, & Grimes, 1991; Courtney, Piliavin, Grogan-Kaylor, & Nesmith, 2001).

Policies should increase the likelihood that more youth will achieve and maintain permanency in a reasonable time period through foster care, reunification, relative placement, guardianship, or adoption. This includes crafting policies to ensure that kinship care families have access to resources needed to raise healthy children in stable home environments.

Adoption policy must address more thoroughly how to better respond to the legal concerns expressed through the Multi-Ethnic Placement Act (MEPA) and Inter-Ethnic Adoption Provisions Act (IEPA) legislation discussed in Table 2.4.

Policymakers need to recognize the seriousness of racial and ethnic disproportionality. Disproportionality and the disparities in outcomes for children of color in the child welfare system are slowly being recognized as major ethical, policy, and program issues, but much needs to be done. First, we need to promote the investment of public resources into gathering critical data about African American, Native American, Asian American, and Hispanic children in the child welfare system. This includes information ranging from the level of access of birth parents for children of color in the child welfare system to data concerning use of substance abuse and mental health services both before entering and during their contact with the system (Hill, 2001; Hines et al., 2004). Second, through this information, officials must enhance national awareness of the disproportionate number of children of color in the foster care system, give the reasons for such disproportion, and address possible solutions. Finally, communities should launch efforts to reduce disparities. The goal of this effort should be to remove race and ethnicity as a predictor of outcome in child welfare services. Table 2.4 outlines additional information about the issue of racial disparity in child welfare.

Finally, performance-based contracting has not been fully implemented. State and county policies to promote and performance-based contracting have been hampered by a lack of knowledge of baseline conditions, sound target goals, and infrastructure funding gaps. Quality improvement systems must be in place to enable agencies to improve performance–based contracting and the implementation of evidence–based practice models (Mordock, 2002; Pecora, Selig, Zirps, & Davis, 1996).

Using Knowledge of Risk, Protection, and Resilience to Achieve Service Integration

We have described the major policies that influence the well-being of children and families in the child welfare system. Fragmented funding and the lack of service integration were noted, along with many of the policy developments that illustrate how risk-reduction strategies could undergird child welfare services. To disrupt the risk mechanisms that lead to child maltreatment and that complicate recovery from victimization, child welfare agencies need adequate funding for key programs, as well as new and more effective ways to link funding to specific indicators of success.

Racial Disproportionality, Bias, and Power in Child Welfare

Many minority leaders argue that because our child welfare system serves minorities and the very poor, it has become a series of interventions that ruptures families, rather than providing a support network that gives them what they need to survive and function healthfully.

Indeed, in several African American communities, growing anger is directed toward child welfare authorities. Speakers at recent community meetings in Bedford Stuyvesant and Harlem drew some stark and painful parallels between modern-day child welfare and nineteenth-century slavery. The child welfare system separates siblings, dismantles families, and terminates parental rights; African American children are a source of income for foster care agencies run by whites. It is a frightening metaphor.

- Between 1995 and 1997, the number of children taken from their parents and placed in foster care in New York City increased 52 percent, from 8,770 to 13,345.
- In New York City, African American children are more than twice as likely as white children to be taken away from their parents following a confirmed report of abuse or neglect.
- One of every 10 children from central Harlem is in foster care today.
- One of every 22 African American children citywide is in foster care, compared with 1 of every 59 Latino children—and only one of every 385 white children.
- One of every four African American foster children remains in foster care 5 years or more. Only 1 in 10 white children remains in the system as long.
- Neighborhoods where the population is largely African American have been hardest hit by Giuliani administration budget cuts to community-based programs designed to prevent the placement of children in foster care.
- Foster care prevention programs are more readily available to white and Latino families than to African American families, even as the need in black communities increases.
- An estimated 3 percent of the 41,198 children in foster care are white, 73 percent are African American, and fewer than 24 percent are Latino.
- Sixty-two percent of the executives and administrators of the city-contracted nonprofit foster care agencies are white, 27 percent are African American, 7.7 percent are Latino, and 3.1 percent are Asian.
- The 10 largest foster care agencies hold contracts worth a total of $302.8 million a year, about half the entire foster care contract budget. They are all traditional, white-run charitable organizations.
- The nine foster care agencies established and operated by people of color in New York City hold contracts worth $46.6 million a year and provide services to 4,782 children, or about 12 percent of all children in foster care.

Source: White, A., Courtney, J., & Fifield, A. (1998). *The race factor in child welfare.* New York: Center for an urban future. Downloaded August 16, 2004, from http://www .nycfuture.org/content/reports/report_view.cfm?repkey=9. Reprinted by permission.

It is worth noting that a number of writers have commented how child welfare agency policy and performance incentive mechanisms are not aligned with current best practices (e.g., Wulczyn & Zeidman, 1997). Critics argue that the child welfare service delivery system needs to be overhauled to better address risk factors leading to child abuse and neglect (Adams & Nelson, 1995; Edna McConnell Clark Foundation, 2004; Specht & Courtney, 1994; Lindsey, 2004; Thomas, 1994; Whittaker & Maluccio, 2002; YMCA of the USA, Dartmouth Medical School and Institute for American Values, 2003). The emerging literature on both protective processes that buffer children from risk and promote recovery once victimization has occurred has much to offer child welfare policy.

To underscore the inherent challenges in doing this, a case study is presented in the accompanying box. The case describes a family in which multiple forms of child neglect are present. This family situation illustrates how child neglect can have serious consequences for child development. The complexity of family situations is evident—where genuine love for children is interwoven with mental health problems, domestic violence, poverty, and deficits in parenting skills. In this scenario, the concepts of risk, resiliency, and protective factors have utility for guiding case decision making and the choice of interventions.

A Case Example

Introduction

This case example involves multiple forms of child neglect. An intergenerational cycle may be at work here: a "passing on of infantilism, mother to daughter, through processes of deprivation leading to detachment (the deprivation-detachment hypotheses), failure to provide stimulation, and the child's identification with an inadequate role model. Hence the cycle of neglect might be said to derive from a cycle of infantilism" (Polansky, Chalmers, Buttenweiser, & Williams, 1981, p. 43). Although it must be emphasized that generalizing these families is not wise because of their diversity, some of the research data depict a group of neglectful caregivers who are generally (a) less able to love; (b) less capable of working productively; (c) less open about feelings; (d) more prone to living planlessly and impulsively; (e) susceptible to psychological symptoms and to phases of passive inactivity and numb fatalism; (f) more likely to live in a situation of family conflict, to be less organized and more chaotic; (h) less verbally expressive; and (i) less positive and more negative in affect (Erikson & Egeland, 1996; Polansky et al., 1981, p. 109; Gaudin, Polansky, Kilpatrick, & Shilton, 1996; Polansky, Gaudin, & Kilpatrick, 1992). Although many families involved with substance abuse never come to the attention of child welfare agencies, when they do they very often are identified as having problems related to child neglect (U.S. Department of Health and Human Services, 1999).

In a sense, the parenting/nurturing instinct has been weakened or distorted in its aim, or overwhelmed by the parent's struggle in personal survival. This stunting or crippling of parenting or nurturing is not often an emergent response to current stress but is predictable from the social history of the parent and the lack of nurturance in his or her childhood (Polansky et al., 1981, pp. 147–157). Some of those risk factors (and family strengths and resources) are illustrated by the following case example.

Children Who Are Not Headliners

The family consists of Mona Stay, twenty-three, and her common-law husband Frank Brown, aged twenty-six. There are three children: Frank Stay, three and a half, Sylvia Stay, eighteen months, and Wilma, seven months. The Stay-Browns have been together over five years. Although they quarrel and separate periodically, they seem very mutually dependent and likely to remain a couple.

Their original referral was from a nurse who had become aware of the eldest child's condition. He was difficult to discipline, was eating dirt and paint chips, and seemed hyperactive. Although over two, he was not speaking. His father reacted to him with impatience. He was often slapped, and hardly ever spoken to with fondness. The case worker got Mona to cooperate in taking young Frank in for a test for lead poisoning, and for a full developmental evaluation. This child had had several bouts with impetigo, had been bitten through the eyelid by a stray dog, and had a series of ear infections resulting in a slight hearing loss. Although physically normal, he appeared already nearly a year delayed.

Often this child was found outside the house alone when the caseworker came to see the family. On one occasion he was seen hanging from a broken fire escape on the second floor. The worker was unable to rouse his mother, or to enter the house until she got help from the nearby landlord, after which she ran upstairs and rescued the child. Only then did the sleeping Mona awaken!

With much effort having been expended on his behalf, this child had been attending a therapeutic nursery. His speech is already improved after four or five months, and his hyperactivity has calmed. He comes through as a lovable little boy.

Sylvia is surprisingly pale . . . and indeed, suffers from severe anemia. This child has had recurrent eye infections, and had a bout with spinal meningitis at age three months which, fortunately, seems to have left no residual effects. Much effort has gone into working with Mona concerning Sylvia's need for proper diet and iron supplement. After a year of contact this is still a problem.

The baby was born after the family had become known to the agency. Despite the agency's urging, Mona refused to go for prenatal care until she was in her second trimester, but she did maintain a fairly good diet, helped by small "loans" from the agency when her money for food ran out. When Wilma was born, she had to remain for a time at the hospital for treatment of jaundice. After she went home, she was left to lie most of the time in her bassinet, receiving very little attention from either parent. At four months of age, Wilma weighed only five pounds and was tentatively diagnosed as exhibiting "failure to thrive" by the hospital. Thereafter the mother avoided going to the clinic, and the caseworker spent much effort concerning the feeding and sheer survival of Wilma. The baby is now slowly gaining weight but is still limp and inactive.

In addition to an active caseworker, a homemaker was assigned to this family for months. Much more was involved than trying to help Mona learn to organize her day: she had almost no motivation to get started. Rather than learning how to manage, she tried to manipulate the homemaker into doing her housework for her. However, with time and patience, Mona has been persuaded to go with the caseworker on shopping trips, is learning how to buy groceries to best advantage, and from time to time manages to get the laundry into and out of the laundromat. So far as her plans for herself, Mona has talked of seeking training as a beauty operator, but has never followed through on this or on other positive plans.

The family's sole support is public assistance. Frank Brown, the father, was on drugs earlier in their relationship, but managed to get off them. Now, however, he drinks heavily, and although he manages to work, he never contributes to the household.

Mona, apparently, was herself a neglected child, and was removed from her parents in infancy. Placed with an adoptive family, there was constant friction during her growing up, and she ran away from home several times. During her teens, she was placed in an institution for incorrigible girls. Later she spent a period in a mental hospital during which she was withdrawn from heroin addiction. It is a commentary on her life that she regards this period in the adolescent ward as one of her happiest ever. Her adoptive mother is now dead, and her father wants nothing more to do with her, so she was more or less living on the streets when she met with Frank and set up their present establishment.

Frank and Mona, despite his obvious exploitativeness, seem to love each other and their children, and to want to keep the family together. They are able to relate to those who try to help them, so at least one is not operating constantly against hostile resistance. Mona is an intelligent woman and now shows adequate ability to handle the children. She can be an excellent cook—when there is food. Yet this remains a disorganized household. Bills are never paid, clothes are thrown around, the children never sleep on clean sheets, trash is piled around the house so that flies and maggots abound. Mona still leaves the youngsters quite alone for brief periods. There is no heat in the house, and the family will soon have to move, with neither any idea where to go nor funds for rent deposits and the like. Mona, at least, is currently wearing an IUD.

The Stay-Brown menage was not invented, although of course we have altered names and some facts to protect all concerned. These are real people, and they are clearly involved in child neglect. The failures center on poor feeding, uncleanliness, extremely bad housing, filthy circumstances which make the children prone to infections, lack of medical care, inadequate supervision and protections from danger, lack of intellectual stimulation, inattentiveness to the children bordering on rejection—one could go on. The fine staff trying to help Mona improve her child care finally gave up and closed her case after about fifteen months of effort.The care was improving slowly, if at all, and there were recurrent instances of regression.

Frank proved superficially amenable to suggestions when he could be seen, but in fact evaded any real responsibility for the household. The time, money, and—more importantly—motivation for hard work with such families are chronically in short supply. So the decision was made to try to help someone else who might be more treatable.

Meanwhile these children are with their parents. Since they have not literally been abandoned, it is uncertain whether a local judge would decide the home is so bad that the children must be removed. If a catastrophe were to occur, if one were to read that these three children had burned to death in a fire, one would be saddened but not greatly surprised. If one of the three were to die of an infectious disease or an undiagnosed appendicitis, one would not be surprised either. For the present, however, they are among the group child-protection workers know well, but that the public does not, because they do not make headlines—or at least not yet.

Source: Polansky, Chalmers, Buttenweiser, & Williams, *Damaged Parents: An Anatomy of Child Neglect,* pp. 5–7. Copyright © 1981. Reprinted with permission of the University of Chicago Press.

Summary

In this chapter, we have reviewed historical and current policies and legislation in American child welfare. A number of critical issues requiring reform have been discussed. The utility of a risk and resilience model for policy reform has been explored. Models that consider the developmental processes of children and families may be useful in future child welfare reform initiatives. Policy experts would be wise to consider this framework as debates about ways to reform child welfare services unfold.

Questions for Discussion

1. What are the implications of the risk and protective factor literature for the design of family support, foster care, and permanency policies and programs?

2. What policy changes would you recommend to better provide an evidence-based and more integrated service delivery system for families with children at risk of child maltreatment?

3. How will the increasing federal and state emphasis upon measurable outcomes be able to promote service delivery approaches that are culturally appropriate and oriented to child well-being?

Additional Reading

Berrick, J. D., Needell, B., Barth., R. B., & Johnson-Reid, M. (1998). *The tender years: Toward developmentally sensitive child welfare services for very young children.* New York: Oxford University Press.

Chibnall, S., Dutch, N., Jones-Harden, B., Brown, A., Gourgine, R., Smith, J., Boone, A., & Snyder, S. (2003). *Children of color in the child welfare system: Perspectives from the child welfare community.* Washington, DC: U.S. Department of Health and Human Services Administration for Children and Families Children's Bureau, Administration for Children and Families.

Child Welfare League of America. (2003). *Making children a national priority: A framework for community action.* Washington, DC: Author.

Shonkoff, J. P., & Meisels, S. J. (Eds.). (2000). *Handbook of early childhood intervention* (2nd ed.) New York: Cambridge University Press.

Notes

1. There were 3 million reports involving the welfare of approximately 5 million children in 2001 and 1.8 million in 2002. For the most recent federal child maltreatment statistics, see U.S. Department of Health and Human Services, Children's Bureau, Administration on Children, Youth and Families, National Clearinghouse on Child Abuse and Neglect Information (2003b), pp. iii and 3. In 1990, there were an estimated 611,924 victims, based on projections using data from 35 states. See U.S. Department of Health and Human Services. (1999), p. 4–2, and for the 2002 statistics see http://www.acf.hhs.gov/programs/cb/publications/cm02/summary.htm

2. These data are from the federal Adoption and Foster Care Analysis and Reporting System (AFCARS), which used data from 45 state and other jurisdictions, including Washington, DC, and Puerto Rico, to derive these estimates. U.S. Department of Health and Human Services, Administration for Children and Families, Children's Bureau (2004), p. 1. See http://www.acf.hhs.gov/programs/cb/dis/tables/entryexit2002 .htm. For total children served in 2002, see http://www.acf.hhs.gov/programs/cb/dis/ afcars/publications/afcars.htm. Note that AFCARS data are periodically updated; therefore, the data cited may not match the data on the current Web site.

3. This section draws from policy briefs and position statements prepared by Casey Family Programs (2004) and Child Welfare League of America (2003).

References

Adams, P., & Nelson, K. (1995). *Reinventing human services: Community and family-centered practice.* Hawthorne, NY: Aldine de Gruyter.

Ainsworth, M. D. S. (1989). Attachments beyond infancy. *American Psychologist,* 44, 709–716.

American Humane Association, Children's Division, American Bar Association, Center on Children and the Law, Annie E. Casey Foundation, Casey Family Services, the Institute for Human Services Management, and The Casey Family Program. (1998). *Assessing outcomes in child welfare services: Principles, concepts, and a framework of core indicators.* Englewood, CO: American Humane Association.

Avery, R. (1998). Public agency adoption in New York State: Phase I report. *Foster care histories of children freed for adoption in New York State: 1980–1993.* Ithaca, NY: Cornell University Press.

Berrick, J. D., Needell, B., Barth, R. B., & Johnson-Reid, M. (1998). *The tender years: Toward developmentally sensitive child welfare services for very young children.* New York: Oxford University Press.

Besharov, D. J. (1994). *When drug addicts have children: Reorienting child welfare's response.* Washington, DC: Child Welfare League of America.

Briere, J. (1992). *Child abuse trauma theory and treatment of the lasting effects.* Newbury Park, CA: Sage.

Bronfenbrenner, U. (1979). *The ecology of human development.* Cambridge, MA: Harvard University Press.

Bronfenbrenner, U. (1986). Ecology of the family as a context to human development: Research perspectives. *Developmental Psychology, 22,* 723–742.

Bronfenbrenner, U., & Morris, P. A. (1998). The ecology of developmental processes. In W. Damon (Ed.). *Handbook of child psychology* (5th ed., pp. 993–1028). New York: John Wiley & Sons.

Brooks-Gunn, J., & Duncan, G. J. (1997). The effects of poverty on children. *The Future of Children, 7,* 55–71.

Brooks-Gunn, J., Klebanov, P. K, & Liaw, F. (1995). The learning, physical, and emotional environment of the home in the context of poverty: The Infant Health and Development program. *Children and Youth Services Review, 17,* 251–276.

Bruns, E. J., & Burchard, J. D. (2000). Impact of respite care services for families with children experiencing emotional and behavioral problems. *Children's Services: Social Policy, Research, & Practice, 3,* 39–61.

Carnegie Council on Adolescent Development. (1989). *Turning points: Preparing youth for the 21st century.* Washington, DC: CCAD.

Casey Family Programs. (2001). *It's my life–A framework for youth transitioning from foster care to successful adulthood.* Seattle: Author.

Casey Family Programs. (2003a). *Family, community, culture: Roots of permanency—A conceptual framework on permanency from Casey Family Programs.* Seattle: Author. (www.casey.org)

Casey Family Programs. (2003b). *Higher education reform: Incorporating the needs of foster youth.* Seattle: Author. (www.casey.org)

Casey Family Programs. (2004). *2005 public policy agenda.* Seattle: Author.

Catalano, R. F., & Hawkins, J. D. (1996). The social developmental model: A theory of antisocial behavior. In J. D. Hawkins (Ed.), *Delinquency and crime: Current theories.* New York: Cambridge University Press.

Chamberlain, P. (2003). *Treating chronic juvenile offenders–Advances made through the Oregon multidimensional treatment foster care model.* Washington, DC: American Psychological Association.

Chibnall, S., Dutch, N., Jones-Harden, B., Brown, A., Gourgine, R., Smith, J., Boone, A., & Snyder, S. (2003). *Children of color in the child welfare system: Perspectives from the child welfare community.* Washington, DC: U.S. Department of Health and Human Services Administration for Children and Families Children's Bureau, Administration for Children and Families.

Child Welfare League of America. (2004). *Making children a national priority: A framework for community action.* Washington, DC: Author.

Children's Defense Fund. (2004). How can I get involved? State fact sheets for grandparents and other relatives raising children. Last retrieved August 20, 2004, from http://www.childrensdefense.org/childwelfare/kinshipcare/fact_sheets/default.asp

Cicchetti, D., & Lynch, M. (1993). Toward an ecological/transactional model of community violence and child maltreatment: Consequences for children's development. *Psychiatry, 56,* 96–118.

Coll, C. G., & Magnuson, K. (2000). Cultural differences as sources of developmental vulnerabilities and resources. In J. P. Shonkoff & S. J. Meisels (Eds.), *Handbook of early childhood intervention* (2nd ed., pp. 94–114). Cambridge, UK: Cambridge University Press.

Cook, R., Fleishman, E., & Grimes, V. (1991). *A national evaluation of Title IV-E foster care independent living programs for youth: Phase 2. Final report,* vol. 1. Rockville, MD: Westat.

Costin, L. B., Bell, C. J., Downs, S. W. (1991). *Child welfare: Policies and practices.* New York: Longman.

Courtney, M., Piliavin, I., Grogan-Kaylor, A., & Nesmith, A. (2001). Foster youth transitions to adulthood: A longitudinal view of youth leaving care, *Child Welfare, 80,* 685–717.

DiNitto, D., & Dye, T. (1989). *Social welfare: Politics and public policy.* Englewood Cliffs, NJ: Prentice-Hall, Inc.

Downs, A. C., & Pecora, P. J. (2004). Application of Erikson's psychosocial theory to the effects of child abuse and ameliorative foster care. (Working Paper No. 2). Seattle: Casey Family Programs. Web site: www.casey.org/research

Edna McConnell Clark Foundation. (2004). Theory of change behind the program for children. New York: Author. Last retrieved August 30, 2004, from http://www.emcf.org/programs/children/indepth/theory.htm

Erikson, E. H. (1959). *Identity and the life cycle.* New York: Norton.

Erikson, E. H. (1985). *The life cycle completed.* New York: Norton.

Erikson, M. F., & Egeland, B. (1996). Child neglect. In Briere, J., Berliner, L., Bulkley, J. A., Jenny, C., & Reid, T. *The APSAC handbook on child maltreatment* (pp. 4–20). Newbury Park, CA: Sage.

Fanshel, D., & Shinn, E. B. (1978). *Children in foster care: A longitudinal investigation.* New York: Columbia University Press.

Fraser, M. W. (Ed.). (2004). *Risk and resilience in childhood: An ecological perspective* (2nd ed.). Washington, DC: NASW Press.

Fraser, M. W., Kirby, L. D., & Smokowski, P. (2004). Risk and resilience in childhood. In M. W. Fraser (Ed.), *Risk and resilience in childhood: An ecological perspective* (2nd ed., pp. 13–66). Washington, DC: NASW.

Garbarino, J., & Ganzel, B. (2000). The human ecology of early risk. In J. P. Shonkoff & S. J. Meisels (Eds.), *Handbook of early childhood intervention* (2nd ed., pp. 76–93). Cambridge UK: Cambridge University Press.

Garmezy, N. (1983). Stressors of childhood. In N. Garmezy & M. Rutter (Eds.), *Stress, coping and development in children* (pp. 43–84). New York: McGraw-Hill.

Garmezy, N. (1985). Stress resistant children: The search for protective factors. In J. E. Stevenson (Ed.), *Recent research in developmental psychopathology* (pp. 76–93). Oxford: Pergamon Press.

Gaudin, J. M., Polanksy, N. A., Kilpatrick, A. C., & Shilton, P. (1996). Family functioning in neglectful families. *Child Abuse & Neglect, 20*(4), 363–377.

Goerge, R., Bilaver, L., Lee, B. L., Needell, B., Brookhart, A., & Jackman, W. (2002). *Employment outcomes for youth aging out of foster care. Final report.* Chicago and Berkeley: Chapin Hall Center for Children at the University of Chicago, and Center for Social Services Research, University of California Berkeley. Retrieved April 15, 2004 from http://aspe.hhs.gov/hsp/fostercare-agingout02/

Goldstein, J. A., Freud, A., & Solnit, A. (1973). *Beyond the best interests of the child.* New York: Free Press.

Graham, M., & Bryant, D. (1993). Characteristics of quality, effective service delivery systems for children with special needs. In D. Bryant & M. Graham (Eds.), *Implementing early intervention: From research to effective practice* (pp. 233–254). New York: Guilford Press.

Hardin, M. (1992). *Establishing a core of services for families subject to state intervention.* Washington, DC: American Bar Association.

Hill, R. B. (2001). The role of race in foster care placements. Paper presented at The Race Matters Forum sponsored by the University of Illinois at Urbana-Champaign, January 9–10, 2001.

Hines, A. M., Lemon, K., Wyatt, P., & Merdinger, J. (2004). Factors related to the disproportionate involvement of children of color in the child welfare system: A review and emerging themes. *Children and Youth Services Review, 26,* 507–527.

Hodges, V. (1994). Assessing for strengths and protective factors in child abuse and neglect: Risk assessment with families of color. Chapter 2. In P. J. Pecora, & D. J. English (Eds.), *Multi-cultural guidelines for assessing family strengths and risk factors in child protective services* (pp. II–1 to 11). Seattle: School of Social Work, University of Washington, and Washington State Department of Social Services.

Johnson, K., Knitzer, J., & Kaufmann, R. (2003). *Making dollars follow sense: Financing early childhood mental health services to promote healthy social and emotional development in young children.* New York: Columbia University, National Center on Children in Poverty.

Karoly, L. M., Kilburn, R. M., Caulkins, J. P., & Cannon, J. S. (2000). *Assessing costs and benefits of early childhood intervention programs: Overview and application.* Santa Monica, CA: The Rand Corporation.

Kessler, R. C., & Magee, W. J. (1993). Childhood adversities and adult depression. *Psychological Medicine, 23,* 679–690.

Kirk, S., Gallagher, J., & Anastasiow, N. (1993). *Educating exceptional children* (7th ed). Boston: Houghton Mifflin.

Larner, M. B., Stevenson, C. S., & Behrman, R. E. (1998). Protecting children from abuse and neglect: Analysis and recommendations. *The Future of Children, 8,* Spring, 4–22.

Light, R. (1973). Abused and neglected children in America: A study of alternative policies. *Harvard Educational Review, 43,* 556–598.

Lindsey, D. (2004). *The welfare of children* (2nd ed.). New York: Oxford University Press.

Lynch, E. W., & Hanson, M. J. (1992). *Developing cross-cultural competence: A guide for working with young children and their families.* Baltimore: Paul H. Brookes.

Maier, H. W. (1978). *Three theories of child development* (3rd ed.). New York: Harper & Row.

Mallon, G. P. (1999). *Let's get this straight: A gay- and lesbian-affirming approach to child welfare.* New York: Columbia University Press.

Maluccio, A. N., Fein, E., & Olmstead, K. A. (1986). *Permanency planning for children: Concepts and methods.* New York: Tavistock.

Maluccio, A. N., & Pecora, P. J. (forthcoming). (Eds.). Foster family care: The United States perspective. In C. McCauley, P. J. Pecora, & W. E. Rose. *Enhancing the well-being of children and families through effective interventions—UK and USA evidence for practice.* Philadelphia: Jessica Kingsley.

Maluccio, A. N., Pine, B. A., & Tracy, E. M. (2002). *Social work practice with families and children.* New York: Columbia University Press.

Massinga, R., & Pecora, P. J. (2003). Providing better opportunities for older children in the child welfare system. *The Future of Children* (Issue No. 30) Volume 14(1), 151–173. (Published electronically from January 2005 forward: www.futureofchildren.org)

McDonald, J., Salyers, N., & Shaver, M. (2004). *The foster care straitjacket: Innovation, federal financing & accountability in state foster care reform—A report by fostering results.* Urbana-Champaign: Children and Family Research Center at the School of Social Work, University of Illinois at Urbana-Champaign. http://www.fosteringresults.org/results/reports/pewreports

Mech, E. V. (Ed.). (1988). Independent-living services for at-risk adolescents. *Child Welfare, 67,* 483–634.

Miller, D. L., Hoffman, F., & Turner, D. (1980). A perspective on the Indian Child Welfare Act. *Social Casework, 61,* 468–471.

Milner, J., Mitchell, L., & Hornsby, W. (2001). The child and family service review: A framework for changing practice. *Journal of Family Social Work, 6,* 5–18.

Mindel, C. H., Habenstein, R. W., & Wright, R. (1988). *Ethnic families in America: Patterns and variations.* New York: Elsevier.

Mordock, J. B. (2002). *Managing for outcomes: A basic guide to the evaluation of best practices in the human services.* Washington, DC: Child Welfare League of America.

Morgan, L. J., Spears, L. S., & Kaplan, C. (2003). *A framework for community action: Making children a national priority.* Washington, DC: Child Welfare League of America.

Mott, P. E. (1976). *Meeting human needs: The social and political history of Title XX.* Columbus, OH: National Conference on Social Welfare.

New York City Administration for Children's Services. (2004). *New York City's child welfare system: Successful reform.* New York: Author.

Osofsky, J. D., & Thompson, D. (2000). Adaptive and maladaptive parenting: Perspectives on risk and protective factors. In J. P. Shonkoff & S. J. Meisels (Eds.), *Handbook of early childhood intervention* (2nd ed., pp. 54–75). Cambridge, UK: Cambridge University Press.

Parish, S. L., Pomeranz, A. E., & Braddock, D. (2003). Family support in the United States: Financing trends and emerging initiatives. *Mental Retardation, 41,* 174–187.

Parish, S. L., & Whisnant, A. L. (2005). Policies and programs for children and youth with disabilities. In J. Jenson & M. Fraser (Eds.), *Social policy for children and families: A risk and resilience perspective* (pp. 167–194). Thousand Oaks, CA: Sage.

Pecora, P. J., Kessler, R. K., Williams, J., Downs, S., English, D., & White, J. (in press). *What works in foster care.* New York: Oxford University Press.

Pecora, P. J., Kessler, R. C., Williams, J., O'Brien, K., Downs, A. C., English, D., White, J., Hiripi, E., White, C.R., Wiggins, T., & Holmes, K. (2005). *Improving family foster care: Findings from the Northwest Foster Care Alumni Study.* Seattle, WA: Casey Family Programs. www.casey.org

Pecora, P. J., Selig, W., Zirps, F., & Davis, S. (Eds.) (1996). *Quality improvement and program evaluation in child welfare agencies: Managing into the next century.* Washington, DC: Child Welfare League of America.

Pecora, P. J., Whittaker, J. K., Maluccio, A. N., & Barth, R. P. (with R. Plotnick). (2000). *The child welfare challenge—Policy, practice, and research* (2nd ed.). New York: Aldine de Gruyter.

Pecora, P. J., Whittaker, J. K., Maluccio, A. N., & Barth, R. P. (with R. Plotnick). (forthcoming). *The child welfare challenge—Policy, practice, and research* (3rd ed.). Piscataway, NJ: Aldine-Transaction Books.

Pecora, P. J., Williams, J., Kessler, R. J., Downs, A.C., O'Brien, K., Hiripi, E., & Morello, S. (2003). *Assessing the effects of foster care: Early results from the Casey National Alumni Study.* Seattle: Casey Family Programs. Web site: http://www.casey.org

Pine, B. A. (1986). Child welfare reform and the political process. *Social Service Review, 60,* 339–359.

Plantz, M. C., Hubbell, R., Barrett, B. J., & Dobrec, A. (1989). Indian Child Welfare Act: A status report. *Children Today, 18,* 24–29.

Polansky, N. A., Chalmers, M. A., Buttenweiser, E., & Williams, D. P. (1981). *Damaged parents: An anatomy of child neglect.* Chicago: University of Chicago Press.

Polansky, N. A., Gaudin, J. M., Jr., & Kilpatrick, A. C. (1992). Family radicals. *Children and Youth Services Review, 14,* 19–26.

Rae-Grant, N., Thomas, B. H., Offord, D. R., & Boyle, M. H. (1989). Risk, protective factors, and the prevalence of behavioral and emotional disorders in children and adolescents. *Journal of American Academy Child and Adolescent Psychiatry, 28,* 262–268.

Ramey, C. T., & Ramey, S. L. (1998). Early intervention and early experience. *American Psychologist, 53,* 109–120.

Rosenberg, M. (1987). New directions for research on the psychological maltreatment of children. *American Psychologist, 42,* 166–171.

Rutter, M. (1979). Protective factors in children's responses to stress and disadvantage. In M. W. Kent & J. E. Rolf (Eds.), *Primary prevention of psychopathology, Vol. 3: Social competence in children* (pp. 49–74). Hanover, NH: University Press of New England.

Rutter, M. (1981). Stress, coping and development: Some issues and some questions. *Journal of Child Psychology & Psychiatry, 22,* 323–356.

Rutter, M. (1985). Resilience in the face of adversity: Protective factors and resistance to psychiatric disorder. *British Journal of Psychiatry, 147,* 598–611.

Rutter, M. (1987). Psychosocial resilience and protective mechanisms. *American Journal of Orthopsychiatry, 57,* 316–331.

Rutter, M. (1989). Intergenerational continuities and discontinuities in serious parenting difficulties. In D. Cicchetti & V. Carlson (Eds.), *Child maltreatment: Theory and research on the causes and consequences of child abuse and neglect* (pp. 317–348). Cambridge, UK: Cambridge University Press.

Rutter, M. (1990). Psychosocial resilience and protective mechanisms. In J. Rolf (Ed.), *Risk and protective factors in the development of psychopathology* (pp. 42–73). New York: Cambridge University Press.

Ryan, J., & Testa, M. (2004). *Child maltreatment and juvenile delinquency: Investigating the role of placement and placement instability.* Champaign-Urbana: University of Illinois at Urbana-Champaign School of Social Work, Children and Family Research Center.

Shonkoff, J., & Phillips, D. (2000). *From neurons to neighborhoods: The science of early childhood development.* Washington, DC: National Research Council and Institute of Medicine.

Singer, J. D., & Butler, J. A. (1987). The Education for All Handicapped Children Act: Schools as agents of social reform. *Harvard Educational Review, 57,* 125–152.

Social Security Administration. (2000). Supplemental Security Income. Determining disability for a child under 18. Final rules. *Federal Register,* September 11, *65,* 54747–54790.

Specht, H., & Courtney, M. E. (1994). *Unfaithful angels: How social work has abandoned its mission.* New York: Free Press.

Stein, T. (1984). The Child Abuse Prevention and Treatment Act. *Social Service Review, 58*(2), 302–314.

Stein, T. (1991). *Child welfare and the law.* New York: Longman.

Thomas, G. (1994). Travels in the trench between child welfare theory and practice: A case study of failed promises and prospects for renewal. *Child and Youth Services Review, 17,* 1–260.

U.S. Department of Health and Human Services, Administration on Children, Youth and Families, Children's Bureau. (2003a). *Safety, permanency and well-being: Child welfare outcomes 1998, 1999 & 2000.* Washington, DC: U.S. Government Printing Office.

U.S. Department of Health and Human Services, Administration for Children, Youth, and Families, Children's Bureau. (2003b). AQ1 *Emerging practices in the prevention of child abuse and neglect.* Washington, DC: Author. This report was prepared by Caliber Associates under contract number 282–98–0025 (Task Order 13) with the Children's Bureau's Office on Child Abuse and Neglect.

U.S. Department of Health and Human Services, Administration for Children and Families Administration on Children, Youth and Families, Children's Bureau. (2004). Adoption and foster care analysis and reporting system (AFCARS). Data as of May 2004. Washington, DC: U.S. Government Printing Office.

U.S. Department of Health and Human Services, Administration on Children, Youth and Families. (1999). Child maltreatment 1997: *Reports from the states to the National Child Abuse and Neglect Data Systems.* Washington, DC: U.S. Government Printing Office. Web site: http://www.calib.com/nccanch

U.S. Government Accounting Office (2004). Child and family services reviews better use of data and improved guidance could enhance HHS's oversight of state performance. Washington, DC: U.S. Government Printing Office. (Report No. GAO-04–333.)

Wald, M. (1976). State intervention on behalf of "neglected" children: Standards for removal of children from their homes, monitoring the status of children in foster care, and termination of parental rights. *Stanford Law Review, 28,* 623, 645.

Walton, E., Sandau-Beckler, P., & Mannes, M. (Eds.) (2001). *Balancing family-centered services and child well-being: Exploring issues in policy, practice, and research.* New York: Columbia University Press.

Weinfield, N. S., Ogawa, J. R., & Sroufe, L. A. (1997). Early attachment as a pathway to adolescent peer competence. *Journal of Research on Adolescence, 7,* 241–265.

Weinstein, E. A. (1960). *The self-image of the foster child.* New York: Russell Sage Foundation.

Werner, E. E. (1989). High-risk children in young adulthood: A longitudinal study from birth to 32 years. *American Journal of Orthopsychiatry, 59,* 72–81.

White, A., Courtney, J., & Fifield, A. (1998). *The race factor in child welfare.* New York: Center for an Urban Future. Retrieved August 16, 2004, from http://www.nycfuture.org/content/reports/report_view.cfm?repkey=9

Whittaker, J. K., & Maluccio, A. N. (2002). Rethinking "child welfare": A reflective essay. *Social Service Review, 76,* 107–134.

Wilson, M. (1984). Mothers' and grandmothers' perceptions of parental behavior in three-generational Black families. *Child Development, 55,* 1333–1339.

Wooden, K. (1976). *Weeping in the playtime of others.* New York: McGraw-Hill.

Wulczyn, F. H., & Zeidman, D. (with A. Svirsky). (1997). HomeRebuilders: A family reunification demonstration project. In J. D. Berrick, R. P. Barth, & N. Gilbert (Eds.), *Child welfare research review* (Vol. II, pp. 252–271). New York: Columbia University Press.

YMCA of the USA, Dartmouth Medical School and Institute for American Values. (2003). *Hardwired to connect: The new scientific case for authoritative communities.* New York: Institute for American Values.

Web-Based Resources

Child Trends for key statistical summaries, child and family trend data and issue summaries http://www.childtrends.org

U.S. Children's Bureau for state outcomes and foster care statistics http://www.acf .hhs.gov/programs/cb/publications

3

Education Policy for Children, Youth, and Families

Andy J. Frey

Hill M. Walker

P ublic education in the United States occurs in the context of a complex and often contentious system composed of diverse interest groups and divergent political views. At the heart of educational policy debates are several competing beliefs about the primary purpose of education. These purposes include preparing students for the workforce, teaching basic academic skills, preparing future citizens to participate in society, and developing social and cognitive skills (Sadovnik, Cookson, & Semel, 2001). This set of interacting purposes creates enormous policy and program challenges.

Recent reports indicate that the current American education system is struggling in its effort to reach all students effectively. Evidence about the overall health of the education system comes from several sources. The National Center for Education found that 50 percent of fourth-grade students and 34 percent of eighth-grade students scored below basic grade level in math ability in 2001. Data from reading tests indicated that 26 percent of eighth graders and 37 percent of fourth graders were below their corresponding basic reading levels in 1998 and 2000, respectively (National Center for Education Statistics, 2004). In 1999, 3.8 million children representing more than 11 percent of the nation's youth dropped out of school before earning a high school diploma. Youth of color are at greatest risk for school dropout, a discussion we will turn to again in a later part of this chapter.

Education has been the target of numerous federal and state-level policy reforms in the past decade. In this chapter, we discuss historical and recent educational policies and programs for children, youth, and their families. Three topics are explored as important components for understanding and creating education policy: (1) risk and protective factors for adjustment and achievement problems experienced by children and adolescents in schools; (2) risk, resilience, and protective influences in education policies and programs; and (3) the application of risk, resilience, and protection to achieve service integration in education policy.

Risk and Protective Factors for School-Related Problems

The term *risk factor* is defined by Fraser and Terzian (in press) as "any event, condition, or experience that increases the probability that a problem will be formed, maintained, or exacerbated" (p. 5). Risk factors for school-related problems may be specific or generic in nature. Within the context of education, nonspecific risk factors such as poverty are not directly related to academic performance. Nevertheless, they have the potential to create maladaptive emotional and behavioral outcomes that in turn have an adverse effect on academic performance (Greenberg, Domitrovich, & Bumbarger, 1999). Academic performance is a broad construct that includes the acquisition of academic and social skills necessary to complete high school and pursue advanced education. Nonspecific risk factors may set into motion what Fraser and colleagues call a "chain of risk" (Fraser, Kirby, & Smokowski, 2004) that may culminate in outcomes such as academic failure.

Other risk factors directly impact the likelihood of academic failure and school problems. For example, factors such as low commitment to school directly contribute to truancy, poor grades, and overall academic performance (Carnahan, 1994). As shown in Tables 3.1 and 3.2, risk factors can be individual in nature or appear in the context of families, schools, communities, or neighborhoods (Jenson & Howard, 1999).

Protective factors are characteristics or traits that buffer exposure to risk. In situations of high risk, protective factors such as attachment to teachers or other adults at school may reduce risk and decrease the likelihood of school-related problems. Closely related is the concept of promotion. Promotive factors are defined as resources that exert positive influences on behavior irrespective of the presence or absence of risk (Sameroff & Gutman,

2004). High intelligence or strong social skills illustrate examples of factors that may promote positive behavioral outcomes irrespective of risk exposure. Tables 3.1 and 3.2 summarize risk, protective, and promotive factors that affect academic performance.

Frameworks for Understanding Risk, Protection, and Resilience

As Jenson and Fraser note in Chapter 1, principles of risk, protection, and promotion interact in the course of a child's developmental process. One

Table 3.1   Risk Factors for Academic Failure by Level of Influence

Level of Influence	Risk Factors
Individual	Learning related social skills (listening, participating in groups, staying on task, organizational skills)
	Social behavior
	Limited intelligence
	Presence of a disability
	Minority status
	Special education status
	Students who fail to read by the fourth grade
Family	Early exposure to patterns of antisocial behavior
	Parent–child conflict
	Lack of connectedness with peers, family, school, and community
School	Large school size
	Limited resources
	High staff turnover
	Inconsistent classroom management
	Percentage of low SES students
	School and classroom climate
	School violence
	Overcrowding
	High student/teacher ratios
	Insufficient curricular and course relevance
	Weak, inconsistent adult leadership
	Overcrowding
	Poor building design
	Overreliance on physical security measures
Neighborhood	Poverty
	Low percentage of affluent neighbors

Table 3.2   Promotive and Protective Factors for Academic Failure by Level of Influence

Level of Influence	Promotive Factors
Individual	Cognitive skills (e.g., intelligence, the ability to work collaboratively with others, and the capacity to focus in the face of distraction) High socioemotional functioning Ability to adapt to changes in school or work schedule Effective and efficient communication skills Ability to use humor to de-escalate negative situations Social skills Understanding and accepting capabilities and limitations Maintaining a positive outlook
School	Positive and safe environment Setting high academic and social expectations Positive relationships with teachers School bonding Positive and open school climate Positive ratings for overall educational performance
	Protective Factors
School	School climate Classroom management strategies that reduce classroom disruption and increase learning School bonding Consistent and firm rules for students
Peer	Acceptance by pro-social peers Involvement in positive peer groups

positive outcome of this interactive process is expressed in the lives of resilient children. Resilient youth are generally defined as young persons who successfully adapt to life circumstances in the presence of multiple risk factors (Arrlington & Wilson, 2000; Luthar, Cicchetti, & Becker, 2000; Olsson, Bond, Burns, Vella-Brodrick, & Sawyer, 2003). Research suggests that one's degree of resilience is related to the frequency, duration, and intensity of risk exposure. The greater the exposure, the more resilient one must be to thrive or be successful.

Children's differential responses to risk have been conceptualized through additive and interactive models (Fraser et al., 2004). Additive models forward the notion that risk and protection operate on a continuum, with the amount of risk directly increasing the probability of poor adaptation, and the amount of protection directly increasing the likelihood of positive adaptation (Masten, 1987). Conversely, as the name implies, interactive models emphasize the interactions that occur between protective factors and varying levels of risk. In this model, one assumes that protective factors have differential protective qualities in the context of high and low risk (Fraser, Richman, & Galinsky, 1999).

We believe that an interactive model of risk and resilience holds the most promise for developing effective education policy and programs. Evidence from efficacious school-based practices supports the need to attend to interactions among key individual, social, and environmental factors. Over the past several decades, our knowledge of "what works" in school-based prevention programs has increased dramatically (Sloboda & David, 1997). For example, we now know that the most successful school-based prevention programs are dual-focused; that is, they employ a comprehensive approach that includes both individual- and school-level change strategies (Sloboda & David). Rather than targeting only individual students, successful school-based practices seek to change the culture and climate of a school (Dupper, 2002). Effective programs clarify and communicate norms about positive behavior and teach social skills to children and youth over extended periods of time (Walker, 2001).

The risk, protective, and promotive characteristics of youth who are more likely to experience academic failure support the need for policies and programs to address key environmental factors that are present in children's lives. For example, Richman, Bowen, and Woolley (2004) cite empirical evidence indicating that youth of color and persons from low socioeconomic families experience high rates of academic failure and dropout. These and other characteristics found to be associated with school problems represent important markers that should inform policy and program efforts. Richman et al. (2004) argue that school dropout, although important, is not the only manifestation of school failure. In an effort to maximize school success for high-risk youth, a wide variety of educational problems must be examined, including truancy and attendance, low performance on achievement tests, and suspension and expulsion rates.

Principles of risk and protection hold great promise for education policy and school-based practices. We review the realized and potential influence of such principles for education policy next.

Educational Policies and Programs: Past and Present

Our review of education policy in the United States begins with the recognition that American educational practices are profoundly influenced by political ideology, most frequently viewed in conservative and liberal terms. Historically, a conservative view of education forwards the idea that individual students have the capacity to earn or not earn their place among the academic elite. Policy approaches based on conservative views tend to emphasize knowledge-centered education, traditional forms of learning and curricula, respect for authority and discipline, and the adoption of rigorous academic standards. In contrast, educational solutions from liberal perspectives tend to support curricula that are responsive to individuals and to social and environmental contexts (Apollonia & Abrami, 1997). Educational policies and programs in the past 100 years are reviewed next and summarized in Table 3.3.

Early Public Policy

From its inception, public education has been conceptualized as a social vehicle for minimizing the importance of class and wealth for determining who will excel economically. In the mid-nineteenth century Horace Mann exemplified this belief, stating that education, more than any other process, was the great equalizer of people from various walks of life (Cremin, 1957). Similarly, Dewey's philosophy of education viewed the role of education as the "leveler" of social reform (Dewey, 1916). Social policy in the late nineteenth and early twentieth centuries was based on the liberal ideas of Mann and Dewey. Policy also stemmed from the conservative notion that mass education was necessary to ensure that the citizenry was able to obey the law, vote, pay taxes, and serve on juries and in the armed forces (Derezinski, 2004). The Massachusetts Compulsory School Attendance Act of 1852 required public school attendance for all able-bodied children of a certain age, unless the parent of the child could establish that the child was obtaining equivalent instruction outside of the public schools. By 1918, 48 states had adopted similar attendance policies (Derezinski). This policy change resulted in programs based on the idea that all children attend school and graduate, assertions that were nonexistent before compulsory attendance laws. At this point, segregated education was determined to be constitutional, as evidenced by the separate-but-equal clause in *Plessey v. Ferguson,* which supported separate transportation systems for African Americans and whites.

Education Policy from 1930 to 1970

In the post–World War I era, debates about academic and social goals of education and whether all children should receive the same quality education dominated educational policy. Although the focus on curriculum and teaching methods remained, a values-based debate ensued that was

Table 3.3   Major American Education Policies, Court Cases, and Public
Reports, 1852–2004

Policy, Court Case, or Public Report	Date	Summary	Influence on Education
Compulsory School Attendance Act	1852	Required public school attendance for all able-bodied children of a certain age, unless the parent of the child could establish that the child was obtaining equivalent instruction outside of the public schools.	Resulted in programs designed to have all children attend school and graduate. Existing programs would need to change to accommodate a very different student population that had not previously attended school.
Plessey v. Ferguson	1896	Commonly referred to as "separate but equal," this decision supported separate transportation systems for blacks and whites.	Validated the belief that separate schools for blacks and whites was a constitutionally sound practice.
Brown v. Board of Education	1954	The Supreme Court ruled that laws assigning students to schools based on race were unconstitutional. The court ruled unanimously that such laws violated the Fourteenth Amendment's guarantee that the rights of all Americans deserved equal protection. The rationale for the verdict was that being separated from white students could result in feelings of inferiority in students of color and compromise their futures.	Desegregation gained momentum and competed for attention in the national spotlight and attempted to force school districts to desegregate.
Numerous Public Reports	Late 1960s and early 1970s	Highlighted the structural inequalities in the educational system (particularly for African American children and those from disadvantaged backgrounds) and the	Justified busing students between schools and between school districts, suggesting that reassigning poor students to schools with middle-class

(Continued)

Table 3.3 (Continued)

Policy, Court Case, or Public Report	Date	Summary	Influence on Education
		relationship between socioeconomic status and unequal educational outcomes.	students would improve poor students' academic achievement.
Head Start Act	1965	Head Start was designed to address a wealth of factors that affect poor children and their families, with the ultimate goal of increasing early school readiness by providing health, educational, nutritional, family support, social, and other services for 3- and 4-year-old children from low-income households.	The first primary prevention program of its kind, designed to prepare disadvantaged children on a universal level for kindergarten.
Elementary and Secondary Education Act (ESEA)	1965	The ESEA of 1965 provided funds for schools that had high percentages of disadvantaged students (Title I). Goals were to promote safe and drug-free learning environments (Title IV), help linguistically diverse children (Title VII), and promote the inclusion and participation of women in all aspects of education (Title IX). These funds were used for whole school reform, compensatory education, and remediation for the country's most disadvantaged children, and to provide free and reduced-cost lunches for children in need.	Title I and Title IV have had the greatest impact on high-risk youth. Title I has been the largest source of federal funding for poor children in schools, serving 10 million children in more than 50,000 schools.
Milliken v. Bradley	1974	The courts declared that if segregation was the result of an individual's choice,	Released a district from desegregation orders after it demonstrated it

Policy, Court Case, or Public Report	Date	Summary	Influence on Education
		school districts could not be forced to remedy the situation.	had done everything possible to desegregate schools. This ruling set a precedent for similar rulings that resulted in an end to racially balanced schools in many American cities.
Education of All Handicapped Children Act, PL-94–142 (later, the Individuals with Disabilities Act)	1975	Provided screening and identification for children with a wide range of disabilities and required schools to provide a variety of services for children based on an individualized education plan developed by a multidisciplinary team.	Altered the education of those with disabilities for many years to come.
A Nation at Risk	1983	Cited high rates of adult illiteracy and low achievement test scores as indicators of declining literacy and educational standards. The report recommended that educational policies strive to improve education for all students and develop more rigorous and measurable standards to assess academic performance. It highlighted the failure of education to ameliorate social problems and blamed these policies for producing mass mediocrity in education that resulted in the decline of authority and standards in schools.	Federal, state, and local policy switched to the improvement of curriculum, school-based management, the tightening of standards, the importance of discipline, and the establishment of academic goals and assessment.
America 2000	1992	President George H. Bush called for voluntary	Began what would become a major movement

(Continued)

Table 3.3 (Continued)

Policy, Court Case, or Public Report	Date	Summary	Influence on Education
		testing in grades 4, 8, and 12, and proposed six goals for education, called America 2000	toward education policy aligned with the conservative ideology.
Goals 2000	1994	President Clinton proposed this initiative, which would have set into law the six national education goals proposed by President George H. Bush.	Continued the trend toward standards and accountability testing.
Gun-Free Schools Act	1994	This Act provided funds only for schools that adopted zero-tolerance policies for guns and drugs on school grounds.	Resulted in the expansion of zero-tolerance policies for less severe student infractions. Led to promising prevention and intervention services such as teacher involvement/ training; the restructuring of schools to increase student engagement, attendance, performance, and family involvement; and the establishment of clear behavior expectations in schools.
No Child Left Behind	2000	NCLB is the most recent reauthorization of the ESEA. It is designed to create a stronger, more accountable education system, seeks to change the culture of education, and purports to use evidence-based strategies found to be effective through rigorous research. NCLB holds students accountable to high educational outcomes and standards. NCLB requires each state to set clear and high standards and to put an assessment system in place to measure student progress toward those standards.	To be determined.

associated with issues of equity and excellence. By 1930, the direction of education policy shifted toward equality in education. During the 1930s, the National Association for the Advancement of Colored People initiated a campaign to overthrow the *Plessey v. Ferguson* decision, with school desegregation a major goal. The achievement gap between advantaged and disadvantaged students became increasingly clear. Subsequently, desegregation gained momentum and competed for policy attention in the national spotlight.

The achievement gap between white and African American and advantaged and disadvantaged children became one of the most important educational issues of the century in the 1940s. The debate that ensued served as a catalyst in efforts to close the achievement gap and to maximize educational opportunities for people of color. The integration movement scored a huge victory in 1954, when the Supreme Court ruled in *Brown v. Board of Education* that laws assigning students to schools based on race were unconstitutional. The court ruled unanimously that such laws violated the Fourteenth Amendment's guarantee that the rights of all Americans deserved equal protection. The rationale for the verdict was that separating African American students from white students could result in feelings of inferiority in students of color and serve to compromise the quality of their education. Unfortunately, it took nearly two decades for every state in the South to comply with the court order, and many of the initial advancements that were achieved by the integration movement have since given way.

During this same time frame, progressive directions in education were attacked by conservatives, who suggested that the American education system was sacrificing intellectual goals for social ones. The discussion between progressives who saw the educational arena as the most legitimate vehicle for leveling the playing field and critics who demanded more academic rigor in education became known as "the great debate" (Ravitch, 1983). The debate was fueled by the Soviet launching of the space satellite *Sputnik*, which served as a warning that the United States might no longer be leading the world in scientific research and development. From the mid-1950s to the mid-1960s the pursuit of excellence, standards-based education, curriculum reform, assessment, and accountability gained momentum. This direction would not take center stage in education policy, however, until the 1980s.

The 1960s witnessed great divisiveness in educational policy illustrated by the tension evident in the eventual move toward a more liberal reform orientation. This change mirrored larger societal issues, predominantly the emphasis on equity issues raised by the Civil Rights Movement. In the 1960s and early 1970s, several influential books highlighted the structural inequalities in the educational system, particularly for African American children and children from disadvantaged backgrounds. These books (Clark, 1965; Kohl, 1967;

Kozol, 1967; Rosenfeld, 1971), along with a report by Coleman entitled *Equality of Educational Opportunity* (1966), highlighted the relationship between socioeconomic status and unequal educational outcomes. The Coleman Report suggested that student composition within schools was highly correlated with student achievement (Sadovnik et al., 2001). The implications of the report were shocking, primarily because Coleman set out to demonstrate that the achievement gap between African American and white students could be attributed to the organizational structure of American schools. The Coleman Report justified busing students between schools and between school districts, suggesting that reassigning poor students to schools with middle-class students would equalize educational opportunities. Seemingly contradicting common sense, the Coleman Report suggested that between-school differences affected educational outcomes only minimally. The report was challenged by many researchers who questioned the premise, method, and findings.

Other progressive policies also emerged in the 1960s. In 1965, the Head Start Act funded an innovative preschool program for disadvantaged children. Head Start was designed to address a wealth of factors that affected poor children and their families. The goal of the program was to increase early school readiness by providing health, educational, nutritional, family support, social, and other services to preschool children from low-income households. The Head Start program was the first federally supported primary prevention program of its kind.

Congress passed the Elementary and Secondary Education Act (ESEA) in 1965. Like Head Start, this legislation was passed on the assumption that inequities in educational opportunities were largely responsible for the achievement gap between advantaged and disadvantaged children. ESEA provided funds for schools that had high percentages of disadvantaged students in order to promote safe and drug-free learning environments (Title IV). The Act also supported linguistically diverse children (Title VII) and promoted the inclusion and participation of women in all aspects of education (Title IX). These funds were used for whole school reform, compensatory education, and remediation for the country's most disadvantaged children, and to provide free and reduced-price lunches for children in need. ESEA has been revised and reauthorized every 5 years since 1965. Provisions of the Act are currently responsible for funding bilingual education, drug education, and school lunch and breakfast programs (Nelson, Palonsky, & McCarthy, 2004).

Title I and Title IV of ESEA have had the greatest impact on vulnerable and high-risk youth. Title I has been the largest source of federal funding for poor children in schools, serving 10 million children in more than 50,000 schools (Slavin, 1999). Title IV provides early screening; remedial academic support; and violence, substance abuse, sexual abuse, and teenage pregnancy prevention programming. Transition programs for youth coming from residential and juvenile justice settings are also supported under Title IV.

Education Policy from 1970 to 2000

The 1970s brought new attempts to integrate schools through complex busing plans and magnet schools designed to attract white students to neighborhood schools that they would not ordinarily attend (Cecelski, 1994). However, desegregation became increasingly difficult to maintain as a host of court cases gradually began to undo the *Brown* mandate. In the 1974 case of *Milliken v. Bradley*, the courts declared that if segregation was the result of an individual's choice, school districts could not be forced to remedy the situation. Put simply, once a district had done all it could to desegregate schools, it was released from further desegregation orders. Similar rulings led to renewed efforts to racially balance schools in many American cities (Nelson et al., 2004).

In 1975, Congress passed the Education of All Handicapped Children Act (EHA), or PL-94–142, which altered educational patterns for students with disabilities. The EHA has undergone several reauthorizations, including a name change, to the Individuals with Disabilities in Education Act (IDEA), in 1990. The Act provides screening and identification for children with a wide range of disabilities and requires schools to offer a variety of services for children based on an individualized education plan developed by a multidisciplinary team. The EHA contained four components that have proved particularly important to high-risk children and youth: (1) screening and identification of children with disabilities; (2) intervention services for children with disabilities; (3) inclusion of students with nondisabled students to the greatest extent possible; and (4) discipline provisions for students with disabilities.

In the late 1970s, many conservative policy proponents pointed to the government's inability to solve social problems in the schools. Some spoke critically of the way in which EHA interfered with individual freedoms (Nelson et al., 2004). Many experts argued that progressive reforms had failed to narrow the achievement gap between advantaged and disadvantaged children and had actually increased discipline and other behavior problems in schools. This belief was fueled by the National Commission on Excellence report titled "A Nation at Risk" (Anyon, 1997). "A Nation at Risk," initiated under Terrel Bell, President Reagan's secretary of education, cited high rates of adult illiteracy and low achievement test scores as indicators of declining literacy and education standards. The report recommended that educational policies strive to improve education for all students and develop more rigorous and measurable standards to assess academic performance (Nelson et al.). This report paved the way for future educational reform efforts. Following the publication of "A Nation at Risk," primary education reform efforts have focused on excellence for all, rather than concentrating on subgroups of children such as disabled or high-risk youth. The report highlighted the failure of education to ameliorate social problems and blamed past policies for producing mass mediocrity in education that resulted in the decline of authority and standards in schools.

Subsequently, federal, state, and local policy switched to the improvement of curriculum, school-based management, tightening of standards, discipline, and the establishment of academic goals and assessment as new policy foci. School-based management emphasized a structural shift away from bureaucratic boards of education to more local forms of control. New policies aimed to engage parents, teachers, and administrators in decision-making processes. Teacher empowerment, closely related to school-based management, was emphasized as a way to give teachers more decision-making power within schools. School choice options, such as vouchers, charter schools, and magnet schools, were created to provide parents with alternatives to the traditional public school offerings. These strategies were based on the belief that the best way to reform education was to include principles of competition and accountability in education policy. This philosophy became a cornerstone of the recently passed No Child Left Behind Act.

Current Federal Education Policy: The No Child Left Behind Act

The momentum created for educational reform gained in the 1990s culminated in the passage of the 2002 No Child Left Behind Act (NCLB). The NCLB has been described as the most sweeping federal reform in education since ESEA was passed in 1965 (Nelson et al., 2004). Technically, NCLB is the most recent reauthorization of ESEA. However, NCLB adds many new initiatives; it is designed to create a stronger, more accountable education system, seeks to change the culture of education, and purports to use evidence-based strategies found to be effective through rigorous research. Rather than providing specific resources for at-risk youth, NCLB proposes assisting children and youth by holding them accountable to high educational outcomes and standards. NCLB requires each state to set clear and high standards and to put an assessment system in place to measure student progress toward those standards (Paige, 2002). Specifically, NCLB requires states to test all students annually in grades 3 through 8 in reading and math. Scores reported by states must be disaggregated by poverty, race, ethnicity, disability, and English language proficiency so that potential achievement gaps can be identified. Schools that fail to make adequate yearly progress toward identifiable goals need to be identified for improvement and are subject to corrective action (Paige). NCLB mandates that teachers use strategies that have proven effective; emphasis is placed on early reading programs. Finally, grants for character education have tripled under NCLB. These policies have affected practice dramatically, placing a premium on standards and assessment, school-based management, teacher empowerment, and school choice (e.g., vouchers, magnet schools, charter schools, and privatization options).

The current era in education policy has also been influenced by the Gun-Free Schools Act of 1994. This law provided funds only for schools that adopted zero-tolerance policies for guns and drugs on school grounds. Public and political concern heightened in the mid-1990s with the outbreak of mass school shootings (Jenson & Howard, 1999). This resulted in the expansion of zero-tolerance policies for less severe infractions. Alternative schools and increased school security strategies were also implemented to address school safety issues. The focus on school safety has also led to many promising prevention and intervention services, and to the restructuring of schools to increase student engagement, attendance, performance, and family involvement. In recent years, there has also been a trend to establish academic excellence for all students by engaging students, teachers, and staff in reform efforts, with a focus on the relationship between school climate and overall academic achievement.

A number of studies suggest that a positive, open school climate increases student achievement (Cummings, 1986; Fine, 1991; Hoy, Hannum, & Tschannen-Moran, 1998; Kagan, 1990; Reyes, 1989) and a school's overall effectiveness (Hoy, Tarter, & Kottkamp, 1991). In fact, school climate has been identified as the most important variable in helping schools exceed their academic expectations (Glidden, 1999). Consistent with this finding, Walker, Sprague, and Severson (2003) suggest that the primary target for school-based prevention efforts should be the peer culture of a school. Programs designed to affect school culture positively, such as conflict resolution programs, peer mediation strategies, and antibullying campaigns, illustrate the growing emphasis on changing peer and institutional culture. Social and economic strategies have also been used in pursuit of academic excellence for all students through innovative services and programs such as school-linked services and community and neighborhood reform. Although the policies underlying these reforms are not particularly new, the dissemination of research findings describing what works in school-based interventions is beginning to have a positive impact on practice (Nelson et al., 2004).

Summary of Federal Policy

Public education in the United States has gone through a number of reform movements in the past century. From the end of World War I until the mid-1940s, education policy focused on equity and attempted to narrow or eliminate the achievement gap between advantaged and disadvantaged youth. From the 1950s to the 1970s, issues of equity dominated federal education policy. Policies favoring equity in education were not without criticism during these years; many critics of equity policies believed intellectual and academic goals were being sacrificed for social ones. These attacks created space for alternative strategies such as the adoption of standards, curriculum reform, and accountability systems. Since the mid-1970s, most education policies and programs have been more closely aligned with conservative ideology that focuses on improving education for all students than with policies aimed at helping children or youth at elevated risk for academic failure.

Principles of Risk, Protection, and Resilience in Education Policy

There is evidence to both support and criticize the effectiveness of the policies and programs discussed in the prior section. Next, we briefly evaluate the degree to which historical and current policies and programs in education have been based on principles of risk and resilience, beginning with those that are clearly within this framework.

Several policies illustrate the relationship between risk, protection, and educational approaches to change and reform. For example, Head Start and IDEA emphasize principles that are consistent with interactive and developmental models of risk and resilience discussed earlier in this chapter. Head Start targets youth who are at highest risk for academic failure due to low socioeconomic status. The program attempts to bolster school readiness skills before entering school and is consistent with evidence suggesting that learning-related social skills gained in early childhood are critical to school success (DeRosier, Kupersmith, & Patterson, 1994; Ladd, 1990; Ladd & Price, 1987; McClelland & Morrison, 2003; McClelland, Morrison, & Holmes, 2000). IDEA intervenes with children before they enter school and targets children at risk of school failure as a result of disability.

Policy efforts and programs that seek to implement schoolwide changes are also compatible with risk and protective factors. These efforts generally strive to improve the learning environment, increase school connectedness or bonding among students, enhance school climate, and increase teacher expectations for students' performance. Positive school and peer cultures have been shown to increase school bonding, which in turn serves as a key protective influence for children (Haberman, 2000; Hawkins, Catalano, Kosterman, Abbott, & Hill, 1999). School-based management strategies aim to increase levels of connectedness among schools, families, and communities, an important protective factor against academic failure.

The recent emphasis on standards-based education sets high academic expectations for all students, itself an identified protective factor against school failure and dropout (Furlong & Morrison, 2000). However, standards-based educational strategies are not directly connected to, or based on, the risk and protection literature. It may also be important to note that such standards have the potential to be counterproductive to children and youth who are not able to compete academically. Some experts have argued that standards-based policies may actually be contrary to principles of risk and resilience because they may lower expectations for teachers and subsequently have a negative impact on achievement (Nelson et al., 2004). Finally, zero-tolerance policies, particularly those that apply to less severe infractions, have been shown to increase risk for poor outcomes among high-risk children and youth (Skiba & Peterson, 1999).

In sum, the application of risk and protective factors to the design of educational policy is inconsistent. Some policies (e.g., the Compulsory School Attendance Act, the Head Start Act, EHA, and IDEA), court cases (e.g., *Brown v. Board of Education*), and programs (e.g., Head Start and special education) support the constructs of risk and resilience. Other policies (e.g., NCLB and Gun-Free Schools Act) and court cases (e.g., *Plessey v. Ferguson* and *Milliken v. Bradley*) ignore or may even reject the constructs of risk and resilience. New and sustained efforts are needed to implement a risk and resilience framework in education policy.

Using Principles of Risk, Protection, and Resilience to Achieve Integrated Education Policy

Principles of risk, protection, and resilience can be applied to education policy in two fundamental ways. One option requires policymakers to specifically focus efforts on youth who are most likely to experience academic failure and school-related problems. Such a strategy tends to concentrate program and policy efforts on youth from disadvantaged backgrounds, since socioeconomic status is a key risk factor for educational failure (Brooks-Gunn & Duncan, 1997). A second approach uses knowledge of risk, protection, and resilience to design promotive educational policies and programs that are beneficial for all children irregardless of risk exposure. We begin our discussion with policy recommendations for programs that promote healthy outcomes for all children and youth.

Promotive Policies and Programs

We recommend that educational policies and programs aimed at promoting social competence, developing caring relationships, and creating high expectations for all students be developed. Policies that promote participation in positive academic and social groups, enhance school bonding or connectedness, and create positive and safe learning environments should also receive priority in the nation's policy and program debates. Policy approaches and programs appear to be most successful when they are implemented schoolwide over the course of several years (Gottfredson & Gottfredson, 1999). Although such programs are believed to be effective across multiple levels of risk, additional research is necessary to verify this assumption.

Simply implementing effective programs is not sufficient to produce broad policy change and educational reform. Policies and programs must also foster service cohesion by addressing the need for multiple interventions within schools in an integrated fashion. Walker, Horner, Sugai, Bullis, Sprague, Bricker, et al. (1996) suggest that there is generally a lack of coordination among prevention efforts because no comprehensive strategic plan for coordinating and linking behavioral supports exists at the school or district level. Although the implementation of systemic interventions may provide the best hope for reducing the intensity and number of children who require additional support, single interventions are unlikely to address all problem behavior within a school. Walker and Sprague (1999) describe the essential components of a comprehensive approach to addressing the mental health needs of students. Their conceptualization of an integrated prevention model is based on a continuum that includes primary, secondary, and tertiary levels of intervention. We suggest that all schools, regardless of risk status, develop a comprehensive schoolwide plan for meeting the needs of students based on this three-tiered model.

A recent report by the Center for Mental Health in Schools (2002) indicates that school-based reform efforts to date have been unsuccessful because projects and services designed to remove barriers to learning are viewed as supplementary in nature. This has left policy experts interested in removing such barriers largely absent from the decision-making table. The result may be seen in the fragmentation of services, marginalization of professionals, and overall inadequacies in policy reform. Service providers, including school social workers, school psychologists, speech language specialists, school nurses, and school counselors, must be trained to support the primary mission of schools. Further, policies must be designed to enhance standards while promoting reasonable professional-to-student ratios for all students.

Promotive programs and policies hold great promise for education. However, policies and programs that specifically target the needs of students with elevated risk are also required to address the needs of children and youth in American schools. We believe that targeted educational policies and programs should focus on schools that have high percentages of students living in poverty and identify and intervene prior to or at the point of school entry. Examples of targeted policies and programs are reviewed next.

Targeted Policies and Programs

Redistribution of Tax Dollars to Support Schools in Poor Neighborhoods

The most obvious recommendation for using principles of risk and protection in targeted educational policy may involve school financing. Nearly 50 percent of school funding comes from local property taxes (Nelson et al., 2004). Therefore, adequately funding schools in poor neighborhoods is an ongoing and persistent challenge to policy officials and school administrators. To address this problem, a larger percentage of school financing may need to come from state and federal taxes rather than from local tax bases. Equalizing the funding base between advantaged and disadvantaged communities is not likely to produce equal educational outcomes, given variations in individual, family, neighborhood, and community risk factors across schools and communities. And providing more money to disadvantaged schools would require people in wealthy districts to partially fund poor districts, a practice that runs counter to the beliefs of many Americans. However, such a strategy may well be necessary to effect positive change and to promote effective policies based on principles of risk and protection.

Early Identification and Intervention at the Point of School Entry

Children raised in conditions of poverty experience severe learning deficits by the time they enter school. Whether in preschool or early elementary school, the importance of early screening for risk factors that lead to poor educational outcomes cannot be overstated. Educators are able to predict with great accuracy which children will require extensive academic or behavioral supports with minimal effort. Systemwide screening, particularly for emotional and behavioral indicators leading to school failure, may be a cost-effective strategy to improve educational outcomes. Many experts believe that enhancing school readiness skills should be the primary focus of policy reforms (Nelson et al., 2004). We concur, and recommend an increase in funding for intervention programs that target school readiness skills.

Several federal programs, including those promoted through Title IV and Title V funds, provide nonspecific funding to address a wide range of educational issues. Title I is consistent with the risk and protection framework described earlier, since the primary criteria to access these funds are tied to students' socioeconomic status. However, there is no mandate that interventions created through these funds address known risk and protective factors. Additionally, there are no mandates that require the funds, or a portion of the funds, to be used for evidence-based practices.

In sum, a series of policy and system reforms is necessary to improve the condition of the country's schools. Principles of risk, protection, and promotion offer a means to begin thinking more systematically about a continuum of education policy defined by levels of service. Integration of policy and programs across other systems of care should be a part of such a continuum.

Strategies to Integrate Education Policy

It is both exciting and challenging to envision integrating educational policies and programs across service domains such as child welfare, substance abuse, mental health, juvenile justice, developmental disabilities, and health. In many respects, the compartmentalized nature in which federal–state funding is provided, and the isolated educational training that professionals in each problem area receive, runs counter to such a vision. Given the number of children involved in the educational system, the amount of time children spend in school, and the ability of schools to mobilize linkages with families and communities, we believe that the education system is an ideal location to identify children in need of services across problem domains.

Cross-system funding for education, health, and social services may be one means to achieve integrated policy. Cross-system funds could be used to (1) promote school readiness skills for high-risk youth; (2) provide early screening to identify children most at risk; (3) deliver case management and wrap-around services to those who display signs of adjustment problems before second grade; (4) provide seamless access to and provision of educational, health, and social services through support service providers and family resource or youth service centers; and (5) implement primary prevention programs at key developmental stages. This vision is consistent with the

---

A Case for Integrated Service Delivery

Jeremy is a 14 year old male who was physically and sexually abused as a young child. His mother was incarcerated when he was six, and her parental rights were terminated when Jeremy was eight. He was placed in six out-of-home placements before he was finally placed in a stable foster care home with loving and supportive parents at age 10. Jeremy has struggled socially and emotionally in the school setting since kindergarten, but was not identified for special education services under the emotionally disturbed category until his current foster parents advocated for an evaluation at age 11. He has done well in some settings but he was suspended 13 times last year during his first year of middle school. Jeremy has been convicted twice for misdemeanor charges and is currently on probation. He receives support from a learning specialist and a school social worker at his middle school, sees a counselor at the local mental health agency, and has a child protection caseworker. Jeremy reports to a probation officer regularly and sees a psychiatrist to monitor medications yearly. These individuals have never met together and many of the services being provided are duplicated across settings.

---

school-linked services movement, which locates social and health services for children and families within or near schools (Dryfoos, 1998). Full-service schools take this notion one step further, bringing community agencies such as child care, parent education, employee training, and health and education services to schools (Dryfoos). Such comprehensive policy and program efforts should be based on building resilience for all children and should focus on improving outcomes across a range of child and youth problems. We use the case of Jeremy to illustrate this point.

An integrated approach to service delivery would be beneficial to Jeremy and his foster parents in several ways. First, if the services provided by his teacher, learning specialist, school social worker, counselor, caseworker, probation officer, and psychiatrist were coordinated, each provider would be aware of how Jeremy is functioning in other aspects of his life. Each provider would also be aware of other services Jeremy is receiving. Such an approach would reduce redundancy in service provision and likely would be more cost-effective. An integrated service delivery system would facilitate communication between professionals and would allow each easy access to the information the others possess. An integrated approach would also result in one set of goals, one treatment plan, and one system to evaluate progress. Additionally, an integrated strategy would be much easier for his foster parents, who find it difficult to attend the requisite meetings associated with each service. Finally, it is exciting to imagine the services that could be put in place if the requisite departments of education, juvenile justice, and child welfare shared costs and interventions for all the services being directed to complex cases such as Jeremy's. Most important, if there had been an integrated approach to assessment and service delivery early in Jeremy's life, it is possible his early antisocial behavior and school failure would have raised warning flags that might have altered Jeremy's path to later destructive outcomes.

Summary

Education policy in the past century has vacillated between progressive and conservative ideologies that have resulted in inconsistent practices in schools. According to Anyon (1997), education policy continues to revolve "around the tensions between equity and excellence, between the social and intellectual functions of schooling, and over differing responses to the questions, Education in whose interests? Education for whom?" (p. 87). Policy directed at the nation's schools has not been guided by a set of consistent principles. Principles of risk, protection, and resilience offer promise as a systematic method of designing and enhancing education policy and programs. Policymakers at all levels would do well to incorporate these principles into the nation's struggling educational system.

Questions for Discussion

1. What are some of the major risk factors for school failure? Which of these should receive the most attention in educational policy and why?

2. How would one approach the concept of risk differently from an additive versus an interactive model?

3. What educational policies and programs over the past 100 years have best served the concept of risk and resilience? Why?

4. What factors inhibit the integration of policies and programs across problem domains?

5. What are some possible solutions to the factors inhibiting the integration of policies and programs across problem domains?

Additional Reading

Fraser, M. W., Kirby, L. D., & Smokowski, P. R. (2004). Risk and resilience in childhood. In M. W. Fraser (Ed.), *Risk and resiliency in childhood: An ecological perspective* (2nd ed, pp. 13–66.). Washington, DC: NASW Press.

Glidden, H. G. (1999). Breakthrough schools: Characteristics of low-income schools that perform as though they were high-income schools. *ERS Spectrum, 17*(2), 21–26.

McClelland, M. M., Morrison, F. J., & Holmes, D. H. (2000). Children at risk for early academic problems: The role of learning-related social skills. *Early Childhood Research Quarterly, 15,* 307–329.

Nelson, J. L., Palonsky, S. B., & McCarthy, M. R. (2004). *Critical issues in education: Dialogues and dialectics* (5th ed.). Boston: McGraw-Hill.

Sadovnik, A. R., Cookson, P. W., & Semel, S. F. (2001). *Exploring education: Introduction to the foundations to education.* Needham Heights, MA: Allyn & Bacon.

Sprague, J. R., & Walker, H. (2000). Early identification and intervention for youth with antisocial and violent behavior. *Exceptional Children, 66*(3), 367–379.

References

Anyon, J. (1997). *Ghetto schooling: A political economy of urban reform.* New York: Teachers College Press.

Apollonia, S., & Abrami, P. C. (1997). Student ratings: The validity of use. *American Psychologist, 52*(11), 1199–1208.

Arrlington, E. G., & Wilson, M. N. (2000). A re-examination of risk and resilience during adolescence: Incorporating culture and diversity. *Journal of Child and Family Studies, 9,* 221–230.

Brooks-Gunn, J., & Duncan, G. J. (1997). The effects of poverty on children. *Future of Children, 7*(2), 55–71.

Carnahan, S. (1994). Preventing school failure and dropout. In R. J. Simeonsson (Ed.), *Risk, resilience, and prevention: Promoting the well-being of all children* (pp. 103–124). Baltimore: Paul H. Brooks.

Cecelski, D. (1994). *Along freedom road.* Chapel Hill: University of North Carolina Press.

Center for Mental Health in Schools (2002). An introductory packet: About mental health in schools. Los Angeles, CA: University of California at Los Angeles, Author. Retrieved July 27, 2005, from http://smhp.psych.ucla.edu/

Clark, K. (1965). *Dark ghetto: Dilemmas of social power.* New York: Harper & Row.

Coleman, J. S. (1966). *Equality of educational opportunity* (No. OE-38001). Washington, DC: National Center for Education Statistics.

Cremin, L. A. (1957). *The republic and the school: Horace Mann on the education of free men.* New York: Teachers College.

Cummings, J. (1986). Empowering minority students: A framework for intervention. *Harvard Educational Review, 56,* 18–36.

Derezinski, T. (2004). School attendance. In P. Allen-Meares (Ed.), *Social work services in schools* (4th ed., pp. 95–118). Boston: Allyn & Bacon.

DeRosier, M. E., Kupersmith, J. B., & Patterson, C. J. (1994). Children's academic and behavioral adjustment as a function of the chronicity and proximity of peer rejection. *Child Development, 65,* 1799–1813.

Dewey, J. (1916). *Democracy and education.* New York: Macmillan.

Dryfoos, J. G. (1998). *A look at community schools in 1998.* New York: Center for Schools and Communities, Fordham University.

Dupper, D. R. (2002). *School social work: Skills and interventions for effective practice.* Hoboken, NJ: John Wiley & Sons.

Fine, M. (1991). *Framing dropouts: Notes on the politics of an urban public high school.* New York: SUNY Press.

Fraser, M. W., Kirby, L. D., & Smokowski, P. R. (2004). Risk and resilience in childhood. In M. W. Fraser (Ed.), *Risk and resiliency in childhood: An ecological perspective* (2nd ed, pp. 13–66). Washington, DC: NASW Press.

Fraser, M. W., Richman, J. M., & Galinsky, M. J. (1999). Risk, protection, and resilience: Towards a conceptual framework for social work practice. *Social Work Research, 23,* 131–144.

Fraser, M. W., & Terzian, M. A. (in press). Risk and resilience in child development: Practice principles and strategies. In G. P. Mallon & P. M. Hess (Eds.), *Handbook of children, youth, and family services: Practices, policies, and programs.* New York: Columbia University Press.

Furlong, M., & Morrison, G. (2000). The school in school violence. *Journal of Emotional & Behavioral Disorders, 8,* 71–82.

Glidden, H. G. (1999). Breakthrough schools: Characteristics of low-income schools that perform as though they were high-income schools. *ERS Spectrum, 17*(2), 21–26.

Gottfredson, G., & Gottfredson, D. (1999). Development and applications of theoretical measures for evaluating drug and delinquency prevention programs. Elliot City, MD: Gottfredson Associates, Inc.

Greenberg, M. T., Domitrovich, C., & Bumbarger, B. (1999). *Preventing mental disorders in school-age children: A review of the effectiveness of prevention programs.* State College: Prevention Research Center for the Promotion of Human Development, College of Health and Human Development, Pennsylvania State University.

Haberman, M. (2000). Urban schools: Day camps or custodial centers? *Phi Delta Kappan, 82*(3), 203–208.

Hawkins, J. D., Catalano, R. F., Kosterman, R., Abbott, R. D., & Hill, K. G. (1999). Preventing adolescent health-risk behaviors by strengthening protection during childhood. *Archives of Pediatrics & Adolescent Medicine, 153,* 226–234.

Hoy, W. K., Hannum, J., & Tschannen-Moran, M. (1998). Organizational climate and student achievement: A parsimonious and longitudinal view. *Journal of School Leadership, 8,* 336–359.

Hoy, W. K., Tarter, C. J., & Kottkamp, R. (1991). *Open school/healthy schools: Measuring organizational climate.* Newbury Park, CA: Sage.

Jenson, J. M., & Howard, M. O. (1999). *Youth violence: Current research and recent practice innovations.* Washington, DC: NASW.

Kagan, D. M. (1990). How schools alienate students at risk: A model for examining proximal classroom variables. *Educational Psychologist, 25,* 105–125.

Kohl, H. (1967). *36 children.* New York: New American Library.

Kozol, J. (1967). *Death at an early age: The deconstruction of the hearts and minds of Negro children in the Boston public schools.* Boston: Houghton Mifflin.

Ladd, G. W. (1990). Having friends, keeping friends, making friends, and being liked by peers in the classroom: Predictors of children's early school adjustment. *Child Development, 61,* 1081–1100.

Ladd, G. W., & Price, J. M. (1987). Predicting children's social and school adjustment following the transition from preschool to kindergarten. *Child Development, 58,* 1168–1189.

Luthar, S. S., Cicchetti, D., & Becker, B. (2000). The construct of resilience: A critical evaluation and guidelines for future work. *Child Development, 71,* 543–562.

Masten, A. (1987). Resilience in development: Implications of the study of successful adaptation for developmental psychopathology. In C. Cicchetti (Ed.), *The emergence of a discipline: Rochester symposium on developmental psychopathology* (pp. 261–294). Hillsdale, NJ: Lawrence Erlbaum.

McClelland, M. M., & Morrison, F. J. (2003). The emergence of learning-related social skills in preschool children. *Early Childhood Research Quarterly, 18,* 206–224.

McClelland, M. M., Morrison, F. J., & Holmes, D. H. (2000). Children at risk for early academic problems: The role of learning-related social skills. *Early Childhood Research Quarterly, 15,* 307–329.

National Center for Education Statistics. (2004). *Nation's report card.* Retrieved June 23, 2004, from http://nces.ed.gov/nationsreportcard/

Nelson, J. L., Palonsky, S. B., & McCarthy, M. R. (2004). *Critical issues in education: Dialogues and dialectics* (5th ed.). Boston: McGraw-Hill.

Olsson, C. A., Bond, L., Burns, J. M., Vella-Brodrick, D. A., & Sawyer, S. M. (2003). Adolescent resilience: A concept analysis. *Journal of Adolescence, 26,* 1–11.

Paige, R. (2002). An overview of America's education agenda. *Phi Delta Kappan, 83*(9), 708–713.

Ravitch, D. (1983). *The troubled crusade: An American education, 1945–1980.* New York: Basic Books.

Reyes, P. (1989). Factors that affect the commitment of children at risk to stay in school. In L. M. Lakebrink (Ed.), *Children at risk* (pp. 18–31). Springfield, IL: Charles C Thomas.

Richman, J. M., Bowen, G. L., & Woolley, M. E. (2004). School failure: An eco-interactional developmental perspective. In M. W. Fraser (Ed.), *Risk and resiliency in childhood: An ecological perspective* (2nd ed., pp. 133–160). Washington, DC: NASW.

Rosenfeld, G. (1971). *"Shut those thick lips!" A study of slum school failure.* New York: Holt, Rinehart, & Winston.

Sadovnik, A. R., Cookson, P. W., & Semel, S. F. (2001). *Exploring education: Introduction to the foundations to education.* Needham Heights, MA: Allyn & Bacon.

Sameroff, A. J., & Gutman, L. M. (2004). Contributions of risk research to the design of successful interventions. In P. Allen-Meares & M. W. Fraser (Eds.), *Intervention with children and adolescents: An interdisciplinary perspective* (pp. 9–26). Boston: Allyn & Bacon.

Skiba, R., & Peterson, R. (1999). The dark side of zero tolerance: Can punishment lead to safe schools? *Phi Delta Kappan, 80,* 381–382.

Slavin, R. (1999). *How Title I can become the engine of reform in America's schools* (No. ERIC Document ED 456 546). Washington, DC: Office of Educational Research and Improvement.

Sloboda, Z., & David, S. L. (1997). *Preventing drug use among children and adolescents.* Washington, DC: National Institute on Drug Abuse.

Spekman, N. J. (1993). An exploration of risk and resilience in the lives of individuals with learning disabilities. *Learning Disabilities Research and Practice, 8*(1), 11–18.

Walker, H. (2001). *School safety issues and prevention strategies: The changing landscape of what we know.* Eugene, OR: Institute on Violence and Destructive Behavior.

Walker, H., Horner, R. H., Sugai, G., Bullis, M., Sprague, J. R., Bricker, D., et al. (1996). Integrated approaches to preventing antisocial behavior patterns among school-age children and youth. *Journal of Emotional & Behavioral Disorders, 4,* 193–256.

Walker, H. M., & Sprague, J. R. (1999). The path to school failure, delinquency and violence: Causal factors and some potential solutions. *Intervention in School and Clinic, 35*(2), 67–73.

Walker, H. M., Sprague, J. R., & Severson, H. H. (2003). Schools and youth violence: What educators need to know about developing healthy students and safe schools. In R. H. A. Haslan & P. J. Vallenutti (Eds.), *Medical problems in the classroom: The teacher's role in diagnosis and management* (4th ed.). Austin, TX: PRO-ED.

Web-Based Resources

The Education Policy Institute http://www.educationpolicy.org/
Education Policy Clearinghouse http://www.edpolicy.org/
Center on Education Policy http://www.ctredpol.org/
Education Commission of the States http://www.ecs.org/
Public Reason Policy Institute http://www.rppi.org/educ.html

4

Child Mental Health Policy: Promise Without Fulfillment?

Mary E. Fraser

hildren and their families are our nation's most valuable and perhaps its most endangered resource. Children and families today face unprecedented challenges, including persistent poverty, eroding family structure, easy access to alcohol and other drugs, and violence. It is no wonder that one of every five children and adolescents in the United States has a diagnosable emotional or behavioral disorder that can lead to school failure, alcohol or other drug use, violent conduct, or suicide (Burns, Costello, Angold, Tweed, Stangl, Farmer, & Erkanli, 1995). According to the Surgeon General's Report on Mental Health (1999), at least 1 in 10 young people—as many as 6 million youth—meet criteria for serious emotional disturbance (SED). Children and adolescents with SED are so ill that their symptoms often disrupt their social, academic, and emotional functioning. Many are in or are at risk for out-of-home placements and have multiple social and health problems that result in referrals to mental health, special education, child welfare, and juvenile justice systems (Brendenberg, Freidman, & Silver, 1990).

The 7-year National Adolescent and Child Treatment Study (NACTS) identified a number of common risk factors among youth with SED. Investigators leading the NACTS investigation found that youth with SED had poorer social skills, lower academic achievement, less financial independence, and more limited interpersonal relationships than youth without SED

(Greenbaum, Deddrick, Friedman, Kutash, Brown, Lardieri, & Pugh, 1996). Youth with SED were also more involved in substance abuse and criminal activity than youth with no SED symptoms.

These results are consistent with those from the National Longitudinal Transitional Study (NLTS) of Special Education students with SED. In this investigation, Davis and Vander Stoep (1997) found that young people with SED were more likely than either youth with other disabilities or the general population to drop out of school, be arrested, and have less competitive employment. Twenty percent of students with SED are arrested at least once before they leave school, compared with 6 percent of all students, and nearly 50 percent of youth with SED are arrested within 5 years of leaving school (U.S. Department of Education, 1994). Without effective policies and interventions that diminish risk and strengthen protection, adult outcomes can be expected to be poor. In this regard, there is a large body of literature on risk factors associated with emotional and behavioral problems in childhood, and the body of evidence on protective factors that can mitigate the effects of these problems is growing. Because children with SED are found in all public child-serving agencies, public policies that promote cross-agency, integrated approaches to effective risk and protection interventions are needed.

This chapter reviews the literature on risk and protective factors related to emotional and behavioral disorders in children and the evolution of child mental health policy in the United States. Two examples of state policy strategies to improve and integrate services to youth with SED are described. Finally, suggestions are made for future policies that combine the risk and resilience perspective with integrated service structures.

Prevalence of Child Mental Health Disorders

A defining feature of the mental health field is the use of a system of classification that relies on diagnostic categories linked to service strategies, both psychosocial and pharmacological. One of the primary classification sources used in the United States is the *Diagnostic and Statistical Manual on Mental Health (DSM)*, published by the American Psychiatric Association. It is currently in its fourth edition. Table 4.1 displays the most common *DSM-IV* (2000) diagnoses found in youth from 9 to 17 years of age. Column A provides national prevalence rates for each diagnosis; column B provides diagnostic prevalence rates within the subgroup of youth who have an SED.

Anxiety is the most common mental health problem found in childhood and adolescence (Costello et al., 1996), and it comes in a variety of forms. These include phobias, separation anxiety disorders, generalized anxiety

Table 4.1   Diagnostic Prevalence Rates for Children 9 to 17 Years Old

Diagnosis	U.S. Population[a]	SED Population[ab]
Anxiety		
Phobias, separation anxiety disorder, generalized anxiety disorder, obsessive–compulsive disorder, posttraumatic stress disorder	8–10%	41%
Depression	6%	19%
Major depressive disorder		
Dysthymia		
Disruptive disorders		
Conduct disorder	4–10%	67%
Oppositional defiant disorder		
Attention deficit hyperactivity disorder	5%	12%
Eating disorders		
Bulimia nervosa	1–3%	
Anorexia nervosa	0.5–1%	
Childhood schizophrenia	0.3%	

a. Friedman, Katz-Levey, Manderschied, & Sondheimer (1996).

b. Greenbaum, Deddrick, Friedman, Kutash, Brown, Lardieri, & Pugh (1996).

disorders, and obsessive compulsive disorders. *Phobias* are unreasonable fears. One of the most common phobias in children and adolescents is social anxiety disorder, which is characterized by an unremitting fear of embarrassment in social and performance situations, sometimes leading to full-blown panic attacks. Children and adolescents with this disorder tend to avoid social situations and try to avoid going to school.

Separation anxiety disorder occurs in about 4 percent of children and young adolescents, and is characterized by irrational fears that parents will be killed or taken away, resulting in clinging behavior, difficulty falling asleep at night, and inability to participate in school and social events away from home. The disorder can last for many years and can be a precursor to panic disorder and agoraphobia in adults.

Generalized anxiety disorder is characterized by excessive and persistent worry. Children and adolescents with this anxiety disorder tend to be perfectionists and insecure.

Obsessive–compulsive disorder (OCD) is characterized by recurrent, time-consuming, obsessive, or compulsive behaviors that cause distress and/or impairment. The obsessions may be intrusive images, thoughts, or impulses. Compulsive behaviors, such as handwashing and other cleaning rituals, are seen as attempts to displace obsessive thoughts. Prevalence estimates range from less than 1 percent in children to as high as 2 percent in adolescents (Surgeon General, 1999).

Posttraumatic stress disorder (PTSD) is a prolonged, pathologic anxiety that may occur following a severe trauma in both adults and adolescents. The onset of PTSD in adolescence is common and may impair the acquisition of life skills needed for independence and self-sufficiency. PTSD is common among youth who are victims of physical and sexual abuse and who witness violent acts in the home or neighborhood.

Major depressive disorder diagnosis requires either a depressed or irritable mood or a diminished interest or pleasure in activities. Accompanying symptoms must include some combination of significant weight change, sleep disturbance, loss of energy or fatigue, psychomotor agitation or retardation, feelings of worthlessness or inappropriate guilt, diminished ability to think or concentrate, and recurrent thoughts of death, which must coexist for at least 2 weeks and produce significant functional impairment. Diagnostic criteria for *dysthymia* also require a depressed or irritable mood, lasting for a period longer than 1 year, and must include many of the same accompanying symptoms as major depression. Although the symptoms of major depressive disorder are similar, they are more debilitating than those of dysthymia. Dysthymia, however, tends to be longer lasting and more chronic in nature.

A disruptive disorder, *conduct disorder,* is based on a repetitive and persistent pattern of behavior in which the basic rights of others or the major age-appropriate social norms or rules are violated. Characteristic behaviors of conduct disorder include aggression toward persons or animals, destruction of property, deceitfulness, or theft. Girls with a conduct disorder are prone to early sexual activity and homelessness. Approximately 40 percent of youth with a conduct disorder develop an antisocial personality disorder and become involved in the criminal justice system. Those with an early onset of conduct disorder have a worse prognosis and a higher risk for adult antisocial disorder. Conduct disorder frequently co-occurs with attention deficit hyperactivity.

Oppositional defiant disorder (ODD) is typically characterized by problem behaviors such as persistent arguing and fighting and frequent loss of temper. Children and adolescents with this disorder frequently test limits, refuse to comply with adult requests, and deliberately annoy others. These behaviors lead to difficulties with family members, peers, and teachers. ODD is sometimes a precursor of conduct disorder.

Attention deficit and hyperactivity disorder (ADHD) is, as its name implies, made up of two distinct sets of symptoms. Although these two problems often occur together, one can be present without the other. Children with attention deficit disorder have difficulty paying attention and are easily distracted. They are often disorganized and have a hard time following through with tasks. The symptoms of hyperactivity include fidgeting, squirming around when seated, and the compulsion to get up and move around. Children with ADHD often perform poorly at school and have difficulties with peer relationships. Hyperactive behavior is often associated with the development of conduct and oppositional defiant disorders.

Eating disorders are potentially life-threatening conditions; 10 percent of cases end in death (Steiner & Lock, 1998). This is particularly of concern, as eating disorders are among the most common chronic illnesses of adolescent girls, following obesity and asthma (Lucas, Beard, O'Fallon, & Kurland, 1991; Stice & Agras, 1998). Anorexia nervosa is characterized by an intense fear of gaining weight and a distorted body image. The symptoms of bulimia nervosa include recurrent episodes of binge eating and purging.

Finally, *childhood schizophrenia* is a rare but serious illness. Children with schizophrenia may experience auditory and visual hallucinations and feel detached from the real world. It is sometimes difficult to distinguish between childhood schizophrenia and autism. Onset of adult schizophrenia usually occurs between puberty and young adulthood. Children with an earlier onset generally have more severe and long-lasting symptoms (American Psychiatric Association, 2000).

In this chapter, the terms *serious emotional and behavioral disorders* and *SED* are used interchangeably. Although not diagnostically specific, either term may include any or several of the diagnostic categories listed earlier. It should be noted, however, that simply having a diagnosis of one of these disorders does not mean that a child is SED. It should also be recognized that different diagnostic categories relate to different risks and intervention strategies. For example, children with eating disorders differ markedly from those with conduct disorders. Thus, child mental health policies must address a wide range of behaviors and conditions that are differentially categorized by diagnostic labels and terms such as SED.

A Risk, Protection, and Resilience Perspective on Mental Health Disorders

Allen-Meares and Fraser (2004) outline a set of empirically supported principles to describe risk, protection, and resilience that are used to inform our discussion of mental health disorders and child mental health policy. They argue that (1) there are identifiable risk and protective factors for social and mental health problems in childhood, (2) cumulative risk is generally more predictive of developmental outcomes than any single risk factor, (3) some risk factors are more responsive than others to change strategies, (4) reduction of risk can produce improved outcomes, and (5) more pronounced outcomes occur when risk factors are reduced and protective factors are increased. Allen-Meares and Fraser (2004) also point out important differences between protective and promotive factors. Protective factors reduce, suppress, and buffer risk and have no effect in the absence of risk. Promotive factors are the opposite of risk factors. They operate to "promote" positive developmental outcomes for all youths. Universal prevention strategies focus on promotive factors, whereas targeted interventions strengthen protective factors to reduce known risks. We apply these definitions to the discussion that follows.

Most serious childhood emotional disorders are considered to be biosocial in nature. Although children endure countless negative life experiences, most children are naturally resilient. That is, when faced with adversity, they tend to make self-righting adaptations. These efforts, however, do not happen in isolation. Resilience results from the nexus of individual effort and facilitating environmental conditions. Most people believe that mental health problems emerge in children and adolescents when there is a combining of adverse environmental factors and a biological vulnerability (Surgeon General, 1999). The principles of risk and resilience can be used to better understand which biological and environmental factors might predict serious emotional and behavioral disorders in children and adolescents as well as which children should be targeted for prevention and early intervention efforts. A touch point for this chapter, these principles can also be used to determine which protective factors need to be bolstered to promote resilience.

Risk Factors

Biological Risk

Shown in Table 4.2, common examples of biological risk factors include genetics, chemical imbalances in the body, and damage to the central nervous system through trauma or prenatal exposure to alcohol and drugs. There are clear genetic links to some conditions, such as ADHD, mood and anxiety disorders, and childhood schizophrenia (Goodman & Stevenson, 1989; Jellinek & Synder, 1998; Maziade & Raymond, 1995; Rutter, Silberg,

O'Conner, & Simonoff, 1999). Having a parent, sibling, or even a grandparent with a mental health problem increases the odds for a mental disorder.

Being born a boy or girl has a differential risk for certain emotional and behavioral disorders in children. For instance, girls are at greater risk for internalizing mental health problems, such as depression, anxiety, and suicide, than boys (Spirito, Bond, Kurkjian, Devost, Bosworth, & Brown, 1993). By age 15, girls are two times more likely to be depressed than are boys (Nolen-Hoeksema & Girgus, 1994). Girls are also more likely to be diagnosed with an eating disorder (Rogers, Resnick, Mitchel, & Blum, 1997) and boys with a conduct disorder and ADHD (Piquero & Chung, 2001; Robins, 1991; Ross & Ross, 1982).

There is evidence that difficult early temperament is related to later emotional and behavioral problems. Agitated and tearful infants have been found to show symptoms of anxiety by the age of 4 (Kagan, Snidman, & Arcus, 1998). Connections between difficult infant temperaments and conduct disorder have also been made (Olds et al., 1998).

Environmental Risk

A child's social environment is an equal—or possibly more important—determinant of later mental health problems than constitutionally based factors (Sameroff & Gutman, 2004). Bronfenbrenner's (1979) empirically supported ecological model of child and adolescent development stresses the importance of contextual factors, including families, communities, and social institutions. Youth at high risk for serious emotional disorders are more likely to come from environments that heighten the effects of biological vulnerability (Resnick & Burt, 1996). Some of the more common environmental risks that exacerbate vulnerability include poverty, dysfunctional family, exposure to violence, and parental psychopathology or criminality.

Poverty is often associated with mental health problems in children and adolescents. Werner and Smith (1992) found that low parental income was the single greatest predictor of emotional disturbances in youth under 18 years of age. Even race and ethnicity, once thought to be a strong predictor of certain emotional and behavioral problems, loses its strength when adjusted for income (Neal, Lilly, & Zakis, 1993; Peeples & Loeber, 1994; Robins, 1991; Siegel, Aneshensel, Taub, Cantwell, & Driscoll, 1998). Early childhood poverty has been found to be associated with depression, antisocial behavior, adolescent anxiety, and adolescent hyperactivity (McLeod & Shanahan, 1996; Pagani, Boulerice, Tremblay, & Vitaro, 1997).

Poverty is also associated with increased violence and substance abuse (Rutter, 1985; Spearly & Lauderdale, 1983). The Children's Defense Fund

Table 4.2   Risk Factors for Child and Adolescent Mental Health Disorders

Individual Level	Familial Level	Extra-Familial Level
Genetic vulnerability to a mental health disorder	Low SES	Frequent violence
Victim of physical or sexual abuse	Multiple moves	High stress
Poor self-esteem	Parental substance abuse	Rejection by peers
Difficult temperament	Parental mental illness	Social isolation

Gender
  Girls: depression, anxiety, eating disorders
  Boys: conduct disorder
	Parental criminality	

Chronic childhood illness or developmental delay	Poor maternal bonding and attachment	
Race/ethnicity	Poor parenting skills	
ADHD: conduct disorder	Four or more siblings in the home	

(1995) estimates that between 3 and 10 million children experience domestic violence yearly. Witnessing violent acts can have a deleterious effect on children (Jenkins & Bell, 1997). Although the risk process is not well understood, the experience of physical and sexual abuse increases a child's risk for major depressive and anxiety disorders (Dykman et al., 1997; Flisher et al., 1997; Silverman, Reinherz, & Giaconia, 1996), conduct disorders (Livingston, Lawson, & Jones, 1993), ADHD (Wolfe, Sas, & Wekerle, 1994), and eating disorders (Douzinas, Fornari, Goodman, Sitnick, & Packman, 1994).

Poor social and economic conditions can lead to family pathology, child abuse, broken homes, and poor parental supervision. However, it may not be poverty itself that causes poor mental health outcomes in children and adolescents. Rather, living in poverty may produce poor child outcomes because the parental experience of financial strain and economic loss often diminishes their capacity to provide involved and supportive parenting (Linver, Fuligni, Hernandez, & Brooks-Gunn, 2004; Oyserman, 2004).

Dysfunctional parenting—rejection, neglect, maltreatment, and inability to provide appropriate structure and supervision—is associated with increased risk of emotional and behavioral disorders in children and adolescents (Johnson, Cohen, Kasen, Smailes, & Brook, 2001; Resnick & Burt, 1996). In one review, Loeber and Stouthamer-Loeber (1996) noted that poor parental supervision and lack of parental involvement in their children's activities were among the strongest correlates of conduct disorder in children. Harsh, abusive, and inconsistent discipline patterns have been linked to serious conduct problems (Lahey et al., 1995; Robins, 1991). In stressed or large families, parental attention can be in short supply and may be unduly focused on negative behaviors. Negative and aggressive behaviors then become reinforced and may lead to antisocial behavioral patterns (Surgeon General, 1999).

In addition, a number of studies have linked poor family management and emotional climate to depression in children. Families with depressed children tend to be less emotionally expressive, more hostile, more critical, and less accepting. Families with depressed children are also less cohesive, more conflictual, and more disorganized than families without depressed children (Gilbert, 2004).

Parents who are depressed themselves find it hard to provide consistent discipline, supervision, and emotionally positive interactions with their children (Zahn-Waxler, Iannotti, Cummings, & Denham, 1990). Parental depression has been found to increase the risk for anxiety disorders, conduct disorders, and alcohol dependence in children and adolescents (Wickramaratne & Weissman, 1998). Parental mental illness itself is associated with poor parenting ability (Oyserman, Mowbray, Allen-Meares, & Firminger, 2000).

Negative life events are also associated with poor emotional and behavioral outcomes in children and adolescents (Goodyer, 1990; Kessler, 1997; Tiet et al., 2001). Examples of negative life events include loss of a parent through death, divorce, or out-of-home placement, multiple moves, physical assault, exposure to violent acts, and injury. Certain groups of disorders are more closely associated with negative life events than others. There also appear to be differences in the effect of negative life events by gender. For example, depression is associated with loss and grief, particularly in girls (Breier et al., 1988; Goodyer, 2001; Moore, Rohde, Seeley, & Lewinsohn, 1999). The earlier a child experiences the loss of a parent or caretaker, the more severe the outcome. Although the event of being a victim of a crime, violent act, or assault is strongly associated with posttraumatic stress and conduct disorder in both girls and boys (Famularo, Kinscherff, & Fenton, 1992), the association between oppositional defiance disorder and being a victim of crime, violence, or assault is particularly strong among girls (Tiet et al., 2001). A parent being arrested and jailed is strongly associated with conduct disorder and dysthymia among boys. The effect for girls is more often seen in cases of conduct disorder and overanxious disorder.

In sum, a number of risk factors are associated with emotional and behavioral disorders in children and adolescents. They can be grouped on individual, familial, and extrafamilial levels. Level of individual risk appears to be related to the number of risk factors a child has in various domains (Fergusson, Horwood, & Lynsky, 1994; Rutter, 1979). Cumulative risk is more important than any single risk factor (Sameroff & Gutman, 2004). Table 4.2 shows risk factors for mental health disorders.

Protective Factors

Protective factors reduce risk. Indeed, the impact of risk factors on children's outcomes can be mediated by protective factors. And, just as increased risk is associated with the number of risk factors, resilience can be a function of the number of protective factors present in a child or adolescent's life (Sameroff, Bartko, Baldwin, Baldwin, & Seifer, 1999). Garmezy (1993) identified three broad sets of variables that operate as possible protective factors. They include (1) child characteristics, such as easy temperament, cognitive skills, and social skills; (2) families that are marked by warmth, cohesion, and structure; and (3) the availability of a support system. Shown in Table 4.3, an important protective factor that is related to most emotional and behavioral disorders is social-adaptive behavior. According to the NACT longitudinal study of youth with SED, adaptive social behavior, such as interpersonal relationship and coping skills, can mitigate risk (Armstrong, Dedrick, & Greenbaum, 2003). Good communication skills have also been found to be protective against hospital readmissions among children with SED (Greenbaum et al., 1996).

Life history reports of adolescents treated for mental health problems indicate that young people who had positive life outcomes tended to have more stable living situations, better family relationships, and more positive relationships with peers than other youth. In addition, children who seemed to prevail over adversities were more goal oriented and experienced more

Table 4.3   Protective Factors against Child and Adolescent Mental Health Disorders

Individual Level	Familial Level	Extra-Familial Level
Good social skills	Parental monitoring	Presence of nurturing/ caring adults
Academic achievement	Good communication and cohesion	Opportunities and support for achievement
Easy going temperament Good problem-solving skills		

successes and fewer stresses than those with poor outcomes (McConaughy & Wadsworth, 2000). Studies sponsored by the World Health Organization suggest that supportive relationships with family or community members minimize the long-term disability associated with childhood schizophrenia (Hopper & Wanderling, 2000). Thus, as poor parenting practices are risk factors for many antisocial behaviors (Loeber et al., 1998), warm, supportive family relationships and parental monitoring appear to function protectively for both boys and girls (Fraser, 2004; Green, 1995; Santilli & Beilenson, 1992). Table 4.3 summarizes protective factors for mental health disorders.

History of Child Mental Health Policy in the United States

Whereas risk and protection are relatively new concepts, the concept of childhood mental illness has a history dating to the late nineteenth century. The first discussion in a textbook of psychological problems in children was Maudsley's chapter on "The Insanity of Early Life" in 1867 (Hergenhahn, 2001). However, the prevailing thought was that children could not "go mad" until they had reached adulthood. Children and adolescents who exhibited serious emotional or behavioral symptoms at that time were hospitalized or imprisoned alongside adults. A public system devoted solely to child mental health did not emerge until 100 years later.

Precursors of Mental Health Policy

The earliest public mental health efforts on behalf of children came as a result of changes in approaches to "wayward" youth at the turn of the century. Public policy in juvenile justice was changing from a punishment to a corrective approach. The nation's first juvenile court was established in Chicago in 1899. In 1909, a group of Hull House board members became impressed with the new juvenile courts and created the Juvenile Psychopathic Institute to study the problems of juvenile offenders. William Healy, M.D., its first director and pioneer in the field, applied emerging psychiatric theory related to children and adolescents to individualize treatment of juvenile offenders. As a result of Healy's influence, juvenile court clinics were developed across the country, providing the first publicly funded community mental health services to troubled youth. Even though mental health theory and practice provided a foundation for much of the evolving juvenile justice and child welfare policies at that time, no formal child mental health policy was developed (Jones, 1999).

During the 1920s, juvenile court clinics began serving more than just children with antisocial problems and became attached to a variety of new structures, such as charities, universities, and teaching hospitals. Referred to as child guidance clinics, school and home problems became the major areas of concentration. Child guidance clinics tended to serve children and adolescents with internalizing problems, and they used Freudian and Ericksonian developmental theories.

The federal government first became involved in child mental health policy in the 1930s, when the federal Children's Bureau began to advocate for the development of a child mental health field. The bureau supported the expansion of child guidance clinics, which became the major source of mental health care for children and youth until the 1970s.

World War II brought an unexpected focus to the mental health needs of children. Because of the huge military draft, background histories were available for hundreds of thousands of young soldiers from varied backgrounds and socioeconomic levels. By the end of the war, it became apparent that soldiers who had behavior problems as children were much more likely to be prematurely discharged, disciplined, wounded, or killed (Schowalter, 2003). The country learned that mental illness is both color and income blind and that the outcomes of mental health problems are costly on both individual and societal levels.

Community Mental Health Centers

In 1963, President Kennedy signed the Mental Retardation Facilities and Community Mental Health Center Act, which changed the face of mental health care nationally. Focused primarily on adults with mental illness, the law established funding for community mental health centers (CMHC). These centers were designed to provide mental health services in community rather than in hospital settings. Like the child guidance movement before it, the Community Mental Health Center Act provided access to mental health services to only a small percentage of children with emotional and behavioral difficulties. The Act did not lead to a mandate requiring affordable mental health services to all children in need (Lourie & Hernandez, 2003), and little or no attention was afforded prevention or early intervention.

Advocacy efforts on behalf of unserved children and youth with emotional problems grew and led to the congressionally established Joint Commission of the Mental Health of Children. In its 1970 report, the commission found that millions of children and youth were not receiving needed mental health services. Many of those receiving care were served in inappropriately restrictive settings, such as state psychiatric hospitals. CMHCs were not required to serve children and youth until the CMHC Amendment Act in 1975.

Although CMHCs were required by law to provide mental health services to children and adolescents, they were slow to respond to the needs of youth with SED. In a 1978 report by President Carter's Commission on Mental Health, CMHCs were criticized for their failure to address the needs of children and youth with serious emotional and behavioral problems (President's Commission on Mental Health, 1978). The commission also noted that few communities were providing the volume or continuum of services needed, and it recommended that a community-based network of integrated services be developed to meet the needs of seriously emotionally disturbed children and adolescents. Although similar recommendations were voiced throughout the 1970s, it was not until the 1987 publication of Jane Knitzer's widely read book *Unclaimed Children* that Congress became mobilized to action. Knitzer boldly stated that of 3 million children and adolescents with serious emotional disturbances in the United States, 2 million did not receive the services they needed. Furthermore, Knitzer reported that at least 40 percent of hospital placements for children were in inappropriately restrictive settings that included facilities for people with mental retardation and adult psychiatric hospital wards. She observed that most states had no specific policies for children with serious emotional disorders and noted that there were millions of "unclaimed" children who were not receiving appropriate mental health services in public health, mental health, education, juvenile justice, and child welfare systems.

Systems of Care

Knitzer documented a lack of services, poor coordination among service providers, overuse of residential and institutional care, and failure of the federal, state, and local governments to respond to the crisis. She suggested ways to improve these conditions and subsequently coined the term *system of care* (SOC) to describe a new approach to mental health policy and service delivery. In 1984, Congress appropriated funds to the National Institute of Mental Health (NIMH), at that time an agency with the Alcohol, Drug, and Mental Health Administration (ADAMHA), to establish a national agenda to deal with the problems outlined by Knitzer. In response, NIMH created the Child and Adolescent Service System Program, or CASSP.

Following the example of the innovative Community Support Program (CSP) for adults with serious and persistent mental illness, CASSP focused on children with severe emotional disorders and provided financial incentives to states to develop systems of care to serve them. The CASSP initiative was the first federal mental health program to clearly identify its target population as youth with severe emotional disturbances. CASSP created a movement and a momentum for change and became the vehicle for the development and articulation of federal and state child mental heath policy.

The CASSP program was based on the following assumptions: (1) children and adolescents with serious emotional disorders were found in all the nation's public health, mental health, education, juvenile justice, and child welfare systems; (2) most children and adolescents with serious problems were served in more than one of these agencies at the same time; (3) no matter with which agencies children were affiliated, their mental health needs were not appropriately addressed; and (4) few states had planning mechanisms to identify children/adolescents who were served across multiple systems. The policy imperative in the CASSP initiative was to develop a multiagency approach to the delivery of mental health services.

In a well-known monograph, Stroul and Friedman (1986) defined a SOC as "a comprehensive spectrum of mental health and other necessary services which are organized into a coordinated network to meet the multiple and changing needs of children and adolescents with severe emotional disturbances and their families" (p. iv). They stated that a SOC should be community based, child centered and family focused, and culturally competent. The multiple needs of each child and family must be met by a full range of services—mental health, social, educational, vocational, substance abuse, recreational, and operational—with case management providing the mechanism to guide the family toward the appropriate mix and timing of services. Figure 4.1 illustrates a model SOC for mental health service delivery.

The ideal system was to be flexible enough to allow families to obtain specific services to meet individual needs, regardless of which agency has overall responsibility for the child or which system offers the services. For example, a child or adolescent with a serious emotional disturbance may have psychological needs that require intervention by a mental health center, special education needs by the school system, and the need for a structured living environment provided by a social services agency.

The concept of a SOC as outlined by Stroul and Friedman (1986) was used by the CASSP program as the blueprint for organizing child mental health services across the county. To receive federal grant funds, states were expected to create a protocol for interagency coordination that would bring all child-serving agencies together. Coordination and development was to start at the state level and then to be replicated at the local level. States were to develop methods of pooling financial resources so that all needed services could be reimbursed, regardless of service eligibility and insurance coverage. By the fall of 1990, all 50 states and the District of Columbia had received CASSP grants. By 1995, all states had at least one state-level, full-time, child

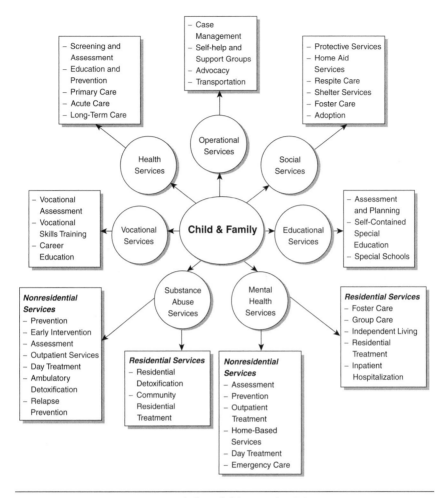

Figure 4.1   A SOC Framework for Children and Adolescents

mental health specialist working to develop a statewide system of care (Davis, Yelton, Katz-Leavy, & Lourie, 1995).

SOC and Mental Health Policy

The policy of creating systems of care to serve the nation's youth with SED became formally endorsed when Congress passed the Children's and Community Mental Health Services Improvement Act in 1992. This Act created the Comprehensive Community Mental Health Services for Children and Their Families program. The program, administered by the Center for Mental Health Services (CMHS) in the Substance Abuse and Mental Health Administration (SAMHSA), provided grants to states to expand the SOC concept. It is the largest federal initiative to date supporting the development of children's mental health services. By the close of the twentieth century, at least 50 percent of states had laws requiring some sort of SOC (Davis, Yelton, & Katz-Leavy, 1995). The initiative provided nearly $460 million in federal funding to 67 local systems of care. These local SOCs served more than 40,000 children across the country (Center for Mental Health Services, 1999).

Systems of care have proven difficult to implement despite the levels of federal and private foundation support allocated to states. The model requires many systems-level alterations, including developing linkages among child-serving agencies, creating a continuum of community-based services, blending financing streams, and creating interagency policy and treatment teams for coordination of care. CMHS conducted a review of SOC implementation in 1995. Researchers found that after 4 years of funding and effort, significant changes had occurred in each site studied. Indeed, there were changes in policies and procedures that facilitated cross-agency training, programming, and co-location of services. They also found enhanced interagency communication and collaborations. However, no site was able to fully implement all the aspects required of a comprehensive SOC model (Vinson, Brannan, Baughman, Wilce, and Gawron, 2001).

Implementation issues

A number of interagency coordination issues emerged as significant stumbling blocks in the SOC approach. Sometimes called "turf problems," these issues include lack of trust, competition, fear of sharing resources, and lack of understanding of other agency mandates and capacity. In addition to these turf problems, the sheer time that it takes to develop meaningful collaborations has probably been the largest barrier to full-scale change (Behar, 2003).

Many states have also found that financing both structural and service elements of a SOC is difficult. Few states are able to support child mental health services with state dollars that are not also attached to federal Medicaid funds. Created in 1965, Medicaid is a jointly managed federal and state health care financing program, governed by federal rules. It pays for about 50 percent of all mental health services provided to children and adolescents (Kenny, Oliver, & Poppe, 2002). Thus, policies flowing from federal and state Medicaid offices are as influential on state child mental health delivery systems as federal policy initiatives that come through NIMH or CMHS.

Unfortunately, state Medicaid spending limits and mental health service expansion initiatives are frequently in conflict with one another. Although federal Medicaid policies have become more flexible over the past 5 years, many state Medicaid spending policies have become more restrictive. State Medicaid policies are frequently focused on cost containment because Medicaid spending has been the highest growth factor in most state budgets and revenues have been down. In contrast, state mental health departments try to make their limited state appropriations stretch farther by matching them to federal Medicaid funds. In addition, Medicaid has some inherent limitations and barriers related to supporting SOC structures. Medicaid lacks mechanisms or incentives that foster joint planning, collaboration, or coordination-of-service approaches.

Slow Pace of Change

Though supportive of the SOC concept, members of child mental health advocacy groups, such as the Federation of Families for Children's Mental Health and the Child and Adolescent Network, a branch of the National Alliance for the Mentally Ill, have become frustrated and critical of the process. They do not see policy rhetoric being translated into significant changes at the child or family level. The *Report of the surgeon general's conference on children's mental health: A national action agenda* (2000) echoed these criticisms. It stated that despite the existence of mental health programs in many communities, the nation still lacks a basic mental health care infrastructure and that "unmet need for services remains as high today as it was 20 years ago" (p. 13). Table 4.4 provides a summary of federal mental health policy initiatives.

Evaluation of Children's Mental Health Policies

Evaluations of child mental health policy have generally been nonsupportive of programs and services implemented in the field. Mental health services to children have been criticized as nontargeted, fragmented, spotty, and generally not empirically supported (Joint Commission on the Mental Health of Children, 1969; Knitzer, 1982; Lourie & Hernandez, 2003; The President's Commission on Mental Health, 1978). Before the 1990s, community mental health centers provided mostly outpatient or inpatient services, with little in between. Many children ended up in juvenile justice or child welfare agencies because there was no other avenue to receive needed residential services. Placement in these settings sometimes required relinquishment of parental

Table 4.4   Summary of Major Federal Mental Health Policy Initiatives

Policy	Date	Impact
Mental Retardation Facilities and Community Mental Health Center Construction Act	1963	Established funding to build and staff community mental health centers
Social Security Amendments of 1965	1965	Provided funding for medically necessary services to low-income families, pregnant women, and persons who are aged, blind, and disabled. Coverage of most mental health services was optional to states.
PL 94–162—Education of All Handicapped Children Act	1974	Required that schools provide mental health services to children with SED as part of their IEP
Community Mental Health Center Amendment Act	1975	Required that CMHCs provide mental health services to children and adolescents
The Omnibus Budget Reconciliation Act (OBRA)	1981	Consolidated funding for social service programs into a single block grant to the states. Act required that 10% of mental health block grant funds be spent on children and adolescents.
Alcohol, Drug, and Mental Health Administration (ADAMHA) Appropriations Act	1984	Directed NIMH to provide incentive grants to states to develop state and local-level child mental health structures to coordinate care to children with SED and their families. NIMH created the Child and Adolescent Service System Program (CASSP)
Children's and Community Mental Health Services Improvement Act	1992	Created the Comprehensive Community Mental Health Services for Children and Their Families Program within the Center for Mental Health Services (CMHS), which provided funding to states to develop systems of care for children with SED
Surgeon General's Reports and President's New Freedom Commission Report on Mental Health	2000–2003	Called for increased research on and use of evidence-based mental health practices

custody, causing increased stress on families and children (Giliberti & Schilzinger, 2000; Lourie & Katz-Leavy, 1991; National Alliance for the Mentally Ill, 2001). In response to these criticisms, Congress supported the creation of systems of care to coordinate and enhance mental health care to youth with SED. Private funders, such as the Robert Wood Johnson and Annie E. Casey Foundations, also contributed millions of dollars to develop model systems of care across the country. Unfortunately, the evaluations of many of these model programs have produced only mixed results.

The Fort Bragg Evaluation

During the early 1990s, the Department of Defense and NIMH funded a major study to test the impact of developing comprehensive and coordinated continuums of care for youth with SED at Fort Bragg, North Carolina. The demonstration program provided services such as in-home crisis stabilization, after-school group treatment, therapeutic foster care, and crisis management to help fill the gap between outpatient therapy and inpatient hospitalization.

The Fort Bragg study demonstrated significant system improvements, such as increased service capacity, reduced use of hospitals and residential treatment facilities, and enhanced collaboration among service agencies. However, it did not produce significant clinical outcomes with regard to alleviation of symptoms, increased functioning, or reduction of impairments (Bickman et al., 1995). Findings from the Robert Wood Johnson Foundation Mental Health Services Program for Youth program, which studied the development of systems of care in eight communities over a 10-year period, showed similar results to those produced in the Fort Bragg project (Cross & Saxe, 1997; Johnsen, Morrissey, & Callaway, 1996).

These disappointing findings caused controversy in the child mental health community. Some researchers advocated for a change in policy emphasis from system development to service effectiveness (Salzer & Bickman, 1997), whereas others continued to support large system reform (Hernandez & Hodges, 2003). Recent policy discourse has suggested requiring both system reform *and* the delivery of evidence-based interventions (Burns, 2001; Rosenblatt & Woodbridge, 2003). Although the risk and resilience framework for targeting interventions is not yet widely used within the mental health field, many policy leaders and advocates are focusing attention on the identification and use of evidence-based practices that will provide cost-effective, client-level improvements.

Using Evidence-Based Practice in Systems of Care

In 1998 the American Psychological Association (APA) convened a special task force to systematically evaluate the "evidence base" for treating individual disorders in children and adolescents. In its report, the APA determined two levels of criteria against which to evaluate the evidence basis of particular interventions. The first, more rigorous one was *well established*; the other, less rigorous, was *probably efficacious*. The major distinction between the two was that well-established treatment is shown to be superior to a placebo or other treatment, whereas a probably efficacious treatment only needs to be superior to a waiting list or to a no-treatment control group. Well-established treatments must be supported by at least two different research teams. Upon conclusion of their review, they found that most known psychosocial interventions for children and adolescents do not meet the first level of empirical support (Lonigan, Elbert, & Johnson, 1998). Table 4.5 shows the APA criteria.

Several well-established treatments have been identified for children and adolescents with the diagnoses of ADHD, conduct disorder, oppositional defiance disorder, and phobia. These include behavioral parent training and classroom behavior modification for ADHD and parent training, functional family therapy, and multisystemic therapy for conduct and oppositional defiance disorders. Graduated exposure, participant modeling, and reinforced practice were found to be well-established interventions for children and adolescents with phobias.

A number of other treatments, including those based on cognitive–behavioral therapy, were identified as probably efficacious. Cognitive–behavioral techniques have been shown to be effective with ADHD; depression; anxiety disorders, including PTSD; conduct disorders; and phobias. Several skills-training interventions also appear to be successful with children with major depression and conduct disorders. Promising interventions not yet on the APA list include school-based contingency management with children for ADHD and conduct disorders (Brestan & Eyberg, 1998; Pelham, Wheeler, & Chronis, 1998), classroom-based social skills training in combination with parent training and systematic communication with teachers for conduct problems (Fraser et al., 2004; Reid, Eddy, Fetrow, & Stoolmiller, 1999), and classroom-based social skills training for depression in elementary school-aged children (Gillam, Reivick, Joaycox, & Seligman, 1995).

Many of the interventions commonly used in the child mental health system either have been untested in controlled research investigations or have not met the scientific rigor necessary for inclusion in the APA Task Force Report. Examples of this include studies assessing the effects of partial hospitalization, day treatment, case management, and home-based services (Surgeon General, 1999). Investigations of these interventions have generally not been rigorous.

To date, there is no national legislation supporting evidence-based practice. States are, however, beginning to enact legislative language requiring

Table 4.5   Well-Established and Probably Efficacious Psychosocial Treatment for Common Child and Youth Mental Health Problems

	Treatments	
Problem	*Well Established*	*Probably Efficacious*
ADHD	Behavioral parent training Behavior modification in school	Cognitive–behavioral therapy
Anxiety	None	Cognitive–behavioral therapy
Autism	None	Contingency management
Depression	None	Behavior self-control therapy Cognitive–behavioral coping skills
Conduct Disorder	Behavioral parent training Functional family therapy Multisystemic therapy	Anger control training Assertiveness training Skills training

Note: This table is adapted from Ollendick and King (2004).

the use of empirically supported interventions in child mental health systems. In this context, state mental health statutes often include the requirement to create interagency systems of care within which evidence-based services are provided to children with SED and their families. Additional research is necessary to evaluate the effects of these efforts.

Child Mental Health Policy from a Risk, Protection, and Resilience Perspective

As noted earlier, an articulated public mental health policy for children and adolescents did not exist until the 1980s. Rather, child mental health has generally followed the policies and initiatives set forth in the adult mental health system. When policies stated that adults with mental health problems were to be confined in institutions, it followed that mentally ill children were also sent to institutions. As Freudian psychotherapy was practiced with primarily affluent adults with neuroses, child guidance clinics served mostly white, non-Latino children with internalizing problems. However, when the Community Mental Health Center (CMHC) Act required community-based services to adults in the late 1960s, services to children were not concurrently mandated. Indeed, CMHCs were not required to provide services to children until 1975. And when block grant funding replaced categorical funding in the 1980s, only 10% of these funds were required to be spent on children.

Forging a coherent and comprehensive policy for children with serious emotional and behavioral problems has been difficult. In response to the lack of clear direction, various public child-serving agencies have provided services. Schools were required to serve children with serious behavioral and emotional disturbances under the Individuals With Disabilities Education Act (IDEA) legislation in 1974. In some states, juvenile justice programs have provided mental health supports to juvenile offenders. As a high percentage of children and adolescents found in child welfare agencies experience trauma and grief, child welfare agencies developed a range of therapeutic living arrangements for children with serious mental health problems.

Finally, in 1984, Congress appropriated funds to the NIMH to create a clear policy direction for child mental health through the CASSP program. CASSP funds were provided to state mental health offices to create systems of care to coordinate mental health services to children with SED, many of whom were served in other child-serving systems. Within each SOC, a broad continuum of community-based care was envisioned. States were encouraged to be creative in designing and delivering new services, relying mostly on underlying values and principles. Emphasis was placed on individualizing services and delivering them in community settings. However, no theoretical framework was suggested for determining what services were needed.

Unfortunately, the knowledge base derived from risk and protective factor research was not applied to mental health practice and policy at that time, and with few exceptions, it is not widely used today. Until recently, the primary policy focus has been on broad system development and reform. Now, with a renewed interest in evidence-based practice as a framework for policy, the risk and resilience perspective may be recognized as a way to target interventions to individuals and groups of high-risk youth.

Service Integration Using a Risk, Protection, and Resilience Framework

A growing body of literature describes the overall characteristics of children with SED and their families (Epstein, Cullinan, Quinn, & Cumblad, 1995; Quinn & Epstein, 1998). Most of these studies report that children with SED have a number of common risk factors, including inadequate social skills, poor academic performance, family violence, and alcohol and drug use, and mental illness. Despite these commonalities, there is no single system of mental health care for these youth. In fact, more youth with SED are found in other service systems than are treated within the child mental health system itself. For example, up to 80 percent of children entering the juvenile justice system have mental health disorders (New Freedom Commission on Mental Health, 2003), and it is estimated that 20 percent of incarcerated youth have SED—double that found in the general population (Urban Institute, 2003). Nearly 20 percent of children with SED are found in the child welfare system, and a whopping 70 percent of youth with SED receive mental health services from local school systems (Burns et al., 1995).

It is clear that children in these separate systems need appropriate mental health care that is individualized to their needs. Over the past two decades, mental health leaders, policymakers, and service providers have been struggling with how to best integrate mental health services into these other systems. The most common integration approaches at the state level involve coordinating mental health, child welfare, and juvenile justice services through one of the following three structures:

1. Separate agencies are maintained as individual departments. In this model, coordination of services is accomplished through formal interagency planning structures.

2. A part or all of the three agencies (mental health, child welfare, and juvenile justice) are housed within a single umbrella department such as a Department of Human Services. Each division maintains its own staff, policy development process, and budget. Coordination is facilitated because each agency reports to a single department director and many departmental rules and procedures inhibiting service integration can be changed without new legislative intervention.

3. All three agencies are combined into a single departmental agency, with a single agency budget and policy-making body.

As one looks at these three options, the decision to combine all child services into a single agency may seem the most advantageous. However, there are costs to this arrangement as well as benefits. Single, integrated agencies tend to be quite large, making management difficult and often inefficient. Turf issues remain problematic. And many child advocates do not like the fact that the allocation of funds across different child populations would occur within a single budget process that may not be open to the public for review and comment.

States have found that restructuring alone may not overcome turf issues, policy conflicts, leadership challenges, and inadequate and disproportional funding. The most important elements of successful service integration may be the agreement on a common target population and blending of funding streams so that a more appropriate set of individually tailored services can be provided. Which agency provides the actual services may not be as important as an arrangement so that services are provided to children who need them, regardless of their custody status or family financial ability.

The value of the risk and protective factor perspective is that it provides a cross-problem, multidisciplinary framework for individualized intervention. A number of exemplary integrated service models are described in the literature. The Ventura County System of Care and the Willie M. Program will be described here as case examples. The Ventura County System of Care was enacted by state statute and focuses primarily on service integration. The Willie M. Program resulted from a class-action lawsuit and is a good example of the use of the risk and resilience framework to individualize care.

Program and Case Examples

Ventura County System of Care

In 1985, the California state legislature passed a landmark bill (AB 3920) that authorized a demonstration program to integrate mental health services across child welfare, public education, and juvenile justice systems. The legislation integrated numerous federal and state statutes addressing public mental health services for children and amended various statutes and regulations to facilitate interagency cooperation. It required publicly funded child-serving agencies in the demonstration counties to engage in interagency planning and to develop interagency protocols and agreements emphasizing services to children in their homes or in the least restrictive setting. Ventura County was selected as one of three demonstration sites under AB 3920.

The Ventura Country System of Care was based on five core concepts in the enabling legislation. These concepts emphasized (1) clearly defining target populations, (2) setting goals to preserve family unity and locally based treatment, (3) developing collaborative programs of services and standards tailored to individual children and their families, (4) creating a continuum of service options and settings that cross agency boundaries, and (5) setting up a mechanism for system evaluation.

Client outcomes for the Ventura County System of Care reflected a cross-agency perspective. Children with serious emotional disturbances were to remain or be reunified with their families, to attend and progress in public schools, and—as appropriate—desist from problem behavior such as delinquency and drug use. A cross-agency SED target population was determined that included mandated service populations within each agency.

The target population focused on emotionally and/or behaviorally disordered youth, including (1) court dependents whose histories included neglect, physical and/or sexual abuse, multiple foster home placements, residential treatment, and psychiatric hospitalization; (2) court wards for whom the public sector had legal responsibility as a result of delinquent behavior and were at risk of out-of-home placement; (3) special education pupils who required mental health services in order to benefit from their Individual Education Plans; and (4) children who were not part of a formal agency other than mental health and were at risk of out-of-home placement into state hospitals or residential treatment.

Mental health treatment was integrated into the service systems of the other major child-serving public agencies. The county mental health department became responsible for serving the mental health needs of target population children in the other three domains—public school, child welfare, and juvenile justice. Mental health staff located their services in places where targeted children lived and went to school. The County Mental Health Department was reorganized to accomplish this. Most of the mental health staff was deployed to agency and school settings to provide and supervise mental health services there. Depending on the needs of the agency, mental health staff provided consultation, assessments, case management, counseling, day treatment, special day classes, in-home care, family therapy, enriched foster home care services, and crisis intervention.

The state legislation facilitated the blending of categorical funds so that each agency domain was able to determine the mental health services it needed. Specific roles and relationships between agencies were delineated in interagency agreements and facilitated by a number of interagency coordinating mechanisms. An interagency juvenile justice council became the policy-making body of the county system. It was set up to serve as a vehicle for identifying problems, developing interagency solutions, and working through agency conflicts. Required membership included the county counselor, public defender, district attorney, sheriff, chief administrative officer of the juvenile court, director of probation, a member of the board of supervisors, the superintendent of schools, and the directors of the Department of Child Welfare and the Department of Mental Health. Still in operation today, the council reviews all agency budgets and looks for ways to mingle and coordinate funding streams.

The demonstration project in Ventura County met the system-level performance outcomes required by the statute. By integrating mental health services into each system, more children were served—especially from ethnic minority backgrounds—and fewer youth required placement in restrictive and costly state hospitals or residential treatment centers. The project resulted in a substantial savings to the state. It was expanded to more counties in 1989. In 1992, the California state legislature enacted the Children's Mental Health Services Act to expand the SOC model to all counties. In 2001, the legislature passed a law requiring an agency-integrated SOC statewide (Shortz, 2003).

The Willie M. Program

North Carolina's Willie M. Program grew out of a class action lawsuit (*Willie M. et al. v. James B. Hunt, Jr. et al.*, 1980) filed on behalf of aggressive children with SED who were institutionalized as a result of inadequate community-based care. Seeing this as an opportunity to improve the service structure, mental health administrators in the North Carolina Division of Mental Health, Developmental Disabilities, and Substance Abuse Services (MH/DD/SAS) used the lawsuit to create a comprehensive continuum of community-based care for high-risk and hard-to-manage children and adolescents.

To be represented by and served under the class action suit, youths had to be under 18 years of age, suffer from a serious emotional or neurological disorder, be violent or chronically aggressive, and have been, or likely to be, placed in public custody or excluded from access to needed treatment or educational services. Although there were many youths who met these criteria, four youths were ultimately named as plaintiffs in the litigation. Willie M., the first of four plaintiffs, was an 11-year-old boy diagnosed as emotionally disturbed with unsocialized aggression.

The Department of Human Services avoided a trial by agreeing to the court's complaints and demands. Each member of the class was guaranteed individualized treatment in the least restrictive setting possible. The treatment was to be based on the child's needs, not the availability of service providers to provide a service or set of services. If needed services did not exist, then they were to be created.

Leaders within the Division of MH/DD/SAS welcomed the challenge and advocated for the development of local systems of care within which to create and provide services to class members. The Willie M. Program became among the first model systems of care in the country. It served up to 1,500 severely aggressive youth with SED a year, two thirds of whom lived in specialized foster care or group homes. Cooperative arrangements were required among the multiple agencies serving these youth. Court officers monitored these relationships, making sure that public education, child welfare, and juvenile justice personnel worked in concert with the Division of MH/DD/SAS on behalf of these children. Wraparound case management was the primary tool used to individualize care to members of the Willie M.

class action suit. Each member was required to have an individual habilitation plan. Beginning in 1995, the individual habilitation plan was based on an assessment process that reviewed both risk and protective factors.

An Assessment and Outcomes Instrument (AOI) was created to assess and to measure the progress of children in the Willie M. Program. The instrument used a risk and protective factor perspective and measured both fixed characteristics (factors that could not be changed through intervention, e.g., parental loss) and dynamic characteristics (factors that were malleable in treatment, such as school performance). Risk factors included living in poverty, parental loss, large family size, parental mental health and substance abuse problems, parental criminality, fetal substance exposure, neurologic or developmental disorders, poor mother–infant attachment, difficult or shy early temperament, witness of violent acts, physical and sexual abuse, school failure, and delinquent behavior. Of the possible 30 risk factors covered on the AOI, the average number experienced by Willie M. class members was 13—a number that far exceeds most definitions of a high-risk youth (e.g., Rutter, 1979). Consistent with the literature on risk and conduct disorders, most Willie M. class members with poor behavioral outcomes had histories of negative parent–child interactions and poor academic performance. Better behavioral outcomes were predicted by protective factors such as good interpersonal, problem-solving, and reading skills; available social support networks, involvement with both family members and pro-social peers; and a parent who was consistently employed (Vance, Bowen, Fernandez, & Thompson, 2002).

Individualized rehabilitation plans were designed to target interventions likely to result in positive behavioral changes. Because most risk factors associated with Willie M. class members were fixed historical experiences and family features not amenable to change, there were not many ways to reduce their impact on current behaviors. However, evaluations of the Willie M. Program found that strengthening protective factors was directly associated with improved behavior outcomes (Bowen & Flora, 2002; Vance et al., 2002). Depending on individual needs, protective factors such as reading skills, relationships with adults, social skills, positive beliefs and attitudes, and involvement in community activities were strengthened through a variety of targeted interventions. Parental and caretaker positive discipline skills were strengthened. The protective factors more highly related to behavioral improvement were increased levels of home and school social skills. Interventions targeting these factors included teaching skills in anger management, empathy development, and getting and keeping friends (Bowen & Flora). Because of these positive behavioral changes, youth served in the Willie M. Program attended school more often and had fewer arrests. Class member and family satisfaction with services was high. As an individualized SOC was successfully developed, the Willie M. class action lawsuit was resolved in 2000.

The Willie M. Program in North Carolina was both successful and expensive. The court demanded the provision of needed services, regardless of cost. Many state legislators resented this open-checkbook approach. As costs went up for class members' services, appropriations to other parts of the mental health system declined or were not increased accordingly. Once the class action lawsuit was resolved and its mandates removed, funding for the Willie M. Program was reduced and realigned within the Division of MH/DD/SAS.

Conclusion

Much can be learned from these case examples. Other lessons about the effectiveness of mental health policies and programs can also be derived from state and local efforts to improve service systems on behalf of children and adolescents with SED. It appears that states have at least several options from which to choose. Ventura County provides an example of a legislative mandate to integrate mental health services into other child-serving systems. On the other hand, the Willie M. Program demonstrates how risk and protective factors can be used as the framework for successful case planning and intervention through a class action lawsuit.

Based on evidence presented in this chapter, at least four core strategies for policy reform in child mental health should be considered:

1. Structures should be developed to integrate mental health services into key child-serving agencies, such as public education, child welfare, and juvenile justice;

2. Systematic assessment should identify malleable risk and protective factors;

3. Evidence-based interventions should be selected and provided to reduce risk and strengthen protective factors; and

4. Services should be developmentally and culturally appropriate, sequenced sufficiently early in childhood to disrupt negative developmental trajectories.

We know that most mental health disorders occur at the same rate in young children that they do in older children and adolescents (Kenny, Oliver, & Poppe, 2002). It is unfortunate that these disorders are not usually diagnosed and treated until youth are much older. State legislatures spend millions of dollars each year treating older youth with serious emotional and behavioral disorders. Too often these funds are expended in the juvenile justice and child welfare systems. One might appropriately ask, "Are these efforts too little, too late?" Increasingly, many experts think this is the case.

In many communities, mental health services are now being integrated into public schools through programs such as school-based health clinics. These clinics improve access to primary health care and provide a less stigmatized entry into mental health services for many youth. School-based health clinics provide preventive and early intervention screenings for many health conditions that inhibit learning. Regular screenings for emotional and behavioral problems can also be included.

In this regard, schools may be the best public setting in which to identify troubled children and to link them with appropriate services. More than 52 million youth attend public school in the United States every day (New Freedom Commission on Mental Health, 2003). The integration of mental health and public school policies to position resources to detect and treat mental health problems before they become florid disorders has the potential to save public money and private heartache. We now know a great deal about risk and protective factors for childhood mental health disorders. Finding, diagnosing, and treating these high-risk children early may interrupt developmental trajectories that lead to poor outcomes in adolescence and adulthood. The ability to prevent and minimize these poor outcomes should become the major challenge facing mental health, child welfare, public education, and juvenile justice policymakers and leaders today.

Questions for Discussion

1. What child mental heath policies and practices have inhibited the integration of mental health services into other child-serving systems, such as juvenile justice and child welfare?

2. Are there reasons to keep these agencies organizationally separate at the state level? Local level?

3. Given what we know about risk factors for a variety of emotional and behavioral disorders, how can mental health and public education resources be combined to support prevention and early intervention strategies?

Additional Reading

Allen-Meares, P., & Fraser, M. W. (2004). *Intervention with children and adolescents: An interdisciplinary perspective.* Boston: Allyn & Bacon.

American Psychiatric Association. (2000). *Diagnostic and statistical manual of mental disorders* (4th ed.). Washington, DC: Author.

Center for Mental Health Services. (1999). *Annual report to Congress on the evaluation of the Comprehensive Community Mental Health Services for Children and Their Families Program.* Atlanta: Macro International.

Costello, E. J., Angold, A., Burns, B. J., Stangl, D. K., Tweed, D. L., Erkanli, A., & Worthman, C. M. (1996). The Great Smoky Mountains Study of Youth. Goals, design, methods, and the prevalence of *DSM-III-R* disorders. *Archives of General Psychiatry, 53,* 1129–1136.

National Alliance for the Mentally Ill (2001). Families on the brink: The impact of ignoring children with serious mental illness. Arlington, VA: National Alliance for the Mentally Ill.

Surgeon General. (1999). *Mental health: A report from the surgeon general.* Washington, DC: DHHS.

Surgeon General. (2000). *Report of the surgeon general's conference on children's mental health: A national action agenda.* Washington, DC: DHHS.

References

Allen-Meares, P., & Fraser, M. W. (2004). *Intervention with children and adolescents: An interdisciplinary perspective.* Boston: Allyn & Bacon.

American Psychiatric Association. (2000). *Diagnostic and statistical manual of mental disorders* (4th ed.). Washington, DC: Author.

Armstrong, K. H., Dedrick, R. F., & Greenbaum, P. E. (2003). Factors associated with community adjustment in young adults with serious emotional disturbance: A longitudinal analysis. *Journal of Emotional and Behavioral Disorders, 1,* 66–76.

Behar, L. B. (2003). Mental health management environments: Children's mental health services—the challenge of changing policy and practice. In W. R Reid & S. B. Silver (Eds.), *Handbook of mental health administration and management* (pp. 149–162). New York: Brunner-Routledge.

Bickman, L., Guthrie, P. R., Foster, E. M., Lamber, E. W., Summerfelt, W. T., Breda, C. S., & Heflinger, C. A. (1995). *Evaluating managed mental health services: The Fort Bragg experiment.* New York: Plenum.

Bowen, N. K., & Flora, D. B. (2002). When is it appropriate to focus on protection in interventions for adolescents? *American Journal of Orthopsychiatry, 72,* 526–538.

Breier, A., Kelsoe, J. R., Kirwin, P. D., Bellar, S. A., Wolkowitz, O. M., & Pickar, D. (1988). Early parental loss and development of adult psychopathology. *Archives of General Psychiatry, 45,* 987–993.

Brendenberg, N., Freidman, R., Silver, S. (1990). The epidemiology of childhood psychiatric disorders: Prevalence findings from recent studies. *Journal of the American Academy of Child and Adolescent Psychiatry, 29,* 76–83.

Brestan, E. V., & Eyberg, S. M. (1998). Effective psychosocial treatments of conduct-disordered children and adolescents: 29 years, 82 studies, and 5,272 kids. *Journal of Child Clinical Psychology, 27,* 180–189.

Bronfenbrenner, U. (1979). *The ecology of human development: Experiments by nature and design.* Cambridge, MA: Harvard University Press.

Burns, B. J. (2001). Commentary on the special issue on the National Evaluation of the Comprehensive Community Mental Health Services for Children and Their Families Program. *Journal of Emotional and Behavioral Disorders, 9,* 71–76.

Burns, B. J., Costello, E. J., Angold, A., Tweed, D., Stangl, D., Farmer, E. M., & Erkanli, A. (1995). Children's mental health service use across service sectors. *Health Affairs (Millwood), 14,* 147–159.

Center for Mental Health Services. (1999). *Annual report to Congress on the evaluation of the Comprehensive Community Mental Health Services for Children and Their Families Program.* Atlanta: Macro International.

Chamberlain, P., & Weinrott, M. (1990). Specialized foster care: Treating seriously emotionally disturbed children. *Children Today, 19,* 24–27.

Children's Defense Fund. (1995). *The state of America's children: 1995.* Washington, DC: Children's Defense Fund.

Costello, E. J., Angold, A., Burns, B. J., Stangl, D. K., Tweed, D. L., Erkanli, A., & Worthman, C. M. (1996). The Great Smoky Mountains Study of Youth. Goals, design, methods, and the prevalence of *DSM-III-R* disorders. *Archives of General Psychiatry, 53,* 1129–1136.

Cross, T. P., & Saxe, L. (1997). Many hands make mental health systems a reality: Lessons from the mental health services program for youth. In C. T. Nixon & D. A. Northrup (Eds.), *Children's mental health services: Research, policy, and evaluation* (pp. 45–72). Thousand Oaks, CA: Sage.

Davis, M., & Vander Stoep, A. (1997). The transition to adulthood for youth who have serious emotional disturbance: Developmental transition and young adult outcomes. *The Journal of Mental Health Administration, 24,* 400–427.

Davis, M., Yelton, S., & Katz-Leavy, J. (1995). *State child and adolescent mental health: Administration, policies, and laws.* Tampa: University of South Florida, Florida Mental Health Institute.

Davis, M., Yelton, S., Katz-Leavy, J., & Lourie, I. (1995). Unclaimed children revisited. *Journal of Mental Health Administration, 22,* 142–166.

Douzinas, N., Fornari, V., Goodman, B., Sitnick, T., & Packman, L. (1994). Eating disorders and abuse. *Child Psychiatric Clinics of North America, 3,* 777–796.

Dykman, R. A., McPherson, B., Ackerman, P. T., Newton, J. E., Mooney, D. M., Wherry, J., & Chaffin, M. (1997). Internalizing and externalizing characteristics of sexually and/or physically abused children. *Integrative Physiological & Behavioral Science, 32,* 62–74.

Epstein, M. H., Cullinan, D., Quinn, K. P, & Cumblad, C. (1995). Personal, family, and service use characteristics of young people served by an interagency community-based system of care. *Journal of Emotional and Behavioral Disorders, 3,* 55–64.

Famularo, R., Kinscherff, R., & Fenton, T. (1992). Psychiatric diagnoses of maltreated children: Preliminary findings. *Journal of American Academy of Child and Adolescent Psychiatry, 31,* 863–867.

Fergusson, D. M., Horwood, L. J., & Lynsky, M. T. (1994). The childhoods of multiple problem adolescents: A 15-year longitudinal study. *Journal of Child Psychology and Psychiatry, 35,* 1123–1140.

Flisher, A. J., Kramer, R. A., Hoven, C. W., Greenwald, S., Alegria, M., Bird, H. R., Canmino, G., Connell, R., & Moore, R. E. (1997). Psychosocial characteristics of physically abused children and adolescents. *Journal of the American Academy of Child and Adolescent Psychiatry, 36,* 123–131.

Fraser, M. W. (Ed.). (2004). *Risk and resilience in childhood: An ecological perspective* (2nd ed.). Washington, DC: NASW.

Fraser, M. W., Day, S. H., Galinsky, M. J., Hodges, V. G., & Smokowski, P. R. (2004). Conduct problems and peer rejection in childhood: A randomized trial of the Making Choices and Strong Families programs. *Research on Social Work Practice, 14,* 313–324.

Friedman, R. M., Katz-Levey, J. W., Manderschied, R. W., & Sondheimer, D. L. (1996). Prevalence of serious emotional disturbance in children and adolescents. In R. W. Manderscheid & M. A. Sonnenschein (Eds.), *Mental health, United States, 1996* (pp. 71–88). Rockville, MD: Center for Mental Health Services.

Garmezy, N. (1993). Children in poverty: Resilience despite risk. *Psychiatry, 56,* 127–136.

Gilbert, C. (2004). Childhood depression: A risk factor perspective. In M. W. Fraser (Ed.). *Risk and resilience in childhood: An ecological perspective* (2nd ed., pp. 315–346). Washington, DC: NASW.

Giliberti, M., & Schilzinger, R. (2000). *Relinquishing custody: The tragic result of failure to meet children's mental health needs.* Washington, DC: Bazelon Center for Mental Health Law.

Gillam, F., Reivick, K., Joaycox, L, & Seligman, M. E. P. (1995). Prevention of depressive symptoms in school children: Two-year follow-up. *Psychological Science, 6,* 343–351.

Goodman, R., & Stevenson, J. (1989). A twin study of hyperactivity. II. The etiological role of genes, family relationships and perinatal adversity. *Journal of Child Psychology and Psychiatry, 30,* 691–709.

Goodyer, I. (1990). *Life experiences, development and childhood psychiatry.* New York: John Wiley.

Goodyer, I. (2001). Life events: Their nature and effects. In I. M. Goodyer (Ed.), *The depressed child and adolescent* (2nd ed., pp. 204–232). New York: Cambridge University Press.

Green, W. (1995). Family, peer and self factors as predictors of male and female adolescent substance abuse at 9th and 12th grade. *Dissertation Abstracts International: Section B: The Sciences and Engineering, 55,* 2771.

Greenbaum, P. E., Dedrick, R. F., Friedman, R., Kutash, K., Brown, E., Lardieri, S., & Pugh, A. (1996). National adolescent and child treatment study (NACTS): Outcomes for individuals with serious emotional and behavioral disturbance. *Journal of Emotional and Behavioral Disorders, 4,* 130–146.

Hergenhahn, B. R. (2001). *An introduction to the history of psychology* (4th ed.). Belmont, CA: Wadsworth.

Hernandez, M., & Hodges, S. (2003). Building upon the theory of change for systems of care. *Journal of Emotional and Behavioral Disorders, 11,* 19–26.

Hoagwood, H., Burns, B. J., Kiser, L., Ringeisen, H., & Schoenwald, S. K. (2001). Evidence-based practice in child and adolescent mental health services. *Psychiatric Services, 52,* 1179–1189.

Hopper, K., & Wanderling, J. (2000). Revisiting the developed versus developing country distinction in course and outcome in schizophrenia: Results from IsoS, the WHO Collaborative Follow-up Project. *Schizophrenia Bulletin, 26,* 835–846.

Jellinek, M., & Synder, J. (1998). Depression and suicide in children and adolescents. *Pediatrics in Review, 19,* 255–265.

Jenkins, E., & Bell, C. (1997). Exposure and response to community violence among children and adolescents. In J. Osofsky (Ed.), *Children in a violent society* (pp. 9–31). New York: Guilford Press.

Johnsen, M. C., Morrissey, J. P., & Calloway, M. O. (1996). Structure and change in child mental health service delivery networks. *Journal of Community Psychology, 24,* 275–289.

Johnson, J. G., Cohen, P., Kasen, S., Smailes, E., & Brook, J. S. (2001). Association of maladaptive parental behavior with psychiatric disorder among parents and their offspring. *Archives of General Psychiatry, 58,* 453–460.

Joint Commission on the Mental Health of Children. (1969). *Crisis in child mental health: Challenges for the 1970's.* New York: Harper & Row.

Jones, K (1999). *Taming the troublesome child: American families, child guidance, and the limits of psychiatric authority.* Cambridge, MA: Harvard University Press.

Kagan, J., Snidman, N., & Arcus, D. (1998). Childhood derivatives of high and low reactivity in infancy. *Child Development, 69,* 1483–1493.

Kazdin, A. E. (1996). Developing effective treatments for children and adolescents. In E. D. Hibbs & P. S. Jensen (Eds.), *Psychosocial treatments for child and adolescent disorders: Empirically based strategies for clinical practice* (pp. 9–18). Washington, DC: American Psychological Association.

Kenny, H., Oliver, L., & Poppe, J. (2002). *Mental health services for children: An overview.* Washington, DC: National Conference of State Legislatures.

Kessler, R. C. (1997). The effects of stressful life events on depression. *Annual Review of Psychology, 48,* 191–214.

Knitzer, J. (1982). *Unclaimed children.* Washington, DC: Children's Defense Fund.

Lahey, B. B., Loeber, R., Hart, E. L., Frick, P. J., Applegate, B., Zhang, Q., Green, S. M., & Russo, M. F. (1995). Four-year longitudinal study of conduct disorder in boys: Patterns and predictors of persistence. *Journal of Abnormal Psychology, 104,* 83–93.

Linver, M., Fuligni, A., Hernandez, M, & Brooks-Gunn, J. (2004). *Poverty and child development: Promising interventions.* In P. Allen-Meares & M. W. Fraser (Eds.), *Intervention with children and adolescents: An interdisciplinary perspective* (pp. 106–129). Boston: Allyn & Bacon.

Livingston, R., Lawson, L., & Jones, J. G. (1993). Predictors of self-reported psychopathology in children abused repeatedly by a parent. *Journal of the American Academy of Child and Adolescent Psychiatry, 32*, 948–953.

Loeber, R., & Stouthamer-Loeber, M. (1996). The development of offending. *Criminal Justice and Behaviour, 23*, 12–24.

Loeber, R., Farrington, D. P., Stouthamer-Loeber, M., & Van Kammen, W. B. (1998). In New perspectives on adolescent risk behavior, R. Jessor (Ed.). *Multiple risk factors for multi-problem boys: Co-occurrence of delinquency, substance use, attention deficit, conduct problems, physical aggression, covert behavior, depressed mood, and shy/withdrawn behavior* (pp. 90–149). Cambridge: Cambridge University Press.

Lonigan, C. J., Elbert, J. C., & Johnson, S. B. (1998). Empirically supported psychosocial interventions for children: An overview. *Journal of Clinical Child Psychology, 27*, 138–145

Lourie, I. S., & Hernandez, M. (2003). A historical perspective on national child mental health policy. *Journal of Emotional and Behavioral Disorders, 2*, 5–9.

Lourie, I. S., & Katz-Leavy, J. (1991). New directions for mental health services for families and children. Families in Society: *The Journal of Contemporary Human Services, 72*, 277–285.

Lucas, A. R., Reard, C. M., O'Fallon, W. M., & Kurland, L. T. (1991). 50-year trends in the incidence of anorexia nervosa in Rochester, MN: A population-based study. *American Journal of Psychiatry, 148*, 917–922.

Maziade, M., & Raymond, V. (1995). The new genetics of schizophrenia. In C. L. Shriqui & H. A. Nasrallah (Eds.), *Contemporary issues in the treatment of schizophrenia* (pp. 61–79). Washington, DC: American Psychiatric Press.

McConaughy, S. H., & Wadsworth, M. E. (2000). Life history reports of young adults previously referred for mental health services. *Journal of Emotional and Behavioral Disorders, 8*, 202–215.

McLeod, J. D., & Shanahan, M. J. (1996). Poverty, parenting and children's mental health. *American Sociological Review, 58*, 351–366.

Moore, S. M., Rohde, P. L., Seeley, J. R., & Lewinsohn, P. M. (1999). Life events and depression in adolescence: Relationship loss as a prospective risk factor for first onset of major depressive disorder. *Journal of Abnormal Psychology, 108*, 606–614.

National Alliance for the Mentally Ill. (2001). Families on the brink: The impact of ignoring children with serious mental illness. Arlington, VA: National Alliance for the Mentally Ill.

Neal, A. M., Lilly, R. S., & Zakis, S. (1993). What are African American children afraid of? *Journal of Anxiety Disorders, 7*, 129–139.

New Freedom Commission on Mental Health. (2003). *Achieving the promise: Transforming mental health care in America.* Final report. DHHS Pub. No. SMA-03-3832. Rockville, MD.

Nolen-Hoeksema, S., & Girgus, J. S. (1994). The emergence of gender differences in depression during adolescence. *Psychological Bulletin, 115,* 424–443.

Olds, D., Henderson, C. R., Jr., Cole, R., Eckenrode, J., Kitzman, H., Luckey, D., Pettitt, L., Sidora, K., Morris, P., & Powers, J. (1998). Long-term effects of nurse home visitation on children's criminal and antisocial behavior: 15 year follow-up of a randomized controlled trial. *Journal of the American Medical Association, 280,* 1238–1244.

Ollendick, T. H., & King, N. J. (2004). Empirically supported treatments for children and adolescents: Advances toward evidence based practice. In P. M. Barrett and T. H. Ollenkick (Eds.), *Handbook of interventions that work with children and adolescents: Prevention and treatment* (pp. 3–25). New York: John Wiley.

Oyserman, D. (2004). Depression during the school-aged years. In P. Allen-Meares & M. W. Fraser (Eds.), *Intervention with children and adolescents: An interdisciplinary perspective* (pp. 264–281). Boston: Allyn & Bacon.

Oyserman, D., Mowbray, C. T., Allen-Meares, P. A., & Firminger, K. B. (2000). Parenting among mothers with a serious mental illness. *American Journal of Orthopsychiatry, 70,* 296–315.

Pagani, L., Boulerice, B., Tremblay, R. E., & Vitaro, F. (1997). Behavioral development in children of divorce and remarriage. *Journal of Child Psychology and Psychiatry, 38,* 769–781.

Peeples, F., & Loeber, R. (1994). Do individual factors and neighborhood context explain ethnic differences in juvenile delinquency? *Journal of Quantitative Criminology, 10,* 141–158.

Pelham, W. E., Jr., Wheeler, T., & Chronis, A. (1998). Empirically supported psychosocial treatments for attention deficit hyperactivity disorder. *Journal of Clinical Child Psychology, 27,* 190–205.

Piquero, A. R., & Chung, H. L. (2001). On the relationships between gender, early onset, and the seriousness of offending. *Journal of Criminal Justice, 29,* 189–206.

President's Commission on Mental Health. (1978). *Report of the sub-task panel on infants, children and adolescents.* Washington, DC: U.S. Government Printing Office.

Quinn, K. P., & Epstein, M. H. (1998). Characteristics of children, youth, and families serviced by local interagency systems of care. In M. H. Epstein, K. Kutash, & A. Duchowski (Eds.), *Outcomes for children and youth with emotional and behavioral disorders and their families: Programs and evaluation best practices* (pp. 81–114). Austin, TX: PRO-ED.

Reid, J. B., Eddy, M. J., Fetrow, R. A., & Stoolmiller, M. (1999). Description and immediate impacts of preventive intervention for conduct problems. *American Journal of Community Psychology, 27,* 483–517.

Resnick, G., & Burt, M. R. (1996). Youth at risk: Definitions and implications for service delivery. *American Journal of Orthopsychiatry, 66,* 172–188.

Robins, L. N. (1991). Conduct disorder. *Journal of Child Psychology and Psychiatry and Allied Disciplines, 32,* 193–212.

Rogers, L., Resnick, M. D., Mitchel, J. E., & Blum, R. W. (1997). The relationship between socioeconomic status and eating disorders in a community sample of adolescent girls. *International Journal of Eating Disorders, 22,* 15–23.

Rosenblatt, A., & Woodbridge, M. W. (2003). Deconstructing research on systems of care for youth with EBD: Frameworks for Policy Research. *Journal of Emotional and Behavior Disorders, 11,* 27–37.

Ross, D. M., & Ross, S. A. (1982). *Hyperactivity: Current issues, research, and theory.* New York: John Wiley.

Rutter, M. (1979). Protective factors in children's responses to stress and disadvantage. In M. W. Kent & J. E. Rolf (Eds.), *Primary prevention of psychopathology, Vol. 3: Social competence in children* (pp. 49–74) Hanover, NH: University Press of New England.

Rutter, M. (1985). Resilience in the face of adversity: Protective factors and resistance to psychiatric disorders. *British Journal of Psychiatry, 147,* 598–611.

Rutter, M., Silberg, J., O'Conner, T., & Simonoff, E. (1999). Genetics and child psychiatry: I. Advances in quantitative and molecular genetics. *Journal of Child Psychology and Psychiatry and Allied Disciplines, 40,* 3–18.

Salzer, M., & Bickman, L. (1997). Delivering effective children's services in the community: Reconsidering the benefits of system interventions. *Applied & Preventive Psychology, 6,* 1–13.

Sameroff, A. J., Bartko, W. T., Baldwin, A., Baldwin, C., & Seifer, R. (1999). Family and social influences on the development of child competence. In M. Lewis & C. Feiring (Eds.), *Families, risk, and competence* (pp. 167–185). Mahwah, NJ: Erlbaum.

Sameroff, A. J., & Gutman, L. M. (2004). Contributions of risk research to the design of successful interventions. In P. Allen-Meares & M. W. Fraser (Eds.), *Intervention with children and adolescents: An interdisciplinary perspective* (pp. 9–26). Boston: Allyn & Bacon.

Santilli, J. S., & Beilenson, P. (1992). Risk factors for adolescent sexual behavior, fertility and sexually transmitted diseases. *Journal of School Health, 62,* 271–279.

Schowalter, J. E. (2003). A history of child and adolescent psychiatry in the United States. *Psychiatric Times, 20.* Retrieved from . . . http://www.psychiatrictimes.com/p030943.html

Shortz, M. (2003). *The tale of two settings: Institutional and community-based mental health services in California since realignment in 1991.* Oakland, CA: California Protection and Advocacy.

Siegel, J. M., Aneshensel, C. S., Taub, B., Cantwell, D. P., & Driscoll, A. K. (1998). Adolescent depressed mood in a multiethnic sample. *Journal of Youth and Adolescence, 27,* 413–427.

Silverman, A. B., Reinherz, H. Z., & Giaconia, R. M. (1996). The long-term sequelae of child and adolescent abuse: A longitudinal community study. *Child Abuse and Neglect, 20,* 709–723.

Spearly, J., & Lauderdale, M. (1983). Community characteristics and ethnicity in the prediction of child maltreatment rates. *Child Abuse and Neglect, 7*, 91–105.

Spirito, A., Bond. A., Kurkjian, J., Devost, L., Bosworth, T., & Brown, L. K. (1993). Gender differences among adolescent suicide attempters. *Crisis, 14*, 178–184.

Steiner, H., & Lock, L. (1998). Anorexia nervosa and bulimia nervosa in children and adolescents: A review of the past 10 years. *Journal of the American Academy of Child and Adolescent Psychiatry, 37*, 352–359.

Stice, E., & Agras. W. S. (1998). Predicting onset and cessation of bulimic behaviors during adolescence: A longitudinal grouping analysis. *Behavior Therapy, 29*, 257–276.

Stroul, B., & Friedman, R. (1986). A system of care for severely emotionally disturbed children and youth. Washington, DC: CASSP Technical Assistance Center, Georgetown University.

Surgeon General. (1999). *Mental health: A report from the surgeon general.* Washington, DC: DHHS.

Surgeon General. (2000). *Report of the surgeon general's conference on children's mental health: A national action agenda.* Washington, DC: DHHS.

Tiet, Q. Q., Bird, H. R., Hoven, C. W., Moore, R., Wu, P., Wicks, J., Jensen, P. S., Goodman, S., & Cohen. (2001). Relationship between specific adverse life events and psychiatric disorders. *Journal of Abnormal Child Psychology, 29*, 153–164.

Urban Institute. (2003). *Addressing the needs of youth with disabilities in the juvenile justice system. The current state of knowledge.* Retrieved on July 22, 2004, from http://www. urban. org/UploadedPDF/410885_youth_with_disabilities.pdf

U.S. Department of Education, Office of Special Education Programs. (1994). *National agenda for achieving better results for children and youth with serious emotional disturbances.* Washington, DC: Department of Education.

Vance, J. E., Bowen, N. K., Fernandez, G., & Thompson, S. (2002). Risk and protective factors as predictors of outcome in adolescents with psychiatric disorder and aggression. *Journal of the American Academy of Child & Adolescent Psychiatry, 41*, 36–43.

Vinson, N. B., Brannan, A. M., Baughman, L. N., Wilce, M., & Gawron, T. (2001). The system-of-care model: Implementation in twenty-seven communities. *Journal of Emotional and Behavioral Disorders, 9*, 30–42.

Werner, E. E., & Smith, R. S. (1992). *Overcoming the odds: High risk children from birth to adulthood.* Ithaca, NY: Cornell University Press.

Wickramaratne, P. J., & Weissman, M. M. (1998). Onset of psychopathology in offspring by developmental phase and parental depression. *Journal of the American Academy of Child and Adolescent Psychiatry, 37*, 933–942.

Wolfe, D. A., Sas, L., & Wekerle, C. (1994). Factors associated with the development of posttraumatic stress disorder among child victims of sexual abuse. *Child Abuse and Neglect, 18*, 37–50.

Zahn-Waxler, C., Iannotti, R., Cummings, E. M., & Denham, S. (1990). Antecedents of problem behaviors in children of depressed mothers. *Development and Psychopathology, 2*, 271–291.

Web-Based Resources

Bazelon Center for Mental Health and Law http://www.bazelon.org/

National Alliance for the Mentally Ill http://www.nami.org/Hometemplate.cfm

National Institute of Mental Health http://www.nimh.nih.gov/

National Mental Health Association http://www.nmha.org/

U.S. Substance Abuse and Mental Health Services Administration http://www
.mentalhealth.samhsa.gov/

5

Health Policy for Children and Youth

Kathleen A. Rounds

Thomas C. Ormsby

Purpose and Overview of Health Policies for Children and Youth

The primary purpose of policies aimed at children and youth is to provide access to preventive and medical care. Access to care is defined as the ability to obtain needed care: Lack of access to care is an indication of unmet health care needs of children and youth (Shi & Singh, 2001). Access to health care includes a number of dimensions: availability (Does the service exist?); cultural acceptability (Is there a fit between the cultural belief system and language of the client and the provider?); accessibility (Does the client have transportation to the service, and can the client access the service at a convenient time?); and affordability (Can the client pay for the service, or does the client have private or public insurance to cover the cost? [Anderson, 1995; Donabedian, 1973]).

The U.S. health care environment is distinguished from health care systems in other industrialized nations by three critical features. First and foremost, the United States is the only country in the Western world that does not have universal health care coverage for its children and adolescents

(Stein, 1997). Second, the health care delivery system is a heavily privatized delivery system financed by public dollars. Federal, state, and local dollars constitute approximately 40 percent of all health care expenditures (Barr, Lee, & Benjamin, 2003). The system is an amalgam of private and government sources that operates in a market-oriented, commodity-oriented economy where many of the key players are driven by a profit motive (Halfon & Hochstein, 1997; Shi & Singh, 2001). Finally, for the most part, U.S. health care is a poorly coordinated system that is primarily characterized by "fragmentation" (Shortell, Gillies, Anderson, Erickson, & Mitchell, 2000).

Halfon and Hochstein (1997) pose two major policy questions regarding the delivery of health care for children and youth. They refer to the first question as the "insurance question," which focuses on expanding access to health insurance for children and youth as well as elimination of other nonfinancial barriers to access (e.g., outreach and transportation). Halfon and Hochstein label the second question the "systems question." This question asks how health care services could be organized and integrated with other systems that serve children and youth to more effectively meet their needs.

Federal health care policies affect all children, youth, and their families. However, these policies more dramatically affect low-income families and their children, who are disproportionately African American, Latino, or members of other ethnic minority groups. According to the Kaiser Commission on Medicaid and the Uninsured, "The gaps in our nation's health coverage system fall at the doorstep of low-income families" (Williams et al., 2004). These families are more likely to have children with health problems (Starfield, 1997), and they are less likely to have health insurance.

Because of special vulnerabilities, some federal health care policies are specifically directed at infants, very young children, or adolescents. For example, eligibility for public health insurance programs, such as Medicaid, has been expanded to include more infants and young children, based on the recognition that these early years are important for preventive care (i.e., well-baby checkups and immunizations) as well as early screening for developmental and health problems. Adolescents are another developmentally vulnerable group because they are more likely to engage in high-risk behaviors, such as unprotected sex and substance use, which have long-term health consequences. It is during early adolescence that most youths develop health behaviors that will last into adulthood (Green & Palfrey, 2000; Greydanus, Patel, & Greydanus, 2003; Knopf & Gordon, 1997).

Federal health policy also targets children who fall under the definition of "children with special health care needs" (CSHCN), that is, "children who have, or are at increased risk for, chronic physical, developmental, behavioral, or emotional conditions and who also require health and related services of a type or amount beyond that required by children generally" (Maternal and Child Health Bureau, 2000a; McPherson et al., 1998). Based on this definition, children with special health care needs comprise 15 percent to 20 percent of the population under 18 years of age (Newacheck & Halfon, 1998). Furthermore, other researchers estimate that about one out of every seven children living in the United States has a chronic health condition or disability. This estimate does not include the "at risk category" included in the definition used by the federal Maternal and Child Health Bureau (Stein & Silver, 1999).

In this chapter, we review the prevalence of four health problems—low birth weight (LBW), asthma, obesity, and sexually transmitted infections— experienced by children and youth, and we identify the risk and protective factors associated with these health problems. We summarize the historical development of child health policy and examine ways in which child health policy has been based on risk and protective factors. Using a case example, we discuss strategies to integrate health care with other service systems that serve children and youth.

Risk and Protective Factors for Health Problems in Childhood and Adolescence

Infants, children, and adolescents in the United States experience a wide range of health problems. LBW, asthma, obesity, and sexually transmitted infections are widespread and affect many children. In this chapter, we focus on the prevalence of these health problems; health disparities associated with race, ethnicity, and socioeconomic status; and risk factors across multiple system levels. (See Table 5.1 for prevalence data on LBW, asthma, overweight, and obesity.) This section concludes with a discussion of protective factors related to access to health care services.

Low Birth Weight

In 2002, 7.8 percent of live births in the United States were LBW infants (LBW—less than 2,500 grams, or 5 pounds, 8 ounces), the highest level in more than 30 years (Centers for Disease Control and Prevention [CDC], 2004c). In the same year, 1.46 percent of live births were very low birth weight (VLBW—less than 1,500 grams) (CDC, 2004c). LBW infants are at increased risk for many problems, including neonatal mortality, neurodevelopmental disorders (Jaffee & Perloff, 2003), and delayed social development (Hediger,

Table 5.1   Estimated Prevalence of Health Conditions Among Children
and Adolescents in the United States

	U.S. Population (all races)	African American (not Hispanic or Latino)	Latino or Hispanic	White (not Hispanic or Latino)
Low Birth Weight				
2001—Percent of Live Births < 2,500 grams	7.68%	13.07%	6.47%	6.76%
2001—Percent of Live Births < 1,500 grams	1.44%	3.08%	1.14%	1.17%
Overweight				
1999–2000— Percent Overweight[a] Children 6–11 years	15.3%	N/A	N/A	N/A
Boys	16.0%	17.6%	(Mexican only) 27.3%	11.9%[b]
Girls	14.5%	22.1%	(Mexican only) 19.6%	12.0%[b]
Adolescents 12–19 years	15.5%	N/A	N/A	N/A
Boys	15.5%	20.5%	(Mexican only) 27.5%	13.0%
Girls	15.5%	25%	(Mexican only) 19.4%	12.2%
2002—Asthma < age 18				
Percent ever told had asthma	12.2%	17.7%	10.3%	11.4%
Percent had asthma attack in past 12 months	5.8%	8.6%	4.4%	5.5%

a. Overweight is defined as BMI at or above the sex- and age-specific 95th percentile BMI cutoff points from the 2000 CDC growth charts.

b. These data are considered unreliable and have a relative standard error of 20% to 30%. The standard error calculations for white boys and white girls aged 6 to 11 are 3.0 and 3.6, respectively.

Overpeck, Ruan, & Troendle, 2002). Compared with normal-birth-weight infants, LBW infants face a greater than fivefold increase in risk of death during the first year, and VLBW infants incur a 100-fold increase of death in the first year (CDC, 2004c).

Racial and ethnic disparities in the incidence of LBW and VLBW infants present a serious public health issue in the United States. The rate of LBW live births among non-Hispanic African American mothers in 2002 (13.4 percent) was approximately twice that of both non-Hispanic white mothers (6.9 percent) and Latino mothers (6.5 percent) (CDC, 2004c). Non-Hispanic African American mothers were also more than twice as likely to have a VLBW live birth than Latino mothers (3.15 percent and 1.17 percent, respectively) (CDC, 2004c). Jaffee and Perloff (2003) suggest that racial/ ethnic disparities in the occurrence of LBW may be attributable to the inequality of living conditions. In a study of 158,174 singleton births in New York City, Rauh, Andrews, and Garfinkel (2001) found that African American women were more likely than white women to receive Medicaid, report substance use during pregnancy, be unmarried at time of birth, and report less years of formal education.

Genetic, lifestyle, and environmental factors may have a significant impact on birth weight outcomes. According to Jaffee and Perloff (2003), risk factors for LBW include smoking during pregnancy, drug use, limited or late utilization of prenatal care, and number of previous births. In the decades since Simpson's report (1957) on the impact of smoking on birth outcomes, maternal smoking during pregnancy has been well established as a major risk factor for LBW. According to Kramer (1987), maternal smoking is the most significant risk factor for LBW in developed countries. In 2001, 11.9 percent of U.S. mothers who smoked during pregnancy had a LBW newborn, compared with 7.3 percent of nonsmoking mothers (CDC, 2004c). Jaakola and Gissler (2004) found a 250-gram average reduction in birth weight of infants among mothers who smoked more than 10 cigarettes daily, as compared with nonsmoking mothers.

Early adolescent childbearing (maternal age 15 and under) has been noted as a significant risk factor for VLBW. In a 1995 study of U.S. singleton first births, Phipps and Sowers (2002) found that the rate of VLBW among very young mothers (age 15 and under) was 24 per 1,000 live births, compared with a rate of 15 per 1,000 live births for 16- to 19-year-old mothers, and 12 per 1,000 live births among mothers who were 20 to 23 years old. Additional findings from Phipps and Sowers revealed that mothers age 15 and under had higher rates of inadequate prenatal care—a well-known risk factor for LBW. Although early adolescent childbirth occurs across the socioeconomic spectrum, Koniak-Griffin and Turner-Pluta (2001) argue that its incidence is much higher among ethnic minority and impoverished young women. They note that the poverty faced by many young women contributes to their late entry into prenatal care and, through poor nutrition, to their increased incidence of medical complications (Koniak-Griffin & Turner-Pluta). One factor that may contribute to the increased prevalence of LBW among adolescent mothers is that, because of the normal adolescent growth period, there is maternal–fetal competition for nutrients within the mother's body (Koniak-Griffin & Turner-Pluta). This competition may be exacerbated in resource-limited households and communities where nutritional foods may be less available or cost-prohibitive.

In recent years, the United States has experienced a significant rise in the rate of multiple births, due, in part, to the increased use of fertility drugs and procedures. Between 1981 and 1997 in the United States, there was a 39 percent increase in the twin birth rate and an astounding 358 percent increase in the triplet birth rate (Blondel et al., 2002). Such increases in multiple births, particularly twin births, have had a significant impact on raising the incidence rate of LBW in the United States (Blondel et al., 2002).

Childhood Asthma

Asthma is the most common chronic illness and the most prevalent cause of disability among children in the United States (Newacheck & Halfon, 1998). Between 1980 and 1996, the prevalence of childhood asthma increased from 3.2 to 6.2 percent, representing an annual average increase of 4.3 percent (Akimbani & Shoendorf, 2002). In 2002, 9 million U.S. children and adolescents under the age of 18 had been diagnosed with asthma at some point in their lives, representing 12.2 percent of the U.S. population under 18 years of age (CDC, 2004a). Also in 2002, 5.8 percent of U.S. children had experienced an asthma attack in the previous 12 months (CDC, 2004a). According to the CDC (2004b), asthma is the third leading cause of hospitalization among those under age 15, and it annually accounts for 14 million missed school days.

The prevalence of asthma varies by race and ethnicity. Non-Hispanic black children (17.7 percent) were more likely than either non-Hispanic white children (11.4 percent) or Latino children (10.3 percent) to have ever been diagnosed with asthma, and they were more likely to have had an asthma attack in the past 12 months (8.6 percent versus 5.5 percent and 4.4 percent, respectively) (CDC, 2004a). In a recent population-based study of 6,004 children in Los Angeles County, the prevalence of childhood asthma among African American children was 15.8 percent, compared with 7.3 percent among whites and 3.9 percent among Latinos (Simon, Zeng,

Wold, Haddock, & Fielding, 2003). Similar disparities in childhood asthma exist in terms of health outcomes and health care utilization. Compared with white children in 1997 and 1998, African American children were three times more likely to be hospitalized due to asthma, and they were four times more likely to die from asthma (Akimbani & Shoendorf, 2002).

A wide array of risk factors, many related to poverty, increases the risk of children developing asthma. Poverty status and family income have been found to be associated with both previous asthma diagnosis and incidence of asthma attacks (CDC, 2004a). Children living below the federal poverty level were more likely to have been diagnosed with asthma (15.0 percent) than those living between 100 percent and 200 percent of federal poverty guidelines (12.1 percent), as well as those living at or above 200 percent of the federal poverty level (11.7 percent) (CDC, 2004a). In 2002, 11 percent of children in families receiving Temporary Assistance for Needy Families (TANF) had asthma, compared with only 6 percent of children in families who did not receive such benefits (Child Trends Databank, 2004). Children receiving Medicaid (15.8 percent) were much more likely to have been diagnosed with asthma at some point in their lives than were children with private insurance or no insurance (11.1 percent and 9.5 percent, respectively) (CDC, 2004a). The lower prevalence of lifetime asthma diagnosis among uninsured children may be partly attributable to limited access to health care, resulting in a decreased likelihood of diagnosis even if asthma exists. Children living in single-mother-headed households were markedly more likely to have been diagnosed with asthma (16.6 percent) than children living with both a father and a mother (11.0 percent) (CDC, 2004a).

It has been well established that certain environmental conditions may be associated with the development of childhood asthma and that several indoor and outdoor environmental pollutants may exacerbate existing asthma (Woodruff et al., 2004). For example, environmental tobacco smoke (ETS), most commonly from parental smoking in the household, is a risk factor for increasing the likelihood of developing childhood asthma, as well as for exacerbating existing asthma in children (Strachan & Cook, 1998). In addition, dust mite and cockroach allergens have been linked to asthma-related health problems among inner-city children (Bradbury, 1997). A recent study found that children who were exposed to cockroaches at some point in their life incurred a significantly increased risk for developing childhood asthma and that cockroach exposure during infancy was associated with a twofold increase in risk for developing asthma (Salam, Li, Langholz, & Gilliland, 2004). In one study of 476 inner-city children with asthma, children who were both allergic and exposed to cockroaches were hospitalized for asthma more often, had more unscheduled asthma-related medical visits, and missed school more often than asthmatic children without significant cockroach exposure (Rosenstreich et al., 1997).

A wide array of other factors also affects the risk of asthma among children. Findings from recent studies suggest that maternal smoking during pregnancy increases the risk of subsequent childhood asthma (Gilliland, Li, & Peters, 2001; Infante-Rivard, Gautrin, Malo, & Suissa, 1999; Jaakola & Gissler, 2004). Another recent study suggests that there is an association between LBW and childhood asthma (Steffenson et al., 2000). Both early day-care attendance and a history of recurrent ear infections have also been found to be associated with increased risk for childhood asthma (Eldeirawi & Persky, 2004; Salam, Li, Langholz, & Gilliland, 2004). A recent study of almost 3,800 young people aged 7 to 18 years found that obese and overweight children were 50 percent more likely to be diagnosed with new-onset asthma and that new-onset asthma was diagnosed twice as often in overweight and obese boys, compared with normal-weight male counterparts (Gilliland et al., 2003).

Overweight and Obesity Among Children and Adolescents

Overweight has grown to epidemic proportions and is the most common health problem facing children in the United States (Strauss & Pollack, 2001). During 1999 and 2000, 15.3 percent of U.S. children aged 6 to 11 were overweight, as defined by the CDC. The CDC defines overweight as the Body Mass Index (BMI) at or above the sex- and age-specific 95th percentile BMI cutoff points from year 2000 CDC growth charts (CDC, 2004c). Overall, boys 6 to 11 years of age were more likely than girls to be overweight (16.0 percent versus 14.5 percent, respectively). Significant disparities exist between racial and ethnic groups (CDC, 2004c). The overweight prevalence rate in 1999–2000 among Mexican boys aged 6 to 11 was 27.3 percent, compared with 17.6 percent among black, non-Hispanic boys, and 11.9 percent in white, non-Hispanic boys (CDC, 2004c). Among U.S. girls aged 6 to 11, the prevalence of overweight was highest among non-Hispanic black girls (22.1 percent), compared with both Mexican and non-Hispanic white girls (19.6 percent and 12.0 percent, respectively) (CDC, 2004c).

Marked racial and ethnic differences in childhood overweight prevalence are also seen among U.S. adolescents aged 12 to 19 (CDC, 2004c). Among U.S. adolescent males aged 12 to 19 in 1999–2000, 27.5 percent of Latino adolescents of Mexican descent were overweight, a significantly higher percentage than both non-Hispanic African Americans and non-Hispanic whites (20.5 percent and 13.0 percent, respectively) (CDC, 2004c). Among female adolescents in the U.S., non-Hispanic African American females

(25.7 percent) were more likely to be overweight than either Mexican Latinas (19.4 percent) or non-Hispanic whites (12.2. percent) (CDC, 2004c). Between 1986 and 1998, overweight prevalence among white children increased by more than 50 percent and increased by more than 120 percent among African Americans and Latinos (Strauss & Pollack, 2001). One recent study of youth aged 13 to 15 in 15 industrialized countries found that U.S. teens were the most likely to be overweight (Lissau et al., 2004). Obesity among older children has been found to be a significant risk factor for subsequent adult obesity, as has early obesity among children with obese parents (Whitaker, Wright, Pepe, Seidel, & Dietz, 1997).

Studies across disciplines have demonstrated that childhood obesity is caused by an interplay of factors (Gable & Lutz, 2000). Findings from a recent study by Stettler, Zemel, Kumanyika, and Stallings (2002) revealed that a pattern of rapid weight gain in the first 3 months of life was associated with childhood overweight at age 7. Findings from another recent study showed an association between clinically significant behavior problems in normal-weight children and an increased risk of becoming overweight 2 years later (Lumeng, Gannon, Cabral, Frank, & Zuckerman, 2003). Excessive television viewing has been identified as a significant risk factor for childhood overweight. Anderson, Crespo, Bartlett, Cheskin, and Pratt (1998) found that children who viewed television 4 or more hours each day had greater body fat and a greater BMI than children who viewed television less than 2 hours daily. One randomized controlled school-based intervention to reduce television, videotape, and videogame use among elementary school students resulted in statistically significant decreases in body mass index as compared with controls (Robinson, 1999). Gable and Lutz posit that food intake and eating habits depend on food availability in the home and that food availability depends largely on parental income and time availability. Gable and Lutz further argue that time to prepare healthy meals may not be available in dual-worker or single-parent homes and that low-income households may not be able to afford nutritional foods.

Sexually Transmitted Infections Among Adolescents

Sexually transmitted infections (STIs) are a significant health problem facing adolescents in the United States. Compared with older adults, adolescents and young adults are at increased risk for acquiring STIs (CDC, 2003a). Although those aged 15 to 24 represent only 25 percent of the sexually experienced population in the United States, almost half (48 percent) of the estimated 18.9 million new STI cases in 2000 were among young people aged 15 to 24 (Weinstock, Berman, & Cates Jr., 2004). Every year, approximately one in four sexually active teens will contract an STI (Alan Guttmacher Institute [AGI], 1999). Despite a steady decline in the teen pregnancy rate in the United States over the past decade, the United States continues to have one of the highest rates of teen pregnancies among developed nations (AGI, 2002). The connection between unintended teen pregnancies and STI risk is crucial, considering that the risky sexual behaviors that may result in pregnancy also place teens at high risk for sexually transmitted infections.

It is difficult to estimate national STI rates due to state differences in reporting requirements. Currently, chlamydia, gonorrhea, syphilis, HIV, and hepatitis B are the only STIs that every state reports to the CDC (CDC, 2003a, 2004d). The accurate collection of incidence and prevalence data is profoundly inhibited by the wide variation in the quality of surveillance data at local and state levels as well as the lack of standardized state reporting mechanisms for many common STIs, including genital herpes and human papilloma virus (HPV). Disparities in reporting between public and private providers further challenge accurate STI data collection, resulting in the potential underestimation of many STIs diagnosed in the private health sector (Rounds, 2004). Additionally, many STIs can be asymptomatic and remain undetected, further contributing to the underestimation of STI rates among adolescents (Rounds). Lack of access to health care, which poses a significant issue among many adolescents, may also add to the underestimation of STI rates.

Among STIs that are required to be reported by states, chlamydia and gonorrhea are more prevalent, and each can cause serious health consequences if undetected or left untreated, particularly in young women (CDC, n.d.). In 2000, 74 percent of all reported chlamydia infections (that included age data) were among young people aged 15 to 24 (Weinstock et al., 2004). Among women in 2002, the highest age-specific reported prevalence rate of chlamydia was in young women aged 15 to 19, with 2,619 cases per 100,000 females, a significantly higher rate than among male age-mates (CDC, 2003a). According to the CDC (2003b), the year 2002 median state-specific chlamydia rate among young women aged 15 to 24 in selected prenatal clinics was 7.4 percent. Compared with many other STIs, syphilis and hepatitis B are relatively rare among adolescents and young adults in the United States. It is estimated that for the year 2000, there were 21 new syphilis cases and 19 new hepatitis B cases per 100,000 young people aged 15 to 24 (U.S. Census Bureau, 2004; Weinstock et al., 2004).

Sixty percent of reported gonorrhea infections in 2000 were among those aged 15 to 24 years (CDC, 2003a). In 2002, gonorrhea was reported highest among women between the ages of 15 and 24 and among men aged

Table 5.2   Common Risk Factors for Risky Adolescent Sexual Behaviors

	System Level	
Individual Characteristics	*Family Conditions*	*Environmental Conditions*
• Inadequate communication skills • Substance abuse • Depression • Sense of invulnerability • Negative attitudes, beliefs, and intentions about safer sex practices • Inadequate perception of risk • Lack of knowledge about sexuality and safer sex practices • Having been sexually abused • Early puberty • Early initiation of sexual activity • Incomplete cognitive development • Intention to initiate intercourse • Inability to use condoms properly	• Poor parental supervision • Family sexual abuse • Older siblings who are sexually active • Chaotic family life • Family norms that accept early initiation of sexual intercourse and multiple partners • Poor parent–adolescent relationship and communication	• Limited sexuality education (e.g., abstinence-only) • Lack of easy/free condom availability in community • Peer pressure • Community norms that accept early initiation of sexual intercourse and multiple partners • Media that sexualizes women and promotes risky sexual practices • Lack of emphasis on prevention • Environments or activities where alcohol and drugs are used • High-risk environment

20 to 24 (CDC, 2003a). In young women aged 15 to 19, there were 675.6 cases of gonorrhea per 100,000 in 2002, representing a slight decrease from 2001 (CDC, 2003a). Among males aged 15 to 19, the gonorrhea prevalence rate in 2002 was significantly lower at 287.9 cases per 100,000 (CDC, 2003a).

As previously noted, states are not required to report cases of herpes simplex virus (HSV) and human papilloma virus (HPV) to the CDC (CDC, 2003a). Both of these viral infections can be asymptomatic and therefore are frequently transmitted to others by those unaware of their infection. There is little precise information about the prevalence or incidence of either STI among adolescents in the United States, though both are widely prevalent among young people.

The overall U.S. STI rates do not reflect the disproportionate impact of STIs on certain high-risk adolescent populations—for example, youth in the juvenile justice system. The presence of chlamydia. In 2002, the median prevalence rate among adolescent females entering juvenile correction facilities was 16.7 percent (positivity was more than 10 percent in 31 of 32 reporting facilities), compared with 3.2 percent of women entering adult corrections facilities (CDC, 2003a). Among young men entering juvenile correctional facilities in 2002, the median prevalence of chlamydia was 6.0 percent (CDC, 2003a). The median site-specific gonorrhea rate among adolescent females entering 22 juvenile correctional facilities in 2002 was 5.6 percent, compared with 1.7 percent among males entering 25 facilities (CDC, 2003a). One study of adolescents in two juvenile detention facilities found that 22.2 percent of females had chlamydia, compared with 8.7 percent of males (Kelly, Bair, Baillargeon, & German, 2000).

Through the Adolescent Women Reproductive Health Monitoring Project, young women under 20 years of age are screened for STIs in nontraditional settings such as school clinics, juvenile corrections facilities, substance abuse treatment facilities, and organizations serving street youth (CDC, 2003a). In 2002, the median site-specific chlamydia rate in school clinics was 13.2 percent. The median site-specific gonorrhea prevalence rate in school clinics was 4.3 percent in 2002 (CDC, 2003a). Chlamydia has also been found to be highly prevalent (median state-specific positivity was 10.1 percent) among economically disadvantaged young women 16 to 24 years of age in the National Job Training Program, through which an average of 20,000 young women have been screened for chlamydia each year since 1990 (CDC, 2003a).

Human immunodeficiency virus (HIV), the virus that over time leads to acquired immunodeficiency syndrome (AIDS), disproportionately impacts adolescents in the United States. Researchers estimate that half of all new HIV infections in the United States occur among young people aged 15 to 24, of which 15,000 (out of 20,000) acquire the virus through sexual transmission (Rosenberg & Biggar, 1998; Weinstock et al., 2004). In areas with confidential reporting, HIV infections in females aged 13 to 24 have accounted for 47 percent of all HIV cases among women (CDC, 2002a). Young women, young men who have sex with men (MSM), and young African Americans are particularly impacted by HIV/AIDS (CDC, 2002a). In a sample of MSM aged 15 to 22 in seven urban areas, researchers found that 7 percent were living with HIV infection (CDC, 2002a). The rate of HIV infection among young white males in this sample was 3 percent, compared with 14 percent of young African American males (CDC, 2002a). In areas with confidential HIV reporting, 56 percent of all HIV cases ever reported for those aged 13 to 24 have been among African Americans (CDC, 2002a). Between 1981 and 2000, African American adolescent females were 3.7 times more likely to report HIV infection than white adolescent females, and African American adolescent males were 1.7 times more likely to report HIV infection than their white counterparts (Maternal and Child Health Bureau, 2003). The link between HIV and infection with other sexually transmitted diseases is important because individuals with STIs other than HIV are at higher risk than uninfected individuals of becoming infected with HIV when exposed to the virus through sexual contact (CDC, 2004e).

Many biological, developmental, and social factors place sexually active adolescents at higher risk than older adults for STIs. (See Table 5.2 for a summary of risk factors that have been found to be associated with risky adolescent sexual behavior.) Adolescents are more likely than older adults to have unprotected sex and multiple sex partners (either concurrent or sequential), resulting in an increased risk of exposure to an STI-infected partner (CDC, n.d.). According to the Youth Risk Behavior Survey in 2001, only half of all sexually active 12th graders reported using a condom during their last sexual intercourse (CDC, 2002b). One in four sexually active high school seniors reported having used alcohol or other drugs before their last sexual intercourse, and more than one in five self-reported having four or more lifetime sex partners (CDC, 2002b). Young women are at increased risk for STIs because, compared with young men, they have an increased biological susceptibility to many STIs, and they have a greater likelihood of choosing older, more experienced, and therefore potentially exposed sexual partners (CDC, n.d.).

One recent study found that adolescent females who self-reported a history of sexual abuse were more likely to have had consensual sexual intercourse before age 14, to have contracted a STI, and to have had three or more sexual partners in the past 3 months (Buzi et al., 2003). Findings from Raj, Silverman, and Amaro (2000) revealed that both adolescent males and females who report a history of sexual abuse also report increased sexual risk behaviors. Shrier, Harris, and Beardslee (2002) found that both female and male adolescents with higher frequency of depressive symptoms were more likely to have been diagnosed with an STI 1 year later. Shrier et al. posit that depressed individuals may engage in risky sexual behaviors as a way of coping with depressive symptoms. In a study of African American adolescent females, body image dissatisfaction was associated with a greater likelihood of unprotected vaginal intercourse, perceived limited control in sexual relationships, and fear of abandonment as a result of negotiating condom use (Wingood, DiClemente, Harrington, & Davies, 2002). Adolescents may face numerous barriers to high-quality STI prevention and treatment services. Lack of insurance or alternative payment source, lack of youth-friendly services, lack of transportation, and confidentiality concerns can all inhibit adolescents from accessing quality services that address sexual health needs (CDC, 2003a).

Access to Care as a Protective Factor

Although research has clearly identified biological, developmental, lifestyle, and environmental risk factors associated with health problems, research on protective factors has been more limited. In the case of children and youth at risk for poor health outcomes, access to health care is a protective factor. A host of factors that facilitate access to health care may also be seen as providing a protective effect. Health insurance and health care delivery models that make health care accessible (e.g., community-based care, school-based care, convenient hours, support services, perceived confidentiality among adolescents, and culturally competent services) have a major impact on whether or not services are accessible and utilized. Access to health care (i.e., an acceptable provider is available, the individual can get to the provider, and the individual has health insurance to pay for medical care) serves as a protective factor when a child needs medical care (Fraser & Terzian, in press). That is, access to medical treatment may reduce or buffer the effect of the health condition. For example, ongoing medical treatment for asthma reduces the likelihood that a child will experience an acute episode requiring treatment in the emergency room. Access to health care can also serve as a protective factor by interrupting a chain of risk (Fraser & Terzian). For instance, early medical treatment for chlamydia, combined with counseling and education on safe sexual practices may reduce the likelihood that an adolescent girl will develop long-term reproductive-health problems. As a protective factor, access to care can also prevent or block the onset of a risk factor (Fraser & Terzian). One example of this aspect of the protective factor is found in the case of a mother of a young child who has access to ongoing preventive health services that may prevent her child from becoming at risk for obesity.

Access to health services, or the lack thereof, is closely related to the discussion of poverty-related risk factors identified for each of the previously discussed childhood and adolescent health problems. Ford, Bearman, and Moody (1999) found that older adolescents, racial/ethnic minorities, sexually active youth, uninsured youth, and those in single-parent homes were more likely to have neglected health care—a significant risk factor for a wide array of health problems. Newacheck, Hughes, Hung, Wong, and Stoddard (2000) found that 7.3 percent of children in the United States had at least one unmet health need. In addition, they found that poor and near-poor children had a threefold increase of risk for having an unmet health need.

Availability of health insurance as one component of access to care is a critical protective factor to increase the likelihood that children and adolescents will receive health care. It is estimated that 12 percent of children in the United States had no form of health insurance in 2001 (Annie E. Casey Foundation, 2004). Newacheck, Brindis, Cart, Marchi, and Irwin (1999) found that 14.1 percent of adolescents were uninsured in 1995 and that older adolescents, minorities, those in low-income families, and those in single-parent households were significantly more likely to be uninsured. Additional findings from the same study revealed that adolescents without health insurance, either public or private, were five times more likely to lack a usual health care provider, four times more likely to have unmet health needs, and twice as likely to miss at least annual contact with a health care provider.

Although the absence of insurance coverage is a major factor related to access to health care (Newacheck et al., 1999), health insurance alone may not be enough to ensure that children and adolescents have access to health care services, particularly among those who are low-income (Rosenbach, Irvin, & Coulam, 1999). As previously noted, having a usual source of care may reduce many barriers to health care services, although it does not ensure that such services will be utilized (Rosenbach et al., 1999). Many nonfinancial factors also appear to affect health care accessibility and utilization. These include delivery system structure, provider availability, preventive care education, enabling services (e.g., transportation and translation), child care, and appointment reminders (Newacheck, Hung, Park, Brindis, & Irwin, 2003; Rosenbach et al., 1999).

Risk, Resilience, and Protection in Health Policy for Children and Youth

In this section, we present a brief overview of the development of child health policy from the beginning of the 20th century to the present. We also examine the effectiveness of health policies in meeting the health care needs of children and youth. We conclude by discussing the degree to which policy has been based on risk and protective factors.

Historical Development of Child Health Policy

Child health policy has developed in a piecemeal way, with policy initiatives often having been episodic responses to the failure of the private marketplace (Barr, Lee, & Banjamin, 2003). Although the federal government was involved to some extent in responding to children's health and mental health needs through the establishment of the Children's Bureau in 1912 and then later through the establishment of the Maternal and Child Health service system, it did not become heavily involved in financing health care for children and youth until the establishment of the Medicaid program in 1965. Table 5.3 provides a chronological listing of major policy initiatives and their primary purposes.

At the turn of the 20th century, living conditions were so poor for many American families that the average state infant mortality rate was 150/1,000. In some industrial cities, it was as high as 180/1,000 (Margolis, Cole, & Kotch, 1997). In response to this high infant mortality rate, social workers joined forces with public health workers and advocates from the fields of education, medicine, and labor to lobby for passage of legislation to establish the Children's Bureau in 1912 (Margolis et al., 1997). The Children's Bureau was initially created with a mandate to study the problem of infant mortality and address the problem by disseminating information on promising interventions to the states. Based on the success of the Children's Bureau, Congress passed the Sheppard–Towner Maternity and Infancy Act in 1921, creating the first national maternal and child health program that provided grants-in-aid to states. The Sheppard–Towner Act represented the first federal effort to establish a maternal and child health infrastructure within the states, and it laid the groundwork for future collaboration between state and federal governments to address maternal and child health (Kessel, Jaros, & Harker, 2003; Margolis et al., 1997). During the 8 years the Act was in effect, the number of permanent maternal and child health centers and state child hygiene and welfare programs increased.

The Sheppard–Towner Act was not renewed in 1929, and the Great Depression had a major impact on the ability of states to provide maternal and child health services. These events contributed to an increase in infant mortality across the nation. In response to rising infant mortality rates and the widespread poverty among women and children, Title V of the Social Security Act was passed in 1935. Title V had three parts that were administered under the Children's Bureau: (1) Maternal and Child Health Services

Table 5.3   Chronology of Key Child Health Policy Legislation 1900 to Present

Legislation	Purpose
1912 Children's Bureau Established	Studied and began to address the high rates of infant mortality
1921 Sheppard–Towner Maternity and Infancy Act	Established the first national Maternal and Child Health program, provided grants-in-aid to states to develop local and state maternal and child health infrastructures
1935 Social Security Act, including Title V Maternal and Child Health Program	Title V—Created a coordinated Maternal and Child Health service system based on a federal–state partnership
1965 Title XIX amended the Social Security Act to establish the Medicaid program	Provided health insurance to children and families in poverty
1981 Omnibus Budget Reconciliation Act of 1981 (OBRA '81) Maternal and Child Health Services Block Grant Amendments to Title V	Shifted program planning, control, and accountability for Maternal and Child Health programs from federal to state and local governments
1989 Omnibus Budget Reconciliation Act (OBRA '89)	Established stricter reporting requirements for Title V and supported development of systems of care for Children with Special Health Care Needs (CSHCN); expanded the Early and Periodic, Screening, Diagnosis, and Treatment (EPSDT) program; mandated Medicaid coverage of children younger than 6 years with family income up to 133% of Federal Poverty Level (FPL)
1996 Personal Responsibility Work and Opportunity Reconciliation Act (PRWORA)	Delinked Medicaid eligibility with public assistance
1997 Title XXI (SSA), State Child Health Insurance Program (SCHIP) established	Expanded the health insurance safety net to cover more low-income children who were not eligible for Medicaid and whose families could not afford private insurance

(MCH) enabled states to expand services that had been provided by the Sheppard–Towner Act, (2) Services for Crippled Children's Program (CCS) enabled states to locate and provide medical and other services for children who had "crippling conditions", and (3) Child Welfare Services (CWS) enabled states to provide services to homeless, dependent, and neglected children (Kessel et al., 2003). Title V funding through the Services for Crippled Children's Program was the only source of federal funding for children with special health care needs (the majority of whom needed orthopedic treatment as a result of the polio epidemic) until 1965, when the Medicaid program was established.

Title V has been amended numerous times over the past decades. The Omnibus Budget Reconciliation Act of 1981, P.L. 97–35, consolidated seven Title V categorical programs into a block grant program. The Omnibus Budget Reconciliation Act of 1989 (OBRA '89), P.L. 101–239, introduced stricter requirements for state planning and reporting regarding use of Title V funds. OBRA '89 gave authority to the Maternal and Child Health Bureau to help develop systems of care for children with special health care needs (CSHCN) and their families, and expanded the mission of CSHCN programs to promote the development of community-based systems of services (McPherson et al., 1998). State health departments administer the Title V MCH Services Block Grant Program (Maternal and Child Health Bureau, 2000b). The federal government requires states to conduct a statewide needs assessment every 5 years and to submit a plan for meeting those needs. Title V Block Grant funds are used primarily for service system development to reduce infant mortality and the incidence of disabilities and to provide and ensure access to health care for women of reproductive age, access to preventive and primary care services for children, and access to family-centered, community-based, coordinated care for children with special health care needs.

The Medicaid program was enacted in 1965 as a joint state and federally funded health insurance program for women who were on public assistance and their children and other persons who were elderly, blind, or disabled. Each state administers its own Medicaid program according to federal guidelines. The federal government provides matching funds for some of the state Medicaid costs (on average about 57 percent of costs are matched). In 1967, the Early and Periodic Screening, Diagnosis, and Treatment Program (EPSDT) was created as a unique prevention component of the Medicaid program to ensure that children receiving Medicaid would receive preventive health services in addition to acute and chronic medical care (Sardell & Johnson, 1998). The EPSDT program requires states to offer age-appropriate screenings and immunizations, follow-up diagnostic services, and medical treatment. Because many states never completely implemented their EPSDT program and in order to increase the number of children receiving preventive care, Congress included provisions in the Omnibus Budget Reconciliation Act (OBRA '89) that expanded EPSDT by requiring states to conduct aggressive outreach and case-finding efforts as well as to provide enabling services such as case management, transportation, and translation services (Rosenbach & Gavin, 1998).

During the 1980s and 1990s, the rates of children and youth covered by private health insurance substantially declined. This was due to several factors, including the loss of manufacturing jobs that often offered employees and their families affordable health insurance and a concomitant rise in lower-paying service jobs, which often did not offer employees affordable health insurance. The proportion of workers who were hired in contract or part-time positions, which typically do not carry health insurance benefits for the worker or his or her family, also increased. In addition, during this period the cost of health insurance for employers rose significantly, and many employers changed policies to cover only the employee and not the family (Moniz & Gorin, 2003; Newacheck et al., 1999).

To deal with the loss of private health insurance coverage and the resulting increase in uninsured children and youth, Congress passed a series of Medicaid expansions beginning in the mid-1980s. For example, the Omnibus Budget Reconciliation Act of 1989 (OBRA '89) required states to cover pregnant women and children up to the age of 6 with family incomes that were up to 133 percent of federal poverty guidelines. The early expansions focused solely on infants and young children. Later, the Omnibus Budget Reconciliation Act of 1990 (OBRA '90) mandated coverage of adolescents up to 16 years of age with family incomes of as much as 100 percent of the federal poverty guidelines (Newacheck et al., 1999).

These Medicaid expansions began the "delinking" of Medicaid with public assistance status. This delinking process was finally completed in 1996 with the passage of the Personal Responsibility Work and Opportunity Reconciliation Act (PRWORA) (Moniz & Gorin, 2003). PRWORA separated the determination of eligibility for Medicaid from Temporary Assistance for Needy Families (TANF). Currently, the federal government requires states to provide Medicaid coverage for children up to age 5 in families with incomes of as much as 133 percent of the poverty guidelines and to cover children from the ages of 6 to 18 in families with incomes as much as 100 percent of the poverty guidelines.

The Balanced Budget Act of 1997 created the State Children's Health Insurance Program (SCHIP) to address the large number of uninsured children of low-income working families who were not eligible for Medicaid because their family income exceeded the eligibility criteria. Unlike Medicaid, SCHIP is not an entitlement program. Under federal legislation, states have been given tremendous flexibility to use SCHIP allocations to create separate SCHIP programs, expand their Medicaid programs, or develop a combination of both. States are also allowed to determine eligibility; among the states, eligibility ranges from 133 percent to 350 percent of the federal poverty guidelines. State dollars are matched by federal dollars. States with lower per capita income receive a higher federal match rate. States are also allowed to require monthly premiums or co-payments for participation in their SCHIP programs; but these may not exceed 5 percent of a family's annual income (Gehshan, 2003).

The success of SCHIP has been highly variable and largely dependent upon each state conducting aggressive and effective outreach, enrollment, and renewal efforts. Although Medicaid and SCHIP "constitute a genuine safety net for most low-income children," there are still close to 8.5 million children who are uninsured, and it is estimated that more than half of these are eligible for Medicaid or SCHIP (Families USA, 2004). Because of barriers to enrollment and renewal, many eligible children are currently not enrolled. In addition, because of constraints on state budgets, outreach efforts have been reduced in many states, and some states have frozen enrollment in their SCHIP programs (Families USA). According to some reports, Medicaid and SCHIP "if implemented effectively—by aggressively enrolling all eligible children, eliminating barriers to coverage for immigrant children, and modestly expanding coverage to more low-income families" could provide coverage to all children in families with incomes under 200 percent of federal poverty guidelines in the United States (Baron, Kleinmann, & Sylvester, 2003).

The Degree to Which Policy Has Been Based on Risk and Protective Factors

As stated earlier in this chapter, for many children and youth, access to care serves as a protective factor in the face of health risk. Federal health policy has primarily attempted to address risk factors associated with poor health outcomes by increasing access to preventive and medical care services. Federal health policy has attempted to increase access in two ways: (1) through the creation of public health insurance programs for low-income children (first through Medicaid and then through SCHIP), and (2) through supporting infrastructure development to ensure that services are delivered in a coordinated and accessible manner (primarily through Title V of the Social Security Act).

Protective Role of Health Insurance

Numerous studies have demonstrated the key role that health insurance plays in increasing access to health care for children and youth (Newacheck et al., 1999; Newacheck, Pearl, Hughes, & Halfon, 1998). Beginning in the 1980s, with the expansion of eligibility for Medicaid and extending through the implementation of the SCHIP program, the federal insurance safety net has covered an increasing percentage of low-income children. However, many children still remain uninsured. In 2002, more than half of the 8 million children who were uninsured were eligible for either Medicaid coverage or SCHIP (Institute of Medicine, 2002).

Some policymakers and researchers argue that the most effective way to ensure that children have health insurance coverage and receive needed care is to approach insurance coverage at the family level as opposed to the individual level. In the Institute of Medicine's *Health Insurance Is a Family Matter* (2002) experts posit that the health of the parents affects children's health, well-being, and opportunities in later life and that the insurance status of parents influences the use of health services by their children. The federal government has yet to take a family approach to providing public health insurance.

Concept of a "Medical Home"

Although public insurance programs such as Medicaid and SCHIP have provided an important health insurance safety net for children and youth, insurance coverage alone is not sufficient for ensuring access to health services (Dubay & Kenney, 2001; Newacheck et al., 2003; Rosenbach et al., 1999). Coordinated systems of care also need to be in place to respond to health care needs of children and youth. Federal policymakers have addressed systems issues primarily through programs funded by Title V of the Social Security Act. For example, one of the hallmarks of coordinated care is to ensure that children have continuous access to routine health care and that medical services are integrated with other child/youth services. The American Academy of Pediatrics and other advocacy groups have worked closely with the Maternal and Child Health Bureau to implement the "medical home" concept for all children, especially children with special health care needs (American Academy of Pediatrics, 2002). Although the term *medical home* was originally defined as a place, it has evolved to define a partnership with families to ensure that children and youth are receiving care that is "accessible, family centered, coordinated, comprehensive, continuous, compassionate, and culturally effective" (Sia, Tonniges, Osterhus, & Taba,

2004). Examining data from the National Survey of Children with Special Health Care Needs, investigators found that when children have a medical home, they experience significantly less delay in seeking care, fewer unmet health care needs, and fewer unmet needs for family support services (Strickland et al., 2004). One of the child health objectives in *Healthy People 2010* is to "increase the proportion of children with special health care needs who have access to a medical home" (U.S. Department of Health and Human Services, n.d.). The Head Start program and the MCHB Title V Block Grant program require that states report on how and to what degree they are achieving this objective.

Another systems approach to increasing access to health care for children and youth is to deliver health care where a majority of children spend a large portion of their day. Policy initiatives to support the development and ongoing operation of school-based and school-linked health centers reflect this approach. Delivering integrated services through school-based health centers will be discussed in the next section on service integration.

The Case of "Abstinence Only" Versus More Comprehensive Programs

One area of controversy regarding how well federal health policy has been informed by risk and protective factors is that of adolescent sexual health. Comprehensive sexual health education can serve as a protective factor by providing youth with the knowledge and skills necessary to make healthy decisions about sexual behavior. In fiscal year 2002, $102 million in federal funds were allocated for abstinence-only education, yet there was no federal program that supported comprehensive sex education to teach young people about both abstinence and contraception (AGI, 2002). Federal law requires that abstinence-only sexuality education teach that sexual activity outside of marriage is wrong and harmful for everyone, irrespective of age (AGI, 2002). This mandate restricts educators from providing information on contraceptive methods, with the exception of emphasizing their ineffectiveness (AGI, 2002). Perhaps most disturbing is that after years of evaluation of abstinence-only programs, no credible evidence has shown that such restrictive education delays adolescent sexual activity (AGI, 2002). However, empirical evidence does suggest that abstinence-only models may reduce contraceptive use among sexually active young people, thereby increasing their risk for STIs and unplanned pregnancies (AGI, 2002). Furthermore, research has demonstrated that the most effective sexuality education programs are comprehensive in nature, incorporating both abstinence promotion and discussion of safer sex options (Centers for Disease Control and Prevention, 2002a). Abstinence-only policies continue to exist widely despite the fact that more than 75 percent of parents support sexuality education that addresses the use of condoms and other contraceptive methods, sexual orientation, and peer pressure to have sex (AGI, 2002).

Using Knowledge of Risk, Protection, and Resilience to Achieve Service Integration in Health Policy

Meeting the needs of children and youth, especially those involved in multiple service systems, requires policies that promote integration and collaboration among service systems. In this section, we use a case study of an adolescent with multiple problems to illustrate how integrated service systems can best meet the needs of children and youth. We use the school-based health center model as an example of how services can be integrated to respond to the multiple challenges of children and youth. School-based health centers (SBHC) serve as an important safety net for primary care—nearly two thirds of students who have access to SBHCs are ethnic minorities and a substantial proportion of schools are in low-income communities (American Academy of Pediatrics Committee on School Health, 2001). These centers have been successful at integrating health and mental health care with educational services because services are delivered where the majority of children and youth spend a large portion of their day. For adolescents in particular, who are more likely to use health care services on a "spontaneous basis" (Pastore & Techow, 2004, p.195), school-based health centers offer location, convenience, confidentiality, and trust—all factors associated with the utilization of health and mental health services by adolescents (Brandis et al., 2003).

Background and Current Status of School-Based Health Centers

During the 1970s, several communities established school-based health clinics to serve low-income children. The Robert Wood Johnson Foundation (RWJ) joined these efforts in 1978 by underwriting a 5-year School Health Services Program that put nurse practitioners in elementary schools serving 150,000 students in Colorado, New York, North Dakota, and Utah. In response to a national concern over the deteriorating health status of children and adolescents, RWJ launched the Community Care Funding Partners Program in 1981. Five of the eight cities in this program located community health centers in secondary schools. Based on the success of this program, in 1986, RWJ launched the School-Based Adolescent Health Care Program to evaluate whether or not school-based health centers could be sustained by communities and could effectively deliver comprehensive medical and mental health services to teens. The foundation used strict criteria to fund 24 centers in 14 cities. The criteria emphasized the need for community advisory committees and coalition building among corporations, foundations, schools, and health and welfare agencies (Brodeur, 2000).

Early Findings

A 1993 evaluation of the School-Based Adolescent Health Care Program found that, although the program had little effect on decreasing high-risk behavior, the centers had increased access to care for students (especially low-income students) who had previously not received care. More than half of the students who were enrolled in the participating schools were receiving care from the centers. Another critical issue revealed in the evaluation was that the centers had not been sufficiently successful in obtaining reimbursement from third-party insurers, including Medicaid.

Through the early 1990s local health departments, private foundations, and the Maternal and Child Health Bureau funded school-based health centers. Because of limited funding to support the development of centers, the RWJ initiated "Making the Grade: State and Local Partnerships to Establish School-Based Health Centers." The goal of this initiative was to reorganize state and local funding policies to support comprehensive health care for children and adolescents as well as to improve administrative procedures enabling school-based health centers to receive reimbursements through Medicaid (Brodeurk, 2000).

Recent Findings

Two recent national reports on school-based health centers indicate that the centers are no longer in a demonstration phase, the number of centers has been growing, and the centers are an effective model for health and mental health care delivery to children and youth (Juszczak, Schlitt, & Odlum, 2003; Schlitt et al., 2000; The Center for Health and Health Care in Schools, 2002). The summary of the results from the national survey conducted by the National Assembly on School-Based Health Care, *Creating Access to Care for Children and Youth: School-Based Health Center Census 1998–1999* (Schlitt et al.,) reported that there are 1,135 centers located in 45 states (51 percent of the centers are located in schools with high school grades). Hospitals, local health departments, and community health centers represent 73 percent of sponsors. Approximately 70 percent of the centers provide mental health services. More than one-half of the centers have opened within the past 4 years, and 70 percent of these centers opened in elementary or middle schools. Once primarily located only in urban areas, school-based health centers have expanded to suburban and rural schools (Juszczak et al., 2003).

Providing Concurrent Health and Mental Health Care Through School-Based Clinics

According to the National Assembly report, nearly all SBHCs offer the following: comprehensive health assessments (90 percent), minor acute illness care (96 percent), psychosocial assessments (80 percent), crisis intervention (79 percent), and brief therapy for mental health problems (67 percent). Approximately 70 percent also offer substance abuse counseling and case management, evaluation, and treatment for mental health problems. In the secondary school centers, 56 percent provide gynecological exams and 60 percent provide diagnosis and treatment of STIs (Juszczak et al., 2003). Other studies have shown that SBHCs are an important secondary access point for teens, especially with regard to behavioral health care services. In Kaplan's 3-year study conducted in Denver, researchers found that teens who were enrolled both in a SBHC and in a managed-care organization were much more likely to use the SBHC for behavioral health care. Only 3 percent of youth who were enrolled in both used the managed-care organization for behavioral health care (Kaplan, Calonge, & Guernsey, 1998). In an evaluation of a SBHC serving two schools in New York City, Pastore and Techow (2004) concluded that "on-site mental health services and their immediate availability for crisis intervention allow teenagers to engage in individual, family, and group treatment before problems become so severe that they interfere with their education" (Pastore & Techow, p. 194).

The following case study illustrates how an SBHC serves as a protective factor by providing access to care to a youth with several risk factors for poor health and mental health outcomes. Because of their location (where the majority of children and youth spend their day) and their collaborative philosophy and interdisciplinary approach to providing services, SBHCs are well positioned to integrate services for children and youth.

Case Study

James, a 14-year-old African American male, lives with his 31-year-old single mother and 8-year-old sister in a public housing project on the outskirts of town. James's mother works in a local fast-food restaurant and has no health insurance. As a freshman in high school, James is experiencing a great deal of anxiety about fitting in with his classmates, often feels sad, is not sleeping well, and is falling behind in his course work because of his lack of motivation and problems concentrating. Like many of his friends, James is experimenting with alcohol, marijuana, and other drugs, and has recently become sexually active. He had unprotected vaginal sex at a party the previous week, and he has been experiencing a firelike burning during urination for the past 2 days. James is worried that he might have gonorrhea, but he has no idea of where to go for help. He is very uncomfortable and does not want to go to school, yet he feels that there is no way he can let his mom find out about his condition.

James is fortunate in that he attends a school with a school-based health center that offers comprehensive services. On the urging of his best friend, who has had several good experiences at the center, James drops by the center for a visit during lunch. Because his mother signed an enrollment form for the health center when he entered high school, he is able to receive confidential services without the center contacting her. A nurse practitioner sees him initially for assessment and medical treatment of his STI. The social worker also conducts an initial psychosocial assessment and schedules a time to meet with James the next day. She plans to follow up with his concerns about school and his feelings of sadness, and to learn more about his recent drug and alcohol use and sexual behavior. James has given the social worker permission to access his school records and talk with his teachers and school counselor. The social worker will be able to contact other staff at the health center for assistance in evaluating James and providing him with needed services. A psychiatrist provides consultation services to the school-based health center staff and conducts psychiatric evaluations and prescribes and monitors psychiatric medications. In addition, the health center staff provides counseling and conducts groups on a number of health and mental health topics, such as substance abuse, sexual health, and coping with relationships. The health center has recently begun participating in an innovative SCHIP outreach initiative to increase the enrollment of eligible youth. The social worker thinks that James probably meets the eligibility criteria and with James's permission she will contact James's mother to assist her in enrolling both of her children. James's enrollment in the SCHIP program will allow the center to be reimbursed for services as well as help the social worker access additional health and mental health services for James if he needs them.

Case Study Questions for Discussion

- What would most likely happen to James if a school-based health center did not exist in his school?
- How would he find out how to get care?
- Where would he receive care and when?
- Who would pay for his care?
- How comprehensive would his care likely be?
- What is the likelihood that James would be assessed and treated for any other conditions or problems than his presenting symptoms (i.e., burning on urination)?

Summary

In this chapter we have reviewed risk factors for several major health problems (LBW, asthma, overweight and obesity, and sexually transmitted infections) experienced by children and youth. Although there are risk factors that are unique to each of these health problems, two major risk factors are common across health problems. These are poverty and living in socially and physically unhealthy environments (Fraser, 2004; Moniz & Gorin, 2003). Access to care, which includes both access to health insurance and to coordinated systems of care, plays a major role in decreasing the risk for poor health outcomes and protecting children and youth from developing health problems.

U.S. health care policy has increased children's access to health services through the creation of public health insurance programs (e.g., Medicaid and SCHIP). Through Title V of the Social Security Act and other initiatives, the federal government has supported the development of a more coordinated and comprehensive service system. The concepts of the "medical home" and SBHCs are recent examples of efforts at coordination and integration. SBHCs are a promising example of integration of health, mental health, and educational services provided in a location that is accessible to children and youth enrolled in schools. However, attempts to fully integrate services for children and youth across major service systems (health, mental health, education, child welfare, and juvenile justice) are still in their infancy and much remains to be accomplished. Furthermore, federal policy has had very limited success in reducing the number of children living in poverty or near poverty or ensuring that children and youth live in healthy environments. To truly make a significant difference in the health of children and youth, federal policy cannot be constrained to the mere creation of coordinated systems of care, though this would be a substantial achievement. It must address also the poverty and social inequities associated with poor health and well-being.

Questions for Discussion

1. Unlike any other industrialized nation, the United States does not have universal health coverage for its children and youth. Why is this?

2. Given the success of school-based health clinics in integrating service systems for children and youth, why has their establishment not been more widespread?

3. What other service delivery models are you aware of that integrate service systems, including health care for children and youth? What policies need to be in place for these service delivery models to be created?

Additional Reading

Alan Guttmacher Institute. (1999). *Facts in brief: Teen sex and pregnancy*. http://www.agi-usa.org/pubs/fb_teen_sex.html

American Academy of Pediatrics Committee on School Health. (2001). School health centers and other integrated school health services. *Pediatrics, 107*, 198–201.

Baron, J., Kleinmann, J. H., & Sylvester, K. (2003). Health insurance for children: Issues and ideas. *The Future of Children, 13*, 1–32.

Green, M., & Palfrey, J. S. (Eds.). (2000). *Bright futures: Guidelines for health supervision of infants, children, and adolescents* (2nd ed.). Arlington, VA: National Center for Education in Maternal and Child Health.

Institute of Medicine. (2002). *Health insurance is a family matter*. Washington, DC: The National Academies Press.

Newacheck, P. W., Hughes, D. C., Hung, Y. Y., Wong, S., & Stoddard, J. J. (2000). The unmet health needs of America's children. *Pediatrics, 105*, 989–997.

Rounds, K. A. (2004). Preventing sexually transmitted infections among adolescents. In M. W. Fraser (Ed.), *Risk and resilience in childhood: An ecological perspective* (2nd ed., pp. 251–280). Washington, DC: NASW.

References

Akimbani, L. J., & Shoendorf, K. C. (2002). Trends in childhood asthma: Prevalence, health care utilization, and mortality. *Pediatrics, 110*, 315–322.

Alan Guttmacher Institute. (1999). *Facts in brief: Teen sex and pregnancy*. Retrieved May 24, 2004, from http://www.agi-usa.org/pubs/fb_teen_sex.html

Alan Guttmacher Institute. (2002). *Facts in brief: Sexuality education*. Retrieved May 24, 2004, from http://www.agi-usa.org/pubs/fb_sex_ed02.pdf

American Academy of Pediatrics. (2002). The medical home. *Pediatrics, 110*, 184–186.

American Academy of Pediatrics Committee on School Health. (2001). School health centers and other integrated school health services. *Pediatrics, 107*, 198–201.

Anderson, R. E., Crespo, C. J., Bartlett, S. J., Cheskin, L. J., & Pratt, M. (1998). Relationship of physical activity and television watching with body weight and level of fatness among children: Results from the third National Health and Nutrition Examination Survey. *Journal of the American Medical Association, 279*, 938–942.

Anderson, R. M. (1995). Revisiting the behavioral model and access to medical care: Does it matter? *Journal of Health and Social Behavior, 36*, 1–10.

Annie E. Casey Foundation. (2004). *Kids count 2004 data book online: Profile for the United States*. Retrieved June 18, 2004, from http://www.aecf.org/cgi-bin/kc.cgi?action=profile&area=United+States

Baron, J., Kleinmann, J. H., & Sylvester, K. (2003). Health insurance for children: Issues and ideas. *The Future of Children, 13,* 1–32.

Barr, D. A., Lee, P. R., & Benjamin, A. E. (2003). Health care and health care policy in a changing world. In H. M. Wallace, G. Green, & K. Jaros (Eds.), *Health and welfare for families in the 21st century* (2nd ed., pp. 26–42). Boston: Jones and Bartlett.

Blondel, B., Kogan, M. D., Alexander, G. R., Dattani, N., Kramer, M. S., Macfarlane, A., et al. (2002). The impact of increasing number of multiple births on the rates of preterm birth and low birth weight: An international study. *American Journal of Public Health, 92,* 1323–1330.

Bradbury, J. (1997). The culprit may be cockroaches. *Lancet, 349,* 1453.

Brandis, C. D., Klein, J., Schlitt, J., Santelli, J., Juszcak, L., & Nystrom, R. (2003). School-based health centers: Accessibility and accountability. *Journal of Adolescent Health, 32S,* 98–107.

Brodeur, P. (2000). School-based health clinics. In S. L. Isaacs & J. R. Knickman (Eds.), *To improve health and health care: The Robert Wood Johnson Foundation anthology* (pp. 121–149). San Francisco: Jossey-Bass.

Buzi, R. S., Tortolero, S. R., Roberts, R. E., Ross, M. W., Addy, R. C., & Markham, C. M. (2003). The impact of a history of sexual abuse on high-risk sexual behaviors among females attending alternative schools. *Adolescence, 38,* 595–605.

The Center for Health and Health Care in Schools. (2002). *2002 state survey of school-based health center initiatives.* Retrieved June 14, 2004, from http://www.healthinschools.org /sbhcs/survey02.htm

Centers for Disease Control and Prevention. (2002a). *Young people at risk: HIV/AIDS among America's youth.* Retrieved May 24, 2004, from http://www.cdc.gov/hiv/pubs/facts/youth.pdf

Centers for Disease Control and Prevention. (2002b). Trends in sexual risk behaviors among high school students—United States, 1991–2001. *Morbidity and Mortality Weekly Report, 51,* 856–859.

Centers for Disease Control and Prevention. (2003a). *Sexually transmitted disease surveillance, 2002.* Retrieved May 24, 2004, from http://www.cdc.gov/std/stats/toc2002.htm

Centers for Disease Control and Prevention. (2003b). *Sexually transmitted disease surveillance 2002 supplement: Chlamydia prevalence monitoring project annual report – 2002.* Retrieved May 24, 2004, from http://www.cdc.gov/std/chlamydia2002/chlamydia2002.pdf

Centers for Disease Control and Prevention. (2004a). *Summary health statistics for U.S. children: National health interview survey, 2002.* Retrieved May 29, 2004, from http://www.cdc.gov/nchs/data/series/sr_10/sr10_221.pdf

Centers for Disease Control and Prevention. (2004b). *Asthma's impact on children and adolescents.* Retrieved May 24, 2004, from http://www.cdc.gov/asthma/children.htm

Centers for Disease Control and Prevention. (2004c). *Health, United States, 2003.* Retrieved May 24, 2004, from http://www.cdc.gov/nchs/products/pubs/pubd/hus/trendtables.htm

Centers for Disease Control and Prevention. (2004d). *Guidelines for viral hepatitis surveillance and case management.* Retrieved May 24, 2004, from http://www.cdc.gov/ncidod/diseases/hepatitis/resource/surveillance

Centers for Disease Control and Prevention. (2004e). *STD prevention: The role of STD detection and treatment in HIV prevention.* Retrieved June 16, 2004, from http://www.cdc.gov/nchstp/dstd/Fact_Sheets/facts_std_testing_and_treatment.htm

Centers for Disease Control and Prevention. (n.d.). *Tracking the hidden epidemics: Trends in the STD epidemics in the United States.* Retrieved May 24, 2004, from http://www.cdc.gov/nchstp/dstd/Stats_Trends/STD_Trends.pdf

Child Trends Databank. (2004). *Health status and disability: Asthma.* Retrieved May 24, 2004, from http://www.childtrendsdatabank.org/indicators/43Asthma.cfm

Donabedian, A. (1973). *Aspects of medical care administration.* Cambridge, MA: Harvard University Press.

Dubay, L., & Kenney, G. (2001). Health care access and use among low-income children: Who fares best? *Health Affairs, 20,* 112–121.

Eldeirawi, K., & Persky, V. W. (2004). History of ear infections and prevalence of asthma in a national sample of children aged 2 to 11 years: The Third National Health and Nutrition Examination Survey, 1988 to 1994. *Chest, 125,* 1685–1692.

Families USA. (2004). *Working without a net: The health care safety net still leaves millions of low-income workers uninsured.* Retrieved May 24, 2004, from www.famliesusa.org

Ford, C. A., Bearman, P. S., & Moody, J. (1999). Foregone health care among adolescents. *Journal of American Medical Association, 282,* 2227–2234.

Fraser, M. W. (2004). The ecology of childhood: A multisystems perspective. In M. W. Fraser (Ed.), *Risk and resilience in childhood: An ecological perspective* (2nd ed., pp. 1–12). Washington, DC: NASW.

Fraser, M. W., & Terzian, M. A. (in press). Risk and resilience in child development: Practice, principles, and strategies. In G. P. Mallon & P. McCartt Hess (Eds.), *Handbook of children, youth, and family services: Practices, policies, and programs.* New York: Columbia University Press.

Gable, S., & Lutz, S. (2000). Household, parent, and child contributions to childhood obesity. *Family Relations, 49,* 293–300.

Gehshan, S. (2003). The state children's health insurance program: A progress report. In H. M. Wallace, G. Green, & K. Jaros (Eds.), *Health and welfare for families in the 21st century* (2nd ed., pp. 259–268). Boston, MA: Jones and Bartlett.

Gilliland, F. D., Berhane, K., Islam, T., McConnell, R., Gauderman, W. J., Gilliland, S. S., et al. (2003). Obesity and the risk of newly diagnosed asthma in school-age children. *American Journal of Epidemiology, 158,* 406–415.

Gilliland, F. D., Li, Y. F., & Peters, J. M. (2001). Effects of maternal smoking during pregnancy and environmental tobacco smoke on asthma and wheezing in children. *American Journal of Respiratory Critical Care, 163,* 429–436.

Green, M., & Palfrey, J. S. (Eds.). (2000). *Bright futures: Guidelines for health supervision of infants, children, and adolescents* (2nd ed.). Arlington, VA: National Center for Education in Maternal and Child Health.

Greydanus, D. E., Patel, D. R., & Greydanus, E. K. (2003). Adolescent health. In H. M. Wallace, G. Green, & K. Jaros (Eds.), *Health and welfare for families in the 21st century* (2nd ed.). Boston, MA: Jones and Bartlett.

Halfon, N., & Hochstein, M. (1997). Developing a system of care for all: What the needs of vulnerable children tell us. In R. E. K. Stein & P. Brooks (Eds.), *Health care for children: What's right, what's wrong, what's next* (pp. 303–338). New York: United Hospital Fund.

Hediger, M. L., Overpeck, M. D., Ruan, W. J., & Troendle, J. F. (2002). Birthweight and gestational age effects on motor and social development. *Pediatric and Prenatal Epidemiology, 16,* 33–46.

Infante-Rivard, C., Gautrin, D., Malo, J. L., & Suissa, S. (1999). Maternal smoking and childhood asthma. *American Journal of Epidemiology, 150,* 528–531.

Institute of Medicine. (2002). *Health insurance is a family matter.* Washington, DC: The National Academies Press.

Jaakola, J. K., & Gissler, M. (2004). Maternal smoking in pregnancy, fetal development, and childhood asthma. *American Journal of Public Health, 94,* 136–140.

Jaffee, K. D., & Perloff, J. D. (2003). An ecological analysis of racial differences in low birthweight: Implications for maternal and child health social work. *Health and Social Work, 28,* 9–22.

Juszczak, L., Schlitt, J., & Odlum, M. (2003). *School-based health centers: National census school year 2001–2002.* Washington, DC: National Assembly on School-Based Health Care.

Kaplan, D. W., Calonge, B. M., & Guernsey, B. P. (1998). Managed care and school-based health centers. *Archives of Pediatric and Adolescent Medicine, 152,* 25–33.

Kelly, P. J., Bair, R. M., Baillargeon, J., & German, V. (2000). Risk behaviors and the prevalence of *Chlamydia* in a juvenile detention facility. *Clinical Pediatrics, 39,* 521–528.

Kessel, W., Jaros, K., & Harker, P. T. (2003). The Social Security Act and maternal and child health services: Securing a bright future. In H. M. Wallace, G. Green, & K. Jaros (Eds.), *Health and welfare for families in the 21st century* (2nd ed.). (pp. 164–170). Boston, MA: Jones and Bartlett.

Knopf, D., & Gordon, T. E. (1997). Adolescent health. In J. B. Kotch (Ed.), *Maternal and child health: Programs, problems, and policy in public health* (pp. 173–217). Gaithersburg, MD: Aspen Publishers.

Koniak-Griffin, D., & Turner-Pluta, C. (2001). Health risks and psychosocial outcomes of early childbearing: A review of the literature. *Journal of Perinatal and Neonatal Nursing, 15,* 1–17.

Kramer, M. S. (1987). Intrauterine growth and gestational duration determinants. *Pediatrics, 80,* 502–511.

Lissau, I., Overpeck, M. D., Ruan, W. J., Due, P., Holstein, B. E., & Hediger, M. L. (2004). Body mass index and overweight in adolescents in 13 European countries, Israel, and the United States. *Archives of Pediatrics and Adolescent Medicine, 158,* 27–33.

Lumeng, J. C., Gannon, K., Cabral, H. J., Frank, D. A., & Zuckerman, B. (2003). Association between clinically meaningful behavior problems and overweight in children. *Pediatrics, 112,* 1138–1145.

Margolis, L. H., Cole, G. P., & Kotch, J. B. (1997). Historical foundations of maternal and child health. In J. B. Kotch (Ed.), *Maternal and child health: Programs, problems, and policy in public health* (pp. 19–43). Gaithersburg, MD: Aspen Publishers.

Maternal and Child Health Bureau. (2000a). *Fact sheet: Division of services for children with special health care needs.* Retrieved May 23, 2004, from www .mchb.hrsa.gov/about/default.htm

Maternal and Child Health Bureau. (2000b). *Understanding Title V of the Social Security Act.* Retrieved May 24, 2004, from ftp://ftp.hrsa.gov/mchb/titleVtoday/ UnderstandingTitleV.pdf

Maternal and Child Health Bureau. (2003). *Child health USA 2002: Adolescent HIV infection.* Retrieved May 24, 2004, from http://www.mchb.hrsa.gov/ chusa02/main_pages/page_38.htm

Maternal and Child Health Bureau. *Division of Services for Children with Special Health Care Needs (DSCSHCN) Fact Sheet.* Rockville, MD: Maternal and Child Health Bureau, Health Resources and Services Administration, U. S. Department of Health and Human Services. Retrieved July 27, 2005, from ftp://ftp.hrsa.gov/mchb/factsheets/dschsn.pdf

McPherson, M., Arango, P., Fox, H., Lauver, C., McManus, M., Newacheck, P. W., et al. (1998). A new definition of children with special health care needs. *Pediatrics, 102,* 137–140.

Moniz, C., & Gorin, S. (2003). *Health and health care policy: A social work perspective.* Boston: Allyn & Bacon.

Newacheck, P. W., Brindis, C. D., Cart, C. U., Marchi, K., & Irwin Jr., C. E. (1999). Adolescent health insurance coverage: Recent changes and access to care. *Pediatrics, 104,* 195–202.

Newacheck, P. W., & Halfon, N. (1998). Prevalence and impact of disabling chronic conditions in childhood. *American Journal of Public Health, 88,* 610–617.

Newacheck, P. W., Hughes, D. C., Hung, Y. Y., Wong, S., & Stoddard, J. J. (2000). The unmet health needs of America's children. *Pediatrics, 105,* 989–997.

Newacheck, P. W., Hung, Y. Y., Park, M. J., Brindis, C. D., & Irwin, C. E., Jr. (2003). Disparities in adolescent health and health care: Does socioeconomic status matter? *Health Services Research, 38,* 1235–1252.

Newacheck, P. W., Pearl, M., Hughes, D. C., & Halfon, N. (1998). The role of Medicaid in ensuring children's access to care. *Journal of the American Medical Association, 280,* 1789–1793.

Pastore, D., & Techow, B. (2004). Adolescent school-based health care: A description of two sites in their 20th year of service. *The Mount Sinai Journal of Medicine, 71*, 191–196.

Phipps, M. G., & Sowers, M. (2002). Defining early adolescent childbearing. *American Journal of Public Health, 92*, 125–128.

Raj, A., Silverman, J. G., & Amaro, H. (2000). The relationship between sexual abuse and sexual risk among high school students: Findings from the 1997 Massachusetts Youth Risk Behavior Survey. *Maternal and Child Health Journal, 4*, 125–134.

Rauh, V. A., Andrews, H. F., & Garfinkel, R. S. (2001). The contribution of maternal age to racial disparities in birthweight: A multilevel perspective. *American Journal of Public Health, 91*, 1815–1824.

Robinson, T. N. (1999). Reducing children's television viewing to prevent obesity. *Journal of the American Medical Association, 282*, 1561–1567.

Rosenbach, M. L., & Gavin, N. I. (1998). Early and periodic screening, diagnosis, and treatment and managed care. *Annual Review of Public Health, 19*, 507–525.

Rosenbach, M. L., Irvin, C., & Coulam, R. F. (1999). Access for low-income children: Is health insurance enough? *Pediatrics, 103*, 1167–1174.

Rosenberg, P. S., & Biggar, R. J. (1998). Trends and HIV incidence among young adults in the United States. *Journal of the American Medical Association, 279*, 1894–1899.

Rosenstreich, D. L., Eggleston, P., Kattan, M., Baker, D., Slavin, R. G., Gergen, P., et al. (1997). The role of cockroach allergy and exposure to cockroach allergen in causing morbidity among inner-city children with asthma. *The New England Journal of Medicine, 336*, 1356–1363.

Rounds, K. A. (2004). Preventing sexually transmitted infections among adolescents. In M. W. Fraser (Ed.), *Risk and resilience in childhood: An ecological perspective* (2nd ed., pp. 251–280). Washington, DC: NASW.

Salam, M. T., Li, Y. F., Langholz, B., & Gilliland, F. D. (2004). Early-life environmental risk factors for asthma: Findings from the children's health study. *Environmental Health Perspectives, 112*, 760–765.

Sardell, A., & Johnson, K. (1998). The politics of EPSDT policy in the 1990s: Policy entrepreneurs, political streams, and children's health benefits. *The Milbank Quarterly, 76*, 175–205.

Schlitt, J., Santelli, J., Juszcak, L., Brindis, C. D., Nystrom, R., Klein, J., et al. (2000). *Creating access to care: School-based health center census 1998–1999.* Washington, DC: National Assembly on School-Based Health Care.

Shi, L., & Singh, D. (2001). *Delivering health care in America: A systems approach* (2nd ed.). Gaithersburg, MD: Aspen Publishers.

Shortell, S. M., Gillies, R. R., Anderson, D. A., Erickson, K. M., & Mitchell, J. B. (2000). *Remaking health care in America: The evolution of organized delivery systems* (2nd ed.). San Francisco: Jossey-Bass.

Shrier, L. A., Harris, S. K., & Beardslee, W. R. (2002). Temporal associations between depressive symptoms and self-reported sexually transmitted disease among adolescents. *Archives of Pediatrics and Adolescent Medicine, 156,* 599–606.

Sia, C., Tonniges, T. F., Osterhus, E., & Taba, S. (2004). History of the medical home concept. *Pediatrics, 113*(5), 1473–1478.

Simon, P. A., Zeng, Z., Wold, C. M., Haddock, W., & Fielding, J. E. (2003). Prevalence of childhood asthma and associated morbidity in Los Angeles County: Impacts of race/ethnicity and income. *Journal of Asthma, 40,* 535–543.

Simpson, W. J. (1957). A preliminary report on cigarette smoking and the incidence of prematurity. *American Journal of Obstetrics and Gynecology, 73,* 808–815.

Starfield, B. (1997). Social, economic, and medical care determinants of children's health. In R. E. K. Stein & P. Brooks (Eds.), *Health care for children: What's right, what's wrong, what's next?* (pp. 39–52). New York: United Hospital Fund of New York.

Steffenson, F. H., Sorenson, H. T., Gillman, M. W., Rothman, K. J., Sabroe, S., Fischer, P., et al. (2000). Low birth weight and preterm delivery as risk factors for asthma and atopic dermatitis in young adult males. *Epidemiology, 11,* 185–188.

Stein, R. E. K. (1997). Changing the lens: Why focus on children's health? In R. E. K. Stein & P. Brooks (Eds.), *Health care for children: What's right, what's wrong, what's next?* (pp. 1–12). New York: United Hospital Fund of New York.

Stein, R. E. K., & Silver, E. J. (1999). Operationalizing a conceptually based noncategorical definition: A first look at US children with chronic conditions. *Archives of Pediatric Adolescent Medicine, 153,* 68–74.

Stettler, N., Zemel, B. S., Kumanyika, S., & Stallings, V. A. (2002). Infant weight gain and childhood overweight status in a multicenter, cohort study. *Pediatrics, 109,* 194–199.

Strachan, D., & Cook, D. (1998). Health effects of passive smoking: Parental smoking and childhood asthma: Longitudinal and case-control studies. *Thorax, 53,* 204–212.

Strauss, R. S., & Pollack, H. A. (2001). Epidemic increase in childhood overweight. *Journal of the American Medical Association, 286,* 2845–2848.

Strickland, B., McPherson, M., Weissman, G., van Dyck, P., Huang, Z. J., & Newacheck, P. (2004). Access to the medical home: Results of the National Survey of Children With Special Health Care Needs. *Pediatrics, 113,* 1485–1492.

U.S. Census Bureau. (2004). *Annual estimates of the population by sex and five-year age groups for the United States: April 1, 2000 to July 1, 2003.* Retrieved June 22, 2004, from http://eire.census.gov/popest/data/national/tables/nc-est2003–01.pdf

U.S. Department of Health and Human Services. (n.d.). *Healthy people 2010.* Retrieved July 20, 2004, from http://www.healthypeople.gov/document/html/objectives/16–22htm

Weinstock, H., Berman, S., & Cates Jr., W. (2004). Sexually transmitted diseases among American youth: Incidence and prevalence estimates, 2000. *Perspectives on Sexual and Reproductive Health, 36,* 6–10.

Whitaker, R. C., Wright, J. A., Pepe, M. S., Seidel, K. D., & Dietz, W. H. (1997). Predicting obesity in young adulthood from childhood and parental obesity. *New England Journal of Medicine, 337,* 869–873.

Williams, C., AZA Consulting, Rosen, J., Hudman, J., O'Malley, M., & The Kaiser Commission on Medicaid and the Uninsured. (2004). *Challenges and tradeoffs in low-income family budgets: Implications for health coverage:* The Henry J. Kaiser Family Foundation.

Wingood, G. M., DiClemente, R. J., Harrington, K., & Davies, S. L. (2002). Body image and African American females' sexual health. *Journal of Women's Health and Gender-Based Medicine, 11,* 433–438.

Woodruff, T. J., Axelrad, D. A., Kyle, A. D., Nweke, O., Miller, G. G., & Hurley, B. J. (2004). Trends in environmentally related childhood illnesses. *Pediatrics, 113,* 1133–1140.

Web-Based Resources

Center for Health and Health Care in Schools http://www.healthinschools.org

Centers for Disease Control and Prevention http://www.cdc.gov/

Child Trends DataBank http://www.childtrendsdatabank.org

Families USA http://www.familiesusa.org

The Future of Children, The David and Lucile Packard Foundation http://www.futureofchildren.org

Kaiser Commission on Medicaid and the Uninsured, The Henry J. Kaiser Family Foundation http://www.kff.org/about/kcmu.cfm

March of Dimes http://www.modimes.org/

Maternal and Child Health Bureau http://mchb.hrsa.gov/

Maternal and Child Health Information Resource Center, Maternal and Child Health Bureau http://www.mchb.hrsa.gov/mchirc/

The National Assembly on School Based Health Care http://www.nasbhc.org/

The Robert Wood Johnson Foundation http://www.rwjf.org

6

Policies and Programs for Children and Youth With Disabilities

Susan L. Parish

Alison I. Whisnant

When disability is defined on the basis of functional limitations in mobility, self-care, communication, or learning, children with disabilities represent approximately 12.3 percent of the population of children aged 5 to 17 in the United States (Hogan, Msall, Rogers, & Avery 1997). Based on U.S. Census data, this was approximately 6.55 million children in 2000. In addition, many more children under the age of 5 have impairments.

This prevalence estimate is useful to grasp the magnitude of the disabled child population. However, it is important to recognize most programs for children with disabilities predicate eligibility on a child's diagnosis or disability category, and diagnostic categories may vary over a child's life course. For the youngest children, identified developmental delays may precede a formal diagnosis of a specific condition, which often occurs when children enter school. Certain diagnoses enable children to obtain income transfers and special education services. As young adults transition out of school, a general label of *developmental disabilities* is frequently applied, which facilitates obtaining employment and long-term care services in some states.

Improved prenatal and perinatal care due to medical and technological advances during the latter half of the 20th century has resulted in dramatic improvements in mortality for children born with impairments. Between 1984 and 1998, for example, there was a fourfold reduction in perinatal mortality in high-risk pregnancies (Creasy & Resnik, 1999). These advances translate into increased numbers of children with disabilities living into adolescence and adulthood, and serve to explain the high prevalence of disability among children in recent years.

Children with disabilities typically need a developmentally appropriate sequence of special, interdisciplinary, or generic services; individualized supports; or other forms of assistance that are usually of lifelong duration (Developmental Disabilities Assistance and Bill of Rights Act of 2000). Children with disabilities often need individualized supports to maximize their cognitive, emotional, academic, and physical development. For example, conditions such as autism, sickle cell anemia, cystic fibrosis, or cerebral palsy result in elevated needs for primary and specialty care. These children's special needs also include ancillary and supportive services, such as rehabilitation therapies, environmental adaptations, assistive devices, personal assistance, mental health, home health, or respite care (Perrin, 2002). Ongoing therapies, specialized interventions, and ancillary and supportive services play a pivotal role in allowing children to maximize independence and fully participate in daily activities and community life. Furthermore, ancillary and supportive services such as respite and other family support services enable parents to care for their children at home rather than seeking expensive out-of-home care (Abelson, 1999; Bruns & Burchard, 2000; Curran et al., 2001), which is usually publicly financed.

A wide array of policies governs the services received by children with disabilities and their families. These may be specifically directed at children with disabilities (e.g., special education, disability income transfers) or may be generic and used by other children (e.g., welfare, Medicaid). Policies directed at families have frequently intended to reduce the likelihood they will seek out-of-home placement for their children, and mitigate the physical, emotional, and financial burdens associated with caring for children with disabilities.

Although the overarching goal of these policies is to enhance the development and adaptation of these children and their families, the best characterization of the service system for children with disabilities may be that it is a fragmented one. The system is fragmented because numerous organizations control the delivery of services (e.g., local school districts, state disability determination offices, state or county social service agencies) and because revenues typically come from two or more levels of government: federal, state, and local. This fragmentation poses tremendous burdens for families seeking assistance to meet their child's needs, and for some families the barriers seem insurmountable.

In the subsequent sections of this chapter, we review risk and protective factors related to childhood disability and outline the major social policies that are directed at children with disabilities and their families. The ways in which concepts of risk and protection are operationalized in these policies will be examined. Finally, recommendations for how greater service integration could be achieved are presented. Before plunging into these tasks, however, we briefly describe the theoretical models that guide our analysis.

Three theoretical frameworks underpin this chapter: the ecological model, models of risk and protective factors, and the social or minority model of disability. The ecological model espoused by Bronfenbrenner (1979, 1986) posits that individual development occurs and can only be understood within a larger family and social–environmental context. In this model, the interplay of factors at the level of the individual, the family, and the environment are all necessary to understand what appear to be individual behavior and individual outcomes. Children's development arises from the complex interplay of these interwoven elements.

Conceptually, risk and protective factors are those elements that influence the chances of adverse outcomes and optimal development, respectively (Fraser, Kirby, & Smokowski, 2004). We build our analysis from the elaboration of this framework presented by Fraser and his colleagues and found in the introductory chapter of this volume. The ecological perspective requires identifying and analyzing risk and protective factors at the levels of the child, his or her family, and the broader society. This analytic scheme is also consistent with recent disability studies scholarship, which has identified a so-called social model of disability that distinguishes between an individual's impairment and his or her disability. The impairment is the individual's biological condition, whereas the disability is what accrues to the individual when society's attitudes, expectations, and built environments do not accommodate the full range of human difference. Lennard Davis (2000) has succinctly described the relationship between disability and impairment as follows:

> Disability is not so much the lack of a sense or the presence of a physical or mental impairment as it is the reception and construction of that difference. . . . An impairment is a physical fact, but a disability is a social construction. For example, lack of mobility is an impairment, but an environment without ramps turns that impairment into a disability. (p. 56)

This social model of disability is entirely consistent with social work's emancipatory and empowerment values and agenda. The goal of this chapter, then, is not to understand how individual impairments place children at risk, but to evaluate how the larger environment, and particularly society's response to impairment, codified in public policy, increases the risk of adverse development or promotes optimal development of children with disabilities. We turn first to the risk and protective factors associated with childhood disabilities.

Risk and Protective Factors for Problems Experienced by Children With Disabilities

Risk Factors

A number of important risk factors are associated with childhood disability, including poverty, greater likelihood of experiencing abuse, social isolation and ostracism from peers and the larger society, difficulty accessing needed supportive services, and problems obtaining medical care when it is needed.

Poverty and childhood disability status are related. Twenty-eight percent of children with disabilities live in households with incomes below the federal poverty level, a level dramatically higher than the 16 percent rate of poverty for nondisabled children (Fujiura & Yamaki, 2000). The elevated risk of living in poverty for children with disabilities is a phenomenon that has been widely described by researchers and policy analysts but that is not well understood. There is even more disturbing evidence that the prevalence of disability actually increased between the early 1980s and the mid-1990s, but only among families living in poverty or those headed by a single mother (Fujiura & Yamaki). Causal ambiguity precludes understanding the direction of effects, and further research is needed to determine the nature of the causal relationship between poverty and disability. A case for effects in both directions can be made. Low-income families are less likely to have access to adequate food, prenatal and other medical care, and safe housing, which can all be implicated in increasing the risk of childhood disability. However, children's extensive care needs may prevent their parents from the employment necessary to bring them out of poverty.

Regardless of the direction of the relationship between poverty and disability, the fact that so many children with disabilities live in poverty has serious negative implications for their well-being. For children generally, living in poverty is associated with a host of negative consequences, including poor physical health, diminished cognitive abilities, emotional and behavioral problems, and reduced educational attainment (Brooks-Gunn & Duncan, 1997). But there is mounting concern that poverty may have more deleterious effects for children with disabilities than it does for typically developing children (Park, Turnbull, & Turnbull, 2002), because children with disabilities require greater care and stimulation to achieve proper development, prevent regression, and avert the development of secondary conditions.

Research on the pathways through which poverty influences child development is in its infancy, and it will likely be some time before these relationships or their applicability to disabled children are clear. We do know the disability-related costs of raising a child are extremely high in the United States, and such costs are burdensome for most families (General Accounting Office, 1999; Parish, Seltzer, Greenberg, & Floyd, 2004), and particularly so for poor families (Lukemeyer, Meyers, & Smeeding, 2000). Public income transfer and insurance programs do not cover most disability-related expenses (General Accounting Office, 1999). Finally, impoverished families of children with disabilities have fewer choices and resources in meeting their child's impairment-related needs (Scorgie, Wilgosh, & McDonald, 1998), and inadequate financial resources are associated with diminished parental ability to cope with the extra health and daily care needs of children with disabilities (Yau & Li-Tsang, 1999). Generally, poverty has a direct negative influence on maternal behavior, and subsequently on the quality of parenting children receive (Brooks-Gunn, Klebanov, & Liaw, 1995). We expect similar relationships in the behavior of poor mothers of disabled children, although this issue has not been studied.

High rates of abuse and neglect also place children with disabilities at risk. Child abuse is widely recognized as placing victimized children at considerable risk for adverse social, developmental, educational, and behavioral outcomes. It is very difficult to determine the rates of abuse for the general population (Pagelow, 1984). It is even more problematic to ascertain abuse rates for children with disabilities; this is especially true when dealing with those whose cognitive and language skills make detection of abuse difficult (Sobsey, 1994). Rates of physical, sexual, and emotional abuse for children with disabilities are significantly higher than those of nondisabled children. One conservative estimate is that children with disabilities are maltreated at rates nearly twice those of nondisabled children (National Center on Child Abuse and Neglect, 1993). However, many researchers believe this estimate is quite low (Sobsey), and one study found abuse rates for children with disabilities to be 4 to 10 times those of nondisabled children (Ammerman & Baladerian, 1993).

Serious risks to emotional well-being are associated with the social isolation children with disabilities often experience, and their ostracism from peers and the larger society. The history of discriminatory and prejudicial treatment of people with disabilities of all ages is a dismal and pervasive aspect of

Western history (Braddock & Parish, 2001), and contemporary reports of children with disabilities indicate these attitudes have not materially diminished. There is long-standing evidence that children interact differently with otherwise rejected and ignored classmates (Chazan, Laing, Jones, Harper, & Bolton, 1983; Dodge, 1983). Because of these different patterns of interactions, children with disabilities, and particularly those with severe impairments, often have limited opportunities for friendships and integration with their peers.

Social isolation, having few friendships, limited reciprocal relationships, and minimal peer interactions follow children with disabilities from early childhood into adolescence and adulthood (Keogh & Bernheimer, 1987; Keogh, Bernheimer, & Guthrie, 2004). Although the long-term effects of this isolation have not been widely studied in disabled children, generally, social skills, networks, and relationships predict later adjustment (Kupersmidt, Coie, & Dodge, 1990; Meyer, Cole, McQuarter, & Reichle, 1990), and childhood disability is associated with negative personal and employment outcomes (Edgar & Levine, 1987; Sitlington, Frank, & Carson, 1992; Whitney-Thomas & Moloney, 2001). Moreover, adolescents and children with disabilities express great dissatisfaction related to their lack of friends and social integration (Keogh et al., 2004).

Evidence has converged to indicate that parents encounter ongoing stress and family disruption over the life course of caring for their children with disabilities (e.g., Farber, 1960; Turnbull, Brotherson, & Summers 1986). These stresses may result from behavior problems in the child, nighttime disturbance, social isolation, adversity in the family, multiplicity of child impairments, chronic ill health, and financial concerns (Singer & Irvin, 1989, p. 7). However, there is also compelling evidence that parents who cope well with their child's unique needs enhance the child's cognitive and social adjustment and minimize further family disruption and distress (Crnic, Friedrich, & Greenberg, 1983; Landesman, Jaccard, & Gunderson, 1989; Summers, Behr, & Turnbull, 1989). Parental adaptation and coping contributes to the most critical protective factor related to childhood disability: strong parental support.

Parental support takes a number of forms across childhood, and often into adulthood, for a person with disabilities. The nature and organization of disability policy in the United States compels parents to serve as their child's advocate, and often as their case manager. This point will be elaborated in subsequent sections, but when parents aggressively champion their child's needs, they are much more likely to receive the services and supports to which the child is entitled. Parental support also bolsters the child's self-esteem, creating resilience to the inevitable rejection most children with disabilities encounter from peers and from society.

A closely related protective factor is the competence and mastery parents develop as their child ages, gained because of the adversity they face in securing services for their child and in coming to terms with their child's impairment. A common developmental trajectory for parents of young children with disabilities is to mourn, at the point of diagnosis, for the child they had anticipated. After this mourning period, most parents report increasing levels of satisfaction with their caregiving abilities and identify their caregiving role as a positive part of their self-identity, although they may revisit grief and depression during transition periods over the course of childhood (e.g., entry into kindergarten, high school graduation). These transition points, for some parents, represent jarring reminders that the child's impairment has altered his or her developmental trajectory. However, parents also overwhelmingly report that their children with disabilities contribute emotionally, socially, and intellectually to the richness of family life (Summers et al., 1989). Protective factors are reviewed next.

Protective Factors

Research on protective and promotive factors associated with childhood disability is far more limited, probably because the medical model of disability that prevailed for much of the 20th century still informs policy and services for children with disabilities. The most important protective factors associated with childhood disability emerge from the family and community context—parental competence as advocates, case managers, and caregivers of their children; supportive peer networks, extended families, and communities; inclusion in communities and activities of daily life; and available medical, educational, and financial resources to allow parents to provide appropriate care for their children.

Extra-familial protective factors include supportive schools and communities, and adequate levels of family support services. These resources can be naturally occurring supports that exist in the community, through churches, community centers, and the like, or disability and advocacy organizations dedicated specifically to children with disabilities and their families. Having sufficient and appropriate supports is a critical factor in helping parents to achieve positive adaptation to their child's disability (Singer & Irvin, 1989). The policies that structure such supports are discussed in the next section. However, there is little research on the ways in which these risk and protective factors directly affect children with disabilities and their families. There is limited evidence of our hypothesis that these protective factors (parental and other supports, responsive public policies, nurturing communities) are directly involved in building disabled children's resilience (Singer & Irvin; Summers et al., 1989).

In summary, the life circumstances and development of children with disabilities are shaped by risk and protective factors that emerge from the environments in which they live. These environmental factors emerge from within the family, community, and larger society and are manifested in the public policies that contribute to different facets of child and family life. Table 6.1 summarizes these significant factors.

Table 6.1   Risk and Protective Factors for Problems Experienced by Children With Disabilities

Risk Factors	Protective Factors
Poverty	Parental competence as advocates, case managers, and caregivers
Increased abuse and neglect	Supportive peer networks, extended families, and communities
Social isolation	Inclusion in community life and activities
Difficulty obtaining supportive services and medical care	Adequate medical, financial, and educational resources to enable parents to meet their children's needs
Ostracism by community and peers	

Risk, Resilience, and Protection in Policies for Children With Disabilities

In the last century, extraordinary changes have occurred in policies for children with disabilities. Extant policy at the beginning of the 20th century was organized at the state level and provided limited custodial care in segregated institutions, to the exclusion of nearly all other services. Beginning in the 1930s, small-scale experimental programs in extra-institutional long-term care were implemented in New York and Ohio, but these did not take hold nationally. Parents began organizing their own educational systems for their children with disabilities, and fledgling parent advocacy groups were inaugurated beginning in the 1940s. Parent advocacy had a lasting impact on the service system for children with disabilities and, ultimately, exerted greater influence over the shape of services than any other force (Braddock & Parish, 2001).

Over the past four decades, assertive and effective advocacy by parents of children with disabilities precipitated the development of policies that support individualized services and that meet the needs of the entire family (Braddock & Parish, 2001). Parent advocacy culminated in passage of mandatory education for children with disabilities in 1975 and facilitated the closure of hundreds of custodial institutions across the United States in the decades since 1970. As parents emerged as champions for their children, adult activists with disabilities also began to demand their civil rights, following the direction of 1960s African American leaders.

These enormous changes resulted in two significant transformations. First, the service system, particularly in education and long-term care, began to reject the prevailing medical model, wherein individuals were defined as inherently defective and in need of professional cures. Supporters of the social model of disability, discussed previously, argue for the thorough inclusion of people with disabilities in all aspects of society, and a society that accommodates them. Advocacy by people with disabilities and their allies ultimately won passage of the Americans with Disabilities Act in 1990, which prohibits discrimination in public settings and requires employers to accommodate people with disabilities (Braddock & Parish, 2001).

A second major transformation was the entrance of the federal government into the service and policy arena for children with disabilities, which began on a large scale in the 1970s. Even when the Social Security Act was passed in 1935, the federal government played a minimal role in funding supports or services for people with disabilities, as money allocated through Title X of the Act provided limited income transfers to the blind. The only exceptions to federal noninvolvement were income transfer and vocational rehabilitation provisions for veterans. For children with disabilities particularly, the federal government did not play a major role through much of the 20th century. This changed in the 1970s, when Medicaid was amended to allow federal reimbursement for medical and long-term care services for children and adults with mental retardation, federal law mandated education of children with disabilities, and the disability income transfer program was expanded to cover children.

These policy transformations evolved concurrently with practice changes. At the beginning of the 20th century, when people with disabilities were considered deviants, the social policy response was segregation and sterilization, to prevent procreation by a group of undesirables. Through most of the 20th century, negative attitudes toward people with disabilities prevailed, and practice models encouraged parents to institutionalize young children with disabilities, abandoning them in warehouse-like facilities that barely provided the rudiments of care (Braddock & Parish, 2001). As attitudes toward people with disabilities shifted, and a civil and human rights perspective emerged, practices began to shift to focus on enhancing and supporting parents to care for their children with disabilities (Braddock & Parish).

At the outset of the 21st century, there are a number of public policies that influence children with disabilities and their families. We describe key federal policies in the areas of income support, education and early intervention, and finally, family support. Medical care, which is also important for children with disabilities, is discussed in Chapter 5 of this volume. Table 6.2 provides an overview of these policies and their features.

Table 6.2   Major Policy Approaches Targeting Children and Youth with Disabilities

	Income Transfers	Education	Early Intervention	Family Support
Policy authority	TANF: Personal Responsibility and Work Opportunity Reconciliation Act of 1996 (federal); SSI: Social Security Act, amended 1972 (federal)	Education for All Handicapped Children Act of 1975; later replaced by Individuals with Disabilities Education Act (IDEA)	Part H added to Education for All Handicapped Children Act in 1986; later replaced by Part C	Varies by state; federal Medicaid funds available to states through Home and Community-Based Services Waiver (Omnibus Budget Reconciliation Act of 1981 that authorized the Home and Community-Based Services Waiver)
Funding	TANF: State and federal; SSI: federal	Local and state; limited federal funding	Local and state; limited federal funding	State; Medicaid programs financed jointly by federal and state
Core features	TANF: time-limited cash assistance to low-income families; work requirements for parents; SSI: monthly payments to low-income children; eligibility based on child disability and family income	Children with disabilities entitled to free appropriate public education in least restrictive environment; IEP guides child's education; parents serve as advocates	Children with disabilities and possible developmental delays eligible to receive services to promote their development; IFSP guides services to entire family	Varies by state; some states offer cash to families; others offer services like respite, parent support groups, etc.; eligibility requirements and breadth/ depth of services vary by state

Income Transfers

Children with disabilities and their families can receive income transfer payments through several different programs: those specifically for people with disabilities, and those for poor people generally. The two major disability income transfer programs in the United States are Disability Insurance and Supplemental Security Income (SSI). The former is targeted at those with work experience who become disabled and their dependents. As such, it is not a major source of income for children with disabilities. SSI, by contrast, specifically includes children with disabilities. The largest income transfer program for poor families, generally, is Temporary Assistance to Needy Families (TANF), the nation's welfare system administered by the states and funded jointly by state and federal governments.

SSI is a means-tested, monthly income program for the elderly and people with disabilities. The program is federally financed and generally federally administered, although some states supplement federal payments and a few administer their own programs directly. Children with disabilities have been able to receive SSI since the program's inception in 1972, and children's eligibility is based on functional limitations (Social Security Administration, 2000a). Parents' income and assets relative to family size are used to determine whether or not a child can receive SSI. In 2004, for a single child with disabilities living in a two-parent home in which parents do not have pension earnings, income must be below $2,945 per month for the child with disabilities to receive SSI payments.

A total of 914,821 children with disabilities under age 18 received SSI benefits in December 2002 (Social Security Administration, 2003). For 2002, the average monthly SSI benefit payment for children was $473 (Social Security Administration, 2003), for an annual rate of $5,675. In 2002, the federal poverty threshold was $8,860 for one person (U.S. Department of Health, 2002). As such, the SSI payment level was approximately 36 percent below the federal poverty level. Approximately 26 percent of children receiving SSI live below the federal poverty level (Grad, 2000), but the SSI program plays a vital role in reducing recipients' poverty. Two thirds of SSI beneficiaries receive at least half of their total income from SSI, and Social Security is responsible for reducing the poverty gap for SSI recipients by an average of 60% (Grad). Although the level of support provided by SSI is limited, reduced poverty for many children with disabilities and their families is an important protective factor.

Evidence indicates that the protective benefits of SSI have eroded recently. The Personal Responsibility and Work Opportunity Reconciliation Act (PRWORA) of 1996 catalyzed important changes in SSI for children with disabilities by constricting child SSI eligibility. Following the new eligibility rules, SSI retrenchment associated with PRWORA had dire consequences for children with disabilities and their families. Between 1996 and 2000, the number of child SSI beneficiaries with mental retardation declined by nearly 76,000, or 22 percent, and receipt by children with all other disabilities declined by 12 percent (Parish, 2003). To compensate for the loss of their children's SSI income, some parents entered the workforce or increased their work hours (Inkelas, Rowe, Karoly, & Rogowski, 1999). Yet increased work activity did not prevent total income from declining for most families, some of whom received other forms of public assistance to compensate for the loss of SSI (Davies, Iams, & Rupp, 2000; Inkelas et al., 1999).

Low-income families of children with disabilities can also receive income transfers through TANF, which is the limited welfare program enacted in 1996 by PRWORA. TANF replaced Aid to Families with Dependent Children (AFDC) and requires parents to work and limits receipt of cash benefits to a lifetime maximum of 60 months.

Under AFDC, parents of disabled children were generally exempted from work requirements (Thompson, Holcomb, Loprest, & Brennan, 1998). When PRWORA was being debated in Congress, the National Commission on Childhood Disability (1995) recommended exempting one parent of a child with disabilities from mandatory work requirements, which excluded parents from being cut from welfare for 2 years following a child's termination from SSI, and prohibited states from counting children's SSI when assessing families' welfare eligibility. However, these recommendations were rejected when the final version of PRWORA passed. TANF allows states to exempt up to 20 percent of their welfare caseload from work requirements, but states have the discretion to establish more strict work participation rules. Seventeen states broadened their work participation rules to include at least some people with disabilities and their caregivers, and an additional 13 states mandated universal participation, regardless of beneficiaries' disability status or caregiving responsibilities (Thompson et al., 1998).

The need for exemptions is a real one—parents of children with disabilities face many barriers to maintaining employment, including children's ongoing and episodic needs for care and a lack of available, affordable child care for children with disabilities (Rosman, McCarthy, & Woolverton, 2001; Shearn & Todd, 2000). In addition, poor families, overrepresented among those of children with disabilities, pay for most child care out-of-pocket, a burden that substantially contributes to their poverty (Lukemeyer et al, 2000; Meyers, Han, Waldfogel, & Garfinkel, 2001; Meyers & Heintze, 1999). The elevated care needs of children with disabilities, and their parents' extraordinary caregiving responsibilities, place parents at elevated risk of unemployment, which is directly associated with family poverty (Lichter & Eggebeen, 1994).

The system of income transfers in the United States provides critical support to children with disabilities and their families. These programs directly address the increased risk of living in poverty for children with disabilities and are attempts, albeit limited ones, to ameliorate the high costs of raising children with disabilities. Although SSI alone does not raise family income above the federal poverty level, there is little doubt that its provisions are important protective factors for the thousands of families who receive it.

Education and Early Intervention

The Individuals with Disabilities Education Act (IDEA) began as the Education for All Handicapped Children Act of 1975 (P.L. 94–142) and gave all children with disabilities the right to a free and appropriate public education. This watershed civil rights law resulted from sustained advocacy by parents of children with disabilities.

Special education has been shaped by the six core principles that formed the nucleus of the Education for All Handicapped Children Act:

1. Zero reject, meaning schools could not opt to exclude any children with disabilities from instruction.

2. Nondiscriminatory evaluation, by which every child receives an individualized, culturally and linguistically appropriate evaluation before being placed in special education.

3. Individualized education plans (IEP) delineate current performance, progress on past objectives, goals and services for the school year, and evaluation of outcomes.

4. Least restrictive environment, a goal stating that children with disabilities are educated to the extent possible in settings with nondisabled children.

5. Due process, which codifies the legal steps to ensure schools' fairness and accountability in meeting the child's needs and how parents can obtain relief via a hearing or by second opinions.

6. Parental participation, whereby parents have the right to access their child's education records and participate in IEP planning (Kirk, Gallagher, & Anastasiow, 1993, pp. 51–52).

These principles have remained fixtures of the Act since its initial passage in 1975. However, the Act has also changed over the years in response to litigation and reauthorizing legislation. We will describe least restrictive environment, IEPs, and some of the issues that have emerged, including school district responsibility to fund and provide needed services, procedures to plan for a child's transition out of school, and reliance on parents to serve as advocates for their children (U.S. Department of Education, 2003).

Least Restrictive Environment

The notion of least restrictive environment exists to ensure that children are served in inclusive and integrated settings and are not segregated from typically developing peers. Since this is a recommendation and not a requirement of IDEA, however, there is great variability among school districts in the proportion of children with disabilities who are educated in inclusive settings. Parents and teachers alike have reported mixed feelings about mainstreaming children with disabilities into least restrictive environments. While regular education teachers generally support mainstreaming, their endorsement appears to deteriorate as they address their own willingness to include children with disabilities in their classrooms (Scruggs & Mastropieri, 1996). Moreover, teachers often are ill equipped or unwilling to adequately include children with special needs in classroom activities. Some parents of nondisabled children fear time will be taken away from their child's learning experience, and some parents of children with disabilities fear their children will not receive the level of attention available in segregated classes (Rallis & Anderson, 1994). Despite this controversy, many agree that mainstreaming is critical for children with disabilities, as it allows them to develop interpersonal and life skills and concurrently allows other students to accept people with disabilities (Osborne & Dimattia, 1994).

Individualized Education Plans

The individualized education plan (IEP) is a legal document created for each student with a disability. It is developed by a multidisciplinary team, including the student, his or her parents, teachers, social workers, speech and physical therapists, psychologists, and whomever else is needed, given the child's needs. The IEP is intended to ensure that the child receives an appropriate education in the least restrictive environment. The IEP is a fluid document and is supposed to be revised annually, or as a child's needs change. IEPs address current educational performance levels, goals, and services provided for inclusion in general education and other considerations as warranted by a child's unique abilities and needs (Sopko, 2003). Despite being mandated by IDEA, parents and teachers recognize numerous barriers in developing appropriate IEPs for children with disabilities. For example, IEPs take considerable time and skill to develop and involve different perceptions and attitudes about interpretations of inclusion and the responsibilities of educators (Sopko, 2003).

A more recent development has been the requirement that IEPs include plans for the transition from school to adult life, which was included in the 1997 reauthorization due to overwhelming evidence of negative outcomes for children with disabilities who left school. The goal of transition planning is to enable children with disabilities to become active and productive citizens and to help them bridge the distance between closely supervised, sheltered educational settings to the less-structured adult world. School districts can include transition planning in a child's IEP, beginning as early as age 14. Transition plans are expected to address instruction, community involvement, employment, and other adult life objectives and should incorporate the child's individual interests and preferences (Sopko, 2003).

Although IDEA guarantees children with disabilities the right to a free appropriate public education, there is frequent disagreement between parents and professionals regarding what constitutes an appropriate education. Schools frequently contest the education and support services requested by parents, and challenges are most common when school districts are asked to provide related services such as transportation, assistive technology, and medical services to assist children in obtaining an education (Katsiyannis & Yell, 2000).

Expensive health services for students with chronic health problems are often among the most controversial. The U.S. Supreme Court ruled in *Cedar Rapids Community School District v. Garret F.* that a school district was required to provide a specially trained nurse as part of a child's special education plan when doing so was necessary for the child's participation in school (Katsiyannis & Yell, 2000). This was an important victory for children whose disabilities require ongoing medical care. For all children with disabilities, this ruling represents a clear statement from the Court that needed ancillary and supportive services remain the school's responsibility.

Extensive litigation surrounding IDEA and schools' ongoing challenges to the rights of children with disabilities translates into a system in which parents must be assertive advocates. The burden parents feel to be their child's advocates and the level of sophistication and resources parents must bring to bear to secure their child's education are considerable. Part of parents' role in IEP planning is to safeguard their child's educational rights, which creates an inherently adversarial relationship between parents and schools. Parents must be active decision makers and are expected to fulfill the role of teacher in the home (Turnbull & Turnbull, 1982). Although these assumptions about parents' abilities to successfully advocate for their children have produced important outcomes like the *Garret* decision, it is unrealistic and unreasonable to expect all parents to be effective advocates. Many parents, and particularly low-income parents, lack the educational and financial resources to champion their children's needs. Lacking a resourceful parent-advocate, a child with disabilities may lose his or her educational rights.

The second part of IDEA that is critically important for children with disabilities is early intervention, which has as its purpose the provision of prevention and treatment services to improve cognitive, social, and emotional development of children under the age of 3. Children receiving early intervention services either are considered at risk for delayed development or have been identified as having a developmental disability (Ramey & Ramey, 1998). Early intervention services have long been recognized as important for helping children with disabilities achieve their developmental potential. Best practices for early intervention programs involve a range of family-centered services, which focus on meeting the needs of the child within the context of his or her family and larger environment. For example, in the course of early intervention, parents may be referred to job assistance or adult education and may receive assistance in obtaining housing and health care.

The philosophy undergirding early intervention is fundamentally grounded in the concepts of protective and promotive factors. Ideally, early intervention services promote well-being and optimal development by providing comprehensive community-based support services to help improve developmental outcomes. Even young children with disabilities are at risk of developing further complications that may exacerbate their impairments or cause secondary conditions (Zimmer & Simeonsson, 2004).

Early intervention in the United States has been structured by a federal mandate since 1986, when Part H (now Part C) was added to the Education for All Handicapped Children Act and mandated the provision of early intervention services (P.L. 99–457). The Act's early intervention mandate is to provide comprehensive services statewide to families of young children from birth to age 3 (Richmond & Ayoub, 1993).

When possible, early intervention services are expected to be provided in the most appropriate natural setting, which includes the home or another community setting. The emphasis on community-based intervention is intended to promote children's integration and inclusion in their home communities (Graham & Bryant, 1993). Between 1999 and 2000, approximately 68 percent of early intervention programs were provided in children's homes (U.S. Department of Education, 2000). Investigators have noted that broad-based early intervention services are essential for young children's cognitive, social, and emotional development (e.g., Graham & Bryant).

Multidisciplinary supports and programs scaffold the early intervention system, including assistive technology devices, audiology services, nutrition, family training and counseling, social work, and physical and occupational therapy. At a minimum, states must identify infants and toddlers deemed to be at risk or have developmental delays. States are also required to obtain Individualized Family Service Plans (IFSPs) and provide data collection methods and evaluation procedures, among others. When a child enters early intervention, an assessment of both the child's and family's strengths and risk factors is conducted (Ramey & Ramey, 1998). The IFSP is subsequently developed collaboratively by parents and professionals, and addresses the child and family as a unit (Ramey & Ramey). This collaborative effort is important for adequately assessing risk and protective factors within the family structure and larger social environment.

Family Support

The greatest responsibility for caring for children with disabilities is borne by families, who constitute the largest group of care providers (Hogan & Msall, 2002). Family support services, which offer important protective factors for children with disabilities, are often a lifeline for families and include services such as respite, environmental adaptations, assistive devices, personal assistance, mental health, and crisis intervention. These supports allow families to care for their children with disabilities at home rather than seeking expensive, and generally publicly financed, out-of-home care (Bruns & Burchard, 2000; Curran, Sharples, White et al., 2001).

The goals of family support services include enabling families to raise their child with disabilities at home by reducing stress and by strengthening and enhancing caregiving capacities (Agosta, 2000). Utilization of formal support services by family caregivers plays a significant role in reducing the burdens and stress associated with caring for a child with disabilities (Floyd & Gallagher, 1997; Freedman & Boyer, 2000; Haveman, van Berkum, Reijinder, & Heller, 1997) and helping families obtain services for unmet needs (Heller, Miller, & Hsieh, 1999).

Despite the extent of care that families provide for their children with disabilities, the actual level of support provided is meager in nearly all states. For example, spending for family support services for children *and* adults with developmental disabilities and their families totaled just $1.0 billion in 2000, a level clearly dwarfed by the $29 billion expenditure for the entire developmental disabilities service system in the states (Parish, Pomeranz, & Braddock, 2003). Family support services across the United States are usually jointly financed by the federal and state governments, often with Medicaid resources, and are typically administered by state or county governments. Not surprisingly, given the vast differences among states in the provision of social services, there is tremendous variability in the level of funding allocated for family support and in the types of available services (Parish et al., 2003).

Families who receive support services encounter extensive barriers to obtaining what they need to care effectively for a family member with disabilities. Freedman and Boyer (2000) found supports demonstrably enhanced family well-being and were critically important to families. However, even among families receiving services, barriers existed, including a lack of flexibility in the types and frequency of services they received, and important access difficulties, such as services not being available when they were most needed (Freedman & Boyer, 2000).

We have reviewed the major public policies that influence the lives of children with disabilities and their families in the United States: income transfers, education, early intervention, and family supports. (Health insurance, another exceptionally important public policy, is discussed in Chapter 5 of this volume.) There is considerable variability in the extent to which knowledge of risk and resilience informed the development of these policies. However, despite the contention about their effectiveness, all are significant in the lives of children with disabilities and their families, and contribute somewhat to promoting the optimal development and successful adjustment of children with disabilities.

Using Knowledge of Risk, Protection, and Resilience to Achieve Service Integration in Disabilities Policy

There are two defining features of the policies related to children with disabilities: (1) the reliance upon parents to be advocates, case managers, and caregivers for their children; and (2) the fragmentation of policy across service domains. Parents are expected to have a central role in the provision of care for their child, from the point of diagnosis, to entry into early intervention, to obtain support services, into the education system, and through transition planning and beyond. In some policies, this role is explicit and direct: Early intervention policy has embraced collaboration between parents and professionals for decades, and the partnership between parents and professionals has long since been regarded as best practices for infants, toddlers, and preschoolers with disabilities (Blue-Banning, Summers, Frankland, Nelson, & Beegle, 2004).

However, there can be little doubt that many parents lack the time, financial, and emotional resources required to be full partners in this endeavor. Within the formal education system, IDEA has established ground rules through which parents can enter an adversarial role with their children's schools in order to obtain the services their children need. Parents speak poignantly of their advocacy, at every step of their child's development, to ensure their children receive needed services. Although sustained advocacy over time often results in parents reporting a sense of mastery and competence in learning the bureaucracies and securing services, by no means is this the optimal way for children with disabilities to obtain what they need. Parents are under enough strain in meeting their child's physical and emotional care needs and should not also have to fulfill roles as advocate and case manager.

Fragmentation across domains of service is the other hallmark of policy for children with disabilities. To obtain the services their children need, parents must navigate numerous different bureaucracies, with separate institutions governing income transfers, early intervention and education, family support, and medical care. All of these programs have different eligibility criteria, paperwork requirements, definitions of disability, revenue sources, and administrative entities. Despite considerable redundancy in terms of the need for parents to "prove" that their child has an impairment, procedures do not exist for streamlined applications or coordination across providers.

Jeremy: A Case Example

To further illustrate the fragmentation and parental advocacy that are hallmarks of disability policy, we will consider the situation of a 9-year-old boy, Jeremy, who has cerebral palsy and mental retardation. Cerebral palsy is a nonprogressive group of chronic conditions that results from a brain injury and affects muscle coordination and motor development. Mental retardation is characterized as below-average intelligence.

Jeremy's IEP recommends he receive speech therapy but no other specialized services. He receives speech therapy in a group with several other classmates. Jeremy's physical therapy was discontinued 2 years ago, when his IEP team, except his mother, felt the therapy was no longer necessary because his progress was limited. His functioning has since deteriorated, but his mother's initial appeal to have the physical therapy put back into his IEP was rejected. She wants to pursue this appeal further but needs to learn how.

Jeremy had a number of orthopedic surgical procedures during his early childhood. Although he has Medicaid, a county clinic has the only providers in the region who accept Medicaid. He and his mother always have lengthy waits for care, and he usually sees different providers at each visit. Jeremy

---

Jeremy

Jeremy lives alone with his mother. Their extended family lives out of state, and his father has not had contact with the family since shortly after Jeremy's diagnosis. Jeremy was slower than other young children to reach early developmental milestones, and his pediatrician's referral to a neurologist confirmed cerebral palsy when Jeremy was 20 months old. He was in a center-based early intervention program until he entered school. Jeremy is in a self-contained classroom with other children with disabilities, but his mother would prefer for him to be mainstreamed into a regular education classroom. Jeremy walks with crutches, has difficulty grasping objects, has limited speech that is difficult to understand, and is incontinent. He is very friendly and outgoing, and is well liked by his teacher, classmates, and other children in his neighborhood. He has a great sense of humor and likes to tell jokes. Jeremy's mother has a close relationship with one neighbor, but this neighbor is not comfortable watching Jeremy. She is employed part time because she cannot find after-school care for him, and he has frequent medical appointments to which she drives him. Because of her low income, Jeremy qualifies for monthly SSI payments and Medicaid. Over the past few years, Jeremy's SSI was cut off twice after being reevaluated, and when his mother's employment temporarily increased. Appealing these termination decisions took his mother several weeks. She did not know that she could ask for aid pending these appeals, because the process is confusing.

---

needs adaptive devices to help him manipulate tools and independently complete activities of daily living (feeding, personal hygiene). His mother has applied through his clinic pediatrician for a number of these devices, specifically to give him greater independence in self-care. Medicaid has denied these applications, and his mother is appealing them. Medicaid does not cover the cost of his diapers, which are expensive.

Jeremy's mother has contacted the regional office of the state's developmental disabilities department to request respite. She would like this care after school, so she could work more. She has completed the application, but it cannot be submitted until the clinic pediatrician finalizes the paperwork certifying his disability, after which they will be placed on the waiting list. She has called the clinic weekly over the past 2 months to check on this paperwork, but it has not been completed yet. The regional office has told her the wait for respite services is at least 18 months long, and when she does receive it, it will be for a maximum of 10 hours per month. After receiving respite services for 1 year, she will again be waitlisted so that other families can receive the service. She has also applied for a cash subsidy to cover the cost of purchasing the adaptive devices Jeremy needs but was told that she is ineligible because her income is too high. Jeremy's situation, like so many others, illustrates the complexity involved in navigating a fragmented service delivery system.

Policy Recommendations

There is widespread recognition that children with disabilities and their families are protected by policies and services that enhance family functioning and provide the therapies disabled children need to maximize their independence and inclusion in society. At present, family support and early intervention are based on principles of risk and protective factors. Special education was developed with a civil rights focus—children with disabilities were entitled to the same educational opportunities as their nondisabled peers. Like SSI payments for children, special education offers some protective benefits but is limited in its scope and success in truly mitigating the risks associated with childhood disability.

The limited availability of family support services across the United States translates into unrealized benefits for most families. The model of early intervention, in which collaborative parent–professional partnerships drive services, has much to offer the broader arena of disability policy for children. In this model, entire families are the focus, and meeting their needs across a spectrum of domains is the goal. Compelled by a single Individualized Family Support Plan (IFSP), care and services are typically coordinated for and with family needs. Our central policy recommendation is related to using an IFSP model to integrate and coordinate services across domains. Expanding the rubric of the IFSP to include family support services from all funding sources, income transfers, and public health insurance would minimize the amount of work parents must do to obtain services their childs needs. A "one-stop shopping" approach would also reduce the fragmentation in care that children receive. If the IFSP model were incorporated in the child's education plan, a holistic framework of serving the child within the context of his or her family would replace the current singular focus on the child's deficits and skills.

Summary

We have described four of the major policies that influence the well-being of children with disabilities and their families: (1) income transfers, (2) education, (3) early intervention, and (4) family support services. We have also presented evidence of the central characteristics of these policies: a reliance on parents as advocates and case managers, and the extraordinary degree of fragmentation that exists across policy domains.

These programs are made more complex and challenging for parents because of the lack of interface between systems, differing eligibility criteria, and the array of separate (and competing) revenue sources that fund them. Although concepts of risk and protective factors are fundamental for early intervention and family support policies, they are applied in very limited ways to education and income transfer policies. In addition, the existing availability of family support is such that it is literally meaningless for many American families. Our final recommendations therefore stem from a desire to allow families to meet the care needs of their children, at a minimum. To accomplish this objective, early intervention must be fully funded, and funding for family support and income transfers should be increased to meet the true needs of low-income families.

Questions for Discussion

1. What are the implications of categorically based eligibility criteria for efforts to integrate policies for children with developmental disabilities with other child/family policies?

2. What policy changes would you recommend to better provide an integrated service delivery system for children and youth with developmental disabilities and their families?

3. How will the transition away from a medical model of disability to a social model of disability influence the delivery of services for children and youth with developmental disabilities and their families in the coming decades?

Additional Reading

Barnes, C., Barton, L., & Oliver, M. (2002). *Disability studies today.* Cambridge, UK: Polity Books.

Cryer, D., & Clifford, R. M. (2003). *Early childhood education and care in the USA.* Baltimore: Brookes.

Pianta, R. C., & Kraft-Sayre, M. (2003). *Successful kindergarten transition: Your guide to connecting children, families, and schools.* Baltimore: Brookes.

References

Abelson, A. G. (1999). Respite care needs of parents of children with developmental disabilities. *Focus on Autism & Other Developmental Disabilities, 14,* 96–101.

Agosta, J. (2000, April). *Family support in the United States: Past, present and emerging systems of support.* Salem, OR: Human Services Research Institute.

Ammerman, R. T. & Baladerian, N. J. (1993). *Maltreatment of children with disabilities*. Washington, DC: National Committee to Prevent Child Abuse.

Blue-Banning, M., Summers, J. A., Frankland, H. C., Nelson, L. L., & Beegle, G. (2004). Dimensions of family and professional partnerships: Constructive guidelines for collaboration. *Exceptional Children, 70*, 167–184.

Braddock, D., & Parish, S. (2001). Disability history from antiquity to the Americans with Disabilities Act. In G. L. Albrecht, K. D. Seelman, & M. Bury (Eds.), *Handbook of disability studies* (pp. 11–68). Thousand Oaks, CA: Sage.

Bronfenbrenner, U. (1979). *The ecology of human development: Experiments by nature and design*. Cambridge, MA: Harvard University Press.

Bronfenbrenner, U. (1986). Ecology of the family as a context for human development. *Developmental Psychology, 22*, 723–742.

Brooks-Gunn, J., & Duncan, G. J. (1997). The effects of poverty on children. *The Future of Children, 7*, 55–71.

Brooks-Gunn, J., Klebanov, P. K, & Liaw, F. (1995). The learning, physical, and emotional environment of the home in the context of poverty: The Infant Health and Development program. *Children and Youth Services Review, 17*, 251–276.

Bruns, E. J., & Burchard, J. D. (2000). Impact of respite care services for families with children experiencing emotional and behavioral problems. *Children's Services: Social Policy, Research, & Practice, 3*, 39–61.

Chazan, M., Laing, A., Jones, J., Harper, G., & Bolton, J. (1983). The management of behavior problems in your children. *Early Childhood Development and Care, 11*, 227–244.

Creasy, R. K., & Resnik, R. (1999). *Maternal–fetal medicine* (4th ed.). Philadelphia: Saunders.

Crnic, K. A., Friedrich, W. N., & Greenberg, M. T. (1983). Adaptation of families with mentally retarded children. *American Journal of Mental Deficiency, 88*, 125–138.

Curran, A. L., Sharples, P. M., White, C., et al. (2001). Time costs of caring for children with severe disabilities compared with caring for children without disabilities. *Developmental Medicine & Child Neurology, 43*, 529–533.

Davies, P., Iams, H., & Rupp, K. (2000). The effect of welfare reform on SSA's disability programs: Design of policy evaluation and early evidence. *Social Security Bulletin, 63*, 3–11.

Davis, L. (2000). Dr. Johnson, Amelia, and the discourse of disability in the eighteenth century. In H. Deutsch and F. Nussbaum (Eds.) *"Defects": Engendering the modern body*. Ann Arbor: University of Michigan Press.

Dodge, K. A. (1983). Behavioral antecedents of peer social status. *Child Development, 54*, 1386–1399.

Edgar, E., & Levine, P. (1987). *A longitudinal follow-along study of graduates of special education*. Seattle: University of Washington Child Development and Mental Retardation Center.

Farber, B. (1960). Family organization and crisis: Maintenance of integration in families with a severely retarded child. *Monographs of the Society for Research in Child Development, 25*, 1–95.

Floyd, F. J., & Gallagher, E. M. (1997). Parental stress, care demands, and use of support services for school-age children with disabilities and behavior problems. *Family Relations, 46,* 359–371.

Fraser, M. W., Kirby, L. D., & Smokowski, P. (2004). Risk and resilience in childhood. In M. W. Fraser (Ed.), *Risk and resilience in childhood: An ecological perspective* (pp. 13–66). Washington, DC: NASW.

Freedman, R. I., & Boyer, N. C. (2000). The power to choose: Supports for families caring for individuals with developmental disabilities. *Health & Social Work, 25,* 59–68.

Fujiura, G. T., & Yamaki, K. (2000). Trends in demography of childhood poverty and disability. *Exceptional Children, 66,* 187–199.

General Accounting Office. (1999, June). *SSI children: Multiple factors affect families' costs for disability-related services* (GAO/HEHS-99-99). Washington, DC: Author.

Grad, S. (2000, December 15). *The role of disability benefits in the economic well-being of beneficiaries.* Paper presented at the National Academy of Social Insurance Conference, Disability Income Policy: Opportunities and Challenges in the Next Decade, Washington, DC.

Graham, M., & Bryant, D. (1993). Characteristics of quality, effective service delivery systems for children with special needs. In D. Bryant & M. Graham (Eds.), *Implementing early intervention: From research to effective practice* (pp. 233–254). New York: Guilford Press.

Haveman, M., van Berkum, G., Reijinder, R., & Heller, T. (1997). Differences in service needs, time demands, and caregiving burden among parents of persons with mental retardation across the life cycle. *Family Relations, 46,* 417–425.

Heller, T., Miller, A. B., & Hsieh, K. (1999). Impact of a consumer-directed family support program on adults with developmental disabilities and their family caregivers. *Family Relations, 48,* 419–427.

Hogan, D. P., & Msall, M. E. (2002). Family structure and resources and the parenting of children with disabilities and functional limitations. *Parenting and the child's world: Influences on academic, intellectual, and social–emotional development.* Mahwah, NJ: Lawrence Erlbaum.

Hogan, D. P., Msall, M. E., Rogers, M. L., & Avery, R. C. (1997). Improved disability population estimates of functional limitation among children 5–17. *Maternal and Child Health Journal, 1,* 203–216.

Inkelas, M., Rowe, M., Karoly, L., & Rogowski, J. (1999). *Policy evaluation of the effects of the 1996 welfare reform legislation on SSI benefits for disabled children: First round case study findings.* Santa Monica, CA: Rand.

Katsiyannis, A., & Yell, M. L. (2000). The Supreme Court and school health services: Cedar Rapids v. Garret F. *Exceptional Children, 66,* 317–326.

Keogh, B. K., & Bernheimer, L. P. (1987). Developmental delays in preschool children: Assessment over time. *European Journal of Special Needs Education, 2,* 211–220.

Keogh, B. K., Bernheimer, L. P., & Guthrie, D. (2004). Children with developmental delays twenty years later: Where are they? How are they? *American Journal on Mental Retardation, 109,* 219–230.

Kirk, S., Gallagher, J., & Anastasiow, N. (1993). *Educating exceptional children* (7th ed). Boston: Houghton Mifflin.

Kupersmidt, J. B., Coie, J. D., & Dodge, K. A. (1990). The role of peer relationships in the development of disorder. In S. R. Asher & J. D. Coie (Eds.), *Peer rejections in childhood* (pp. 17–59). New York: Cambridge University Press.

Landesman, S., Jaccard, J., & Gunderson, V. (1989). The family environment: The combined influences of family behavior, goals, strategies, resources, and individual experiences. In M. Lewis & S. Feinman (Eds.), *Social influences on development* (pp. 63–96). New York: Plenum.

Lichter, D. T., & Eggebeen, D. J. (1994). The effect of parental employment on child poverty. *Journal of Marriage and the Family, 56,* 633–645.

Lukemeyer, A., Meyers, M. K., & Smeeding, T. (2000). Expensive kids in poor families: Out of pocket expenditures for the care of disabled and chronically ill children and welfare reform. *Journal of Marriage and the Family, 62,* 399–415.

Meyer, L., Cole, D. A., McQuarter, R., & Reichle, J. (1990). Validation of the assessment of social competence for children and young adults with developmental disabilities. *Journal of the Association for Persons with Severe Handicaps, 15,* 57–68.

Meyers, M. K., Han, W. J., Waldfogel, J., & Garfinkel, I. (2001). Child care in the wake of welfare reform: The impact of government subsidies on the economic well-being of single-mother families. *Social Service Review, 75,* 29–59.

Meyers, M. K., & Heintze, T. (1999). The child care subsidy shortfall: Is the subsidy system working? *Social Service Review, 73,* 37–64.

National Center on Child Abuse and Neglect. (1993). *A Report on the Maltreatment of Children With Disabilities.* U.S. Department of Health and Human Services, Administration on Children, Youth, and Families, Washington, DC.

National Commission on Childhood Disability. (1995, October). *Supplemental Security Income for children with disabilities: Report to Congress.* Washington, DC: Author.

Osborne, A. G., & Dimattia, P. (1994). The IDEA's least restrictive environment mandate: Legal implications. *Exceptional Children, 61,* 6–14.

Pagelow, M. D. (1984). *Family violence.* New York: Praeger.

Parish, S. L. (2003). Mental retardation and federal income transfers: The political and economic context. *Mental Retardation, 41,* 446–459.

Parish, S. L., Pomeranz, A. E., & Braddock, D. (2003). Family support in the United States: Financing trends and emerging initiatives. *Mental Retardation, 41,* 174–187.

Parish, S. L., Seltzer, M. M., Greenberg, J. S., & Floyd, F. J. (2004). Economic implications of caregiving at midlife: Comparing parents of children with developmental disabilities to other parents. *Mental Retardation, 42,* 413-426.

Park, J., Turnbull, A. P., & Turnbull, H. R. (2002). Impacts of poverty on quality of life in families of children with disabilities. *Exceptional Children, 68,* 151–170.

Perrin, J. M. (2002). Health services research for children with disabilities. *The Milbank Quarterly, 80,* 303–324.

Rallis, S. F., & Anderson, G. (1994). *Building inclusive schools: Places where all children can learn.* Occasional Paper Series, Volume IX, Number 2. Andover, MA: Regional Laboratory for Educational Improvement of the Northeast & Islands.

Ramey, C. T., & Ramey, S. L. (1998). Early intervention and early experience. *American Psychologist, 53,* 109–120.

Richmond, J., & Ayoub, C. C. (1993). Evolution of early intervention philosophy. In D. Bryant & M. Graham (Eds.), *Implementing early intervention: From research to effective practice* (pp. 1–17). New York: Guilford Press.

Rosman, E., McCarthy, J., & Woolverton, M. (2001). *Child care: Adults with mental health needs and children with special needs.* Washington, DC: Georgetown University Child Development Center.

Scorgie, K., Wilgosh, L., & McDonald, L. (1998). Stress and coping in families of children with disabilities: An examination of recent literature. *Developmental Disabilities Bulletin, 26,* 22–42.

Scruggs, T. E., & Mastropieri, M. (1996). Teacher perceptions of mainstreaming/inclusion, 1958–1995: A research synthesis. *Exceptional Children, 63,* 59–74.

Shearn, J., & Todd, S. (2000). Maternal employment and family responsibilities: The perspectives of mothers of children with learning disabilities. *Journal of Applied Research in Intellectual Disabilities, 13,* 109–131.

Singer, G. H. S., & Irvin, L. K. (1989). *Support for caregiving families.* Baltimore: Brookes.

Sitlington, P., Frank, A., & Carson, R. (1992). Adult adjustment among high school graduates with mild disabilities. *Exceptional Children, 59,* 221–233.

Sobsey, D. (1994). *Violence and abuse in the lives of people with disabilities: The end of silent acceptance?* Baltimore: Brookes.

Social Security Administration. (2000a; September 11). Supplemental Security Income. Determining disability for a child under 18. Final rules. *Federal Register, 65,* 54747–54790.

Social Security Administration. (2000b, December 29). Final Rules. Old-Age, Survivors, and Disability Insurance and Supplemental Security Income for the aged, blind, and disabled; substantial gainful activity amounts; "Services" for trial work period purposes—monthly amounts; student child earned income exclusion. *Federal Register, 65,* 82905–82912.

Social Security Administration. (2003). *Annual statistical supplement to the Social Security Bulletin.* Washington, DC: Author.

Sopko, K. M. (2003). *The IEP: A synthesis of current literature since 1997.* Alexandria, VA: National Association of State Directors of Special Education.

Summers, J. A., Behr, S. K., & Turnbull, A. P. (1989). Positive adaptation and coping strengths of families who have children with disabilities. In G. H. S. Singer & L. K. Irvin (Eds.), *Support for caregiving families* (pp. 27–40). Baltimore: Brookes.

Taylor, S. J., Bogdan, R., & Racino, J. A. (1991). *Life in the community: Case studies of organizations supporting people with disabilities.* Baltimore: Brookes.

Thompson, T. S., Holcomb, P. A., Loprest, P., & Brennan, K. (1998). *State welfare-to-work policies for people with disabilities*. Washington, DC: Urban Institute.

Turnbull, A. P., Brotherson, M. J., & Summers, J. A. (1986). Family lifecycle: Theoretical and empirical implications and future directions for families with mentally retarded members. In J. J. Gallagher & P. M. Vietze (Eds.), *Families of handicapped persons: Research, programs and policy issues* (pp. 45–66). Baltimore: Brookes.

Turnbull, A. P, & Turnbull, H. R. (1982). Parent involvement in the education of handicapped children: A critique. *Mental Retardation, 20,* 115–122.

U.S. Department of Education. (2000). *Twenty-fourth annual report to Congress on the implementation of the Individuals with Disabilities Education Act*. Washington, DC: Author.

U.S. Department of Health and Human Services. (2002, February 14). Annual update of the HHS poverty guidelines. *Federal Register, 67,* 6931–6933.

U.S. Department of Education. (2003). *Twenty-fifth annual report to Congress on the implementation of the Individuals with Disabilities Education Act*. Washington, DC: Author.

Whitney-Thomas, J., & Moloney, M. (2001). "Who I am and what I want": Adolescents, self-definition, and struggles. *Exceptional Children, 67,* 375–389.

Yau, M. K., & Li-Tsang, C. W. (1999). Adjustment and adaptation in parents of children with developmental disabilities in two-parent families: A review of the characteristics ancillary attributes. *British Journal of Developmental Disability, 45,* 38–51.

Zipper, I. N., & Simeonsson, R. J. (1997). Promoting the development of young children with disabilities. In M. Fraser (Ed.), *Risk and resilience in childhood: An ecological perspective* (pp. 244–264). Washington, DC: NASW.

Web-Based Resources

Bazelon Center for Mental Health Law http://www.bazelon.org/
Children's Defense Fund http://www.childrensdefense.org/
Family Voices http://www.familyvoices.org/
Institute for Community Inclusion http://www.communityinclusion.org/
Kids Together, Inc. http://www.kidstogether.org/
Tash, Equal Opportunity and Inclusion for People With Disabilities http://www.tash.org/
The Arc http://www.thearc.org/

7

Policies and Programs for Adolescent Substance Abuse

Jeffrey M. Jenson

Elizabeth K. Anthony

Matthew O. Howard

A dolescent substance abuse has been the subject of frequent discussion in local, state, and federal policy circles since the 1960s. Substance abuse among children and youth has also attracted the attention of the American public. An opinion poll conducted by the Harvard School of Public Health and the Robert Wood Johnson Foundation revealed that 67 percent of Americans ranked drugs as among the most pressing problems facing teenagers (Blendon, 2000). Eighty-two percent of respondents viewed adolescent drug abuse as one of the top 10 health problems in the country.

The visible and often devastating effects of substance abuse on individuals—coupled with the societal and economic costs associated with abuse—have been the targets of repeated social intervention in the past century. Demands for policy and program reform have come from a range of constituents and organizations. A recent report compiled by the Physician Leadership on National Drug Policy (PLNDP, 2002) outlined the need for greater policy directives aimed at preventing adolescent substance abuse in the United States. The National Institute on Drug Abuse (NIDA) and the Substance

Abuse and Mental Health Services Administration (SAMHSA) are placing considerable emphasis on informing the practice community about efficacious ways to prevent and treat adolescent substance abuse (Robertson, David, & Rao, 2003; Schinke, Brounstein, & Gardner, 2002). Researchers and practitioners are uncovering new knowledge about the risk and protective factors associated with the onset and use of alcohol and illicit drugs that is being used to inform policy and programming (Hawkins, Catalano, & Arthur, 2002; Kaftarian, Robertson, Compton, Davis, & Volkow, 2004).

In this chapter, we identify risk and protective factors and review past and current policy and program responses to treating and preventing adolescent substance abuse. The utility of a public health framework that emphasizes risk, protection, and resilience for the development of innovative policy and programs is examined. We begin with a brief discussion of recent trends in adolescent substance use.

Trends in Adolescent Substance Use

Adolescent substance use exists on a continuum that includes no use, nonproblematic use, abuse, and dependence. Although substance abuse and dependence create the most concern to practitioners and policy officials, even low levels of use by children and youth can be problematic, given the many developmental tasks they encounter to be successful at school and in the community. Our review of trends in substance use therefore includes reports of experimental and regular use.

The nation's most accurate prevalence estimates for adolescent substance use come from the Monitoring the Future Study (MTF) (Johnston, O'Malley, & Bachman, 2004), sponsored by NIDA and the University of Michigan. MTF is an annual assessment of alcohol and drug use in a random sample of approximately 16,000 public and private high school students. In-school surveys with nationally representative samples of high school seniors have been conducted since 1975. Eighth- and 10th-grade students have been surveyed since 1991.

There have been several notable trends in adolescent substance use since the 1970s. Lifetime illicit drug use—marijuana, hallucinogen, cocaine, heroin, and other opiate use and use of stimulants, barbiturates, or tranquilizers that are not under a doctor's order—peaked among seniors in 1981. Sixty-six percent of 12th graders in 1981 had used an illicit drug at least once in their lives; 43 percent had used an illicit drug other than marijuana. Lifetime use of illicit drugs reached its lowest point in 1992; only 41 percent of seniors had used any illicit drug, and 25 percent had used an illicit drug other than marijuana. In 1993, seniors reversed a decade-long pattern of declining illicit drug use; 43 percent had used an illicit drug, and 27 percent had used an illicit drug other than marijuana. Rates of illicit drug use rose to 54 percent by 1997 and have changed very little since 1998. Use of illicit drugs other than marijuana increased to 30 percent by 1997 and remained at similar levels through 2002.

Lifetime alcohol and tobacco use by seniors reached their highest levels in the late 1970s and early 1980s. Approximately 93 percent of seniors reported lifetime alcohol use between 1977 and 1985. Lifetime prevalence of alcohol use decreased moderately between 1985 and 1993; 87 percent of students in the class of 1993 used alcohol. In 2003, 77 percent of seniors reported lifetime alcohol use. Lifetime cigarette smoking peaked in 1977; 76 percent of seniors smoked cigarettes that year, compared with 54 percent of seniors in 2003.

Substance use among younger adolescents is of particular concern to policymakers and practitioners because early initiation is positively related to later problem use (e.g., Hawkins, Catalano, & Miller, 1992). The number of eighth-grade students reporting lifetime use of any illicit drug increased from 19 percent in 1991 to 23 percent in 2003. Illicit drug use among 10th grade students increased from 31 percent to 41 percent between 1991 and 2003 (Johnston et al., 2004).

Males continue to use most drugs at higher rates than females. However, recent MTF results show a decrease with regard to gender differences in drug use. In 2002, the difference in annual illicit drug use between boys and girls in the eighth grade was only three percentage points; 19 percent of boys, compared with 16 percent of girls, reported annual illicit drug use in 2002. MTF results indicate that alcohol and drug use are more prevalent among European American students than among African American or Hispanic students (Johnston et al., 2004). In 2002, annual prevalence of illicit drug use among eighth graders was 15 percent for African American, 18 percent for European American, and 25 percent for Hispanic students.

MTF results provide a fairly accurate picture of substance use among American youth. However, it is important to acknowledge that the MTF study may underestimate the magnitude of substance use among youth in the United States because it does not include school dropouts (an estimated 15 to 20 percent of students in this age group), a group at high risk for alcohol and drug use. Estimates of drug and alcohol use among minority groups may be particularly affected, because more American Indian and Hispanic high school seniors drop out of school than African American, Asian American, or white seniors (Johnston et al., 2004).

Trends in adolescent substance use point to the need for a continuum of policy and practice responses. Prevention strategies are needed to delay initiation and to interrupt the progression of substance use that often begins with alcohol or tobacco and culminates with more serious drug use. Conversely, treatment options are necessary for individuals exhibiting symptoms of abuse or dependence. Specific policy and program approaches should be based on principles of risk, protection, and resilience.

The Etiology of Adolescent Substance Abuse: Principles of Risk, Protection, and Resilience

Knowledge generated by investigations examining the relationship among risk and protective factors and adolescent substance use has led to significant advancements in the etiology, assessment, and prevention of drug abuse (for a review of such investigations, see Belcher & Shinitzky, 1998; Hawkins, Catalano, & Miller, 1992; Hawkins, Kosterman, Maguin, Catalano, & Arthur, 1997; Jenson, 2004; Weinberg, Rahdert, Colliver, & Glantz, 1998). Yet definitions and policy applications underlying concepts of risk and protection are clouded with controversy. Most researchers, practitioners, and public health specialists agree that risk factors for adolescent substance use can be empirically identified. As noted in Chapter 1, there is considerably less agreement about the concept and definition of protection. Some authors (Luthar, 1991; Sameroff, Bartko, Baldwin, Baldwin, & Seifer, 1998) assert that risk and protective factors act as polar opposites of one another. Other investigators (Rossa, 2002; Rutter, 2000) argue that protective factors are characteristics and conditions that moderate or mediate levels of risk for problem behaviors like substance abuse. The following discussion of protective factors, consistent with the interpretation presented in Chapter 1, is based on the view that protective factors are traits, conditions, and characteristics that influence or modify risk for substance abuse.

Risk Factors

Risk factors for adolescent substance abuse occur at environmental, interpersonal, social, and individual levels. These factors are summarized next and in Table 7.1.

Environmental Risk Factors

Community laws and norms favorable to drug use, such as low legal drinking ages and low taxes on alcoholic beverages, increase the risk of substance use during adolescence (Joksch, 1988). Studies examining the relationship

Table 7.1   Risk Factors for Adolescent Substance Abuse

Environmental Factors

Laws and Norms
- Low taxation and weak regulation of alcohol and drugs
- Permissive cultural and social norms about substance use

Availability of Alcohol and Drugs

Poverty

Limited Economic Opportunity

Neighborhood Factors
- Neighborhood disorganization
- Low neighborhood attachment
- High rates of residential mobility
- High rates of adult criminality
- High population density

Interpersonal and Social Factors

Family Factors
- Family conflict
- Poor family management practices
- Dysfunctional family communication patterns
- Parent and sibling substance use
- Poor parent–child bonding

School Failure

Low Commitment to School

Rejection by Conforming Peer Groups

Association With Drug-Using Friends

Individual Factors

Family History of Alcoholism

Sensation-Seeking Orientation

Poor Impulse Control

Attention Deficits

Hyperactivity

Table adapted from Jenson (2004).

between legal age for drinking and adolescent drinking and driving have shown that lowering the drinking age increases underage drinking and teen traffic fatalities (Joksch, Saffer & Grossman, 1987). Laws and norms that express intolerance for use of alcohol and illicit drugs by adolescents are associated with a lower prevalence of alcohol and drug use (Johnston, 1991).

In 2003, 17 percent of children under the age of 18 lived in conditions of poverty (U.S. Census Bureau, 2003). Poverty is associated with many adverse adolescent outcomes, including conduct problems, delinquency, and unwanted pregnancy (Cauce, Stewart, Rodriguez, Cochran, & Ginzler, 2003; Farrington, Gallagher, Morley, St. Leger, & West, 1988). Poverty may also have an indirect effect on adolescent substance use. Family income is associated with many other risk factors for drug use (e.g., parenting practices and academic difficulties); low family income may affect drug use indirectly through such risk factors.

Low neighborhood attachment, school transitions, and residential mobility are associated with drug and alcohol abuse (Felner, Primavera, & Cauce, 1981; Murray, 1983). Neighborhoods with high population density and high rates of adult crime also have high rates of adolescent crime and drug use (Simcha-Fagan & Schwartz, 1986). Neighborhood disorganization may also indirectly affect risk for drug abuse by eroding the ability of parents to supervise and control their children.

Interpersonal and Social Risk Factors

Interpersonal and social risk factors for adolescent substance abuse occur in family, school, and peer settings. Children whose parents or siblings engage in serious alcohol or illicit drug use are themselves at greater risk for these behaviors (Biederman, Faraone, Monuteaux, & Feighner, 2000; Brook, Whiteman, Gordon, & Brook, 1988; Hill, Shen, Lowers, & Locke, 2000). Children raised in families with lax supervision, excessively severe or inconsistent disciplinary practices, and little communication and involvement between parents and children are also at high risk for later substance abuse (Baumrind, 1983). Similarly, studies have shown that parental conflict is related to subsequent alcohol or drug use by adolescent family members (Kumpfer & DeMarsh, 1986).

School failure, low degree of commitment to education, and lack of attachment to school are school-related factors that increase the risk of substance abuse during adolescence (Fleming, Kellam, & Brown, 1982; Holmberg, 1985). Adolescent drug users are more likely to skip classes, be absent from school, and perform poorly than non–drug users (Gottfredson, G., 1981; Kim, 1979).

Associations with friends who use drugs is among the strongest predictors of adolescent substance abuse (Elliott, Huizinga, & Ageton, 1985; Fergusson & Horwood, 1999; Jenson & Howard, 1999; Reinherz, Giacconia, Carmola Hauf, Wasserman, & Paradis, 2000). Peer rejection in elementary grades is associated with school problems and delinquency (Coie, 1990; Kupersmidt,

Coie, & Dodge, 1990), which are also risk factors for drug abuse (Hawkins, Jenson, Catalano, & Lishner, 1988). Some investigators hypothesize that rejected children form friendships with other rejected children and that such groups become delinquent or engage in drug use during adolescence (Patterson, 2002; Patterson, Reid, & Eddy, 2002; Tremblay, 1988).

Individual Risk Factors

Psychosocial and biological factors are related to drug and alcohol abuse during adolescence. For example, evidence from adoption, twin, and half-sibling studies supports the notion that alcoholism is an inherited disorder (Cadoret, Cain, & Grove, 1980). Several studies have found that a sensation-seeking orientation predicts initiation and continued use of alcohol and other drugs (Cicchetti & Rogosch, 1999; Cloninger, Sigvardsson, & Bohman, 1988; Sussman, Dent, & Galaif, 1997). Research also indicates that attention deficit disorders, hyperactivity, and poor impulse control before the age of 12 predict the age of onset of drinking and drug use (Shedler & Block, 1990).

In a recent longitudinal investigation, Jenson and Potter (2003) and Potter and Jenson (2003) found three distinct patterns of co-occurring mental health and substance use patterns among a sample of 154 detained youths. Adolescents who were most likely to abuse alcohol and other drugs also had high levels of self-reported depression, paranoia, hostility, and suicidal ideation. This and other investigations (Loeber, Farrington, Stouthamer-Loeber, & van Kammen, 1998a, 1999b; Teplin, 2001; Timmons-Mitchell, et al., 1997) suggest that mental health problems may play an important role in a youth's decision to experiment and to persistently use alcohol or other drugs.

Protective Factors

Many adolescents develop healthy relationships and succeed in school and the community despite being exposed to multiple risk factors. Empirical research devoted to identifying individual and environmental characteristics that protect youth from substance abuse has lagged behind similar efforts aimed at identifying risk factors for drug use. However, an increasing number of investigators have begun to examine the relationship between protective factors and substance use in recent years (Johnson, et al., 1998; Pollard, Hawkins, & Arthur, 1999; Rutter, 2000; Stouthamer-Loeber, et al., 1993; Tolan, Guerra, & Kendall, 1995; Werner, 1994). When identified in children and adolescents, protective factors can be established or enhanced to reduce risks for substance abuse. Protective factors for alcohol and other drug use are summarized next and in Table 7.2.

Table 7.2   Protective Factors Against Adolescent Substance Abuse

Environmental, Interpersonal, and Social Factors

Family Factors

- Being a firstborn child
- Being raised in a small family
- Low parental conflict
- Caring relationships with siblings
- Caring relationships with extended family members
- Attachment to parents

Social Support From Nonfamily Members

Commitment to School

Involvement in Conventional Activities

Belief in Pro-social Norms

Individual Factors

Social and Problem-Solving Skills

Positive Attitude

Positive Temperament

High Intelligence

Low Childhood Stress

Table adapted from Jenson (2004).

Environmental, Interpersonal, and Social Protective Factors

Environmental, interpersonal, and social protective factors are attributes that buffer community, neighborhood, family, school, and peer risk factors. The most comprehensive study of protective factors among children has been conducted by Werner and colleagues. Werner and Smith (1989) began following a cohort of high-risk children in Kauai, Hawaii in 1955. Analysis of the children's outcomes as adolescents and adults has contributed to knowledge about factors that prevent youth from abusing alcohol and other drugs.

Werner (1994) found that being raised in a family with four or fewer children, experiencing low parental conflict, and being a firstborn child reduce the effects of poverty and other risk factors for substance abuse. Children who abstained from drug use during adolescence and early adulthood had positive parent–child relationships in early childhood and caring relationships with siblings and grandparents. Children abstaining from alcohol and other drugs also received social support and frequent counsel from teachers, ministers, and neighbors (Werner, 1994).

A positive family milieu and community supports are protective factors for drug abuse among children exposed to multiple risk factors. Garmezy (1985) found low childhood stress among high-risk children living in supportive family environments and in adolescents who had strong external support systems. Because stress increases risk for drug use in later adolescence and early adulthood (Rutter, 1985), such findings have implications for preventing childhood and early adolescent drug abuse.

Strong social bonds to parents, teachers, and pro-social peers are significant factors in children's resistance to drug use (Berrueta-Clement, Schweinhart, Barnett, Epstein, & Weikhard, 1984; Hawkins, Catalano, & Associates, 1992). Four elements of the social bond have been found to be inversely related to adolescent drug abuse: (1) strong attachments to parents (Brook, Brook, Gordon, Whiteman, & Cohen, 1990), (2) commitment to school (Friedman, 1983), (3) involvement in pro-social activities such as church or community organizations (Miller, Davies, & Grenwald, 2000), and (4) belief in the generalized norms and values of society (Jenson & Howard, 1999; Krohn & Massey, 1980).

Understanding the processes by which strong social bonds develop is necessary to develop strategies that increase healthy bonding in high-risk youth. Social learning (Bandura, 1989) and social development (Catalano & Hawkins, 1996) theorists indicate that three conditions are critical to the formation of strong social bonds: (1) opportunities for involvement in pro-social activities, (2) possession of the requisite behavioral and cognitive skills necessary to achieve success in such activities, and (3) rewards or recognition for positive behaviors. To promote healthy bonds, policies should support intervention strategies that provide opportunities, enhance skills, and offer rewards to high-risk youth.

Individual Protective Factors

Individual protective factors are psychosocial and biomedical characteristics that inhibit drug use. Competence in social and problem-solving situations is associated with abstinence and reductions in teenage drug use and delinquency. In a sample of high-risk urban children, Rutter (1985) found that problem-solving skills and strong self-efficacy were associated with successful adolescent outcomes. Youth who possessed adequate problem-solving skills, and the ability to use skills, were less likely to engage in drug use and delinquency. Jenson, Wells, Plotnick, Hawkins, and Catalano

(1993) found that strong self-efficacy decreased the likelihood of drug use 6 months following drug treatment among adjudicated delinquents. These findings suggest that social and problem-solving skills moderate the effects of multiple risk factors for drug abuse and other adolescent outcomes.

Attitude and temperament are protective factors for substance abuse. Positive social orientation and positive temperament reduce the likelihood of adolescent drug abuse in several studies of high-risk youth (e.g., Jenson & Howard, 1999). Low intelligence (Werner, 1994) is also related to drug use.

Resilience

In Chapter 1, Jenson and Fraser note the importance of resilience—an individual's ability to succeed in the face of adverse life circumstances—in the prevention of adolescent problem behaviors such as substance abuse. Anecdotal accounts detailing a person's ability to overcome substance abuse and addiction are common in American popular literature (Agnew & Robideaux, 1998; Burroughs, 2003; Hamill, 1994; Knapp, 1996). However, the concept of resilience as an empirical construct in the explanation, prevention, or treatment of adolescent substance use remains a relatively new area of investigation (Luthar & Zelazo, 2003; Meschke & Patterson, 2003).

Studies indicate that some children and adolescents display high levels of functioning despite being surrounded by adverse familial or environmental influences (Fergusson & Horwood, 2003; Zucker, Wong, Puttler, & Fitzgerald, 2003). Zucker et al. (2003) examined the relationship between levels of resilience and subsequent childhood and adolescent outcomes among sons of alcoholic fathers and found that resilient youth were significantly more likely than nonresilient youth to resist substance use and other antisocial behaviors. Other studies have focused on the role of resilience in overcoming conditions of poverty (Cauce et al., 2003) and exposure to violence (Gorman-Smith & Tolan, 2003). Additional research is needed to better understand the direct and indirect effects of resilience on substance use.

Summary

Risk factors for substance use have been shown to be relatively stable over the past several decades. The factors summarized earlier consistently predict alcohol and drug use even though social norms about the acceptability of substance use have changed several times during this period. This suggests that policies and programs should encourage the development of strategies that target risk factors at multiple levels, including differential vulnerability, poor child-rearing practices, school achievement, social influences, social learning, and broad social norms.

Protection and resilience hold great promise in understanding, preventing, and treating substance abuse. Knowledge gained from studies examining the complex relationships among risk, protection, and resilience should be considered in policy and program design.

Risk, Protection, and Resilience in Substance Abuse Policy

The Evolution of Drug Policy: A Brief Overview

Drug policy in the United States reflects cultural beliefs about the risks associated with substance use and the role of governmental regulation in people's personal and social lives. Cultural beliefs about substance use and opinions about the best way to prevent or treat substance abuse are in turn affected by a host of social, political, and economic conditions (DuPont & Voth, 1995). The evolving nature of these beliefs may best be seen in the underlying tension that is evident between policy approaches favoring control and regulation and those strategies that emphasize prevention and treatment. The relative emphasis placed on control strategies versus prevention and treatment alternatives has a significant impact on the nature of policies, programs, and services for children and adolescents available at any given point in time (McBride, VanderWaal, & Terry-McElrath, 2001; Musto, 1996). The good news for prevention and treatment advocates may be that a recent increase in federal funding for adolescent health has led to a greater array of substance abuse prevention and treatment alternatives for children and youth (Dougherty, 1993; Irwin, Burg, & Cart, 2002). Major American drug policies of the past century are reviewed next and are shown in Table 7.3.

Early Drug Policy

American drug policy emerged at the turn of the century with the passage of several important acts. The Pure Food and Drug Act of 1906 required labeling of all drugs sold in the country. The Harrison Narcotics Act of 1914 and the 1919 Volstead Act prohibited the sale of narcotics or alcohol (DuPont & Voth, 1995). Prohibition against illicit drugs was used as a public policy approach well into the 1950s, when the federal government implemented drug trafficking laws and enacted strict penalties for drug violations.

Table 7.3   Major Federal Substance Abuse Policies for Children, Youth, and Families, 1990 to Present

Legislation	Purpose
1906 Pure Food and Drug Act	Required the patent medicine industry to list product ingredients
1914 Harrison Narcotics Act	Prohibited the manufacture, sale, and possession of narcotics
1919 Volstead Act & Eighteenth Amendment to the Constitution	Prohibited the sale of alcohol
1937 Marijuana Tax Act	Prohibited the nonmedical use of marijuana
1966 Narcotic Addict Rehabilitation Act	Established civil commitment system (treatment) for federal offenders rather than prosecution
1970 Comprehensive Drug Abuse Prevention and Control Act	Consolidated previous drug laws and reduced penalties for marijuana possession; included the Controlled Substances Act, which established five schedules for regulating drugs based on medicinal value and potential for addiction or abuse
1986 and 1988 Anti-Drug Abuse Acts	Emphasized law enforcement in general, with the 1988 Act also attending to treatment and prevention; created the Office of National Drug Control Policy (ONDCP) and the Substance Abuse and Mental Health Services Administration (SAMHSA)
1997 Title XXI (SSA), State Child Health Insurance (SCHIP) established	Expanded health insurance coverage for children and allowed flexibility in resource distribution

1960–1980

The "drug revolution" of the 1960s and 1970s created an increase in demand for illicit drugs that was unparalleled in prior years. Changing social norms reflecting greater tolerance for experimental drug use led to a shift from the predominantly punitive stance that was common before 1960 to an interest in decriminalizing marijuana and other less serious drugs. As "recreational" and experimental drug use became more common, increased public awareness of the health risks associated with substance use coincided with the development of prevention and treatment strategies for illicit drug abuse (McBride et al., 2001). Passage of the Narcotic Addict Rehabilitation Act of 1966 reflected society's desire to help individuals suffering from addiction. And, in 1967, the American Medical Association endorsed the disease theory as the predominant explanation of alcohol addiction, a change that was to have a profound effect on American social policy (Freeman, 2001).

The 1970s witnessed several key pieces of drug-related legislation. Predating President Nixon's declaration calling for a "War on Drugs" by just 1 year, Congress passed the Comprehensive Drug Abuse Prevention and Control Act in 1970. The Act consolidated several former federal laws and categorized addictive drugs for purposes of control and regulation. While reducing the penalties for certain types of possession offenses, the Act also strengthened law enforcement efforts. The emphasis on rehabilitation, however, remained an important part of the 1970 legislation.

1980–Present

An increase in drug use among the nation's youth at the end of the 1970s marked a reversal in public opinion about the nature of substance use policy. "Get-tough" approaches began to replace policies favoring community-based treatment and the subsequent passage of the Anti-Drug Abuse Acts of 1986 and 1988 reinforced a return to policies favoring law enforcement and control (McBride et al., 2001). The federal Office of National Drug Control Policy (ONDCP) was created in 1988 to better coordinate drug policy across states and international borders. By the late 1980s, all states raised the legal drinking age to 21 in response to growing concerns about the dangers and consequences of adolescent alcohol abuse. Arrest, conviction, and incarceration rates for drug-related offenses—particularly among poor and minority youth—increased following tougher policy provisions passed in the 1980s (Mauer & Huling, 1995; Snyder, 1990).

Some policy experts have noted an apparent return to drug policies favoring prevention and rehabilitation in the past decade (PLNDP, 2002). This change coincides with a newfound interest in viewing adolescent substance abuse as a public health problem and applying principles of risk and protection to substance policy and programs (Hawkins et al., 2002). Next, we discuss specific federal policies across the domains of law enforcement, prevention, and treatment. Though not exhaustive, these selected policies highlight major trends in policy approaches aimed at adolescent substance abuse.

Law Enforcement

Law enforcement has always been a critical component of American drug policy (Morin & Collins, 2000; PLNDP, 2002). Funding for law enforcement efforts aimed at combating adolescent substance abuse has increased substantially each year since 1980. Federal spending for the control of illicit drugs alone increased from $1.5 billion in 1981 to $17.9 billion in 1999 (Robert Wood Johnson Foundation, 2001). More than 75 percent of federal funds distributed to state and local communities for illicit drug use control is devoted to law enforcement activities (Kleiman, 1998).

The 2003 National Drug Control Strategy earmarked 67 percent of the $19.2 billion drug control budget for the supply reduction strategies of interdiction and law enforcement. The remaining 33 percent of the overall budget was allocated to prevention and treatment (ONDCP, 2002). As Figure 7.1 demonstrates, federal spending for supply reduction has increased and remains disproportionate to spending levels for prevention and treatment (ONDCP, 2004).

Domestic and international law enforcement and interdiction policies comprise what is known as a supply reduction strategy. Intended to disrupt the drug trade market and to limit access to drugs, supply reduction relies on practices such as taxation and law enforcement to control alcohol and illicit drug use. Initiatives to dismantle illicit drug trafficking networks are also included in supply reduction strategies. The federal drug control budget provides funding through various initiatives to increase the capacity of organizations such as the Drug Enforcement Administration, Federal Bureau of Investigation, U.S. Customs Service, Border Patrol, and Coast Guard to implement these approaches.

The effectiveness of law enforcement and drug interdiction can be evaluated by assessing the cost of illicit drugs and by monitoring rates of adolescent substance use. Based on these outcome measures, the results of law enforcement and drug interdiction efforts have achieved limited success. Despite spending more than $18 billion a year on international law enforcement and interdiction, evidence suggests that the relative price of many "hard drugs" has actually decreased in recent years (Bach & Lantos, 1999; Kleiman, 1998) and that access to illicit drugs has not diminished (Robert Wood Johnson Foundation, 2001). In 2003, more than 50 percent of adolescents tried an illicit substance by the time they graduated from 12th grade (Johnston et al., 2004), a finding that offers at least cursory evidence to suggest that law enforcement and interdiction efforts alone are not effective in reducing adolescent substance use.

Supply reduction strategies restricting access and increasing taxes for alcohol and other drugs appear to have produced greater success in reducing

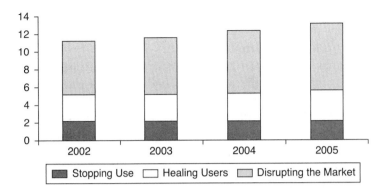

Figure 7.1   Federal Spending for Substance Abuse Policy and Programs:
The National Drug Control Budget ($ Billions), 2002–2005.

This figure is adapted from the National Drug Control Strategy, FY 2005 Budget Summary,
by ONDCP, 2004, Washington, DC: The White House.

substance abuse. For example, an increase in the minimum drinking age
is associated with a decline in alcohol consumption and in alcohol-related
auto fatalities (Cook & Tauchen, 1984). Further, federal taxes on alcohol
and tobacco have generated government revenue that has been used to fund
efficacious prevention and treatment services in many states (Robert Wood
Johnson Foundation, 2001).

Many experts assert that policy debates about the merits of supply reduction strategies do not lie in the specific findings regarding the effectiveness
of law enforcement, interdiction, taxation, and restrictive access strategies
(Kleiman, 1998; Morin & Collins, 2000). Rather, the primary concern of
many policy officials is the disproportionate allocation of federal funding
that has historically relegated prevention and treatment alternatives to a
secondary priority. Continuing to increase funding for law enforcement and
interdiction during periods of limited funding for prevention and treatment
illustrates this source of major policy contention. Given the enormous cost of
interdiction and enforcement and the ongoing increases necessary to reduce
the illicit drug trade, many public health officials are advocating higher levels
of funding for prevention and treatment.

Prevention

The history of adolescent substance abuse prevention efforts dates to at
least the 1960s. Early prevention efforts educated children and youth about
different types of drugs and informed young people about the physical

effects of using alcohol and other substances. These "information only" programs fell short of providing interactive experiences to young people and relied on didactic learning approaches to educate adolescents about substance abuse. Other programs employed "scared-straight" tactics to warn adolescents about the adverse individual and social consequences of alcohol and illicit drugs (Lynam et al., 1999; Rosenbaum, 1999; U.S. Department of Education, 1998). Perhaps not surprisingly, programs relaying only information about alcohol and other drugs or exposing youth to the risks of drug use produced few positive results.

The evolution of substance abuse prevention advanced slowly following the early 1970s. It was not until the mid-1980s that an emerging group of prevention researchers began to introduce school-based curricula as a new approach to prevent substance abuse (Botvin, 2004; Hansen, 1992; Hawkins et al., 2002; Kellam & Anthony, 1998). These curricula were based on known correlates of substance abuse and relied on interactive and structured activities that involved children in the concept of prevention. Subsequent longitudinal studies of these interventions revealed that well-designed prevention curricula could effectively prevent the initiation of drug use among young people (e.g., Hansen). The common thread among the programs was the use of a risk and protective factor framework as a guiding source of program design.

Policies and programs supporting substance abuse prevention have increased significantly since the initial program evaluations of the mid-1980s. It is widely agreed that the adoption of the risk-based prevention paradigm is largely responsible for the increase in attention paid to prevention policy and to prevention research (Robertson et al., 2003). NIDA, SAMHSA, and governmental entities such as the Office of Juvenile Justice and Delinquency Prevention (OJJDP) all recognize the utility of a public health prevention framework and have taken efforts to implement principles of risk, protection, and resilience in their current program and policy initiatives (Howell, 2003; Robertson et al., 2003; Schinke et al., 2002). Programs targeting factors that increase and guard against risk for substance abuse now represent the most commonly used prevention strategy in the United States (American Academy of Pediatrics, 2001; Robertson et al., 2003). The results from a number of longitudinal investigations of risk-based prevention programs implemented in school, family, and community settings reveal positive outcomes with regard to substance use (for reviews, see Foxcroft, Ireland, Lister-Sharp, Lowe, & Breen, 2003; Gottfredson & Wilson, 2003).

Federal Policy Initiatives

Several important federal policy directives support the use of a public health framework for substance abuse prevention. The *Drug-Free*

Communities Program initiated in 1997 supports community and antidrug coalitions that create collaborative efforts among prevention agencies and organizations (ONDCP, 2004). The Department of Education and SAMHSA provide funds for school- and community-based prevention programs under this initiative.

Changing social norms about substance use is a primary objective of several media campaigns and education programs that have received generous federal support (ONDCP, 2004). In 1998; the National Youth Anti-Drug Media Campaign, a program of ONDCP, received $195 million in federal funding and $2 billion in public and private funds to combat media images promoting substance use (Kelder, Maiback, Worden, Biglan, & Levitt, 2000).

In collaboration with the Ad Council and Partnership for a Drug-Free America, the 5-year media campaign is one of the most visible prevention strategies in the country. The program's primary objective is to educate children, youth, and parents about drug use and to promote young people's ability to reject illegal drugs through personal and social skill development (ONDCP, 2004). The campaign aims to change social norms about drug use by communicating messages about youth who do not use substances, discussing the negative effects of drugs, and portraying the positive aspects of a drug-free lifestyle (ONDCP, 1997). An evaluation of the campaign revealed that nearly 80 percent of youth and 70 percent of parents who were polled about the campaign recalled seeing at least one message delivered through media sources each week (Westat & the Annenberg school for communication, 2003). However, like the information-only and scared-straight efforts before it, the media campaign has produced little direct evidence of reducing substance use. Despite this result, the campaign is scheduled to continue. President Bush's budget for fiscal year 2005 allocates $145 million to the National Youth Anti-Drug Media Campaign.

Education has been a primary location of substance abuse prevention activities. Funding for school-based drug education formally began in the 1980s, when Congress allocated approximately $500 million a year for prevention activities (Burke, 2002; Wyrick, Wyrick, Bibeau, & Fearnow-Kennedy, 2001). Federal government involvement in substance abuse prevention, however, has had an uneven history. In the late 1980s and early 1990s, significant amounts of government dollars were devoted to a drug abuse resistance education program called Project D.A.R.E. The popular program brought police officers and law enforcement officials to school classrooms. Officers warned children about the dangers of alcohol and other drug use and worked to reduce negative stereotypes of law enforcement. Evaluations of Project D.A.R.E. revealed that the program was no more effective than routine prevention approaches being used in the nation's schools and classrooms to prevent substance use (e.g., Lynam et al., 1999). To their credit, the developers of D.A.R.E. used these findings to retool the program to include more interactive and skills-based teaching strategies in the curriculum. Still, the enormous sum of money allocated to an ineffective program has been a stark lesson to policymakers about the risk of funding untested prevention approaches.

In 1997, the U.S. Department of Education's Safe and Drug-Free School and Communities Program took an important step in prevention policy by requiring all programs that receive federal funds to select and implement interventions that had demonstrated some degree of effectiveness in preventing substance use. Efforts to increase the number of empirically supported interventions in prevention settings have positively affected the quality and outcomes of school-based prevention programs since 1997 (Burke, 2002; Gottfredson & Wilson, 2003). NIDA supports considerable substance abuse prevention research and has developed specific action steps for school and community-based programs that are based on principles of risk and protection (Robertson, David, & Rao, 2003).

Prevention research continues to advance what is known about effective ways to delay or prevent substance use initiation. Efforts are now under way to bring efficacious programs to a larger scale across school districts and communities (Botvin, 2004). No matter how effective such efforts become, the need for treatment services for children and youth experiencing more serious substance use problems must also be an important part of a policy and program continuum.

Treatment

Several public health organizations, including the PLNDP (2000) and the American Academy of Pediatrics (2000), are at the forefront of advocacy efforts aimed at increasing federal funding for substance abuse treatment. A recent position paper on adolescent drug policy published by PLNDP (2002) called for the use of evidence-based interventions in drug treatment. PLNDP (2000) also suggested that levels of substance abuse funding should be similar to funds provided for diseases such as diabetes and heart disease. The PLNDP (2002) argues that the long-standing federal emphasis on law enforcement policy has mitigated the potential of treatment as a means of reducing substance abuse problems.

There is currently no national standard of care for treating adolescent substance abusers in the United States. Substance abuse treatment varies by region, state, and locality and is generally considered to be poorly funded and difficult to access. The surgeon general's office estimates that approximately

75 percent of children who need help fail to receive it (U.S. Department of Health and Human Services, 1999). Other estimates indicate that as few as 1 in every 10 adolescents who need substance abuse treatment actually receive it and that only 25 percent of those participating in treatment receive the appropriate type and level of assistance (Center for Substance Abuse Treatment, 2002; NIDA, 2002). Access to care appears to be strongly related to inadequate health insurance coverage and to complicated managed-care regulations that limit time allotted for treatment (American Academy of Pediatrics, 2001).

A major concern affecting access to care for many children and adolescents is the fragmented nature of substance abuse treatment. Policies and programs supporting adolescent substance abuse treatment come from such disparate domains as education, juvenile justice, child welfare, labor, and health. Each system has its own eligibility criteria, and each operates independently from the other. The result is a fragmented system of care (SOC) in which many youth may be shuffled from program to program with little coordination across service sectors.

Youth with substance abuse problems are also more likely to experience other mental health problems. In many cases, treatment facilities in one system are not equipped to handle multiple problems. For example, estimates indicate that 60 to 80 percent of youth involved in the juvenile justice system also have a substance use disorder (Dembo, Williams, & Schmeidler, 1993; Teplin, 2001). Few resources currently exist to treat youth with multiple problems.

Public sources provide funding for alcohol and drug treatment through a combination of Medicaid and state and local funds. Funds for public substance abuse treatment are limited, and restrictions placed on the type of eligible service often prevent integration across systems of care (PLNDP, 2002). For example, the Medicaid program provides health insurance coverage for more than 16.4 million children. However, Medicaid programs display considerable variation in the services they fund, ranging from comprehensive treatment benefits in some states to only inpatient detoxification in other states (Gehshan, 1999). Medicaid reimbursement rates are also typically quite low, which has led to less incentive to provide treatment services (American Academy of Pediatrics, 2001).

Expansion of health care coverage for low-income children was included as a provision in a 1997 bill that created the State Children's Health Insurance Program (SCHIP). This program allows states to access federal funds for children who are not eligible for other coverage. Funds are provided via the Medicaid program or through a separate program established specifically for SCHIP participants. Although coverage still varies considerably by state, all states using SCHIP generally pay for detoxification and for some types of outpatient substance abuse treatment (Gehshan, 1999).

Medicaid and SCHIP are required to implement the Early and Periodic Screening, Diagnosis, and Treatment Program (EPSDT). Many experts believe that EPSDT could be an effective way to increase substance abuse treatment services for troubled youth (e.g., Rosenbaum, Johnson, Snonsky, Markus, & DeGraw, 1998). However, a general lack of awareness about EPSDT in the professional community has led to underutilization. Weak coordination between Medicaid and SCHIP has also limited use of EPSDT as a referral source for substance abuse treatment.

Federal block grants provide resources that seek to improve access to substance abuse treatment services. These grants typically provide funds that are channeled through federal and state agencies. For example, prevention services funded by the Substance Abuse Prevention and Treatment Block Grant are administered by the Center for Substance Abuse Prevention. Corresponding treatment services are funded and administered by the Center for Substance Abuse Treatment, SAMHSA, and the U.S. Department of Health and Human Services. With many states rolling block grant money into specialty "carve-out" arrangements, one recent policy concern is that substance abuse services may be inappropriately offered by mental health providers rather than by trained substance abuse treatment specialists (PLNDP, 2001).

Finally, numerous financial barriers to substance abuse treatment exist. Treatment services are generally not funded at the same level as other medical services, and benefit limitations, higher co-payments, and separate deductibles all apply to substance abuse benefits (Buck & Umland, 1997). The Mental Health Parity Act of 1996 (P.L. 104–204) dictates that the same annual and lifetime maximums should be provided for mental health treatment as for general medical care. However, no such legislation exists for substance abuse benefits.

Several public health organizations have recently made policy recommendations calling for a more thoughtful and integrated continuum of care in adolescent substance abuse prevention and treatment (American Academy of Pediatrics, 2001; PLNDP, 2002; Robert Wood Johnson Foundation, 2001). We explore these ideas more fully in the next section.

Using Knowledge of Risk, Protection, and Resilience to Achieve Service Integration

Principles of risk, protection, and resilience are key components of effective substance abuse intervention. The potential of these principles for public policy has yet to be fully realized. To be effective, knowledge of risk, protection, and resilience should undergird policy and programs in all systems of care for children and youth.

A Continuum of Substance Abuse Policy

Substance use disorders are prevalent among children and youth in nearly all public sectors of care in the United States. Aarons and colleagues (Aarons, Brown, Hough, Garland, & Wood, 2001) examined prevalence rates for substance use disorders among adolescents who were receiving care in five service systems in San Diego County. Prevalence estimates ranged from 19 percent for youth in the child welfare system to 41 and 62 percent for adolescents in the mental health and juvenile justice systems, respectively (Aarons et al., 2001). The high prevalence of substance abuse across systems of care points to the need for better integration and coordination of prevention and treatment policy and programs.

Policies aimed at adolescent substance abuse, like policies targeting other childhood and adolescent problems, have largely been incremental and fragmented. That is, programs and interventions tend to develop as a result of localized conditions that fail to consider national trends vis-à-vis substance abuse or empirical evidence regarding the relative effectiveness of prevention and treatment approaches. To confound matters, service sectors for high-risk youth develop responses to problems that tend to be very similar to one another. Creating an integrated continuum of care must begin with assessment and screening policies and practices.

Assessment and Screening Policies

An integrated SOC for children and youth must first acknowledge the need to assess and screen youth for a variety of problem behaviors, including substance abuse. Once appropriate assessment data are collected, appropriate placements and sanctions can be more easily determined. Policies are needed to create centralized assessment centers that serve diagnostic and referral needs across major systems of care for children and adolescents. Provisions of these policies should include standardized diagnostic tools that offer interpretative guidelines for juvenile justice, mental health, child welfare, and substance abuse practitioners. Standardized assessment procedures might also lead to more systematic placement criteria and decision making, and would allow cross-system comparisons of risk and protective factors found to be prevalent among youth and their family members. Knowledge of these factors, in turn, could be used to inform the direction of prevention and treatment programs.

Prevention Policies

Perhaps the single greatest policy need in substance abuse prevention lies in funding. Prevention has historically been underfunded when compared with competing demands made by treatment providers and law enforcement (PLNDP, 2002). In recent years, longitudinal studies have indicated that prevention programs are not only effective in preventing and reducing substance abuse but also more cost-effective than treatment and law enforcement (Bukoski & Evans, 1998). Data from two effective interventions— the Strengthening Families and Preparing for the Drug-free Years—have reported savings of between 5 and 10 dollars in future costs for every dollar spent (Spoth, Guyull, & Day, 2002). The increasing availability of effective programs through the dissemination efforts of entities such as SAMHSA (Schinke, et al., 2002), the Center for the Study and Prevention of Violence (Mihalic & Irwin, 2003), and collaborations dedicated to advancing evidence-based practice such as the Campbell Collaboration (Campbell Collaboration Library, 2004) is further argument for the adoption of prevention policy as a national priority for children, youth, and families.

To reach more children, youth, and families, prevention policy must bring effective programs to scale at the school, neighborhood, and community levels. Members of the Social Development Research Group at the University of Washington are currently testing a model called *Communities That Care* (CTC), which represents this type of effort. CTC is designed to help community leaders identify risk and protective factors for substance abuse that are common among children and youth in their neighborhoods and schools. Once identified, these factors become the targets of specific intervention efforts (Arthur, Hawkins, Pollard, Catalano, & Baglioni, 2002). The CTC model is currently being implemented and tested in six states and holds great promise as a strategy that links risk, protection, policy, and practice. To date, CTC has demonstrated that risk-focused prevention planning can be an effective way to organize communities (Arthur et al., 2002).

Treatment Policies

Historically, treatment for young people has mirrored that provided to adults; 12-step and self-help interventions based on a disease model of addiction have dominated the field (Jenson, et al., 2004). Reviews of controlled trials of adolescent substance abuse treatment reveal fewer than 20 investigations before 2001 (Deas & Thomas, 2001; Jenson, Howard, & Vaughn). Cognitive-behavioral interventions promoting skill development and family-based

---

A Prevention Case Example

Bishopville is a (fictitious) suburban community on the east coast that has recently become alarmed about increases in adolescent substance abuse. Anecdotal reports about all-night drug parties (i.e., raves) involving alcohol, marijuana, and hallucinogens have surfaced in local schools and neighborhoods. A recent party led to the arrest of six local teenagers and alerted officials that action steps were necessary.

The CTC model (Hawkins, Catalano, & Associates, 1992; Hawkins, 2004) was chosen by officials as a means of better understanding and addressing the problem of adolescent substance abuse in Bishopville. Using the model, Bishopville employed the following action steps that led to the creation of a city-wide prevention policy:

Step One: *Organizing and Mobilizing*. Leaders of Bishopville selected key individuals to guide the prevention planning process. This included the mayor, educators, business representatives, and other elected officials. The group subsequently formed a community prevention board that was charged with organizing and mobilizing other community advocates and constituency groups.

Step Two: *Developing a Community Profile of Strengths, Resources, and Challenges*. Risk and protective factors for adolescent substance use were assessed using a CTC Survey with a random sample of children and adolescents in grades 6 to 12 (Hawkins, 2004). Survey results were used to rank the most common risk and protective factors found among children and youth in Bishopville. A community-needs assessment aimed at identifying existing and needed services for children and youth was also conducted in this phase.

Step Three: *Creating a Strategic Prevention Plan*. In this phase, the Bishopville Community Prevention Board reviewed and selected several efficacious prevention strategies that will be implemented in their local schools and neighborhoods. A school-based curriculum that targets early onset of substance use and a community-level media campaign were among the strategies selected for implementation.

Step Four: *Evaluating and Monitoring the Plan*. Steps were identified to monitor and evaluate the prevention strategies selected by the board. Outcome measures and other methodological decisions were made in consultation with local and national experts to ensure a rigorous evaluation process.

Please see Hawkins, Catalano, and Associates (1992) and Hawkins (2004) for a more detailed description of using the CTC model in a community setting.

---

therapeutic approaches are among the most effective treatment strategies for adolescents.

Proponents of evidence-based practice (Chambless & Hollon, 1998; Rosen & Proctor, 2003) argue that treatments for substance use disorders must be selected on the basis of effectiveness. Clearly, more controlled studies of adolescent substance use treatment are needed to create the knowledge base necessary to recommend and disseminate efficacious programs to the practice community. Only limited empirical evidence is available to form the basis of a policy continuum reflecting different levels of treatment for adolescent substance abuse. Standards of care for treatment connected to evidence-based interventions also need to be made available to professionals in the treatment community (PLNDP, 2002).

Years of anecdotal evidence suggests that a lack of communication between drug treatment agencies and poor coordination across systems of care have interacted to create a mix of programs that have not adequately met the needs of adolescent substance abusers. Several treatment initiatives show promise with regard to improving the disjointed treatment system. Drug courts, an initiative funded by the federal government under the National Drug Control Strategy (ONDCP, 2004), are one alternative for juvenile offenders with substance abuse problems. As part of the program, youth may be referred to treatment and receive mandatory drug sanctions in lieu of traditional case processing (Kimbrough, 1998).

The Tribal Youth Program administered by OJJDP emerged in response to the problem of violent crime and co-occurring substance use disorders among American Indian youth. The Departments of Health and Human Services, Education, Interior, and Justice collaborated to design and implement the program in 1999. Program objectives include providing a range of assessment and treatment prevention strategies aimed at addressing the unique needs of substance-abusing American Indian youth (OJJDP, 2000). The Tribal Youth initiative represents the type of cross-system coordination needed to implement integrated policies and service for troubled youth.

These initiatives represent only the surface of adolescent substance abuse treatment needs in the United States. Efficacy trials of treatment approaches, community advocacy efforts, and standards of care are needed to inform the direction of substance abuse treatment. Coordination across agencies and systems of care should be a top priority in treatment policy discussions.

Summary

Principles of risk, protection, and resilience hold great promise for substance abuse programs and policies. A prevention and treatment continuum based on risk and protective factors should offer a cogent solution to legislators and policy officials charged with developing effective ways to prevent and reduce adolescent substance abuse. A public health model that incorporates

A Treatment Case Example

A case history. Johnny is a 16-year-old boy who is currently under jurisdiction and supervision of the juvenile justice system. He has a history of property offending dating back some 6 years to when he was arrested for stealing on several occasions. In recent years, Johnny's behavior escalated to more serious crimes, including assault. He first experimented with alcohol and marijuana at age 12 and now admits to using marijuana, cocaine, and hallucinogens "whenever and wherever" they are available. Johnny was placed in the juvenile justice for assaulting a boy in his neighborhood. He reports that he had been drinking and was high on cocaine at the time of the incident.

Johnny's family life had been unstable. His father left home when Johnny was 5 years old; they have had relatively little contact since that time. Johnny has heard from other relatives that his father frequently uses alcohol and that he has been incarcerated on several occasions. Johnny's mother has worked a series of low-paying jobs but has no history of substance abuse. Two years ago, his mother invited her boyfriend into the family home. Johnny was initially resentful of this decision and has adapted to the situation by largely ignoring the boyfriend. Johnny has two sisters, both of whom are younger in age. Johnny's mother reports that Johnny tends to be withdrawn and sad much of the time. He spends long periods of time alone in his room and has recently stopped seeing many of his friends.

System response. Johnny's case represents a profile that is common among youth in the juvenile justice system. Perhaps what is most typical is the presence of multiple and overlapping behavior problems. In our case, Johnny's problems include antisocial conduct, substance abuse, and undiagnosed symptoms of depression.

Theoretically, the presence of these problems could logically lead to placement in the juvenile justice system for antisocial conduct, the substance abuse treatment network for drug-using behaviors, or the mental health system for symptoms of depression. The challenge for treating Johnny—and the thousands of young people like him—lies in integrating system responses and treatments in a manner that addresses Johnny's multiple problems. In Johnny's case, policies that create and support a centralized assessment process might best lead to a coordinated response across multiple systems of care.

risk and protection as guiding principles is also consistent with the current evidence-based practice movement.

Efforts toward integrating substance abuse policy should begin by examining overlapping initiatives in juvenile justice and mental health. Co-occurring drug use and mental health problems are well documented among young people. Many youth with concomitant problems are subsequently placed in the nation's juvenile justice and mental health systems. Efforts to improve coordination must also include the array of treatment providers who contract for services with public systems of care. Community-based programs that offer outpatient care, day treatment, and residential care must be added to policy discussions across the multiple systems of care for children, youth, and families. A public health approach emphasizing risk, protection, and resilience may provide a common language and effective organizing framework for adolescent substance programs and policies.

Questions for Discussion

1. What have been the dominant public policy approaches to adolescent substance abuse in the past three decades? Which strategy has received the greatest percentage of funding?

2. What are the organizational implications of a shift to a public health approach to substance abuse prevention and treatment?

3. What are the challenges in integrating service systems for the delivery of adolescent substance abuse treatment and prevention?

4. What policy recommendations would you make to address the disjointed delivery system?

Additional Reading

American Academy of Pediatrics. (2001). Improving substance abuse prevention, assessment, and treatment financing for children and adolescents. *Pediatrics, 108,* 1025–1029.

Botvin, G. J. (2004). Advancing prevention science and practice: Challenges, critical issues, and future directions. *Prevention Science, 5,* 69–72.

Foxcroft, D. R., Ireland, D., Lister-Sharp, D. J., Lowe, G., & Breen, R. (2003). Longer term primary prevention for alcohol misuse in young people: A systematic review. *Addiction, 98,* 397–411.

Hawkins, J. D., Catalano, R. F., & Arthur, M. (2002). Promoting science-based prevention in communities. *Addictive Behaviors, 90,* 1–26.

Hawkins, J. D., Catalano, R. F., & Associates. (1992). *Communities that care: Action for drug abuse prevention.* San Francisco: Jossey-Bass.

Office of National Drug Control Policy. (2004). *The President's National Drug Control Strategy, 2004.* Washington, DC: Executive Office of the President.

Physician Leadership on National Drug Policy. (2002). *Adolescent substance abuse: A public health priority: An evidence-based, comprehensive, and integrative approach.* Providence, RI: Center for Alcohol and Addiction Studies, Brown University.

Robert Wood Johnson Foundation. (2001). *Substance abuse: The nation's number one health problem: Key indicators for policy.* Update. Princeton, NJ: RWJF.

Wagner, E. F., & Waldron, H. B. (2001). *Innovations in adolescent substance abuse interventions.* New York: Pergamon Press.

Note

1. This reduction, however, may be an artifact of a change in item wording pertaining to alcohol use in the Monitoring the Future surveys following 1993 (Johnston, O'Malley, & Bachman, 2004). The question for lifetime alcohol use was changed in 1993 to refer to drinks of "more than a few sips." Prior to 1993, lifetime use included any use of alcohol.

References

Aarons, G. A., Brown, S. A., Hough, R. L., Garland, A. F., & Wood, P. A. (2001). Prevalence of adolescent substance use disorders across five sectors of care. *Journal of the American Academy of Child and Adolescent Psychiatry, 40,* 419–426.

Agnew, E., & Robideaux, S. (1998). *My mama's waltz.* New York: Pocket Books.

American Academy of Pediatrics. (2000). Insurance coverage of mental health and substance abuse services for children and adolescents: A consensus statement. *Pediatrics, 106,* 860–862.

American Academy of Pediatrics. (2001). Improving substance abuse prevention, assessment, and treatment financing for children and adolescents. *Pediatrics, 108,* 1025–1029.

Arthur, M. W., Hawkins, J. D., Pollard, J. A., Catalano, R. F., & Baglioni, A. J., Jr. (2002). Measuring risk and protective factors for substance use, delinquency, and other adolescent problem behaviors: The Communities That Care Youth Survey. *Evaluation Review, 26,* 575–601.

Bach, P. B., & Lantos, J. (1999). Methadone dosing, heroin affordability and the severity of addiction. *American Journal of Public Health, 89,* 662–665.

Bandura, A. (1989). Human agency in social cognitive theory. *American Psychologist, 14,* 1175–1184.

Baumrind, D. (1983, October). *Why adolescents take chances—and why they don't.* Paper presented at the National Institute for Child Health and Human Development, Bethesda, MD.

Belcher, H. M., & Shinitzky, H. E. (1998). Substance abuse in children: Prediction, protection, and prevention. *Archives of Pediatrics and Adolescent Medicine, 152,* 952–960.

Berrueta-Clement, J. R., Schweinhart, L. J., Barnett, W. S., Epstein, A. S., & Weikhard, D. P. (1984). *Changed lives: The effects of the Perry Preschool Program on youths through age 19.* Ypsilanti, MI: High/Scope Press.

Biederman, J., Faraone, S. V., Monuteaux, M. C., & Feighner, J. A. (2000). Patterns of alcohol and drug use in adolescents can be predicted by parental substance use disorders. *Pediatrics, 106,* 792–797.

Blendon, R. (2000). *Report on public attitudes toward illegal drug use and drug treatment.* Harvard School of Public Health and the Robert Wood Johnson Foundation. Unpublished data.

Botvin, G. J. (2004). Advancing prevention science and practice: Challenges, critical issues, and future directions. *Prevention Science, 5,* 69–72.

Brook, J. S., Brook, D. W., Gordon, A. S., Whiteman, M., & Cohen, P. (1990). The psychosocial etiology of adolescent drug use: A family interactional approach. *Genetic, Social and General Psychology Monographs,* No. 116. (Whole No. 2).

Brook, J. S., Whiteman, M., Gordon, A. S., & Brook, D. W. (1988). The role of older brothers in younger brothers' drug use viewed in the context of parent and peer influences. *Journal of Genetic Psychology, 151,* 59–75.

Buck, J. A., & Umland, B. (1997). Covering mental health and substance abuse services. *Health Affairs (Millwood), 16,* 120–126.

Bukoski, W. J., & Evans, R. I. (Eds.) (1998). Cost-benefit/cost-effectiveness of drug abuse prevention: Implication for programming and policy (NIDA Research Monograph No. 176). Rockville, MD: National Institute on Drug Abuse.

Burke, M. R. (2002). School-based substance abuse prevention: Political finger-pointing does not work. *Federal Probation, 66,* 66–71.

Burroughs, A. (2003). *Dry: A memoir.* New York: St. Martin's Press.

Cadoret, R. J., Cain, C. A., & Grove, W. M. (1980). Development of alcoholism in adoptees raised apart from alcoholic biologic relatives. *Archives of General Psychiatry, 37,* 561–563.

Campbell Collaboration Library (2004). (Database). Retrieved on July 17, 2004, from http:/www.campbellcollaboration.org/Fralibrary.html

Catalano, R. F., & Hawkins, J. D. (1996). The social development model: A theory of antisocial behavior. In J. D. Hawkins (Ed.), *Delinquency and crime: Current theories* (pp. 149–197). New York: Cambridge University Press.

Cauce, A. M., Stewart, A., Rodriguez, M. D., Cochran, B., & Ginzler, J. (2003). Overcoming the odds? Adolescent development in the context of urban poverty. In S. S. Luthar (Ed.), *Resilience and vulnerability: Adaptation in the context of childhood adversities* (pp. 343–363). Cambridge, UK: Cambridge University Press.

Center for Substance Abuse Treatment. (2002). *Treatment Episode Data Set, 2002* (Data file). Available from the Substance Abuse and Mental Health Data Archive Web site, www.icpsr.umich.edu/SAMHDA/das.html

Chambless, D. L., & Hollon, S. D. (1998). Defining empirically supported therapies. *Journal of Consulting and Clinical Psychology, 66,* 7–18.

Cicchetti, D., & Rogosch, F. A. (1999). Psychopathology as risk for adolescent substance use disorders: A developmental psychopathology perspective. *Journal of Clinical Child Psychology, 28,* 355–365.

Cloninger, C. R., Sigvardsson, S., & Bohman, M. (1988). Childhood personality predicts alcohol abuse in young adults. *Alcoholism: Clinical and Experimental Research, 12,* 494–503.

Coie, J. D. (1990). Towards a theory of peer rejection. In S. R. Asher & J. D. Coie (Eds.), *Peer rejection in childhood* (pp. 365–398). New York: Cambridge University Press.

Cook, P. J., & Tauchen, G. (1984). The effect of minimum drinking age legislation on youthful auto fatalities, 1970–1977. *Journal of Legal Studies, 13,* 169–190.

Deas, D., & Thomas, S. E. (2001). An overview of controlled studies of adolescent substance abuse treatment. *The American Journal on Addictions, 10,* 178–189.

Dembo, R., Williams, L., & Schmeidler, J. (1993). Addressing the problems of substance abuse in juvenile corrections. In J. A. Inciardi (Ed.), *Drug treatment in criminal justice settings.* Newbury Park, CA: Sage.

Dougherty, D. M. (1993). Adolescent health: Reflections on a report to the U.S. Congress. *American Psychologist, 48,* 193–201.

DuPont, R. L., & Voth, E. A. (1995). Drug legalization, harm reduction, and drug policy. *Annals of Internal Medicine, 123,* 461–465.

Elliott, D. S., Huizinga, D., & Ageton, S. A. (1985). *Explaining delinquency and drug use.* Beverly Hills, CA: Sage.

Farrington, D. P., Gallagher, B., Morley, L., St. Leger, R., & West, D. (1988). Are there any successful men from criminogenic backgrounds? *Psychiatry, 51,* 116–130.

Felner, R. D., Primavera, J., & Cauce, A. M. (1981). The impact of school transitions: A focus for preventive efforts. *American Journal of Community Psychology, 9,* 449–459.

Fergusson, D. M., & Horwood, L. J. (1999). Prospective childhood predictors of deviant peer affiliations in adolescence. *Journal of Child Psychology and Psychiatry and Allied Disciplines, 40,* 581–592.

Fergusson, D. M., & Horwood, L. J. (2003). Resilience in childhood adversity: Results of a 21-year study. In S. S. Luthar (Ed.), *Resilience and vulnerability: Adaptation in the context of childhood adversities* (pp. 130–155). New York: Cambridge University Press.

Fleming, J. P., Kellam, S. G., & Brown, C. H. (1982). Early predictors of age at first use of alcohol, marijuana, and cigarettes. *Drug and Alcohol Dependence, 9,* 285–303.

Foxcroft, D. R., Ireland, D., Lister-Sharp, D. J., Lowe, G., & Breen, R. (2003). Longer term primary prevention for alcohol misuse in young people: A systematic review. *Addiction, 98,* 397–411.

Freeman, E. M. (2001). *Substance abuse intervention, prevention, rehabilitation, and systems change strategies: Helping individuals, families, and groups to empower themselves.* New York: Columbia University Press.

Friedman, A. S. (1983). *Clinical research notes.* Rockville, MD: National Institute on Drug Abuse.

Garmezy, N. (1985). Stress-resistant children: The search for protective factors. In J. E. Stevenson (Ed.), *Recent research in developmental psychology* (pp. 213–233). Oxford: Pergamon Press.

Gehshan, S. (1999). *Substance abuse treatment in State Children's Health Insurance Programs.* Washington, DC: National Conference of State Legislatures.

Gorman-Smith, D., & Tolan, P. H. (2003). Positive adaptation among youth exposed to community violence. In S. S. Luthar (Ed.), *Resilience and vulnerability: Adaptation in the context of childhood adversities* (pp. 392–413). New York: Cambridge University Press.

Gottfredson, D. C., & Wilson, D. B. (2003). Characteristics of effective school-based substance abuse prevention. *Prevention Science, 4,* 27–38.

Gottfredson, G. D. (1981). Schooling and delinquency. In S. E. Martin, L. B. Sechrest, & R. Redner (Eds.), *New directions in the rehabilitation of criminal offenders.* Washington, DC: National Academy Press.

Hamill, P. (1994). *A drinking life: A memoir.* Boston: Little, Brown.

Hansen, W. B. (1992). School-based substance abuse prevention: A review of the state of the art in curriculum: 1980–1990. *Health Education Research, 7,* 403–430.

Hawkins, J. D. (2004). Using *Communities that Care* to Promote Healthy Child Development and Academic Success. Presentation at the Annual Program Meeting of the Society for Prevention Research. Quebec City, Canada. May 27, 2004.

Hawkins, J. D., Catalano, R. F., & Arthur, M. (2002). Promoting science-based prevention in communities. *Addictive Behaviors, 90,* 1–26.

Hawkins, J. D., Catalano, R. F., & Associates. (1992). *Communities That Care: Action for drug abuse prevention.* San Francisco: Jossey-Bass.

Hawkins, J. D., Catalano, R. F., & Miller, J. Y. (1992). Risk and protective factors for alcohol and other drug problems in adolescence and early adulthood: Implications for substance abuse prevention. *Psychological Bulletin, 112,* 64–105.

Hawkins, J. D., Jenson, J. M., Catalano, R. F., & Lishner, D. L. (1988). Delinquency and drug abuse: Implications for social services. *Social Service Review, 62,* 258–284.

Hawkins, J. D., Kosterman, R., Maguin, E., Catalano, R. F., & Arthur, M. W. (1997). Substance use and abuse. In R. T. Ammerman & M. Hersen (Eds.), *Handbook of prevention and treatment with children and adolescents: Intervention in the real world context* (pp. 203–237). New York: John Wiley.

Hill, S. Y., Shen, S., Lowers, L., & Locke, J. (2000). Factors predicting the onset of adolescent drinking in families at high risk for developing alcoholism. *Biological Psychiatry, 48,* 265–275.

Holmberg, M. B. (1985). Longitudinal studies of drug abuse in a fifteen-year-old population. I. Drug career. *Acta Psychiatrica Scandinavia, 71,* 67–79.

Howell, J. C. (2003). *Preventing and reducing juvenile delinquency: A comprehensive framework.* Thousand Oaks, CA: Sage.

Irwin, C. E., Burg, S. J., Cart, C. U. (2002). America's adolescents: Where have we been, where are we going? *Journal of Adolescent Health, 31,* 91–121.

Jenson, J. M. (2004). Risk and protective factors for alcohol and other drug use in childhood and adolescence. In M. W. Fraser (Ed.), *Risk and resilience in childhood: An ecological perspective* (2nd ed., pp. 183–208). Washington, DC: NASW.

Jenson, J. M., & Howard, M. O. (1999). Hallucinogen use among juvenile probationers: Prevalence and characteristics. *Criminal Justice and Behavior, 26,* 357–372.

Jenson, J. M., Howard, M. O., & Vaughn, M. G. (2004). Assessing social work's contribution to controlled studies of adolescent substance abuse treatment. *Journal of Social Work in the Addictions, 4,* 54–66.

Jenson, J. M., & Potter, C. C. (2003). The effects of cross-system collaboration on mental health and substance abuse problems of detained youth. *Research on Social Work Practice, 13,* 588–607.

Jenson, J. M., Wells, E. A., Plotnick, R. D., Hawkins, J. D., & Catalano, R. F. (1993). The effects of skills and intentions to use drugs on posttreatment drug use of adolescents. *American Journal of Drug and Alcohol Abuse, 19,* 1–17.

Johnson, K., Bryant, D. D., Collins, D. A., Noe, T. D., Strader, T. N., & Berbaum, M. (1998). Preventing and reducing alcohol and other drug use among high-risk youths by increasing family resilience. *Social Work, 43,* 297–308.

Johnston, L. D. (1991). Toward a theory of drug epidemics. In L. Donohew, H. E. Sypher, & W. J. Bukoski (Eds.), *Pervasive communication and drug abuse prevention* (pp. 93–131). Hillsdale, NJ: Erlbaum.

Johnston, L. D., O'Malley, P. M., & Bachman, J. G. (2004). Monitoring the Future. National results on adolescent drug use: Overview of key findings, 2003. Bethesda, MD: National Institute of Drug Abuse. Available from http://www.monitoringthefuture.org/pubs.html

Joksch, H. C. (1988). *The impact of severe penalties on drinking and driving.* Washington, DC: AAA Foundation for Traffic Safety.

Kaftarian, S., Robertson, E., Compton, W., Davis, B. W., & Volkow, N. (2004). Blending prevention research and practice in schools: Critical issues and suggestions. *Prevention Science, 5,* 1–3.

Kelder, S. H., Maibach, E., Worden, J. K., Biglan, A., & Levitt, A. (2000). Planning and initiation of the ONDCP National Youth Anti-Drug Media Campaign, *Journal of Public Health Management Practice, 6,* 14–26.

Kellam, S. G., & Anthony, J. C. (1998). Targeting early adolescents to prevent tobacco smoking: Findings from an epidemiologically based randomized field trial. *American Journal of Public Health, 88,* 1490–1495.

Kim, S. (1979). *An evaluation of Ombudsman Primary Prevention program on student drug abuse.* Charlotte, NC: Charlotte Drug Education Center.

Kimbrough, R. J. (1998). Treating juvenile substance abuse: The promise of juvenile drug courts. *OJJDP Juvenile Justice Journal, 2,* 11–18. Washington, DC: Office of Juvenile Justice and Delinquency Prevention.

Kleiman, M. A. (1998). Drugs and drug policy: The case for a slow fix. *Issues in Science and Technology, 15,* 45–52.

Knapp, C. (1996). *Drinking: A love story.* New York: Delta.

Krohn, M. D., & Massey, J. L. (1980). Social control and delinquent behavior: An examination of the elements of the social bond. *Developmental Psychology, 18,* 359–368.

Kumpfer, K. L., & Alder, S. (2003). Dissemination of research-based family interventions for the prevention of substance abuse. In W. J. Bukoski & Z. Sloboda (Eds.), *Handbook of drug abuse prevention: Theory, science, and practice* (pp. 75–100). New York: Kluwer.

Kupersmidt, J. B., Coie, J. D., & Dodge, K. A. (1990). The role of poor peer relationships in the development of disorder. In S. R. Asher & J. D. Coie (Eds.), *Peer rejection in childhood* (pp. 274–305). New York: Cambridge University Press.

Loeber, R., Farrington, D. P., Stouthamer-Loeber, M., & van Kammen, W. B. (1998a). *Antisocial behavior and mental health problems: Explanatory factors in childhood and adolescence.* Mahwah, NJ: Lawrence Erlbaum.

Loeber, R., Farrington, D. P., Stouthamer-Loeber, M., & van Kammen, W. B. (1998b). Multiple risk factors for multi-problem boys: Co-occurrence of delinquency, substance use, attention deficit, conduct problems, physical aggression, covert behavior, depressed mood, and shy/withdrawn behavior. In R. Jessor (Ed.), *New perspectives on adolescent risk behavior* (pp. 91–149). New York: Cambridge University Press.

Luthar, S. S. (1991). Vulnerability and resilience: A study of high-risk adolescents. *Child Development, 62,* 600–616.

Luthar, S. S., & Zelazo, L. B. (2003). Research on resilience. In S. S. Luthar (Ed.), *Resilience and vulnerability: Adaptation in the context of childhood adversities* (pp. 510–550). New York: Cambridge University Press.

Lynam, D. R., Zimmerman, R., Novak, S. P., Logan, T. K., Martin, C., & Leukefeld, C., et al. (1999). Project DARE: No effects at 10-year follow-up. *Journal of Consulting and Clinical Psychology, 67,* 590–593.

Mauer, M., & Huling, T. (1995). *Young Black Americans and the criminal justice system: Five years later.* Washington, DC: National Institute on Drug Abuse.

McBride, D. C., VanderWaal, C. J., & Terry-McElrath, Y. M. (2001). *The drug-crime wars: Past, present and future directions in theory, policy and program interventions.* Research Paper Series (14). Washington, DC: The National Institute of Justice.

Meschke, L. L., & Patterson, J. M. (2003). Resilience as a theoretical base for substance abuse prevention. *The Journal of Primary Prevention, 23,* 483–514.

Mihalic, S. F., & Irwin, K. (2003). Blueprints for violence prevention: From research to real-world settings—factors influencing the successful replication of model programs. *Youth Violence and Juvenile Justice, 1,* 307–329.

Miller, L., Davies, M., & Greenwald, S. (2000). Religiosity and substance use and abuse among adolescents in the National Comorbidity Survey. *Journal of the American Academy of Child and Adolescent Psychiatry, 39,* 1190–1197.

Morin, S. F., & Collins, C. (2000). Substance abuse prevention: Moving from science to policy. *Addictive Behaviors, 25,* 975–983.

Murray, C. A. (1983). The physical environment and community control of crime. In J. Q. Wilson (Ed.), *Crime and public policy* (pp. 67–91). San Francisco: Institute for Contemporary Studies.

Musto, D. F. (1996). Alcohol in American history. *Scientific American, 274,* 78–82.

National Institute on Drug Abuse. (2002). *Monitoring the future, 2002.* (Data file). Available from the Substance Abuse and Mental Health Data Archive Web site, www.icpsr.umich.edu/SAMHDA/das.html

Office of Juvenile Justice and Delinquency Prevention. (2000). *Tribal youth program:* Program announcement: FY 2000. U.S. Department of Justice, Office of Justice Programs, Office of Juvenile Justice and Delinquency Prevention,

Washington, DC. Retrieved July 12, 2004, from http://www.ojjdp.ncjrs.org/grants/000424.pdf

Office of National Drug Control Policy. (1997). *The national youth anti-drug media-campaign: Communication strategy statement.* Washington, DC: Office of National Drug Control Strategy.

Office of National Drug Control Policy. (2002). Drug abuse in America. PowerPoint Presentation, #13. Washington, DC: Executive Office of the President.

Office of National Drug Control Policy. (2004). The President's National Drug Control Strategy, 2004. Washington, DC: Executive Office of the President.

Patterson, G. R. (2002). The early development of coercive family process. In J. B. Reid, G. R. Patterson, & J. Snyder (Eds.), *Antisocial behavior in children and adolescents: A developmental analysis and model for intervention* (pp. 25–44). Washington, DC: American Psychological Association.

Patterson, G. R., Reid, J. B., & Eddy, J. M. (2002). A brief history of the Oregon model. In J. B. Reid, G. R. Patterson, & J. Snyder (Eds.), *Antisocial behavior in children and adolescents: A developmental analysis and model for intervention* (pp. 3–24). Washington, DC: American Psychological Association.

Physician Leadership on National Drug Policy. (2000). *Position paper on drug policy.* Providence, RI: Center for Alcohol and Addiction Studies, Brown University.

Physician Leadership on National Drug Policy. (2001). *Best practices initiative: State-level issues for Medicaid, welfare, and substance abuse treatment.* Providence, RI: Center for Alcohol and Addiction Studies, Brown University.

Physician Leadership on National Drug Policy. (2002). *Adolescent substance abuse: A public health priority: An evidence-based, comprehensive, and integrative approach.* Providence, RI: Center for Alcohol and Addiction Studies, Brown University.

Pollard, J. A., Hawkins, J. D., & Arthur, M. W. (1999). Risk and protection: Are both necessary to understand diverse behavioral outcomes in adolescence? *Social Work Research, 23,* 145–158.

Potter, C. C., & Jenson, J. M. (2003). Cluster profiles of multiple problem youth: Mental health problem symptoms, substance use, and delinquent conduct. *Criminal Justice and Behavior, 30,* 230–250.

Reinherz, H. Z., Giaconia, R. M., Carmola Hauf, A. D., Wasserman, M. S., & Paradis, A. D. (2000). General and specific childhood risk factors for depression and drug disorders by early childhood. *Journal of the American Academy of Child and Adolescent Psychiatry, 39,* 223–231.

Robert Wood Johnson Foundation. (2001). Substance abuse: The nation's number one health problem. Key indicators for policy. Update. Princeton, NJ: RWJF.

Robertson, E. B., David, S. L., & Rao, S. A. (2003). *Preventing drug use among children and adolescents: A research-based guide for parents, educators, and community leaders* (2nd ed.). Bethesda, MD: U.S. Department of Health and Human Services.

Rosen, A., & Proctor, E. K. (Eds.). (2003). *Developing guidelines for social work intervention: Issues, methods, and research agenda.* New York: Columbia University Press.

Rosenbaum, M. (1999). *Kids, drugs, and drug education: A harm reduction approach.* San Francisco: National Council on Crime and Delinquency.

Rosenbaum, S., Johnson, K., Snonsky, C., Markus, A., and DeGraw, C. (1998). The children's hour: The state of children's health insurance program. *Health Affairs, 17,* 75–89.

Rossa, M. W. (2002). Some thoughts about resilience versus positive development, main effects, versus interaction effects and the value of resilience. *Child Development, 71,* 567–569.

Rutter, M. (1985). Resilience in the face of adversity: Protective factors and resistance to psychiatric disorder. *British Journal of Psychiatry, 147,* 598–611.

Rutter, M. (2000). Psychosocial influences: Critiques, findings, and research needs. *Development and Psychopathology, 12,* 375–405.

Saffer, H., & Grossman, M. (1987). Beer taxes, the legal drinking age, and youth motor vehicle fatalities. *Journal of Legal Studies, 16,* 351–374.

Sameroff, A. J., Bartko, W. T., Baldwin, A., Baldwin, C., & Seifer, R. (1998). Family and social influences on development of child competence. In M. Lewis & C. Feiring (Eds.), *Families, risk, and competence* (pp. 161–185). Mahwah, NJ: Lawrence Erlbaum.

Schinke, S., Brounstein, P., & Gardner, S. (2002). Science-based prevention programs and principles, 2002. DHHS Pub No. (SMA) 03–3764. Substance Abuse and Mental Health Services Administration, Rockville, MD.

Shedler, J., & Block, J. (1990). Adolescent drug use and psychological health: A longitudinal inquiry. *American Psychologist, 45,* 612–630.

Simcha-Fagan, O., & Schwartz, J. E. (1986). Neighborhood and delinquency: An assessment of contextual effects. *Criminology, 24,* 667–703.

Snyder, H. (1990). *Growth in minority detentions attributed to drug law violators.* Washington, DC: Office of Juvenile Justice and Delinquency Prevention.

Spoth, R., Guyull, M., & Day, S. (2002). Universal family-focused intervention in alcohol-use disorder prevention: Cost effectiveness and cost-benefit analysis of two interventions. *Journal of Studies on Alcohol, 63,* 219–228.

Stouthamer-Loeber, M., Loeber, R., Farrington, D. P., Zhang, Q., van Kammen, W., & Maguin, E. (1993). The double edge of protective and risk factors for delinquency: Interrelations and developmental patterns. *Development and Psychopathology, 5,* 683–701.

Sussman, S., Dent, C. W., & Galaif, E. R. (1997). The correlates of substance abuse and dependence among adolescents at high risk for drug abuse. *Journal of Substance Abuse, 9,* 241–255.

Teplin, L. (2001). Assessing alcohol, drug, and mental disorders in juvenile detainees (Fact Sheet No. 2). Washington, DC: U.S. Department of Justice, Office of Juvenile Justice and Delinquency Prevention.

Timmons-Mitchell, J., Brown, C., Schulz, S. C., Webster, S. E., Underwood, L. A., & Semple, W. E. (1997). Comparing the mental health needs of female and male incarcerated juvenile delinquents. *Behavioral Sciences and the Law, 15,* 195–202.

Tolan, P. H., Guerra, N. G., & Kendall, P. C. (1995). A developmental–ecological perspective on antisocial behavior in children and adolescents: Toward a unified risk and intervention framework. *Journal of Consulting and Clinical Psychology, 63*, 579–584.

Tremblay, R. (1988). *Peers and the onset of delinquency.* Paper prepared for the Onset Working Group Program on Human Development and Criminal Behavior, Castine, Maine.

U.S. Census Bureau. (2003). *Statistical abstract of the United States.* Washington, DC: Author.

U.S. Department of Education (1998). *Drug education curricula: A guide to selection and implementation.* Washington, DC: Government Printing Office.

U.S. Department of Health and Human Services (1999). Mental health: A report of the Surgeon General. Rockville, MD: U.S. Department of Health and Human Services.

Weinberg, N. Z., Rahdert, E., Colliver, J. D., & Glantz, M. D. (1998). Adolescent substance abuse: A review of the past 10 years. *Journal of the American Academy of Child and Adolescent Psychiatry, 37*, 252–261.

Werner, E. E. (1994). Overcoming the odds. *Developmental and Behavioral Pediatrics, 15*, 131–136.

Werner, E. E., & Smith, R. S. (1989). *Vulnerable but invincible: A longitudinal study of resilient children and youth.* New York: Adams, Bannister, and Cox.

Westat & the Annenberg School for Communication. (2003). *Evaluation of the National Youth Anti-Drug Media Campaign: 2003 report of findings executive summary* (Contract No: N01DA-8–5063). Washington, DC: National Institute on Drug Abuse.

Wyrick, D., Wyrick, C. H., Bibeau, D. L., & Fearnow-Kenney, M. (2001). Coverage of adolescent substance use prevention in state frameworks for health education. *Journal of School Health, 71*, 437–442.

Zucker, R. A., Wong, M. M., Puttler, L. I., & Fitzgerald, H. E. (2003). Resilience and vulnerability among sons of alcoholics: Relationship to developmental outcomes between early childhood and adolescence. In S. S. Luthar (Ed.), *Resilience and vulnerability: Adaptation in the context of childhood adversities* (pp. 76–103). New York: Cambridge University Press.

Web-Based Resources

Monitoring the Future www.monitoringthefuture.org
National Institute on Drug Abuse www.nida.nih.gov
Physician Leadership on National Drug Policy www.PLNDP.org
Robert Wood Johnson Foundation www.impacteen.org
Social Development Research Group www.sdrg.u.washington.edu
Substance Abuse and Mental Health Services Administration www.samhsa.gov

8

Juvenile Justice Policies and Programs

William H. Barton

Juvenile justice policy and practices are greatly influenced by knowledge, events, and values that are viable at any given point in time. After decades of "getting tough" with young offenders and flirting with the treatment model *du jour,* the juvenile justice system now finds itself at a policy and programmatic crossroad. Recent advances in theory, research, and practice that are based on principles of risk, protection, and resilience hold promise for a more rational, comprehensive set of juvenile justice policies and practices. Nevertheless, such optimism must be tempered by the inevitable role that societal values, politics, and public perceptions will continue to play and by limitations in the knowledge base itself.

This chapter outlines this conceptual advance, places it in a historical context, and suggests ways it can be used to improve current and future juvenile justice policies and practices. The first section presents an overview of juvenile justice policy—its goals and stakeholders. The second and third sections review what is known about the prevalence and incidence of delinquency and discuss risk and protective factors for delinquent behavior. The fourth section traces the history of juvenile justice policies, noting the extent to which presumed risk and protective factors have exerted an influence. The final sections apply what we have learned about risk, protection, and resilience to juvenile justice policies and practices.

Purpose and Overview of Juvenile Justice Policy

Prior to the 20th century, the United States did not have a juvenile justice policy per se. Although age was considered a factor in mitigating punishment, children who committed crimes were under the jurisdiction of the adult court. The first juvenile court was established in Chicago in 1899, and by 1925, all but two states had followed suit (Bernard, 1992). The juvenile court was the expression of the first formal juvenile justice policy—that juveniles were distinct from adults and that the system was to act in the best interests of the child. Specialized juvenile probation services emerged to monitor juveniles while under the jurisdiction of the court (National Center for Juvenile Justice, 1991).

This two-tiered system created a tension between the goals of rehabilitation and punishment that continues to this day. As will be described later in this chapter, the parade of policy reforms during the 20th century reflects alternating emphases on these two primary goals. Historically, relatively "lenient" policies favoring treatment have been followed by "get tough" policies mandating punishment. Table 8.1 summarizes events that have impacted juvenile justice policy during the last century.

To whom do juvenile justice policies apply? Young people who meet the definition of a juvenile in a given state are subject to juvenile court jurisdiction if a petition is filed alleging a delinquent act (which would be a crime if committed by an adult as well) or a status offense (behavior, such as school truancy or running away from home, not considered criminal if committed by an adult). Once a petition is filed, the juvenile probation department prepares a predisposition report summarizing the facts and context of the case and containing recommendations to the judge for corrective action. Should the judge "adjudicate" the child as delinquent (analogous to a determination of guilt in adult criminal court), dispositional options may include probation supervision, placement in a nonresidential program, or residential placements of varying restrictiveness.

The definition of a juvenile, that is, of those who come under the jurisdiction of the juvenile court, varies from state to state. In most states, the upper age of juvenile court jurisdiction is 17, but in some, such as Connecticut, New York, and North Carolina, it is 15, and in 10 other states, including Georgia, Massachusetts, Michigan, and Texas, it is 16 (Sickmund, 2003). Further complicating the definition of a juvenile are policies in some states that extend juvenile court jurisdiction to age 20 for status offenses and that allow extended juvenile court supervision of placements of delinquents until 20 in most states to as old as age 24 in a few others, including California (Sickmund, 2003).

Table 8.1   Chronology of Events Impacting U.S. Juvenile Justice Policy

Date	Event	Comments
<1899		Children treated the same as adults under the law.
1899	First juvenile court established in Cook County, Illinois	*Parens patriae* philosophy—juvenile court was to act in the best interests of the child.
1900–1950	All states establish juvenile courts	
1960s–1980s	Interest in delinquency prevention, diversion, and deinstitutionalization programs	Community organization approaches (e.g., Mobilization for Youth), diversion and deinstitutionalization are (see common JJDPA below) 1974.
1966	*Kent v. United States*	Courts must provide the "essentials of due process" in transferring juveniles to the adult system.
1967	*In re* Gault	In hearings that could result in commitment to an institution, juveniles have four basic constitutional rights (notice, counsel, questioning witnesses, protection against self-incrimination).
1968	Juvenile Delinquency Prevention and Control Act	Children charged with status offenses were to be handled outside the court system
1970	*In re* Winship	In delinquency matters, the State must prove its case beyond a reasonable doubt.
1971	*McKeiver v. Pennsylvania*	Jury trials are not constitutionally required in juvenile court hearings.
1974	Juvenile Justice and Delinquency Prevention Act (JJDPA)	Deinstitutionalization of status offenders; separation of juvenile and adult offenders
1975	Lipton, Martinson, & Wilks report	Results misinterpreted by most as indicating that "nothing works" in juvenile corrections.
1975	*Breed v. Jones*	Waiver to criminal court following adjudication in juvenile court constitutes double jeopardy.
1977–1979	*Oklahoma Publishing Co. v. District Court/Smith v. Daily Mail*	The press may report juvenile court proceedings under certain circumstances.

(Continued)

Table 8.1 (Continued)

Date	Event	Comments
1980	Amendment to the JJDPA	Juveniles removed from adult jails and lockups.
1982	*Eddings v. Oklahoma*	Reversed the death sentence of a 16-year-old tried in adult court—ruled that a defendant's young age should be considered a mitigating factor.
1984	*Schall v. Martin*	Preventive "pretrial" detention of juveniles is allowable under certain circumstances.
1988	Maloney, Romig, & Armstrong introduce the "Balanced Approach"	Some juvenile justice jurisdictions adopt the three goals of public safety protection, accountability, and competency development.
1988	*Thompson v. Oklahoma*	Ruled that the Eighth Amendment prohibited the death penalty for persons under 16.
1989	*Stanford v. Kentucky*	Ruled that the Eighth Amendment does not prohibit the death penalty for crimes committed at age 16 or 17.
1980s–1990s	Several highly publicized violent acts by juveniles; states "toughen" juvenile codes	More juveniles are transferred to the adult system; many states adopt mandatory sentences; juvenile court confidentiality provisions are weakened; special programs target serious juvenile offenders; "scared-straight" and boot camp programs proliferate.
1990s	Many states adopt blended sentencing policies	Extends sanctions beyond upper age of juvenile court jurisdiction. Creates a middle ground between juvenile and adult sanctions.
1990s	Many schools adopt "zero-tolerance" policies	More youths excluded from school; often end up in the juvenile justice system.
1993	OJJDP introduces its "Comprehensive Strategy"	Approach favoring prevention, risk assessment and classification, and adoption of evidence-based treatment programs—adopted by several states.
1995	OJJDP launches "Balanced & Restorative Justice" Project (BARJ)	Restorative justice philosophy begins to appear in some jurisdictions (e.g., victim–offender mediation, family group conferences, teen courts).

Sources: Bazemore & Umbreit (1995), Bernard (1992), McNeese (1998), Skiba et al., (2003), Snyder & Sickmund (1999), Wilson & Howell (1993).

States have long been able to use judicial waiver to transfer young offenders to adult court jurisdiction under certain conditions. In the 1990s, many states modified their juvenile codes to define young people who commit certain crimes as adults, even though their age would otherwise define them as juveniles. So, for example, a 14- or 15-year-old charged with murder or certain other serious crimes is now processed automatically in adult court in many states. In addition, most states have other mechanisms of transferring jurisdiction from juvenile to adult court by judicial waiver, prosecutorial discretion, or both.

Many other stakeholders are affected by juvenile justice policies. These include, most obviously, the family members of young offenders, but also the neighborhoods in which they live, the broader community, and public and private service providers who administer juvenile justice programs. Thus, as juvenile justice policies shift emphases among the system's goals, there are ongoing implications for family stability, neighborhood social capital, and the economy. Taxpayers pay for most juvenile justice services. In recent years, more intensive treatments, more restrictive settings, and greater duration of services have led to rapidly increasing costs.

Delinquency and Delinquents

It was noted earlier that the term *delinquency* technically refers to acts committed by juveniles that would be crimes if committed by adults as well. Colloquially, however, the term refers to the full range of problem behaviors exhibited by young persons that could result in their appearance in juvenile court. A complication emerges when we realize that some behaviors currently not enveloped by the conceptual definition of delinquency may have been in times past, whereas other forms of delinquency may be more contemporary constructions of behavior that might not have been labeled as delinquent or problematic in other times. In prior eras, for example, delinquency even included such things as being seen near an unsavory establishment, or merely being poor and congregating in public with other poor children (Bernard, 1992). In more modern times, some altercations among youth that previously would have been ignored or handled informally by parents, neighbors, or schools may now lead to formal charges. Delinquency is a concept defined through a combination of behavioral indicators and societal definitions and responses, and these definitions and responses tend to change over time. The dynamic nature of the concept poses some problems for a discussion of risk and protective factors, since there is at least an implicit assumption that the outcome that is being "predicted" is at the individual level.

Prevalence and Incidence of Delinquency

Despite the preceding caveat, there is merit in describing the current prevalence and distribution of delinquency to gain a sense of its scope. There are two ways to approach this task. First, since this chapter focuses on juvenile justice policies and these apply to those who come in contact with the juvenile justice system, we will summarize recent data on juvenile arrests and court processing. Then, since not all delinquent behavior is detected or formally processed, but is presumably related to (at least most of) the same etiological factors, we will summarize what is known from self-report studies.

In 2001, the most recent year with available data, there were 2.27 million arrests of people under the age of 18 in the United States, accounting for 17 percent of all arrests and 15 percent of all violent crime arrests (Snyder, 2003). Most crimes in the country are committed by people between the ages of 10 and 49. Persons aged 10 to 17 make up approximately 19 percent of that population (Snyder & Sickmund, 1999). Thus, juveniles are overrepresented in arrests for such crimes as arson (49 percent), vandalism (39 percent), burglary (31 percent), larceny-theft (30 percent), robbery (24 percent), weapons offenses (23 percent), and liquor law violations (23 percent), but underrepresented in arrests for such crimes as murder (10 percent), drug abuse (13 percent), aggravated assault (14 percent), and forcible rape (17 percent) (Snyder).

Another way to look at juvenile offense patterns is to consider the proportion of juvenile arrests accounted for by various crimes. Of the 2.27 million juvenile arrests in 2001, 4.2 percent were for violent index offenses (murder, nonnegligent manslaughter, forcible rape, robbery, aggravated assault), 21.6 percent were for property crime index offenses (burglary, larceny-theft, motor vehicle theft, arson), 10.5 percent for other assault, 8.9 percent for drug offenses, 7.5 percent for disorderly conduct, 7.0 percent for alcohol offenses, 4.6 percent for vandalism, 12.2 percent for truancy or curfew violations, and the remaining 23.4 percent for other nonindex offenses (based on Snyder, 2003). When expressed as arrest rates per 100,000 juveniles ages 10 to 17 in 2001, about 7 percent of all juveniles were arrested, with about 1.5 percent arrested for property index crimes and about one third of 1 percent arrested for a violent index crime in 2001 (Snyder). Juvenile arrest rates for nearly all crimes declined noticeably in the late 1990s, from a high point in the mid-1990s (Snyder). The decline was even more pronounced for black youths than for white youths (Snyder).

The official record data described earlier are indicative of the volume of delinquency processed by law enforcement and the courts. However, juvenile arrest data do not give a very good estimate of the overall incidence or prevalence of delinquent behavior. Much delinquent activity goes undetected or unprocessed by the system. Moreover, arrests are case specific rather than person specific or crime specific. That is, the same juvenile may account for several arrests, a single arrest may result from several crimes committed by an individual, and a single crime may result in the arrest of multiple individuals (Snyder, 2003). Therefore, studies of self-reported delinquency can be a useful supplement to official data.

Self-report delinquency studies have a long history in criminology research, with the general consensus being that youths' self-reports of delinquent activity are reasonably reliable and valid when collected under appropriate conditions of anonymity or confidentiality (Elliott & Ageton, 1980; Farrington, Loeber, Stouthamer-Loeber, Van Kammen, & Schmidt, 1996; Hindelang, Hirschi, & Weis, 1981; O'Malley, Bachman, & Johnston, 1983). Studies based on samples of general school populations have consistently found that approximately 80 percent of adolescents report having engaged in behavior that could have gotten them in trouble with the law if detected. A relatively high number report use of alcohol and illegal substances, truancy, and minor fights (Elliott, Huizinga & Ageton, 1985; Farrington et al., 1996). A smaller number of adolescents report involvement in serious offenses against persons or property. Relatively few report frequently committing such offenses, and most do not go on to commit crimes as adults (Elliott et al., 1985; Farrington et al., Moffitt & Caspi, 2001). Thus, although nearly all adolescents engage in some misconduct, relatively few, about 6 to 8 percent according to several studies (Hamparian, 1978; Wolfgang, Figlio, & Sellin, 1972; Wolfgang, Thornberry, & Figlio, 1987), are the chronic, serious juvenile offenders who account for most of the serious juvenile crime. Risk and protective factors for delinquent conduct are described next.

Risk and Protective Factors for Delinquency

The risk and protection framework for understanding delinquency has evolved from somewhat separate lines of research and theory. Some researchers have adopted an epidemiological approach to the study of youth problem behaviors, such as psychopathology, substance abuse (Hawkins, Catalano, & Miller, 1992), delinquency (Dryfoos, 1990; Elliott, 1994; Thornberry, Huizinga, & Loeber, 1995; Tremblay & Craig, 1995), school dropout (Wehlage, Rutter, Smith, Lesko, & Fernandez, 1989), and teenage pregnancy (Dryfoos, Franklin, Grant, Corcoran, O'Dell, & Bultman, 1995). From a different perspective, other researchers have attempted to understand why some individuals achieve positive developmental outcomes despite resembling in many ways those at highest risk for failure (Anthony, 1987;

Rutter, 1985; Werner & Smith, 2001). These streams of research and theory have converged in recent decades to identify a common set of risk and protective factors associated with various developmental outcomes.

Risk factors are defined by Fraser, Kirby, and Smokowski (2004) as "any influences that increase the chances for harm or, more specifically, influences that increase the probability of onset, digression to a more serious state, or maintenance of a problem condition" (p. 14). *Protective factors* operate in the presence of risk to mediate or buffer the effect of risk, thus enhancing positive adaptation (Garmezy, 1985; Masten, 1994; Rutter, 1985). Some scholars suggest using the term *promotive factors* for those influences associated with positive developmental outcomes for all people, reserving the term *protective factors* for those that operate only or more strongly in the presence of risk (Fraser et al., 2004; Fraser & Terzian, in press; Sameroff, 1999). Risk, promotive, and protective factors each may operate in either domain-specific (i.e., related to specific developmental outcomes) or general ways.

This distinction between protective and promotive factors brings with it conceptual clarity and a methodological recommendation for risk and resilience research. To truly claim to have identified a protective factor, an interactive model of analysis is required (Fraser & Terzian, in press). That is, it must be shown that a purported protective factor's effect varies with the degree of risk present, exerting a stronger influence in the presence of high risk, and weaker or no influence in the absence of risk. As noted by Fraser and Terzian relatively few studies to date clearly demonstrate this interactive effect.

Several recent reviews summarize the research regarding risk factors, protective factors, and resilience in general (Durlak, 1998; Fraser et al., 2004; Werner & Smith, 2001) and for delinquency and violence in particular (Hawkins et al., 2000; Howell, 2003; Lipsey & Derzon, 1998; Office of the Surgeon General, 2001; Stouthamer-Loeber, Loeber, Wei, Farrington, & Wikström, 2002; Williams, Ayres, Van Dorn, & Arthur, 2004). Table 8.2 lists risk, protective, and promotive factors identified at various ecological levels by their reviews.

Individual Level

Some risk and protective factors are biological or genetic in origin. Males are at higher risk than females for antisocial behavior (e.g., Patterson, Reid, & Dishion, 1992). Recent work suggests that the absence of the genetically controlled monoamine oxidase (MAOA) enzyme is associated with aggressive behavior (Rowe, 2001). The role of temperament in resilience has been identified by several researchers who noted that, from an early age, children with an "easy" temperament fared better than those with a "difficult"

Table 8.2   Risk, Protective, and Promotive Factors for Juvenile Delinquency

Level	Risk Factors	Protective/Promotive Factors
Individual: Biological and Genetic	Gender (male) (b) (c) (d) (e) Absence of MAOA gene (b) Neuropsychological defects (h) Cognitive defects—low IQ (c) (d) (e) (g) (h) Difficult temperament (d) (h) Hyperactivity/ADHD (c) (e) (h) Perinatal trauma (g) (h) Neurotoxins (h) Maternal AOD use in pregnancy (h)	Gender (female) (h) High IQ (b) (e) (f) (g) Easy temperament (b) (g) (h)
Individual: Psychological and Behavioral	Aggression (c) (d) (e) Beliefs favorable to deviance (c) (e) Alienation (e) (d) (h) Rebelliousness (h) Impulsiveness (d) Risk taking (c) (d)	Assertiveness (g) Pro-social beliefs (h) (e) (f) Social problem-solving skills (a) (g) (h) Self-efficacy (a) (b) Self-esteem (b) Internal locus of control (g)
Family	Family management problems (b) (c) (d) (e) (h) Family conflict (b) (d) (e) (h) Lack of parental involvement (c) (d) (e) (h) Low level of parental education (g) Child maltreatment (b) (c) (d) (e) (g) Family history of crime (c) (d) (e) (h) Parental antisocial personality (h) Parental psychopathology (b) (g) Parental attitudes favoring deviance (c) Parent–child separation (c) (d) (e) (g) Divorce (e) (d) (g) (h) Large family size (d)	Positive discipline techniques (b) (h) Supportive relationships (a) (b) (f) (g) (h) Monitoring & supervision (h) Parent w/HS education or more (g) Good communication (f) Family advocacy (h) Achievement orientation (h) Strong spiritual values (h) Racial pride (h) Extended family bonds (h) Fewer siblings (g)
Other Adults		Presence of caring adult (b) (g)
Peers	Antisocial peers (c) (d) (e) (h) Delinquent siblings (c) Gang membership (c) (e)	Pro-social peer group (a) (f) (g) (h)
School	Early academic failure (c) (d) (e) (g) (h) Low school commitment (c) (d) (e) (h)	Academic success (b) (f) (g) (h) Positive bonding to school (e) (f) (g) (h)

(Continued)

Table 8.2 (Continued)

Level	Risk Factors	Protective/Promotive Factors
	Aggressive behavior in school (h) Poor-quality schools (d) Truancy (c) (d) Frequent school transitions (c)	High-quality schools (a)
Neighborhood	High population density (h) High population mobility (h) Physical deterioration (d) (h) High crime rates (c) (e) (h) Availability of drugs/weapons (c) (h) Lack of social cohesion (h) Low resident attachment (h)	Collective efficacy (b) Non-disadvantaged neighborhood (f) Low neighborhood crime (f)

	Antisocial community norms/laws (h)
	Exposure to violence (c)
	Racial prejudice and
	  discrimination (b) (c)
	Few education/employment
	  opportunities (b)
	Poverty (b) (c) (d) (e) (g) (h)	

Society/
  Community
		Pro-social community norms/
		  laws (a) (h)
		Support (h)
		Empowerment (h)
		Many education/employment
		  opportunities (b)
		Boundaries and
		  expectations (h)
		Constructive use of time (h)
		Regular church
		  involvement (g)

Sources: (a) Durlak (1998); (b) Fraser, Kirby, & Smokowski (2004); (c) Hawkins, Herrenkohl, et al. (2000); (d) Lipsey & Derzon (1998); (e) Office of the Surgeon General (2001); (f) Stouthamer-Loeber et al. (2002); (g) Werner & Smith (2001); and (h) Williams et al. (2004).

temperament (Moffitt & Caspi, 2001; Werner & Smith, 2001). Presumably, the child's natural temperament elicits responses in kind from parents and others. Hyperactivity in young children is associated with later behavioral problems and delinquency (Loeber, Farrington, & Petechuk, 2003). Intelligence, as measured by IQ tests, can be seen as a protective factor when high (Masten, 1994) and a risk factor when low (Loeber, Farrington, Stouthamer-Loeber, & van Kammen, 1998). Hawkins, Catalano, and Miller

(1992) report a relationship between a mother's alcohol and drug use during pregnancy and a child's later delinquency.

Other factors at the individual level are psychological or behavioral. Risk factors include early aggressive behavior (Farrington, 1991; Hawkins et al., 2000), rebelliousness (Williams et al., 2004), and alienation (Williams et al., 2004). Attitudes and beliefs favorable to deviance are a risk factor (Hawkins et al., 2000), whereas pro-social beliefs act as a protective factor (Williams et al., 2004; Office of the Surgeon General, 2001). Internal locus of control and assertiveness (Werner & Smith, 2001), social problem-solving skills (Durlak, 1998; Werner & Smith, 2001; Williams et al., 2004), self-efficacy, and self-esteem (Fraser et al., 2004) have been identified as protective or promotive factors.

Family Level

The family represents the most salient social context for children, so it is not surprising that the literature identifies a number of important risk and protective or promotive factors within the family. A relatively consistent picture emerges. Through attachment and modeling, the family exerts a profound effect on children's behavior. Nearly all reviews cite inconsistent or harsh discipline practices, parental criminality, child maltreatment, lack of parental involvement, and divorce as risk factors, while mentioning warm relationships with pro-social parents who are involved in their children's lives and provide consistent monitoring and discipline as perhaps the strongest protective or promotive factor (Durlak, 1998; Fraser et al., 2004; Hawkins et al., 2000; Lipsey & Derzon, 1998; Office of the Surgeon General, 2001; Stouthamer-Loeber et al., 2002; Werner & Smith, 2001; Williams et al., 2004). Werner and Smith (2001) noted the role of parental education, with a high school education or more as the line tipping the scale from a risk factor to a protective factor. Williams et al. (2004) cite several protective factors that appear to apply specifically to African American families. These include a strong achievement orientation, presence of strong spiritual values, racial pride, and bonds to extended family members.

Peers

Association with delinquent peers is a frequently cited and relatively strong predictor of delinquency, more so for adolescents than for younger children (Hawkins et al., 2000; Moffitt, 1993; Office of the Surgeon General, 2001). On the other hand, association with prosocial peers may provide protection (Durlak, 1998; Stouthamer-Loeber et al., 2002; Werner & Smith, 2001).

Other Adults

A relationship with a caring adult outside of the immediate family is an important protective factor or asset (Eccles & Gootman, 2002; Fraser et al., 2004; Scales & Leffert, 1999; Werner & Smith, 2001). Such a relationship may emerge naturally with an extended family member, a neighbor, or teacher. Alternatively, this relationship may be arranged in formal mentoring programs, such as Big Brothers and Big Sisters. This program has been successful in reducing recidivism among young offenders (Tierney, Grossman, & Resch, 1995).

Schools

Next to the family, schools are the most important social arena for children and adolescents. The literature consistently indicates that school commitment and performance are linked to developmental outcomes, with low commitment and poor performance as risk factors and strong commitment and good performance as protective factors (Fraser et al., 2004; Hawkins et al., 2000; Lipsey & Derzon, 1998; Office of the Surgeon General, 2001; Stouthamer-Loeber et al., 2002; Werner & Smith, 2001; Williams et al., 2004). Moreover, there is evidence that the quality of the school environment plays an important role in the onset and prevention of delinquency (Durlak, 1998; Gottfredson, 2000; Lipsey & Derzon).

Neighborhood and Community

Poverty is one of the most frequently cited correlates of delinquency (Fraser et al., 2004; Hawkins, Catalano, & Miller, 1992; Hawkins et al., 2000; Lipsey & Derzon, 1998; Office of the Surgeon General, 2001; Werner & Smith, 2001). The availability of drugs and weapons, and neighborhood disorganization in general (e.g., high population mobility, physical deterioration, high crime rates, and lack of social cohesion), are risk factors for delinquency (Hawkins et al., 2000; Nash & Bowen, 1999; Sampson, Raudenbush, & Earls, 1997; Williams et al., 2004). On the other hand, communities and neighborhoods with high collective efficacy are presumed to exert informal social control that helps protect against delinquency (Fraser et al., 2004; Nash & Bowen; Sampson et al., 1997).

Community norms more broadly affect delinquency through formal laws and policies and informal means (Durlak, 1998; Hawkins, Catalano, & Miller, 1992; Williams et al., 2004). For example, a community that vigorously pursues enforcement of age limits for the purchase of alcohol might be expected to have lower delinquency rates. Fraser et al. (2004) note that limited opportunities for education and employment and the presence of racial discrimination are risk factors for delinquency, whereas the presence of many education and employment opportunities provides protection.

Summary

In addition to illustrating the ecological nature of risk and protection, several key themes emerge from this review:

- Many risk, promotive, and protective factors are malleable (e.g., the presence of social support, the development of social skills, parenting skills, etc.); others are not (IQ, temperament, gender).
- The effect of risk factors is not linear; that is, the presence of multiple risk factors increases the probability of undesirable outcomes exponentially (Pollard, Hawkins, & Arthur, 1999; Rutter, 2001).
- There is both overlap among the risk, protective, and promotive factors and co-occurrence among adolescent problem behaviors—common risk and protective factors are associated with a range of problems (Dryfoos, 1990; Hawkins, Catalano, & Miller, 1992; Huizinga, Loeber, Thornberry, & Cothern, 2000).
- The effect of some risk and protective factors is developmentally specific (Hawkins et al., 2000; Office of the Surgeon General, 2001).
- Risk and protective factors appear to operate similarly across cultural and ethnic groups (Elliott, Huizinga, & Menard, 1989; Hawkins, Laub, & Lauritsen, 1998; Williams, Ayres, Abbott, Hawkins, & Catalano, 1999).
- Risk factors can combine either simultaneously or cumulatively over time, in either case increasing the probability of undesirable outcomes.
- In general, risk factors and protective factors are inversely distributed across social strata; that is, those at highest risk generally have fewer natural protections than those at lower risk (Pollard et al., 1999).

Although much of the research base on risk and protection uses the presence or absence of delinquency as the primary dependent variable, merely preventing delinquent or antisocial behavior may not be the only positive goal of risk- and resilience-based interventions. The resilience literature and positive youth development literature remind us that being "problem-free isn't fully prepared" (Pittman & Irby, 1996, p. 3). The juvenile justice system is primarily concerned with preventing the recurrence of delinquency, and, as will be discussed later in this section, risk and protection research can offer some guidance here. On the other hand, by embracing the more universal goals of positive youth development—competence, character, connections, confidence, and contribution—communities have the opportunity not only to prevent youth problem behaviors but also to promote long-term, healthy development (Hamilton, Hamilton, & Pittman, 2004). At the same time, many positive youth development initiatives seem to lose sight of the real differences in the distribution of risk in our society. The evidence suggests that risk factors are more powerful than protective or promotive factors in influencing behavior, so that interventions really need to focus on *both* lowering risk and enhancing protection (Fraser & Terzian, in press; Pollard et al., 1999).

The social development model (Catalano & Hawkins, 1996), a synthesis of social control theory, social learning theory, and differential association theory, provides a useful theoretical framework for summarizing knowledge of risk, protection, resilience, and developmental outcomes. Although developed as an explanation for antisocial behavior, it is applicable to developmental outcomes more broadly. At the heart of the theory are four purported socialization processes affecting children: "(1) perceived opportunities for involvement in activities and interactions with others, (2) the degree of involvement and interaction, (3) the skills to participate in these involvements and interactions, and (4) the reinforcement they perceive as forthcoming from performance in activities and interactions" (Catalano & Hawkins, p. 156). Through these processes, the child develops a social bond with the socializing unit, with its strength dependent upon the consistency of the socializing processes. Bonding, consisting of attachment, commitment, and beliefs, then influences subsequent behavior as the child seeks to maintain the connection. Antisocial behavior results from (1) a weakening of the bond with pro-social socialization agents, (2) a situation in which, even in the presence of a pro-social bond, the situational inducements to deviance are sufficiently compelling, or (3) the child's development of a strong bond to antisocial socialization agents, including parents or peers. Finally, the theory contains developmentally specific submodels reflecting changes in salient socialization agents at different ages (e.g., the progression from family to school). From this model, it can be seen that behavior emerges from ecological interplay of individual characteristics, social interactions, and environmental supports/constraints, with the direction of the developmental trajectory (pro-social or antisocial) dependent upon the array of risk, protective, and promotive factors, as summarized earlier.

Despite the advances in research and theory regarding risk and resilience, one should not assume that knowledge of risk and protective profiles can predict long-term developmental outcomes with much accuracy. Attempts to quantify the effect sizes of various risk factors, for example, have shown that the predictive power of even the most powerful risk factors is modest (Hawkins et al., 2000; Office of the Surgeon General, 2001). Evidence from longitudinal studies suggests that turning points, such as military service and, especially, marriage, can have a profound effect on positively redirecting developmental trajectories (Laub & Sampson, 2003; Werner & Smith, 2001). The "error variance" in predictive models may be due to incomplete specification of the predictors, or it may indicate that chance, personal agency, and individuals' interpretation of the immediate context play major roles in eliciting behavior. As Lösel and Bender (2003) note, "errors in prediction of antisociality in childhood and adolescence should not just be viewed as a technical deficit. They are also indicators of general phenomena of multifinality and equifinality in development" (p. 131). In sum, while the growing knowledge base of the risk and resilience framework may have great relevance for policies and practices, it must be applied cautiously and with recognition of its limits.

Risk, Resilience, and Protection in Juvenile Justice Policy

In the century since the founding of the juvenile court, juvenile justice policies have evolved amid the dialectic between the goals of punishment and rehabilitation of young offenders. Bernard (1992) has captured this fluctuating history well, describing the "cycle of juvenile justice" as beginning with the observation that delinquency is a serious and escalating problem, blaming the problem on the current tenor of policies (either "get tough" or "lenient"), advocating "reforms" moving to the other pole, discovering that the problem remains unsolved, blaming the then current tenor of policies, switching to the other pole again, and so on.

Juvenile courts were meant to function "in the best interests of the child," and early juvenile correctional programs were supposed to be treatment programs rather than prisons. As delinquency and recidivism concerns remained high, however, juvenile court and juvenile correctional practices became tougher, and the court's discretion, intended to reduce the punitiveness of the adult courts, became suspect, since juveniles lacked many due process protections. A series of Supreme Court challenges gradually brought many of those due process protections into the juvenile court by the latter part of the 20th century (Bernard, 1992; Snyder & Sickmund, 1999). However, the increasing formality of the juvenile court system rendered it more like the adult system, and perhaps paved the way for policies such as "three strikes," mandatory sentence lengths for some offenses, and the increasing use of transfer to the adult system via judicial waiver, prosecutorial direct file, or statutory exclusion.

Throughout the checkered history of juvenile justice, there has been a continuing reliance upon secure, residential placements, both preadjudication (detention) and postadjudication (training schools and private secure residential facilities). In recent years, a number of studies have provided evidence that many secure residential facilities

1. are overused—that is, many youths in secure residential facilities are not serious and/or chronic offenders and could be placed in less restrictive settings (Snyder & Sickmund, 1999);

2. house youths in poor conditions characterized by overcrowding (Sickmund, 2002) or unsafe environments (Lerner, 1986; Parent, et al., 1994); and

3. are relatively ineffective—that is, gains made while incarcerated, if any, tend to dissipate upon youths' return to the community (Whittaker & Pecora, 1984), and recidivism outcomes are often no better than would be found in less restrictive, community-based settings (Lipsey, 1992; Loeber & Farrington, 1998).

Some policy officials have advocated for greater use of community-based programs at all stages of the juvenile justice system. In many instances, community-based responses have served to divert youths from more formal processing through the system. In other instances, they have served as integral parts of the formal system (e.g., probation) or as complementary components (e.g., community-based treatment programs). For a review of community-based programs in juvenile justice, see Barton (2002).

Until recently, juvenile justice policies and programs have not been based on knowledge of risk, protection, and resilience in any sophisticated way. This in itself is not surprising, since this knowledge base has only been extensively used in the last few decades. Instead, policies and practices appear to have been based primarily on deterrence, incapacitation, and retribution, with an occasional dose of developmental psychology. Juvenile justice policies and programs have sought to protect the community and reform offenders by teaching them a lesson that delinquency leads to unpleasant consequences and either closely supervising their behavior or keeping them off the streets for some time. At the same time, treatment programming has used behavioral contingencies and, more recently, cognitive–behavioral approaches to modify behavior and/or the thinking patterns presumed to lead to offending behavior. There has been some recognition of the importance of peer influences on adolescents, expressed in treatment models such as Guided Group Interaction (McCorkle, Elias & Bixby, 1958) and Positive Peer Culture (Vorath & Brendtro, 1974). Yet, whatever the treatment modality, recidivism has remained high, with recent studies finding recidivism rates between 55 percent and 90 percent of youths released from juvenile correctional facilities (Krisberg, Austin, & Steele, 1991; Krisberg & Howell, 1998).

Since the mid-1990s, knowledge of risk and protective factors has found its way into mainstream juvenile justice policy discussions, heavily promoted by the Office of Juvenile Justice and Delinquency Prevention (OJJDP) in its "Comprehensive Strategy" (Howell, 1995; Wilson & Howell, 1993). As a result, it has become increasingly common for state and local jurisdictions to incorporate risk assessments in various stages of the juvenile justice system. Sometimes these are accompanied by needs assessments as well. These policies are intended to classify youths more objectively and to design treatment plans accordingly.

Risk, protection, and resilience are explicitly ecological concepts, yet the tendency is to apply them primarily at the individual level. Thus, we see the contemporary extension of the typological enterprise, with an emphasis on developing risk and need profiles of individual youths and making juvenile justice system decisions (e.g., detention placements, dispositional placements, treatment plans) at least partly on the basis of these assessments. This may or may not be much of an improvement. The evidence suggests that although risk and protective factors have some explanatory power at the aggregate level, they do not do a very good job of predicting individual level outcomes (Laub & Sampson, 2003; Office of the Surgeon General, 2001; White, Moffitt, Earls, Robins, & Silva, 1990). While representing an improvement over pure chance predictions, the rate of false-positive and false-negative predictions is high. False-positive predictions are characterized by individuals with high-risk profiles who do not go on to commit more offenses. Conversely, false-negative predictions involve youths with low-risk profiles who do go on to commit crimes. In some sense, the advances in risk and protective factor research may have provided juvenile justice policymakers and practitioners with an exaggerated sense of confidence.

This confidence may be seen in such reports as those of OJJDP's Study Group on Very Young Offenders (Loeber & Farrington, 2001; Loeber, Farrington, & Petechuk, 2003). These reports suggest that disruptive behavior at very early ages is a precursor to early onset of delinquency (first juvenile court contact before age 12), which, in turn, predicts subsequent serious and chronic delinquency. Among the evidence they cite is an increase in child arrests during the 1990s, especially for violent crimes (Loeber et al., 2003). Yet they also indicate that a review of self-report studies shows little change in the self-report rates for major forms of delinquency among children under the age of 12 between 1976 and 1998 (Loeber et al., 2003). This at least raises the possibility that the increase in arrests and court cases involving very young children is as much or more a function of the definitions applied to children's behavior as to the behavior itself. That is, behavior that may formerly have been ignored or handled informally may now be defined as delinquent and processed through the system. If there is a correlation with later arrests and court appearances, might this suggest that a risk factor for delinquency is system involvement itself?

Incorporating Knowledge of Risk, Protection, and Resilience Into Juvenile Justice Policy

A burgeoning literature on "what works" in juvenile justice has emerged in recent decades as a counter to the now infamously misinterpreted "nothing works" mantra of the 1970s (Lipton, Martinson, & Wilks, 1975). Major reviews and meta-analyses of juvenile correctional treatment programs have indicated that there are many approaches that, if implemented correctly and targeted toward the most appropriate youths, can reduce recidivism (Andrews, Zinger, Hoge, Bonta, Gendreau, & Cullen, 1990; Lipsey, 1992; Lipsey & Wilson, 1998). The financial burden of programs is also an important consideration. Aos and colleagues applied a sophisticated cost–benefit analysis to a wide range of crime prevention and intervention programs for juveniles and adults (Aos, Phipps, Barnoski, & Lieb, 2001). Table 8.3 presents a summary of its major findings for juvenile programs.

From a meta-analysis of relevant evaluation studies, Aos et al. (2001) estimated the average crime reduction effect size of each type of program listed in Table 8.3. Then, based upon the cost of the program and estimated benefits of crimes prevented to taxpayers and to potential crime victims, they were able to compute an estimated cost-effectiveness ratio, or total benefit amount per dollar spent. As can be seen from the right-hand column in Table 8.3, most of the programs were estimated to be cost-effective, with returns of between $1.28 and $45.91 per dollar spent. Programs with poor returns included the Job Training Partnership Act, boot camps, and "scared-straight" programs, none of which is remotely informed by the risk and resilience framework. In contrast, prevention programs that strengthen families, provide mentoring, or foster school success or social skills, and intervention programs—Multi-Systemic Therapy, Functional Family Therapy, Coordinated Services (wraparound)—that either are explicitly ecological or target key risk factors are shown to be highly cost effective. It is no accident that these approaches are either informed by or consistent with the risk and resilience framework.

Table 8.3   Comparative Costs and Benefits of Delinquency Prevention/
Intervention Programs

	Net Direct Cost of the Program per Participant	Estimated Benefits[a] per Dollar Spent
Early Childhood Programs		
Nurse Home Visitation (for low-income single mothers)	$7,733	$3.06
Early Childhood Education for Disadvantaged Youth	$8,938	$1.78
Middle Childhood and Adolescent (Nonoffender) Programs		
Seattle Social Development Project	$4,355	$4.25
Quantum Opportunities Program	$18,964	$1.87
Mentoring	$1,054	$5.29
National Job Corps	$6,123	$1.28
Job Training Partnership Act	$1,431	–$7.44
Juvenile Offender Programs **Specific "Off-the-Shelf" Programs**		
Multi-Systemic Therapy	$4,743	$28.33
Functional Family Therapy	$2,161	$28.81
Aggression Replacement Training	$738	$45.91
Multidimensional Treatment Foster Care	$2,052	$43.70
Adolescent Diversion Project	$1,138	$24.91
General Types of Treatment Programs		
Diversion With Services (vs. regular juvenile court processing)	–$127	na[b]
Intensive Probation (vs. regular probation)	$2,234	$4.00
Intensive Probation (as alternative to incarceration)	–$18,478	na[b]
Intensive Parole Supervision (vs. regular parole)	$2,635	$3.32
Coordinated Services	$603	$25.59
Scared-Straight Programs	$51	na[c]
Other Family-Based Therapy Approaches	$1,537	$21.13
Juvenile Sex Offender Treatment	$9,920	$3.38
Juvenile Boot Camps	–$15,424	na[b]

Source: Adapted from Aos, S., Phipps, P., Barnoski, R., & Lieb, R., *The Comparative Costs and Benefits of Programs to Reduce Crime: Version 4.0.* Reprinted with permission.

a. Benefits per participant reflect the combined savings to taxpayers from reduced criminal justice processing costs (if any) and the value of crime victim benefits based on the program's estimated effect on preventing future crimes, net of program costs.

b. Since these programs actually represent immediate cost savings, one cannot calculate a cost–benefit ratio. Aos et al. estimate the total benefits per participant for Diversion With Services to be $5,579. Intensive Probation as an alternative to incarceration produces no differences in recidivism but is substantially less expensive, with an estimated $18,000 to $19,000 in savings per participant. Juvenile boot camps, despite their lower up-front cost than regular juvenile correctional institutions, have been found to increase recidivism, and Aos et al. estimate a negative bottom line of $3,587 per participant.

c. Scared-straight programs have been found to increase recidivism; Aos et al. estimate their bottom line as a negative $24,531 per participant.

Fraser and Terzian (in press) outline three basic practice principles from the risk and resilience framework: (1) strengthen protection and reduce risk—both must be addressed; (2) understand the effect of the social and developmental context on protection and risk; and (3) identify and disrupt risk mechanisms—the "sequencing of events that elevate risk" (p. 20). The cost-effective programs identified by Aos, and the following discussion of additional ways to incorporate the risk and resilience framework into juvenile justice, can be seen as congruent with these practice principles.

Prevention

Where knowledge of risk, protection, and resilience can be most useful for juvenile justice may be at the periphery of the system. The best example is prevention, where this knowledge can inform efforts to lower the risks and increase the protection in entire communities or to focus efforts on targeting risks and strengthening protection in the more specific contexts of schools or families. The *Communities That Care* (CTC) approach of Hawkins, Catalano, and Associates (1992) is an example of community-wide prevention developed in considerable detail. CTC components include a framework for community mobilization, local assessment of risk and protective factors, and a menu of evidence-based programs that can be tailored to meet specific communities' needs. A recent evaluation of CTC in several Pennsylvania communities showed CTC counties with modestly reduced delinquency rates, although implementation was inconsistent (Greenberg & Feinberg, 2002).

There is evidence that school-based prevention programs targeting risk factors can be effective (Hawkins & Herrenkohl, 2003). These programs address the major school-based risks, including early aggressive behavior, academic failure, and low commitment to school. Among the promising approaches reviewed by Hawkins and Herenkohl (2003) were attempts to improve organizational climate and classroom management, engaging families in supporting academic achievement, increasing opportunities for bonding to school, teaching emotional skills for self-control and social interaction, and promoting pro-social norms.

Similarly, Tremblay and Japel (2003) review a number of programs that appear effective in preventing delinquency by improving parents' skills and supports, addressing children's cognitive skills, and reducing early disruptive behavior among children. Their review shows that several perinatal and preschool programs were found to change parenting behavior in at-risk families (e.g., communication, attitudes, discipline techniques) in ways that would appear to reduce risks and strengthen protection. Another group of studies supported the notion that very early interventions with at-risk families, including parent training, environmental stimulation, and parent support could improve children's cognitive functioning and reduce early disruptive behaviors. Tremblay and Japel conclude, "The general impression from the review of the twenty-eight prevention experiments is that early childhood interventions can have a positive impact on the three most important risk factors for juvenile delinquency: disruptive behavior, cognitive skills, and parenting" (p. 237).

Aftercare

The other key opportunity for incorporating the risk and resilience framework at the periphery of juvenile justice is aftercare, as best exemplified by the Intensive Aftercare Program model (IAP) developed by Altschuler and Armstrong (1991, 1998). IAP has the following key components: (1) case management services; (2) a collaborative network of community services; (3) services that are "backed in" to the residential facility (i.e., the case manager meets with the youth, conducts assessments, develops release plans, and arranges for relevant community-based service providers to visit the youth in the facility prior to release); (4) a step-down process, in which youths move first into a transition phase, gradually experiencing more community interaction during the last weeks of incarceration, and then go on to closely supervised release, and finally to decreased supervision; and (5) a system of graduated sanctions to help control behavior during aftercare (Altschuler & Armstrong, 1998; Altschuler, Armstrong, & MacKenzie, 1999). The Boys & Girls Clubs of America is currently attempting to blend IAP and strengths-based principles in juvenile aftercare programs in several sites.

A case example illustrating ways to incorporate strengths into aftercare programming is discussed in the box.

Juvenile Justice Interventions

Within the core of the juvenile justice system itself, the benefits of incorporating knowledge of risk, protection, and resilience in policy and practice may be limited. For example, what we know about risk factors for delinquency would constitute a strong argument for eliminating any programs that separate juvenile offenders from other adolescents and treat them as a group. Why would a program attempting to reduce the risk factors for delinquency require that juvenile offenders limit their peer contact exclusively to other juvenile offenders, as occurs in residential programs? At the same time, there is some evidence that mixing offenders and nonoffenders

Incorporating Strengths in Juvenile Aftercare[1]

When Raymond was 12 he was committed for possession of a firearm on school property. He was sent to one of two maximum security facilities for boys in the state. He struggled with the program at the facility and spent 2 years before he was released to live with his mother and was on parole for about 6 months. Just after he completed his parole, while staying with his father in a nearby county, he was arrested on a battery charge. He was placed back with his mother and ordered to serve home detention for 3 months. The day after he was released from home detention, he left the house without permission; he used drugs he stole from his aunt, who lived in the house; and his mother reported him to the police. He resisted arrest and was committed back to the state. This time he was sent to the second maximum security facility at age 15.

He completed the treatment program this time with few problems and could have been released after 10 months, except that there were concerns about him living with either parent. The mother lived in a trailer with four children and a husband. The father owned a strip club and was at work every night for the entire night. Consequently, there would have been no supervision in his home. He preferred to live with his father; his mother resented this and acted to prevent it. Their relationship was very strained as a result. He does not even know how to get in touch with her anymore. Finally, arrangements were made for Raymond to be released to a group home. He spent 7 days there before he was picked up for shoplifting. He was recommitted to the secure care facility. He is now 17 and is expected to be released this fall.

This time he has had access to an aftercare program that has begun working with him in the facility. In addition to many risk factors (early involvement with the system, aggression, broken home, strained relationship with his mother, negative peer involvement), his aftercare worker has identified several strengths in Raymond. He is strong academically, has athletic skills, uses assertiveness in avoiding peer pressure, is eager to please adults and people in authority, is developing skills in decision making and problem solving, and is able to reflect critically on his own thinking, choices, and behavior. He has good insights into his relationships with his family, wants to work with a mentor, and is open to asking for assistance. He enjoys working on service projects and will play a leadership role if allowed.

He has a good relationship with his father, who also cares about him and who is planning to remarry (his new wife will be able to help with evening supervision), so a placement with his father may be possible this time. Raymond expects to complete his GED while in the facility and wants to go to college. His aftercare worker will help him apply to the local technical college. Other components of his reentry plan include providing him with an opportunity to participate in Youth as Resources service projects with other, pro-social youth, and perhaps working at a Boys & Girls Club, where he can combine his athletic interests with leadership skills. He will be referred for counseling to help him deal with his feelings about his relationship with his mother. An important aspect of this aftercare program is the continuity of the mentoring relationship with the aftercare worker begun in the facility and continuing into the community.

1. Adapted from Dr. Roger Jarjoura, Director, Aftercare for Indiana Through Mentoring, personal communication, June 10, 2004. Used with permission.

may be deleterious to the nonoffenders (Dishion, McCord, & Poulin, 1999). So what is one to do? There are thus practical as well as conceptual limits to the extent to which juvenile justice policies and programs can be based on knowledge of risk, protection, and resilience.

One increasingly common application of risk principles, albeit not resilience, to juvenile justice has been the use of structured risk assessment instruments in making placement and treatment decisions (Howell, 2003; Wiebush, Baird, Krisberg, & Onek, 1995). Many jurisdictions now employ such instruments at various points in the juvenile justice system for decisions regarding placement in secure detention, probation supervision levels, dispositional placement restrictiveness, and aftercare planning (Wiebush et al., 1995). I have argued elsewhere (Barton, 1997) that the use of risk assessments in decisions involving potential deprivation of liberty may be inappropriate for three reasons: (1) some of the items used in risk assessment instruments (such as age at first offense) are static; (2) risk assessments are based on aggregate predictions that, when applied to an individual, may effectively punish the individual for something he or she *might* do in the future; and (3) the degree of predictive accuracy is limited, as discussed previously in this chapter.

Nevertheless, there are some ways that the risk and resilience perspective can inform juvenile justice policies and practices. Chief among these is the use of truly individualized, collaborative case coordination in system-of-care (Duchnowski, Kutash, & Friedman, 2002; Stroul & Friedman, 1986) or wraparound service models (Burchard, Bruns, & Burchard, 2002; Goldman, 1999; VanDenBerg & Grealish, 1996). The wraparound approach explicitly values culturally competent, strengths-based assessment and practice (Saleebey, 1997); involves youths, parents, and informal sources of support and professionals as partners in service planning; and operates through a formal collaboration among provider agencies that span traditional service arenas (Goldman). Evidence is growing that wraparound services are at least promising (Burchard et al., 2002) and cost-effective (Aos et al., 2001).

In the 1980s, Maloney, Romig, and Armstrong (1988) provided a major advance in conceptualizing juvenile justice goals by articulating the "balanced approach" to probation. According to this approach, juvenile justice policymakers must consciously balance concern for three system goals: (1) public safety protection, (2) accountability (of the juvenile and the system), and (3) competency development. In other words, every decision point in the system must take account of all three goals. Several states subsequently adopted the balanced approach in their juvenile codes or agency mission statements.

More recently, advocates of restorative justice (e.g., Bazemore & Terry, 1997; Bazemore & Umbreit, 1995) have sought to replace the traditional retributive paradigm of juvenile justice in which crimes are viewed as committed against society with a new paradigm in which crimes are viewed as upsetting the balance of rights and obligations, with victims and offenders seeking a mediated restoration of that balance. Although the restorative justice paradigm has not been adopted fully in most places, elements of restorative justice have increasingly appeared, usually targeting minor or first-time offenders, including such practices as family group conferences (McGarrell, Olivares, Crawford, & Kroovand, 2000) and teen courts (Butts, Buck, & Coggeshall, 2002). This approach is, in many ways, consistent with the principles of risk, protection, and resilience.

A more radical way of embracing the risk and resilience framework might be to divorce the juvenile justice system from treatment programming altogether. Others have advocated splitting the legal and social welfare programming aspects of the court (e.g., Feld, 1999), but for slightly different reasons. Recall the three goals of juvenile justice articulated in the Balanced Approach as described earlier (Maloney et al., 1986). It may be that the juvenile justice and correctional culture is inhospitable to the risk and resilience framework and cannot effectively pursue all three of those goals. It is difficult for justice system actors to transcend long-standing beliefs in the effectiveness of deterrence and punishment, despite evidence to the contrary. It is also difficult for them to take an ecological view when confronted with a steady stream of individuals. Perhaps the juvenile justice system should concentrate on what it could do best—public safety protection and accountability enforcement from a *just deserts* framework, transferring responsibility for competency development to community service providers more aligned with the risk and resilience framework. That is, there would still be juvenile court proceedings and probation oversight and enforcement of the terms of accountability. But probation would work in partnership with community service providers and other community stakeholders who would both participate in the development of dispositional recommendations to the court and provide the individualized case management services.

In a sense, this is what already occurs in wraparound programs such as Wraparound Milwaukee (Kamradt, 2000) and the Dawn Project in Indianapolis (Indiana Behavioral Choices, Inc., 2001). Designed to serve youth with mental health needs who enter the juvenile justice system, these programs rely on care coordination teams, partnerships with juvenile justice and other system providers, and blended funding. They report promising results in terms of reduced residential placements and lowered recidivism (Indiana Behavioral Choices, Inc., 2001; Kamradt, 2000).

The wraparound concept could be flexibly extended to most, if not all, cases currently entering the juvenile justice system or transitioning from residential placements. The intensity of services could vary based upon the assessed needs and strengths of the individuals, their families, and contexts. Not all would require lengthy and expensive services, and the use of and length of stay at costly residential placements would likely decrease.

Summary

Juvenile justice policies and practices are society's way of confronting and dealing with juvenile delinquency. The United States historically has vacillated between an emphasis on punishment and treatment of juvenile delinquents, with neither approach proving very effective. The juvenile court was established in 1899 to formally recognize that children were distinct from adults. In the last century, however, the vacillation between punishment and treatment emphases has intensified. To illustrate, the juvenile court has taken on more of the trappings of the adult system, and toward the end of the century we have seen a wave of "get tough" policies such as zero tolerance and the use of transfers to the adult court, despite a decline in juvenile crime rates in the late 1990s.

An examination of juvenile justice policy and practice trends reveals little explicit connection to the research and theory that has grown from the risk and resilience perspective in recent decades. The risk and resilience framework evolved from two initially separate streams of research: developmental psychopathology, using epidemiological methods to identify the causes of youth problem behaviors, and longitudinal studies of resilience seeking to understand why some people attained positive developmental outcomes in the face of high risk or adversity. By now, a reasonable consensus has emerged regarding an array of risk and protective/promotive factors at various ecological levels—the individual, family, peers, neighborhood, community, and society—that influence the probability of delinquency and other youth problems.

It is logical to assume that this knowledge can inform the juvenile justice system to develop policies and practices that, by reducing risk and enhancing protection, prevent delinquency or its recurrence. At present, the most common application of at least part of this framework has been the proliferation of risk assessment instruments to guide placement and/or treatment decisions at various points in the system. This chapter has argued that this approach, although perhaps an improvement over purely discretionary, clinical judgment, has limitations, primarily because it presumes a degree of predictive accuracy at the individual level that does not exist, despite the impressive aggregate claims of the risk and resilience research.

Several more promising strategies for incorporating risk and resilience into the juvenile justice system were presented in this chapter. These included community-wide prevention initiatives, more targeted prevention in schools or with families, and interventions such as individualized wraparound services that aim to work across system boundaries. In the end, however, because of its political environment and long-standing internal culture, the juvenile justice system may not be the most hospitable venue within which the risk and resilience framework can take hold. A system based on restorative rather than on retributive justice might be preferable, but this too is unlikely to completely replace the current system. The most feasible way to incorporate risk and resilience into juvenile justice may be to make the boundaries of that system more permeable through formal collaborations with other community entities, as occurs in wraparound programs. In this way, it is the partnering agencies and stakeholders who may be able to work more fully from the risk and resilience framework to foster youths' competency development, thereby complementing the juvenile justice system's role in pursuing its remaining two goals of accountability and public safety protection.

Questions for Discussion

1. What are the main obstacles to incorporating the principles of risk, protection, and resilience into juvenile justice policies and practices?

2. In what ways is the strengths perspective compatible with the principles of risk, protection, and resilience?

3. What are major factors leading to "reforms," or modifications, of juvenile justice policies and practices? Which, if any, are most apt to lead to sustained changes? Why?

4. How do risk and protective factors for juvenile delinquency compare to those identified for other youth problems, such as substance abuse, poor school adjustment, and so on?

Additional Reading

Bazemore, G., & Walgrave, L. (Eds.). (1999). *Restorative juvenile justice: Repairing the harm of youth crime.* Monsey, NY: Criminal Justice Press.
Bernard, T. J. (1992). *The cycle of juvenile justice.* New York: Oxford University Press.

Hamilton, S. F., Hamilton, M. A., & Pittman, K. (2004). Principles for youth development. In S. F. Hamilton & M. A. Hamilton (Eds.), *The youth development handbook: Coming of age in American communities* (pp. 3–22). Thousand Oaks, CA: Sage.

Howell, J. C. (2003). *Preventing and reducing juvenile delinquency: A comprehensive framework.* Thousand Oaks, CA: Sage.

Mendel, Richard A. (2000). *Less hype, more help: Reducing juvenile crime, what works—and what doesn't.* Washington, DC: American Youth Policy Forum.

References

Altschuler, D. M., & Armstrong, T. L. (1991). *Intensive community-based aftercare prototype: Policies and procedures.* Baltimore: Johns Hopkins University, Institute for Policy Studies.

Altschuler, D. M., & Armstrong, T. L. (1998). Recent developments in juvenile aftercare: Assessment, findings, and promising programs. In A. R. Roberts (Ed.), *Juvenile justice: Policies, programs, and services* (2nd ed., pp. 448–472). Chicago: Nelson-Hall.

Altschuler, D. M., Armstrong, T. L. & MacKenzie, D. L. (1999). *Reintegration, supervised release, and intensive aftercare.* OJJDP Juvenile Justice Bulletin. Washington, DC: U.S. Department of Justice, Office of Juvenile Justice and Delinquency Prevention.

Andrews, D. A., Zinger, I., Hoge, R. D., Bonta, J., Gendreau, P., & Cullen, F. T. (1990). Does correctional treatment work? A clinically relevant and psychologically informed meta-analysis. *Criminology, 28,* 369–404.

Anthony, E. J. (1987). Children at high risk for psychosis growing up successfully. In E. J. Anthony & B. J. Cohler (Eds.). *The invulnerable child* (pp. 147–184). New York: Guilford Press.

Aos, S., Phipps, P., Barnoski, R., & Lieb, R. (2001). *The comparative costs and benefits of programs to reduce crime: Version 4.0.* Olympia, WA: Washington State Institute for Public Policy.

Barton, W. H. (1997). Resisting limits on discretion: Implementation issues of juvenile dispositional guidelines. *Criminal Justice Policy Review, 8,* 169–200.

Barton, W. H. (2002). Juvenile justice: Community treatment. In J. Dressler (Ed.-In-Chief), *Encyclopedia of crime and justice* (2nd ed., pp. 917–927). New York: Macmillan Reference.

Bazemore, G., & Terry, W. C. (1997). Developing delinquent youths: A reintegrative model for rehabilitation and a new role for the juvenile justice system. *Child Welfare, 76,* 665–716.

Bazemore, G., & Umbreit, M. (1995). *Balanced and restorative justice: Program summary.* Washington, DC: U.S. Department of Justice, Office of Juvenile Justice and Delinquency Prevention.

Bernard, T. J. (1992). *The cycle of juvenile justice.* New York: Oxford University Press.

Burchard, J. D., Bruns, E. J., & Burchard, S. N. (2002). The wraparound approach. In B. J. Burns & K. Hoagwood (Eds.), *Community treatment for youth: Evidence-based interventions for severe emotional and behavioral disorders* (pp. 69–90). New York: Oxford University Press.

Butts, J. A., Buck, J., & Coggeshall, M. B. (2002). *The impact of teen court on young offenders.* Washington, DC: Urban Institute, Justice Policy Center.

Catalano, R. F., & Hawkins, J. D. (1996). The social development model: A theory of antisocial behavior. In J. D. Hawkins (Ed.), *Delinquency and crime: Current theories* (pp. 149–197). Cambridge, UK: Cambridge University Press.

Dishion, T. J., McCord, J., & Poulin, F. (1999). When interventions harm. Peer groups and problem behavior. *American Psychologist, 34,* 755–764.

Dryfoos, J. G. (1990). *Adolescents at risk: Prevalence and prevention.* New York: Oxford University Press.

Duchnowski, A. J., Kutash, K., & Friedman, R. M. (2002). Community-based interventions in a system of care and outcomes framework. In B. J. Burns & K. Hoagwood (Eds.), *Community treatment for youth: Evidence-based interventions for severe emotional and behavioral disorders* (pp. 16–37). New York: Oxford University Press.

Durlak, J. A. (1998). Common risk and protective factors in successful prevention programs. *American Journal of Orthopsychiatry, 68,* 512–520.

Eccles, J., & Gootman, J. A. (Eds.). (2002). *Community programs to promote youth development.* Board on Children, Youth, and Families, Division of Behavioral and Social Sciences and Education, National Research Council and Institute of Medicine. Washington, DC: National Academy Press.

Elliott, D. S. (1994). Serious violent offenders: Onset, developmental course, and termination—The American Society of Criminology 1993 Presidential Address. *Criminology, 32,* 1–21.

Elliott, D. S., & Ageton, S. (1980). Reconciling race and class differences in self-reported and official estimates of delinquency. *American Sociological Review, 45,* 95–100.

Elliott, D. S., Huizinga, D., & Ageton, S. (1985). *Explaining delinquency and drug use.* Beverly Hills, CA: Sage.

Elliott, D. S., Huizinga, D., & Menard, S. (1989). *Multiple problem youth: Delinquency, substance use and mental health problems.* New York: Springer-Verlag.

Farrington, D. P. (1991). Childhood aggression and adult violence. In D. Pepler & K. H. Rubin (Eds.), *The development and treatment of childhood aggression* (pp. 2–29). Hillsdale, NJ: Lawrence Erlbaum.

Farrington, D. P., Loeber, R., Stouthamer-Loeber, M., van Kammen, W. B., & Schmidt, L. (1996). Self-reported delinquency and a combined delinquency seriousness scale based on boys, mothers, and teachers: Concurrent and predictive validity for African-Americans and Caucasians. *Criminology, 34,* 493–517.

Feld, B. C. (1999). *Bad kids: Race and the transformation of the juvenile court.* New York: Oxford University Press.

Franklin, C., Grant, D., Corcoran, J., O'Dell, P., & Bultman, L. (1995). *Effectiveness of prevention programs for adolescent pregnancy: A meta-analysis.* Austin, TX: University of Texas at Austin, School of Social Work.

Fraser, M. W., Kirby, L. D., & Smokowski, P. R. (2004). Risk and resilience in childhood. In M. W. Fraser (Ed.), *Risk and resilience in childhood: An ecological perspective* (2nd ed., pp. 13–66). Washington, DC: NASW.

Fraser, M. W., & Terzian, M. A. (in press). Risk and resilience in child development: Practice principles and strategies. In G. P. Mallon & P. McCartt Hess (Eds.), *Handbook of children, youth, and family services: Practices, policies and programs.* New York: Columbia University Press.

Garmezy, N. (1985). Stress-resistant children: The search for protective factors. In J. E. Stevenson (Ed.), *Recent research in developmental psychopathology* (pp. 213–233). New York: Pergamon Press.

Goldman, S. K. (1999). The conceptual framework for wraparound: Definition, values, essential elements, and requirements for practice. In B. J. Burns & S. K. Goldman (Eds.), *Systems of care: Promising practices in children's mental health, 1998 Series: Vol. IV* (pp. 27–34). Washington, DC: Center for Effective Collaboration and Practice, American Institutes for Research.

Gottfredson, D. C. (2000). *Schools and delinquency.* New York: Cambridge University Press.

Greenberg, M., & Feinberg, M. (2002). An evaluation of PCCD's Communities that Care delinquency prevention initiative. Final report. Harrisburg, PA: Pennsylvania Commission on Crime and Delinquency. Retrieved June 2, 2004, from http://www.pccd.state.pa.us/pccd/LIB/pccd/juvenile/Final%20Report-PSUCTCeval.pdf

Hamilton, S. F., & Hamilton, M. A. (Eds.). (2003). *The youth development handbook: Coming of age in American communities.* Thousand Oaks, CA: Sage.

Hamparian, D. (1978). *The violent few: A study of dangerous juvenile offenders.* Lexington MA: Lexington Books.

Hawkins, D. F., Laub, J. H., & Lauritsen, J. L. (1998). Race, ethnicity, and serious juvenile offending. In R. Loeber & D. P. Farrington (Eds.), *Serious and violent juvenile offenders: Risk factors and successful interventions* (pp. 30–47). Thousand Oaks, CA: Sage.

Hawkins, J. D., Catalano, R. F., & Associates. (1992). *Communities That Care: Action for drug abuse prevention.* San Francisco: Jossey-Bass.

Hawkins, J. D., Catalano, R. F., & Miller, J. Y. (1992). Risk and protective factors for alcohol and other drug problems in adolescence and early adulthood: Implications for substance abuse prevention. *Psychological Bulletin, 112,* 64–105.

Hawkins, J. D., & Herrenkohl, T. I. (2003). Prevention in the school years. In D. P. Farrington & J. W. Coid (Eds.), *Early prevention of adult antisocial behaviour* (pp. 265–291). Cambridge, UK: Cambridge University Press.

Hawkins, J. D., Herrenkohl, T. I., Farrington, D. P., Brewer, D., Catalano, R. F., Harachi, T. W., & Cothern, L. (2000). *Predictors of youth violence.* Juvenile Justice Bulletin. Washington, DC: U.S. Department of Justice, Office of Juvenile Justice and Delinquency Prevention.

Hindelang, M. J., Hirschi, T., & Weis, J. G. (1981). *Measuring delinquency.* Beverly Hills, CA: Sage.

Howell, J. C. (Ed.). (1995). *Guide for implementing the comprehensive strategy for serious, violent, and chronic offenders.* Washington, DC: U.S. Department of Justice, Office of Juvenile Justice and Delinquency Prevention.

Howell, J. C. (2003). *Preventing and reducing juvenile delinquency: A comprehensive framework.* Thousand Oaks, CA: Sage.

Huizinga, D., Loeber, R., Thornberry, T. P., & Cothern, L. (2000). Co-occurrence of delinquency and other problem behaviors. *Juvenile Justice Bulletin.* Washington, DC: U.S. Department of Justice, Office of Juvenile Justice and Delinquency Prevention.

Indiana Behavioral Choices, Inc. (2001). The Dawn Project. Indianapolis; [author]. Retrieved May 28, 2004, from http://www.kidwrap.org/

Kamradt, B. (2000). Wraparound Milwaukee: Aiding youth with mental health needs. *Juvenile Justice Journal, 7.* Retrieved May 28, 2004, from http://www.ncjrs.org/html/ojjdp/jjjnl_2000_4/wrap.html

Krisberg, B. A., Austin, J., & Steele, P. (1991). *Unlocking juvenile corrections.* San Francisco: National Council on Crime and Delinquency.

Krisberg, B., & Howell, J. C. (1998). The impact of the juvenile justice system and prospects for graduated sanctions in a comprehensive strategy. In R. Loeber & D. P. Farrington (Eds.), *Serious and violent juvenile offenders: Risk factors and successful interventions* (pp. 346–366). Thousand Oaks, CA: Sage.

Laub, J. H., & Sampson, R. J. (2003). *Shared beginnings, divergent lives.* Cambridge, MA: Harvard University Press.

Lerner, S. (1986). *Bodily harm: The pattern of fear and violence at the California Youth Authority.* Bolinas, CA: Common Knowledge Press.

Lipsey, M. (1992). Juvenile delinquency treatment: A meta-analytic inquiry into the viability of effects. In T. Cook, D. Cordray, H. Hartman, L. Hedges, R. Light, T. Louis, & F. Mosteller (Eds.), *Meta-analysis for explanation: A casebook* (pp. 83–127). New York: Russell Sage Foundation.

Lipsey, M. W., & Derzon, J. H. (1998). Predictors of violent and serious delinquency in adolescence and early adulthood: A synthesis of longitudinal research. In R. Loeber & D. P. Farrington (Eds.), *Serious and violent juvenile offenders: Risk factors and successful interventions* (pp. 86–105). Thousand Oaks, CA: Sage.

Lipsey, M. W., & Wilson, D. B. (1998). Effective intervention for serious juvenile offenders: A synthesis of research. In R. Loeber & D. P. Farrington (Eds.), *Serious and violent juvenile offenders: Risk factors and successful interventions* (pp. 313–345). Thousand Oaks, CA: Sage.

Lipton, D., Martinson, R., & Wilks, J. (1975). *The effectiveness of correctional treatment: A survey of treatment evaluation studies.* New York: Praeger.

Loeber, R., & Farrington, D. P. (Eds.). (1998). *Serious & violent juvenile offenders: Risk factors and successful interventions.* Thousand Oaks, CA: Sage.

Loeber, R., & Farrington, D. P. (Eds.). (2001). *Child delinquents: Development, intervention and service needs.* Thousand Oaks, CA: Sage.

Loeber, R., Farrington, D. P., & Petechuk, D. (2003, May). Child delinquency: Early intervention and prevention. *Child Delinquency Bulletin Series.* Washington, DC: Office of Juvenile Justice and Delinquency Prevention. Retrieved May 19, 2004, from http://www.ncjrs.org/pdffiles1/ojjdp/186162.pdf

Loeber, R., Farrington, D. P., Stouthamer-Loeber, M., & van Kammen, W. B. (1998). *Antisocial behavior and mental health problems: Explanatory factors in childhood and adolescence.* Mahwah, NJ: Lawrence Erlbaum.

Lösel, F., & Bender, D. (2003). Protective factors and resilience. In D. P. Farrington & J. W. Coid (Eds.), *Early prevention of adult antisocial behaviour* (pp. 130–204). Cambridge, UK: Cambridge University Press.

Maloney, D., Romig, D., & Armstrong, T. (1988). Juvenile probation: The balanced approach. *Juvenile and Family Court Journal, 39,* 1–62.

Masten, A. S. (1994). Resilience in individual development: Successful adaptation despite risk and adversity. In M. C. Wang & E. W. Gordon (Eds.), *Educational resilience in inner-city America: Challenges and opportunities* (pp. 3–25). Hillsdale, NJ: Lawrence Erlbaum.

McCorkle, L. W., Elias, A., & Bixby, F. L. (1958). *The Highfields story: A unique experiment in the treatment of juvenile delinquents.* New York: Holt.

McGarrell, E. F., Olivares, K., Crawford, K., & Kroovand, N. (2000). *Returning justice to the community: The Indianapolis Restorative Justice Experiment.* Indianapolis, IN: Hudson Institute, Crime Control Policy Center.

McNeese, C. A. (1998). Juvenile justice policy: Current trends and twenty-first century issues. In A. R. Roberts (Ed.), *Juvenile justice: Policies, programs, and services* (2nd ed., pp. 21–39). Chicago: Nelson-Hall.

Moffit, T. E. (1993). Adolescence-limited and lift-course-persistent antisocial behavior: A developmental taxonomy. *Psychological Review, 100,* 674–701.

Moffitt, T. E., & Caspi, A. (2001). Childhood predictors differentiate life-course persistent and adolescence-limited antisocial pathways among males and females. *Development and Psychopathology, 132,* 355–375.

Nash, J. K., & Bowen, G. L., (1999). Perceived crime and informal social control in the neighborhood as a context for adolescent behavior: A risk and resilience perspective. *Social Work Research, 23,* 171–186.

National Center for Juvenile Justice. (1991). *Desktop guide to good juvenile probation practice.* Washington, DC: U.S. Department of Justice, Office of Juvenile Justice and Delinquency Prevention.

Office of the Surgeon General. (2001). *Youth violence: A report of the Surgeon General.* Washington, DC: U.S. Department of Health and Human Services. Retrieved June 1, 2004, from http://www.surgeongeneral.gov/library/youthviolence/

O'Malley, P. M., Bachman, J. G., & Johnston, L. D. (1983). Reliability and consistency in self reports of drug use. *International Journal of Addictions, 18,* 805–824.

Parent, D. G., Leiter, V., Kennedy, S., Levins, L., Wentworth, D., & Wilcox, S. (1994). *Conditions of confinement: Juvenile detention and corrections facilities. Research summary.* Washington, DC: U.S. Department of Justice, Office of Juvenile Justice and Delinquency Prevention.

Patterson, G. R., Reid, J. B., & Dishion, T. J. (1992). *Antisocial boys.* Eugene, OR: Castalia.

Pittman, K., & Irby, M. (1996). *Preventing problems or promoting development: Competing priorities or inseparable goals?* Baltimore, MD: International Youth Foundation.

Pollard, J. A., Hawkins, J. D., & Arthur, M. W. (1999). Risk and protection: Are both necessary to understand diverse behavioral outcomes in adolescence? *Social Work Research, 23,* 145–158.

Rowe, D. C. (2001). *Biology and crime.* Los Angeles: Roxbury Press.

Rutter, M. (1985). Resilience in the face of adversity: Protective factors and resistance to psychiatric disorders. *British Journal of Psychiatry, 147,* 598–611.

Rutter, M. (2001). Psychosocial adversity: Risk, resilience and recovery. In J. M. Richman & M. W. Fraser (Eds.), *The context of youth violence: Resilience, risk, and protection* (pp. 13–41). Westport, CT: Praeger.

Saleebey, D. (1997). *The strengths perspective in social work practice* (2nd ed.). New York: Longman.

Sameroff, A. J. (1999). Ecological perspectives on developmental risk. In J. D. Osofsky & H. E. Fitzgerald (Eds.), *WAIMH handbook of infant mental health: Volume 4, Infant mental health groups at high risk* (pp. 223–248). New York: Wiley.

Sampson, R. J., Raudenbush, S. W., & Earls, R. (1997). Neighborhoods and violent crime: A multilevel study of collective efficacy. *Science, 277,* 918–924.

Scales, P. C., & Leffert, N. (1999). *Developmental assets: A synthesis of scientific research on adolescent development.* Minneapolis: Search Institute.

Sickmund, M. (2002, December). *Juvenile residential facility census, 2000: Selected findings.* Juvenile Offender and Victims National Report Series Bulletin. Washington, DC: Office of Juvenile Justice and Delinquency Prevention. Retrieved May 19, 2004, from http://www.ncjrs.org/pdffiles1/ojjdp/196595.pdf

Sickmund, M. (2003, June). Juveniles in court. *Juvenile Offender and Victims National Report Series Bulletin.* Washington, DC: Office of Juvenile Justice and Delinquency Prevention. Retrieved May 19, 2004, from http://www.ncjrs.org/pdffiles1/ojjdp/195420.pdf

Skiba, R., Simmons, A., Staudinger L., Rausch, M., Dow, G., & Feggins, R. (2003, May). Consistent removal: Contributions of school discipline to the school-prison pipeline. Presented at the School to Prison Pipeline Conference, Harvard Civil Rights Project, Cambridge, MA.

Snyder, H. N., (2003, December). Juvenile arrests 2001. *Juvenile Justice Bulletin.* Washington, DC: Office of Juvenile Justice and Delinquency Prevention. Retrieved May 19, 2004, from http://www.ncjrs.org/pdffiles1/ojjdp/201370.pdf

Snyder, H. N. & Sickmund, M. (1999). *Juvenile offenders and victims: 1999 national report.* Pittsburgh: National Center for Juvenile Justice.

Stouthamer-Loeber, M., Loeber, R., Wei, E., Farrington, D. P., & Wikström, P. H. (2002). Risk and promotive effects in the explanation of persistent serious delinquency in boys. *Journal of Consulting and Clinical Psychology, 70,* 111–123.

Stroul, B. A., & Friedman, R. M. (1986). *A system of care for seriously emotionally disturbed children and youth.* Washington, DC: CASSP Technical Assistance Center, Georgetown University Child Development Center.

Thornberry, T. P., Huizinga, D., & Loeber, R. (1995). The prevention of serious delinquency and violence: Implications from the program of research on the causes and correlates of delinquency. In J. C. Howell, B. Krisberg, J. D. Hawkins, & J. J. Wilson (Eds.), *Serious, violent, and chronic juvenile offenders: A sourcebook* (pp. 213–237). Thousand Oaks, CA: Sage.

Tierney, J., Grossman, J., & Resch, N. (1995). *Making a difference: An impact study of Big Brothers/Big Sisters.* Philadelphia: Public/Private Ventures.

Tremblay, R. E., & Craig, W. M. (1995). Developmental crime prevention. In M. Tonry & D. P. Farrington (Eds.), *Building a safer society: Strategic approaches to crime prevention* (pp. 151–236). Chicago: University of Chicago Press.

Tremblay, R. E., & Japel, C. (2003). Prevention during pregnancy, infancy, and the preschool years. In D. P. Farrington & J. W. Coid (Eds.), *Early prevention of adult antisocial behaviour* (pp. 205–264). Cambridge, UK: Cambridge University Press.

VanDenBerg, J. E., & Grealish, M. E. (1996). Individualized services and supports through the wraparound process: Philosophy and procedures. *Journal of Child and Family Studies, 5,* 7–21.

Vorath, H., & Brendtro, L. K. (1974). *Positive peer culture.* Chicago: Aldine.

Wehlage, G., Rutter, R. A., Smith, G. A., Lesko, N., & Fernandez, R. R. (1989). *Reducing the risk: Schools as communities of support.* London: Falmer Press.

Werner, E. E., & Smith, R. S. (2001). *Journeys from childhood to midlife: Risk, resilience, and recovery.* Ithaca, NY: Cornell University Press.

White, J. L., Moffitt, T. E., Earls, F., Robins, L. N., & Silva, P. A. (1990). How early can we tell? Predictors of childhood conduct disorder and adolescent delinquency. *Criminology, 29,* 507–533.

Whittaker, J. K., & Pecora, P. J. (1984). A research agenda for residential care. In T. Philpot (Ed.), *Group care practice: The challenge of the next decade* (pp. 71–87). Sutton, Surrey, UK: Community Care/Business Press International.

Wiebush, R. G., Baird, C., Krisberg, B., & Onek, D. (1995). Risk assessment and classification for serious, violent, and chronic juvenile offenders. In J. C. Howell, B. Krisberg, J. D. Hawkins, & J. J. Wilson (Eds.), *Serious, violent, & chronic juvenile offenders: A sourcebook* (pp. 171–212). Thousand Oaks, CA: Sage.

Williams, J. H., Ayers, C. D., Abbott, R. D., Hawkins, J. D., & Catalano, R. F. (1999). Racial differences in risk factors for delinquency and substance use among adolescents. *Social Work Research, 23 (4),* 241–256.

Williams, J. H., Ayers, C. D., Van Dorn, R. A., & Arthur, M. W. (2004). Risk and protective factors in the development of delinquency and conduct disorder. In M. W. Fraser (Ed.), *Risk and resilience in childhood: An ecological perspective* (2nd ed., pp. 209–249). Washington, DC: NASW.

Wilson, J. J., & Howell, J. C. (1993). *A comprehensive strategy for serious, violent, and chronic juvenile offenders: Program summary.* Washington, DC: U.S. Department of Justice, Office of Juvenile Justice and Delinquency Prevention.

Wolfgang, M. E., Figlio, R. M., & Sellin, T. (1972). *Delinquency in a birth cohort.* Chicago: University of Chicago Press.

Wolfgang, M., Thornberry, T. P., & Figlio, R. M. (1987). *From boy to man, from delinquency to crime: Follow up to the Philadelphia birth cohort of 1945.* Chicago: University of Chicago Press.

Web-Based Resources

Building Blocks for Youth http://www.buildingblocksforyouth.org/

Center for the Study and Prevention of Violence http://www.colorado.edu/cspv/index.html

National Center for Juvenile Justice http://ncjj.servehttp.com/NCJJWebsite/main.htm

NCJJ's Statistical Briefing Book http://www.ojjdp.ncjrs.org/ojstatbb/index.html

Office of Juvenile Justice and Delinquency Prevention (OJJDP) http://ojjdp.ncjrs.org/

9

Toward the Integration of Child, Youth, and Family Policy

Applying Principles of Risk, Resilience, and Ecological Theory

Jeffrey M. Jenson

Mark W. Fraser

The chapters in this book describe policies and programs aimed at many of the most pressing problems facing American children, youth, and parents. These policies—and the services created by them—represent a complex array of legislative, administrative, and, occasionally, judicial responses to child and adolescent problems. Identifying and analyzing major policy responses to the social and health problems confronted by children is a difficult undertaking for the best student, policy official, or scholar. Imagine, then, the confusion experienced by a child, adolescent, or parent receiving assistance in one or more of the systems of care reviewed in this book. Unfortunately, no road map exists to guide family members through the labyrinth of programs and agencies that provides services for children and youth. For many families, what we call the "service system" is a maze of programs and procedures that have confusing eligibility requirements and service definitions. In their complexity, these systems too often wind up compromising the good intentions of advocates, policy-makers, and practitioners.

To try to make sense of public policies in terms of their historical development and current dimensions, chapter authors have applied a risk and resilience framework—informed by elements of ecological theory. Using the constructs of risk and protection, we summarize their findings next. A developmental process to guide the creation and implementation of a logical continuum of policies and programs for children, youth, and families is then outlined.

Policies and Programs Across Systems of Care

This book has traced the origins and evolution of public policies that define major American systems of care for children, youth, and families. Chapter authors used principles of risk and resilience to describe and assess policy responses to a range of child and adolescent problems and conditions. Each chapter began with a review of risk and protective factors that were relevant to problem behaviors or to conditions within particular policy domains, such as child welfare and mental health.

Although the systems of care in child welfare, developmental disabilities, education, health, juvenile justice, mental health, and substance abuse are usually vertically developed with separate funding streams, services, and administrative structures, one is immediately struck by the similarity of risk and protective factors across substantive domains. This is not a new observation. Prior reviews of risk and protection have noted the overlap of risk and protective factors across problem domains (Fraser, Kirby, & Smokowski, 2004; Hawkins, Catalano, & Miller, 1992; Howard & Jenson, 1999; Howell, 2003). However, the similarity of factors related to different systems of care is a clue both to the complexity of public responses to issues confronting children and families and to the potential for reform. In Chapter 1 we identified common risk and protective factors for childhood and adolescent problems at the environmental, interpersonal, social, and individual levels of influence. These characteristics and conditions were present across the policy domains discussed in the book.

The presence of common risk and protective factors for different childhood and adolescent behaviors and conditions affords a special opportunity to think systematically about creating policies that address the root causes of problem behaviors. For example, the authors in this volume have indicated that a number of common environmental factors—poverty, poor parenting, and community disorganization—are associated with juvenile delinquency, substance abuse, and child maltreatment. It follows, then, that these risk factors should become the targets of coordinated and integrated policy and program responses in the juvenile justice, substance abuse, and child welfare systems.

A parallel theme emerging from each chapter, however, concerns the lack of attention that has historically been afforded the underlying correlates of child and adolescent problems in the policy development process. On balance, chapters describe an incremental and reactive approach to the creation of policies that form the basis for programs in public systems of care for children, youth, and families. Policies tend to be the product of ongoing reform cycles that stem from changes in the nature and prevalence of social or health problems. For example, the rubella epidemic of the mid-1960s increased the number of children with severe auditory and visual disabilities. It contributed to the reform of special education policies that, through the Education for All Handicapped Children Act (P.L. 94–142) in 1975, provided public schools with resources to serve children with disabling conditions once considered so severe that only institutional care was thought appropriate. When incidence and prevalence rates increase dramatically, public and policy attention is diverted to particular systems of care. When the prevalence of problems increases, policy reforms tend to be introduced at a fast pace, often with inadequate consideration of unintended consequences or long-term effects.

This is a common pattern. In Chapter 8 Barton notes the cyclical nature of juvenile justice policy—characterized by a shifting emphasis on rehabilitation and punishment—that has defined a myriad of reforms, ranging from the creation of probation in the first juvenile courts in the early 1900s to recent judicial waiver procedures that permit some juvenile offenders to be tried in criminal courts and exposed to adult sanctions. Fraser (Chapter 4) identifies fluctuations in mental health policy based on evolving beliefs about the appropriate role of institutional and community-based care for those with serious mental illnesses. And Pecora (Chapter 2) traces the evolution of child welfare policy through periods of time during which social norms about the handling of child abuse and neglect changed dramatically.

One would be naïve not to recognize the important contribution of social norms and public perceptions to public policy. After all, legislation is largely a result of the public's reaction to social conditions and behavioral patterns. Frey and Walker's discussion of the recently passed No Child Left Behind Act (P.L. 107–110) in Chapter 3 illustrates the power of public perception in reshaping education. Public outcry for school reform and accountability in the latter part of the 1990s is clearly reflected in many provisions of the

Act. Similar examples can be drawn from the evolution of public policies in the health (Chapter 5) and developmental disabilities (Chapter 6) fields.

It is the confluence of public concern and substantive knowledge that should yield policy. However, the urgency created by public perception and pressure sometimes catalyzes changes that produce reforms with unintended and negative side effects. When pressured to respond to real or apparent changes in the nature of a child or adolescent problem behavior, officials frequently turn to convenient policy solutions that fail to address the underlying risk and protective factors associated with that problem (Jenson & Howard, 1998). The result of this process is seen in the form of ineffective, fragmented, and short-lived programs that sometimes do more harm than good. But perhaps their greater effect is that they add to bureaucratic inertia, making systems more complicated, slower to respond to true reform (witness the case of systems of care reform in mental health), and less generative in creating innovations.

Few systems of care for children, youth, and families have developed a deliberate or effective continuum of care. Nearly all chapter authors noted that primary systems of care tend to offer a maze of programs and services that are seldom delivered to children and families in sequential or orderly fashion. One exception might be the comprehensive strategy for the prevention, treatment, and control of juvenile delinquency that was adopted by the juvenile justice system in the late 1990s. This strategy, developed by the Office of Juvenile Justice and Delinquency Prevention (Howell, 2003), outlines a clear continuum of care and graduated sanctions (punishments related to the seriousness of offenses) that many states are now using as a framework for handling young offenders. The strategy emphasizes a continuum of service that matches the individual needs (often identified through systematic risk assessment) and offending histories of delinquent youth to appropriate interventions and sanctions. If it continues to be implemented, the approach may provide valuable lessons for other systems of care.

Finally, careful analysis of the policies and programs reviewed in this volume reveals that untested and ineffective policies and programs are repeated over time. One example is the reoccurring use of media campaigns as a way to increase awareness about the dangers of substance use. Jenson, Anthony, and Howard note in Chapter 7 that this strategy had little effect on reducing substance use in the 1970s and early 1980s. However, recent public awareness of increasing drug use among adolescents has rekindled interest in media and information campaigns that alert young people and their parents to the dangers of alcohol and other illicit drug use. As Jenson and colleagues note in Chapter 7, this interest is reflected in the large allocation of federal funds to a national media campaign in recent years.

Perhaps most glaring in each author's historical review of public policy is the lack of an underlying framework to guide policy development. No common model or framework for policy development could be found across the seven systems of care reviewed by authors. We believe that principles of risk and resilience—grounded in ecological theory—offer a useful framework for considering the conditions that affect children and that, through a risk and protective factor perspective, we can better design social programs to address these conditions. Next, we offer some thoughts about how these principles might be used to develop child, youth, and family policy.

Risk and Resilience: An Ecological Perspective for Developing Child, Youth, and Family Policy

Rooted in ecological theory, principles of risk, protection, and resilience have been successfully applied to prevention and treatment settings with children and adolescents. Substance abuse and delinquency prevention programs, in particular, have been based on risk and protective factors occurring at levels of influence (e.g., environmental, interpersonal and social, individual) that are compatible with ecological theory (Germain, 1991). The utility of risk, protection, and ecological theory for policy development has, however, been relatively untapped.

Using a risk- and protection-based approach to creating policies for children, youth, and families requires participation in a number of predetermined action steps. These steps are outlined next and summarized in the developmental policy process shown in Figure 9.1.

Step 1: Evaluate Risk and Protective Factors

Policy making begins with developing an understanding of the risk and protective factors associated with a targeted child or adolescent problem behavior. Consistent with ecological theory, factors should be assessed or summarized at environmental, interpersonal, social, and individual levels. Chapter authors have identified reviews of risk and protective factors associated with each of the problem behaviors and conditions discussed in this book. Because risk and protective factors have been identified for many social and health problems, it may not be necessary for policymakers to conduct basic risk or protective factor assessments. In most fields, research studies already specify predominate risk and protective factors (for a review, see, Fraser, 2004). However, differences in local environmental conditions may necessitate assessments in some circumstances. For example, an urban center may be concerned about the disproportionate nature of poverty or the

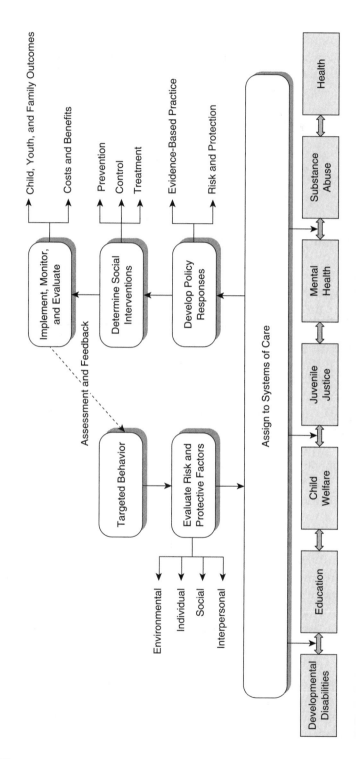

Figure 9.1 A Developmental Process of Child, Youth, and Family Policy

needs of racial groups in certain geographic areas. The ways risk and protective factors vary by region, gender, and race/ethnicity is the subject of much current research. Though there are common risk and protective factors, risk factors clearly vary from the tribal lands of the mountain and plains states to the urban centers of the east and west coasts. These differences complicate risk assessment and pose a major challenge for policymakers. Nevertheless, in thinking about policy from a risk and protection perspective, we have two advantages. First, we use a common language across policy domains. This gives policymakers, advocates, practitioners, and researchers a vocabulary through which to describe related behaviors, to set program objectives, and to assess program outcomes. Second, because the ideas of risk and protection arise from research in child development and prevention science, we can build upon scientific knowledge. This knowledge base is expanding rapidly, and it already holds the potential—as demonstrated in juvenile justice—to reform service systems across the country.

Step 2: Assign Policy Responsibility in Ways That Promote Service Integration Across Systems of Care

Policies based on empirical evidence about the risk and protective factors that are associated with child and youth problems should be developed and implemented across the seven systems of care addressed in this book. Integrating key programs and services identified or implied by policies across and within systems of care should be a priority. Questions to consider in policy development and integration processes include the following:

1. Which systems of care have primary responsibility for the programs and services defined or implied by the policy?

2. Where does fiscal accountability for the programs and services defined or implied by the stated policy lie?

3. Does the stated policy explicitly develop linkages between and within the major systems of care for children, youth, and families?

4. Do adequate implementation resources exist within or across the primary systems of care to achieve service integration?

5. How can systems of care share existing or new program resources, including staff, physical locations, training curricula, and evaluation tools and methods?

Locating and integrating program components defined by social policies within and across systems of care are challenging undertakings. Collaborative partnerships between researchers, policy experts, and administrators are

The Value of Collaboration and Integration:
The Case of Early and Unwanted Teen Pregnancy

Early and unwanted adolescent pregnancy rates fell by 24 percent between 1996 and 2001 (U.S. Centers for Disease Control and Prevention, 2002). The decline, although likely influenced by a host of individual and social factors, has been partially attributed to improvements in the coordination of policies and programs between the nation's health care and educational systems. Steps and responsibilities in this collaborative effort included:

a.   The systematic dissemination of information by public health departments, government agencies, and schools to educate the public about the high rates of adolescent pregnancy in the United States.
b.   The implementation of school-based prevention efforts aimed at delaying the onset of sexual activity and educating students about the risks associated with unprotected sex.
c.   The creation of school-based health clinics to reach adolescents who may not have access to medical care and thus may be at highest risk for early and unwanted pregnancy.
d.   Targeted federal, state, and local funding of community-based health clinics that educate young men and women at risk for early and unwanted pregnancy and offer treatment for young families.

The recent decline in adolescent pregnancy rates comes at a time of increased collaboration between the nation's health care and educational systems. This fruitful collaboration represents the potential of policy and program integration for reducing child and adolescent problems.

necessary to achieve the more fluid delivery and integration of policies aimed at children, youth, and families. An example of collaboration between systems of care that illustrates policy and program efforts aimed at integration is given in the accompanying box.[1]

A similar example revealing the positive effects of system collaboration and integration on adolescent behavior can be found in recent efforts to treat co-occurring substance abuse and mental health problems. Jenson and Potter (2003) tested an experimental intervention created as a result of legislation passed by the Colorado state legislature. A legislative note mandated mental health and juvenile justice systems to find innovative ways to treat co-occurring substance use and mental health problems among young offenders. The state systems responded by assessing risk and protective factors for adolescent substance abuse and mental health problems. An integrated intervention that placed mental health case managers in juvenile justice facilities was selected as an intervention approach. In a longitudinal investigation of the program, Jenson and Potter found significant reductions in self-reported depression, anxiety, and substance use following treatment for youth referred to the program.

This type of cross-system integration holds great promise for reducing child and adolescent problem behaviors. Examples of integrated programs that cross traditional boundaries established by the systems of care discussed in this book are increasing (e.g., Burns et al., 2001). Policy experts and practitioners are beginning to recognize the benefits of policies, programs, and services that use coordinated and collaborative efforts. Indeed, exemplified by California's Ventura County Project (Chapter 4), some state legislatures are mandating the development of coordinated, collaborative services.

Step 3: Use Evidence to Create Public Policy Responses

Empirical evidence gained from studies of risk and protective factors should be used to create child, youth, and family public policies. This will require the dissemination of aggregate level information about the etiology of child and adolescent problems to policymakers during the deliberation processes that lead to the creation of public policy. Empirical evidence needs to be translated to legislators and policy experts in a manner that is immediately useable and practical.

Recent developments in evidence-based practice offer an opportunity to advance the notion of creating policies from an empirical framework. Speaking in terms of mental health practice and policy, Hoagwood, Burns, and Weisz (2002) define evidence-based practice as "a body of knowledge, obtained through carefully implemented scientific methods, about the prevalence, incidence, or risks for mental disorders, or about the impact of treatments or services on mental health problems" (p. 329). In more generic terms, Sackett and colleagues (Sackett, Rosenberg, Gray, Haynes, & Richardson, 1996) refer to evidence-based practice as the process of using the best available evidence in the decision-making process. Simply stated, using evidence-based principles in the policy process implies paying close attention to knowledge about the onset and persistence of child and youth problems, and about the effects of social interventions aimed at ameliorating such problems.

Step 4: Determine the Course of
Specific Individual and Social Interventions

To determine the course of individual and social interventions, policy officials should consider evidence that identifies efficacious programs and services for children and adolescents. Policy creation that uses principles of risk, resilience, and evidence-based practice requires a comprehensive review of empirical evidence about the efficacy of alternative intervention approaches. In essence, determining the appropriate course of social intervention begs an answer to the old question, "What works best for whom under what conditions?"

Several outlets have surfaced as sources for obtaining information about effective interventions for children and youth. In Chapter 1, we noted the work of the University of Colorado's Center for the Study and Prevention of Violence. The Center has identified a number of efficacious violence prevention programs that can be selected as the basis for a community or state's violence prevention efforts (Mihalic & Irwin, 2003). In addition, interdisciplinary groups such as the international Campbell and Cochrane collaborations have made available systematic reviews of the treatment outcome literature across a range of adolescent problems. These reviews offer a rich source of information for policy officials who are engaged in the process of recommending or selecting interventions in public systems of care (Campbell Collaboration Library, 2004; Cochrane Library, 2004).

There is growing evidence that decision makers have begun to consider program effectiveness when selecting interventions. Howell (2003) describes steps taken by the state of Washington to select and implement empirically supported programs in its juvenile justice system. Burns (2002) notes the increased use of efficacious interventions such as multisystemic therapy (Henggeler, Schoenwald, Borduin, Rowland, & Cunningham, 1998), wraparound interventions (Burchard, Burns, & Burchard, 2002), and treatment foster care (Chamberlain, 2002) in the child mental health system.

To make better use of the research literature on the effectiveness of interventions for children and adolescents (for a review, see Allen-Meares & Fraser, 2004) and to implement the kind of collaborative programs that are described in every chapter, state and local officials must find ways to break through organizational isomorphism and exert leadership in overcoming the turf issues that have confounded previous reform efforts (e.g., the implementation of the Children's and Community Mental Health Services Improvement Act of 1992, which attempted to create systems of care within mental health). Mihalic and Irwin (2003) reviewed implementation obstacles faced by 42 communities who chose to use efficacious violence prevention programs in their state or communities. They found that quality of technical assistance, consistent staffing, and community support were among the most important influences on successful program implementation. Based on efforts to date, the difficulty of replicating effective programs—particularly those developed in highly controlled clinical settings—has been underestimated. These factors should be considered by states and communities as they progress from policy and intervention decision making to program implementation.

Step 5: Implement, Monitor, and Evaluate Policies and Interventions

In the development of systems of care, greater emphasis on monitoring and evaluating interventions will be necessary. The energy and enthusiasm of reforms must be converted into systematic procedures that monitor the implementation of new programs, provide feedback, and articulate consequences for failed implementation. This implies using fidelity checks to ensure that interventions are being implemented as they were intended to be, conducting cost–benefit analyses to assess the economic consequences of programs and policies, and assessing child, youth, and parent outcomes. Monitoring and evaluation allow policy experts to determine the outcomes of policies and programs; effective efforts can be refunded and ineffective approaches can be redesigned.

Conclusion

In this book, we have suggested that a new framework for child, youth, and family policy is needed in this country. Specifically, we have argued that a risk and resilience model, grounded in principles of ecological theory, offers great potential for creating policies and programs that will lead to effective interventions for a host of child and adolescent problem behaviors.

The time for a new paradigm that will improve the developmental processes and outcomes associated with child, youth, and family policy is ripe. Opinion polls assessing public willingness to fund early intervention and rehabilitation programs for children and youth reveal strong support for collaborative and community-based efforts (Moon, Cullen, & Wright, 2003). Recent advances in strengths-based practice approaches have emerged that should prove complimentary to the risk, protection, and resilience framework set forth in this volume (Maton, Schellenbach, Leadbeater, & Solarz, 2004). While more research is needed to better understand the interactive processes inherent in a strengths-based approach, the potential of the model for policy development should not be understated. And, finally, recent trends in the acceptance of evidence-based practice have brought researchers and policy experts together in ways that were unseen in past years.

The principles of risk and resilience arose from recent research on developmental psychopathology and prevention science. In these fields, major advances have occurred in articulating the developmental trajectories of children who drop out of school, become delinquent, use illicit substances, experience serious emotional disorders, or have other poor developmental outcomes. At the same time, this knowledge has been used to design effective prevention programs, many of which are described in the previous chapters. These programs attempt to reduce risk and alter developmental trajectories (Dodge, 2001). Findings from them are promising (e.g., Allen-Meares & Fraser, 2004).

In the glow of promise from these programs, we ask, "Is it adequate to construct policy on the basis of risk factors alone?" We think risk reduction alone is an insufficient public policy goal, though its achievement would be a significant step forward. It is the hope incumbent in the concept of resilience, where children at high risk prevail over adversity, that gives us pause. Policy must clearly be driven, in part, by a moral imperative to reduce risk. From resilient children, we learn that risk reduction must be complemented with strategies that ameliorate or buffer adversities. In studying these protective processes, we often find that what protects children at risk also serves to promote positive developmental outcomes for all children (e.g., Fraser, 2004).

From this perspective, public policy for children and youths should be guided by attempts to reduce risk *and* promote protection. For all children (including those at risk), it should promote competence in social and academic settings, confidence, and a sense of having control over one's life, connection to others who provide support and mentoring, character or moral integrity regarding right and wrong behaviors, and caring or compassion for others who may be less fortunate (Lerner, Fisher, & Weinberg, 2000). Too often, policy development is influenced by changes in problem rates or by catalyzing events such as epidemics or disasters. Of course, it is important to respond when rates rise or events create great need. But public policy for children and youth should be proactive and positive rather than reactive and risk focused. It should promote protective processes that nurture developmental outcomes for all children, especially those at great risk. In the sense of *Healthy People 2010* (U.S. Department of Health and Human Services, 2000), the intent of public policy for children, youth, and families should extend beyond the prevention of delinquency, substance abuse, or other social and health problems. It should express health-promoting societal goals related to positive developmental outcomes for all children and the creation of widely accessible means for achieving these outcomes. Though there may always be a need for specialized programs to help children who have special needs (e.g., children who are victimized by individual disadvantage or tragic events), public policy for children should be rooted in core commitments that strengthen families, improve schools, and reinvigorate neighborhoods.

Much remains to be done to solve the fragmented nature of child, youth, and family policy in the United States. This fact is underscored in recent testimony offered by Timothy Kelly (2002) to the President's New Freedom Commission on Mental Health. Kelly, Commissioner of the Virginia State Department of Mental Health from 1994 to 1997, speaking of the fragmentation evident in that state's system said:

> In my view the problem is not primarily a lack of funds, though additional funds are always welcomed. Neither is it the providers, many of whom are very talented and deeply dedicated to those they serve. The problem is that the mental health service system as a whole is stuck on a status quo approach that accepts tradition and mediocrity rather than demanding innovation and excellence (p. 1).

Kelly's statement very likely applies to all the systems of care discussed in this book. Each system employs skilled practitioners, and each can point to exemplary programs and innovative service delivery patterns. Yet, child, youth, and family policies continue to suffer from the lack of an underlying and unifying framework that integrates services across problem domains and systems of care. A risk and resilience perspective, coupled with ecological theory, holds promise as an effective organizing framework for future public policy efforts directed at the nation's young people. It is their future and our challenge.

Note

1. Biglan, Brennan, Foster, and Holder (2004) used a similar format with a different example to demonstrate the importance of collaboration in developing effective strategies for working with high-risk youth.

References

Allen-Meares, P., & Fraser, M. W. (Eds.). (2004). *Intervention with children and adolescents: An interdisciplinary perspective.* Needham Heights, MA: Allyn & Bacon.

Biglan, A., Brennan, P. A., Foster, S. L., & Holder, H. D. (2004). *Helping adolescents at risk. Prevention of multiple problems.* New York: Guilford.

Burchard, J. D., Burns, E. J., & Burchard, S. N. (2002). The wraparound approach. In B. J. Burns & K. Hoagwood (Eds.), *Community treatment for youth: Evidence-based interventions for severe emotional and behavioral disorders* (pp. 69–90). New York: Oxford University Press.

Burns, B. J. (2002). Reasons for hope for children and families: A perspective and overview. In B. J. Burns & K. Hoagwood (Eds.), *Community treatment for youth: Evidence-based interventions for severe emotional and behavioral disorders* (pp. 1–15). New York: Oxford University Press.

Burns, B. J., Landsverk, J., Kelleher, K., Faw, L., Hazen, A., & Keeler, G. (2001). Mental health, education, child welfare, and juvenile justice service use. In R. Loeber & D. P. Farrington (Eds.), *Child delinquents: Development, intervention, and service needs* (pp. 273–304). Thousand Oaks, CA: Sage.

Campbell Collaboration Library. (2004). (Database). Retrieved on August 1, 2004, from http://www.campbellcollaboration.org/Fralibrary.html

Chamberlain, P. (2002). Treatment foster care. In B. J. Burns & K. Hoagwood (Eds.), *Community treatment for youth: Evidence-based interventions for severe emotional and behavioral disorders* (pp. 117–138). New York: Oxford University Press.

Cochrane Library. (2004). (Database). Retrieved on August 6, 2004, from http://www.update-software.com/cochrane/default.htm

Dodge, K. A. (2001). The science of youth violence prevention: Progressing from developmental epidemiology to efficacy to effectiveness to public policy. *American Journal of Preventive Medicine,* Supplement to 20, 63–70.

Fraser, M. W. (Ed.). (2004). *Risk and resilience in childhood: An ecological perspective* (2nd ed.). Washington, DC: NASW.

Fraser, M. W., Kirby, L. D., & Smokowski, P. R. (2004). Risk and resilience in childhood. In M. W. Fraser (Ed.), *Risk and resilience in childhood: An ecological perspective* (2nd ed., pp. 13–66). Washington, DC: NASW.

Germain, C. B. (1991). *Human behavior in the social environment: An ecological view.* New York: Columbia University Press.

Hawkins, J. D., Catalano, R. F., & Miller, J. Y. (1992). Risk and protective factors for alcohol and other drug problems in adolescence and early adulthood: Implications for substance abuse prevention. *Psychological Bulletin, 112,* 64–105.

Henggeler, S. W., Schoenwald, S. K., Borduin, C. M., Rowland, M. D., & Cunnigham, P. B. (1998). *Multisystemic treatment of antisocial behavior in children and adolescents.* New York: Guilford.

Hoagwood, K., Burns, B. J., & Weisz, J. R. (2002). A profitable conjunction: From science to service in children's mental health. In B. J. Burns & K. Hoagwood (Eds.), *Community treatment for youth: Evidence-based interventions for severe emotional and behavioral disorders* (pp. 327–338). New York: Oxford University Press.

Howard, M. O., & Jenson, J. M. (1999). Causes of youth violence. In J. M. Jenson & M. O. Howard (Eds.), *Youth violence: Current research and recent practice innovations* (pp. 19–42). Washington, DC: NASW.

Howell, J. C. (2003). *Preventing and reducing juvenile delinquency: A comprehensive framework*. Thousand Oaks, CA: Sage.

Jenson, J. M., & Howard, M. O. (1998). Youth crime, public policy, and practice in the juvenile justice system: Recent trends and needed reforms. *Social Work, 43*, 324–334.

Jenson, J. M., & Potter, C. A. (2003). The effects of cross-system collaboration on mental health and substance abuse problems of detained youth. *Research on Social Work Practice, 13*, 588–607.

Kelly, T. A. (2002). Dealing with fragmentation in the service delivery system. Testimony to the President's New Freedom Commission on Mental Health. Arlington, Virginia. December 4.

Lerner, R. M., Fisher, C. B., & Weinberg, R. A. (2000). Toward a science for and of the people: Promoting civil society through the application of developmental science. *Child Development, 71*, 11–20.

Maton, K. I., Schellenbach, C. J., Leadbeater, B. J., & Solarz, A. L. (2004). *Investing in children, youth, families, and communities. Strengths-based research and policy*. Washington, DC: American Psychological Association.

Mihalic, S. F., & Irwin, K. (2003). Blueprints for violence prevention. From research to real-world settings—Factors influencing the successful replication of model programs. *Youth Violence and Juvenile Justice, 1*, 307–329.

Moon, M. M., Cullen, F. T., & Wright, J. P. (2003). It takes a village: Public willingness to help wayward youths. *Youth Violence and Juvenile Justice, 1*, 32–45.

Sackett, D. L., Rosenberg, W. M. C., Gray, J. A. M., Haynes, R. B., & Richardson, W. S. (1996). Evidence-based medicine: What it is and what it isn't. *British Medical Journal, 312*, 71–72.

U.S. Centers for Disease Control and Prevention. (2002). Special tabulations of first births from the 1997–2002 natality data sets, numbers 9–16, series 21.

U.S. Department of Health and Human Services. (2000). *Healthy people 2010*. Washington, DC: U.S. Government Printing Office.

Index

About the Editors

Jeffrey M. Jenson, Ph.D., is the Bridge Professor of Children, Youth, and Families at the Graduate School of Social Work, University of Denver. He is principal investigator of the Youth Matters Denver Public Schools Prevention Project, a group-randomized trial assessing the effects of a structured curriculum on aggression and substance use among elementary school students in 28 Denver public schools. Dr. Jenson has written numerous articles and chapters on topics pertaining to adolescent substance abuse and juvenile delinquency. His 1999 book (with Matthew O. Howard), *Youth Violence: Current Research and Recent Practice Innovations*, examines advances in understanding, preventing, and treating aggression and violence among children and adolescents. Dr. Jenson received the University of Denver Distinguished Scholar Award in 2003.

Mark W. Fraser, Ph.D., holds the John A. Tate Distinguished Professorship for Children in Need at the School of Social Work, University of North Carolina at Chapel Hill. He directs the Making Choices Project, a school-based prevention program focused on third-grade children and their families. Editor of the Practice Resources Book Series of NASW Press, Dr. Fraser has written numerous chapters and articles on risk and resilience, child behavior, child and family services, and research methods. With colleagues, he is the co-author or editor of six books. These include *Families in Crisis*, a study of intensive family-centered services, and *Evaluating Family-Based Services*, a text on methods for family research. In *Risk and Resilience in Childhood*, he and his colleagues explore ways children prevail over adversity. They describe resilience-based perspectives for child maltreatment, school dropout, substance abuse, violence, unwanted pregnancy, and other social problems. In *Making Choices*, Dr. Fraser and his co-authors outline a program to help children build enduring social relationships with peers and adults. In *The Context of Youth Violence*, he explores violence from the perspective of resilience, risk, and protection. In his most recent book, *Intervention with Children and Adolescents*, Fraser and his colleagues review advances in intervention knowledge for social and health problems.

About the Contributors

Elizabeth K. Anthony, M.S.W., is a doctoral student at the Graduate School of Social Work, University of Denver. Ms. Anthony's professional experience includes direct practice with children, youth, and families. She is currently Research Coordinator for the Bridge Project, an after-school program for high-risk youth located in three public housing projects in Denver, Colorado. Ms. Anthony's doctoral work is examining the utility of risk and resilience models for the prevention of adolescent problem behaviors.

William H. Barton, Ph.D., is Professor and Director of the Office of Research Services at the Indiana University School of Social Work in Indianapolis. His interests include juvenile justice practice and policy, delinquency prevention and youth development, and the applied methodology of program evaluation. Dr. Barton has published numerous articles on topics related to juvenile delinquency and the juvenile justice system. Prior to joining the faculty at Indiana University, he conducted postdoctoral research at the University of Michigan's Institute for Social Research and the Center for the Study of Youth Policy.

Andy J. Frey, Ph.D., is an Assistant Professor in the Kent School of Social Work at the University of Louisville. Dr. Frey's research interests and publications address school-based services and interventions for children with serious emotional disorders. Prior to his appointment at the University of Louisville, he was a social worker and behavioral consultant to several urban school districts in Colorado.

Mary E. Fraser, D.S.W., has worked as a program and policy consultant to mental health departments in three states. Dr. Fraser wrote the Child and Adolescent Service System Program grant for the state of Utah in 1991 and served as that office's first director. She worked in the capacity of executive staff member to the North Carolina Legislative Oversight Committee on Mental Health Reform in 2000. Dr. Fraser's numerous publications focus on mental health policy and practice for children and families. She was previously a clinical adjunct professor in social work and psychiatry at the University of North Carolina at Chapel Hill.

Matthew O. Howard, Ph.D., is Professor of Social Work and Professor of Psychiatry at the University of Michigan in Ann Arbor, Michigan. Dr. Howard has published more than 80 epidemiological, health services, and treatment outcome studies in the chemical dependency and juvenile justice areas. Prior to coming to the University of Michigan, Dr. Howard was a Research Assistant Professor in the Department of Psychiatry and Behavioral Sciences at the University of Washington, a Research Associate Professor in the Department of Psychiatry at Oregon Health Sciences University, and an Associate Professor of Social Work at Washington University.

Thomas C. Ormsby, B.A., is completing master's degrees in the Schools of Social Work and Public Health at the University of North Carolina at Chapel Hill. His current interests include adolescent sexual and reproductive health, international women's health, infant mortality, and prevention of mother-to-child HIV transmission. Mr. Ormsby's most recent work addresses HIV/AIDS prevention among women, adolescents, and children. Prior to beginning graduate studies, he served with the Peace Corps in Morocco and Kenya.

Susan L. Parish, Ph.D., is Assistant Professor in the School of Social Work at the University of North Carolina at Chapel Hill. Dr. Parish's research and publications address the impact of disability, health, and poverty policy on poor families affected by disability. She has served as an expert witness in three federal class-action lawsuits concerned with the rights of people with developmental disabilities and their families. Prior to joining the faculty at the University of North Carolina, Dr. Parish completed an NIH postdoctoral fellowship at the University of Wisconsin's Waisman Center. She also has 8 years of prior experience in administering residential and family support programs for people with disabilities.

Peter J. Pecora, Ph.D., is Senior Director of Research Services for the Casey Family Programs and Professor, School of Social Work, University of Washington, Seattle, Washington. Dr. Pecora's many co-authored books and articles focus on child welfare program design, administration, and research. He has provided training to program leaders in the United States and other countries and has served as an expert witness for a number of states. Dr. Pecora is currently leading a multidisciplinary study of foster care alumni in Oregon and Washington in conjunction with Harvard University and the University of Michigan. He was formerly a line worker and program coordinator in a number of child welfare service agencies in Wisconsin.

Kathleen A. Rounds, Ph.D., is a Professor in the School of Social Work, University of North Carolina at Chapel Hill. Her research has included evaluation of support services for people with HIV, services for pregnant and postpartum women who are using drugs and alcohol, and adolescent parenting programs. Her practice interests focus on social work in public health and community health settings, particularly in the area of maternal and child health. Dr. Rounds is the director of the Maternal and Child Health Public Health Social Work Leadership Training Program and the co-director of the Behavioral Healthcare Resource Program at the School of Social Work. In 2002 she was selected by the U.S. Department of Health and Human Services as a recipient of the Secretary's Primary Health Care Policy Fellowship.

Hill M. Walker, Ph.D., is Professor of Special Education, co-director of the Institute on Violence and Destructive Behavior, and director of the Center on Human Development in the College of Education at the University of Oregon. His research interests include social skills assessment, curriculum development and intervention, longitudinal studies of aggression and anti-social behavior, and the development of early screening procedures for detecting students who are at risk for social–behavioral adjustment problems and/or later school dropout. Dr. Walker is the co-author, along with Herbert Severson, of *Systematic Screening for Behavior Disorders*; author of *The Acting Out Child: Coping with Classroom Disruption*; co-author, with Phillip Strain and Michael Guralnick, of *Children's Social Behavior: Development, Assessment and Modification*; co-author, with Geoffrey Colvin and Elizabeth Ramsey, of *Antisocial Behavior in School: Strategies and Best Practices*; and co-editor, with Michael Epstein, of *Making Schools Safer and Violence Free: Critical Issues, Solutions, and Recommended Practices*. His two most recent books are *Interventions for Academic and Behavior Problems II: Preventive and Remedial Approaches*, co-edited with Mark Shinn and Gary Stoner, and the second edition of *Antisocial Behavior in School: Evidence-Based Practices*, co-authored with Elizabeth Ramsey and Frank Gresham.

Alison I. Whisnant, B.A., is currently pursuing dual master's degrees in social work and public health at the University of North Carolina at Chapel Hill. Her professional experiences include direct practice with youth with developmental disabilities, homeless families, and low-income women. Ms. Whisnant aspires to improve the health and well-being of women and children through program and policy development.